Dear Sisters

OTHER WORKS BY ROSALYN BAXANDALL

America's Working Women: A Documentary History (with Linda Gordon)

Picture Windows: How the Suburbs Happened (with Elizabeth Ewen)

Words on Fire: The Life and Writing of Elizabeth Gurley Flynn

OTHER WORKS BY LINDA GORDON

Woman's Body, Woman's Rights Birth Control in America

Cossack Rebellions: Social Turmoil in the 16th-Century Ukraine

Heroes of Their Own Lives: The Politics and History of Family Violence

Pitied but Not Entitled: Single Mothers and the History of Welfare

Women, the State and Welfare

The Great Arizona Orphan Abduction

Rosalyn Baxandall and Linda Gordon

DEAR SISTERS
Dispatches from the Women's Liberation Movement

BASIC
BOOKS

A Member of the
Perseus Books Group

Copyright © 2000 Rosalyn Baxandall and Linda Gordon

Published by Basic Books, A Member of the Perseus Books Group.

Designed by Jenny Dossin

A CIP catalog record for this book is available from the Library of Congress.

ISBN 0-465-01706-1

00 01 02 03 04 / 10 9 8 7 6 5 4 3 2 1

To the feminists of the future,

may you learn from our achievements and our mistakes

Contents

I
Origins

II
Bodies

III
Institutions

A Note on the Text

Many of the documents reproduced here originated as mimeographed leaflets, posters, or articles in periodicals that no longer exist. In the citations at the back of the book, we have given the sources from which we took the items we publish here, although many of them were reprinted repeatedly in other publications and the versions may vary. Some of the written documents reproduced here have been edited to make them shorter and we did not want to burden the reader with many dots indicating ellipses.

We have given the date of production of an item whenever we know it. If there is no date listed, that is because the original had no date – typical of many women's liberation leaflets and posters that were intended for immediate circulation and without self-consciousness about the historical importance of what was being created.

If no author is listed, that is because the document was created by a group or anonymously, but whenever possible the source list gives the geographical location from which the document originated.

Rosalyn Baxandall and Linda Gordon

Contents

Part II: Bodies

Part III: Institutions

Introduction

THIS IS A BOOK about a social movement that changed America. The women's liberation movement, as it was called in the 1960s and 1970s, or feminism, as it is known today, reached into every home, school, and business, into every form of entertainment and sport. Like a river overflowing its banks and seeking a new course, it permanently altered the landscape. Some think its impact has been excessive and others—like us—believe that much more progress toward sex equality is needed. But all agree that it has left an indelible mark on women, men, and children everywhere.

Women's liberation was the largest social movement in the history of the U.S. Yet at the end of the twentieth century, very little had been written that examines the movement's breadth and variety, and no publication presents the movement both in historical perspective and in the voices of its own activists. *Dear Sisters* invites readers to listen in on a conversation among women who were discovering and exploring new territories, in the society and in their own lives, grassroots testimony in the form of posters, tracts, poems, manifestos, songs, cartoons, slogans, and serious art. It includes the evidence of conflict as well as cooperation, without which the movement could not have grown. The documents collected here are the flesh, bones, and spirit of the women's movement and they carried its dispatches across the country and all over the world. We feature the earliest years of the movement, from the mid-1960s to about 1977, because this was the period of the most yeasty ferment, creativity, and mass participation.

We created this book from two intersecting vantage points. As historians, we have taught women's history to thousands of college students over the last three decades, and as feminists we were active participants in women's liberation: taking part in consciousness raising, demonstrating, writing leaflets, engaging in street theater, helping build new institutions. Although our activities were similar, we were in different cities and different organizations with different outlooks—Rosalyn Baxandall in radical-feminist New York Radical Women, Linda Gordon in socialist-feminist Bread and Roses in Boston. Because of our double perspective—scholarly and participatory—we are in a position to reflect on the movement's history and at the same time to recall the personal intensities of discovery and solidarity that the movement generated. Precisely because we are committed to the goals of women's liberation, we consider it imperative to evaluate critically the movement's strengths and weaknesses.

Although we were part of the movement, we have not relied on memory to re-create this rich historical period. *Dear Sisters* rests on research in archives throughout the U.S. and in privately owned papers and other memorabilia. Some of what we found surprised us and led us to revise our own understandings of the movement, illustrating the uncertainty of memory. For example: We discovered that women of color played a larger part in the early movement than had been previously believed. We found that, although the movement was indeed decentralized and varied, there was substantial accord even among groups that considered themselves at odds at the time.

Just as we came to a fuller understanding of women's liberation in creating this book, we hope the book will correct widespread misconceptions about the movement. These exist not because the public is foolish or hostile to feminism. In fact, 1998 Roper polls found that 51 percent of Americans believe feminists have been helpful to women, 53 percent that feminists are "in touch with the average American woman," 65 percent that black feminists help the black community. The misimpressions derive in part from widely published misinformation. Indeed, it is hard to imagine an historical event as widespread and powerful as the women's liberation movement that has been so poorly documented and reported. You can count on your fingers the scholarly studies and well-researched journalism about the American women's movement. Even our most feminist students have absorbed inaccurate ideas and cliches.

Part of this problem is the movement's success. Its achievements—the broad range of work women now do, the equal treatment they expect, the direct way women express themselves—have become the very air we breathe, so taken for granted as to be invisible, and so we do not ask how these changes came about. Furthermore, the largest grassroots part of the women's movement is difficult to study precisely because it was so big, so decentralized, so varied, and often left few records. It is hardly surprising that most of what has been written has focused on the main national feminist organization, the National Organization for Women, and its leaders, such as Gloria Steinem and Betty Friedan, because this aspect of the movement was more centralized, less outrageous, more focused—and kept better records. By contrast, the larger, mass women's liberation movement has been less studied and more misrepresented.

There are deeper reasons, too, for the lack of reliable studies and the perpetuation of false stereotypes. Despite the huge changes in our society brought about by the women's movement, feminism's fundamental ideas are still controversial—indeed, they are at the root of the hottest debates of our times: abortion rights, contraception for teenagers, welfare, women in the armed forces, gay marriage, affirmative action. The media—and not only conservative sources—often portray the women's movement through unrepresentative anecdotes and outright falsehoods; it is easy enough to find a few crazies in a movement so vast and varied. In turn, such poor journalism arises in part from the lack of scholarly research upon which reporters can draw.

Three biases from three different perspectives infuse the misinformation about women's liberation: an overtly hostile, conservative perspective that demonizes the movement as acting against nature, even doing the work of the devil; the perspective of those feminist activists who, disap-

pointed by the movement's incomplete success, consider it a failure; and a trivializing view of the movement as a lifestyle rather than politics, as personal self-transformation rather than social change, as a digression from traditional politics. These biases give rise to widespread myths about women's liberation. Depending on one's particular bias, women's libbers:

- were privileged, white young women who had neither knowledge about nor concern for working-class women or women of color.

- rejected motherhood and considered children only a burden.

- ignored bread-and-butter economic issues and focussed only on sex, violence, and personal issues.

- drew energy away from movements aimed at correcting major social and economic problems, such as militarism, racism, and poverty, and prevented the formation of strong coalitions or united efforts.

- hated being women and rejected everything feminine, from bras and long hair to shaved legs and high heels.

- were man-haters who tried to belittle and compete with men, often rejecting them entirely and becoming lesbians.

- were losers, bitter because men rejected them.

- were humorless and prudish, quick to take offense.

- were spoiled, self-centered, and self-pitying women who whined about life's difficulties and exaggerated the discrimination against women.

Like most myths, some of these contain kernels of truth. Yes, feminists did reject confining clothing such as high heels and girdles. Many stopped dieting and curling, straightening, processing, dyeing, shaving, plucking their hair. Yes, feminists wanted help raising children, from husbands and organized day care, as more and more women joined the workforce. Yes, feminists were angry at men who beat them, harassed them, belittled them, and kept them in inferior and dead-end jobs. Yes, women's liberation was particularly strong among college-educated young women. Yes, in order to be heard, especially because women had a history of being timid, soft-spoken, and ignored, feminists sometimes shouted and oversimplified.

But some of these myths contain not a grain of truth. Feminists never rejected motherhood; rather, they sought to improve its conditions. Not only were most feminists romantically involved with men, but all had sons, brothers, fathers, male friends, or coworkers whom they loved. Far from being losers, feminists were typically the most achieving and self-confident of women. Feminist humor was so popular it became mainstream—think of Lily Tomlin and Nicole Hollander. Anything but prudes, feminists dedicated themselves to liberating women's sexuality. They were doers, not complainers. They identified discrimination for the purpose of trying to change it.

SOCIAL ROOTS OF WOMEN'S LIBERATION

Women's liberation was a movement long overdue. By the mid-1950s a majority of American women found themselves expected to function as full economic, social, and political participants in the nation while still burdened with handicaps. As wage-earners, as parents, as students, as citizens, women were denied equal opportunity and, often, even minimal rights and respect. Many women experienced sharp conflict among the expectations placed on them—education, employment, wife- and motherhood. Looking back at the beginning of the twenty-first century, we can see feminism as a necessary modernizing force and, not surprisingly, one which rapidly became global. Within the U.S., the movement gained widespread support so quickly because it met real needs, because the great majority of women stood to benefit from reducing discrimination,

harassment, and prejudice against them. A movement that might at first have seemed to promise to rationalize the current political and economic system by integrating women into it quickly took off—as many social movements do—into uncharted territory, exposing the degree to which basic social structures had rested on a traditional gender system. The radical challenge to these fundamental structures can be measured by the virulence of the later worldwide backlash, from the Taliban to the Christian Coalition.

How did an apparently arch-conservative decade like the 1950s produce a movement so radical? To answer that we have to look beneath a veneer that concealed discomforts and discontents. The period between the end of World War II and the birth of women's liberation at the end of the 1960s has usually been described as an era of prosperity, stability, and peace, leading to the conclusion that it was also an era of satisfaction and little change. An intensely controlled and controlling official and commercial culture seemed to provide evidence for that conclusion. The domestic correlate of the cold war and the Korean War was the hysterical anticommunism that stigmatized nonconformity, including that related to family, sex, and gender. Anxiety about the Soviet threat made family stability seem critical and linked women's domestic roles to the nation's security. Just as schoolchildren were drilled in ducking under their desks and covering their heads to protect themselves from atomic bombs, so teenage girls were taught the imperatives of beauty and domesticity. Far from interpreting these women's obligations as constraints, cold war American culture regarded them as freedom. That American middle-class women did not seem to need jobs and enjoyed an expanding array of household appliances demonstrated the superiority of American institutions over Soviet society, where dowdy women grew heavily muscled from their hard labor and could shop only for a narrow array of dreary clothes and consumer goods. In the early 1960s future feminist Betty Friedan was to name this view of women's appropriate destiny the "feminine mystique," a term now used by historians to describe the domestic gendered face of the cold war. Twenty years later historian Elaine Tyler May observed that the concept of containment, first used to characterize the U.S. policy of preventing Soviet expansion, could characterize equally well the stifling of female ambitions, the endorsement of female subordination, and the promotion of domesticity by cold war gender culture. Resistance to these norms was un-American, and that label became a heavy club with which to beat misfits and dissidents.

The domestic political aspect of this culture has been called McCarthyism, after the senator from Wisconsin who became its most vicious advocate, ultimately so fanatic and irrational that he helped discredit it. The gendered aspects of the McCarthyist attack on communism have not yet been fully studied. Not only liberals, progressive labor officials, artists, and journalists suffered from the congressional investigations of "un-Americans"; so did many women's organizations and individual women in politics. Richard Nixon began his national political career defeating Democratic Congresswoman Helen Gahagan Douglas by smearing her as a communist. Another victim of McCarthy was Dorothy Kenyon, U.S. representative to the U.N. Commission on the Status of Women. The Un-American Activities committees went after the distinguished Women's International League for Peace and Freedom.

Cold war culture demanded sexual as well as political and gender conformity. The witch hunts targeted not only alleged communists but also homosexuals, and drove many people out of their employment. Films and magazines depicted the lesbian as a moral threat, a symbol of decay, chaos, and predatory evil. Vice control units of local police departments, along with private moral crusade organizations like the American Society for Social Hygiene and public health officials, routinely rounded up those engaged in "immoral" sexual activities. Psychiatrists labeled homosexuals and discontented women alike as sick and in need of rehabilitation.

Girls grew up in this cold war era barred from wearing blue jeans or sneakers to school, required to sit with their knees together and to set their hair in pin curls. Nothing in the culture encouraged them to become strong or competitive. Girls grew to hate athletics and dread physical education in school, where they were required to wear unfashionable tunics or bloomers. Girls were not encouraged to fantasize about careers, about what they would "become" when they grew up. They were expected to break a date with a girlfriend if a boy asked for a date. They watched movies and TV in which married couples slept in twin beds and mothers were full-time housewives. The people of color on TV were stereotypes, comic or worse: step-and-fetch-it black servants, marauding Apaches, or fat lazy Mexicans. Rape, illegitimacy, abortion—some of women's real problems—were among many tabooed subjects, whispered about but rarely seriously or openly discussed.

But this official feminine-mystique culture obscured an unofficial but probably more widespread reality that was, ironically, designated as deviant. A small band of historians has been uncovering the story of what turns out to be the majority of American women who did not, and often could not, conform. We belonged to that majority. Neither of our families was like *Leave It to Beaver* or *Father Knows Best*. Our mothers "worked," which meant, of course, employment for wages, and we thought they were unusual. In fact, in contrast to official norms, women's labor-force participation climbed rapidly throughout the fifties and by 1954 women's employment had equaled that during World War II. Most women displaced from well-paid, industrial jobs at the war's end did not return to domesticity but found work in traditionally female low-paying jobs in the expanding service and clerical sectors. As has long been true in American history, African American women and poor women of all colors had particularly high rates of employment, so that the domesticity myth was in part a racist assumption that elite white norms were universal. Women in "pink collar" employment swelled the membership of unions, such as the Hotel Employees and Restaurant Employees and the National Federation of Telephone Workers. And these working women were not only young and single: By 1960, 30 percent of married women were employed, and 39 percent of mothers with school-age children were in the labor force. By 1955, 3 million women belonged to unions, constituting 17 percent of union members. In unions in which women made up a significant part of the membership, they wielded considerable power, especially at the local level.

The number of married women seeking employment rose fastest in the middle class. Women benefited from an enormous expansion in higher education after World War II. Government investment in universities after the war had multiplied educational opportunity, especially in public institutions. In 1940, 26 percent of American women completed college; in 1970, 55 percent. These relatively privileged American women faced a particular dilemma: educated with men and often achieving, despite discrimination, the same levels of knowledge, discipline, and sophistication as the men of their social class, they were still expected to forego professional or intellectual pursuits after college to become full-time housewives and mothers. Those who resisted this directive and sought employment, through choice or economic necessity, usually found themselves limited to clerical or low-level administrative jobs.

In part as a response to this restriction, many women, like both our mothers, defied the limits of domesticity through community and political activism. Even in the suburbs, where women seemed to be conforming to the "feminine mystique" by staying home with small children, many were active in churches, schools, libraries, and parks. New forms of organizing appeared: In 1956, for example, the first all-female La Leche group met to encourage breast feeding. Other groups, alarmed by Rachel Carson's studies of the dangers of pesticides like DDT, had the audacity to challenge official science. Women Strike for Peace, composed largely of left-wing women, attacked military spending priorities, raised an alarm about strontium-90 fallout in milk, and directly challenged the cold war and American military buildup by contesting U.S. government propaganda about the threat of Soviet expansionism. Even conservative women, while paying official homage to the ideal of women's domesticity, were organizing in the Ku Klux Klan, White Citizen's Councils, John Birch Society, and Republican Party.

Some forms of deviance from the official domestic norms were more private. At the edges of mainstream culture a counterculture began to emerge in the early 1950s, reflecting a mood of depression, alienation, and anger at the shallowness of dominant standards. True, the "beat" poets and artists were mainly male, but they attracted female groupies who preferred this alternative masculinity and identified with the rejection of respectability and conformity. Beatnik women, dressed in black with heavy black eye makeup and uncurled hair, hung around coffeehouses in New York and San Francisco. Rebelling against consumerism and conformity, yearning for something more genuine, some embraced Zen Buddhism and existentialism.

Even popular commercial culture was riddled with contradictions, ambivalence, competing voices, and transgressions. Later, when the contrast between the cultures of the 1950s and that created by the rebirth of feminism was so great, these hints of dissidence paled. Only now, as the women's movement can be seen in historical context, have historians looked back again and noticed the complexity of the cultural messages. In addition to emphasizing femininity and domesticity, many women's magazines featured and honored women who made a mark beyond their homes. Magazine articles glorified housewives, but they also offered tips to women managing wage work along with housework and openly praised participation in community activism and politics. Readers met, for example, Dorothy McCullough Lee, who cultivated the image of a pale, frail housewife but as mayor of Portland single-handedly defeated the heavyweights of organized crime; Louise Williams, mother of two, a great cook but an even better mechanic at American Airlines; and Babe Didrikson Zaharias, a champion golfer and pole vaulter who continued competing despite cancer. *Reader's Digest* placed Mary McLeod Bethune among the world's greatest living women, despite the fact that she was the highest-ranking African American in the New Deal and had been accused of being a communist by McCarthy. Honoring women's work and public activity was especially pronounced in black journalism: magazines like *Ebony* and *Jet* promoted marriage and motherhood but also professional and artistic achievement.

Doris Day, the movie star whose image was as wholesome as cornflakes—freckled, happy, and antiseptic in her pastel sweaters and shorty pajamas—was no conventional passive housefrau. She played a tomboy in *Calamity Jane*, a pushy wife who drives her husband's career in *I'll See You in My Dreams*, and a resourceful clever woman, much the sexual initiator, who catches Rock Hudson in *Pillow Talk.* Marilyn Monroe, epitome of the dumb blonde bombshell, tried to complicate that image in her screen roles. In *Diamonds Are a Girl's Best Friend,* when a guy says, "I thought you were dumb," she insists, "I can be smart when I want to, but most men don't like it." She first married major league baseball player Joe DiMaggio, an icon of American virtue, and then blacklisted playwright Arthur Miller; the FBI tracked her as a subversive.

Dissidence in the 1950s was, of course, particularly pronounced in youth culture. Rebellious adolescent voices competed with homogenized "Archie" comic book people and Disney's cute, servile Annette Funicello. Young people identified as "rebels without a cause," the phrase sent reverberating through America by James Dean, Hollywood's symbol of alienated middle-class youth. The idea that they didn't have "a cause" came from their affluence, the fact that they "had everything." But these rebels did have a cause—they just couldn't name it—and the affluence of their parents only heightened their discontent. They rejected the false facades of family, the suburbs, and corporate careers, the measurement of success by large houses and consumer goods. They sought authenticity instead among male outsider figures—cowboys, hoods, oddballs, delinquents, but also blacks and Latinos. As with the beats, women remained followers, but some were choosing geeks or boys on motorcycles instead of jocks. Rebellion among less privileged groups took different forms, less covered by the mainstream media and less shocking to middle-class whites, who considered the norms of poor people and people of color outside established culture anyway. But the protest was there, among young Chicanos dressing in flashy "zoot suits" and "low-riding" their jazzed-up cars, among the hoods and rockers with their greased ducktail hairdos.

Nowhere was the youth rebellion as intense or as contagious as in music, and the transcendence of race segregation was the proximate cause. The officially dominant 1950s white sound (Peggy Lee, Jo Stafford, Rosemary Clooney, and Pat Boone) combined inane lyrics, like "How Much Is That Doggie in the Window," with soothing melodies, bland orchestration, and ballad rhythms. Yet this is the decade that produced rock and roll, a revolution in popular music. The term was first applied to black rhythm and blues by Alan Freed, the white disk jockey who promoted black music to white audiences. The breakthrough singer was Elvis Presley, the "white boy who could sing black." Not only did whites start to buy records by black artists but they also attended huge concerts where for the first time white and black youth mingled and danced. In Los Angeles, for example, racially mixed rock concerts were busted up by the police. Conservatives considered rock and roll the music of the devil, dangerous, degenerate, mongrel, oversexualized, and in a way they were right: it is difficult to overestimate the impact of rock and roll on the men and women who moved from the inchoate, half-conscious alienation of rebels without a cause to the organized radical movements that began with the civil rights movement.

POLITICAL ROOTS OF WOMEN'S LIBERATION

From the vantage point of the new century, the women's liberation movement appears extravagant, immoderate, impatient, as well as young and naive. It was all those and more, but how one weighs its radicalism, positively or negatively, and how one measures its naivete depend on understanding its historical context. Thirty years later our culture has been so transformed, the expectations of young women so altered, that it is hard to grasp the unique combination of anger and optimism that made second-wave feminism so determined to change so much so fast.

Women coming into adulthood at the end of the 1960s, both middle- and working-class, faced an economy that was producing an ever larger number of jobs for women and for the men they might marry. Even more important, women had unprecedented access to education. But many were disappointed in the jobs they could get. They went from being the equals or even the superiors of men in educational achievement to working as secretaries or "administrative assistants" for the same class of men. Although they faced discrimination in their colleges and universities, they also encountered professors who recognized and challenged their intelligence. Yet their studies, no matter how rigorous, offered them no way to escape the cultural imperative that directed them toward marriage and family as their fundamental and often exclusive source of identity and satisfaction.

If economic and educational abundance opened windows for the women who began women's liberation in 1968, the passionate new social activism of the 1950s and 1960s opened doors and invited women in. But these movements, like the economy as a whole, also sent women a double message. Whenever there have been progressive social change movements in modern history, women's movements have arisen within them, and for similar reasons: in the crucible of activism for civil rights, for peace, for the environment, for free speech, for social welfare, women have been valued participants who gained skills and self-confidence. At the same time they have been thwarted, treated as subordinates, gophers, even servants, by the men in charge—including men who considered themselves partisans of democracy and equality. Within these movements women learned to think critically about social structures and ideologies, to talk the language of freedom and tyranny, democracy and domination, power and oppression. Then they applied these concepts to question their own secondary status. It is precisely this combination of raised aspirations and frustration that gives rise to rebellion.

The first chapter of *Dear Sisters* illustrates this dynamic, with examples from civil rights, from the student movement, and from the anti–Vietnam War movement that show how women experienced the double message of pride and humiliation. In addition to understanding individual motivation, we need to understand the political culture of these movements and the optimism they generated, even for those millions who only watched. By the 1960s, there was a sense of unity among progressive campaigns for social justice; in fact, they came to be collectively called "the movement," a singular designation. Reflecting the relative prosperity of the period, its mood was optimistic, even utopian. Its members came largely from the middle class,

but working-class people also participated. The movement was as critical of commercialization, conformity, and moral hypocrisy as of poverty. Its guiding principle was challenge to received wisdom and hierarchical authority. Quintessentially a movement of young people, it was correspondingly impatient and preferred direct action to political process. In dress, in sexual behavior, in its favorite intoxicants, and above all in its beloved music, it distinguished itself sharply from grown-ups.

By the mid-1960s, the more ideologically Left currents within the movement were called the New Left, because they differed fundamentally from the older Lefts: communism, socialism, and New Deal progressivism. At least a decade earlier, the civil rights movement had been the first to break with conventional politics, helped by its high proportion of student activists, ability to stimulate mass participation, decentralized and pluralist organization, and commitment to direct but nonviolent action. Like all mass movements, the civil rights movement had no defined beginning, although the 1955 Montgomery bus boycott announced to the country that something big was happening. Thousands of African Americans were challenging three hundred years of apartheid, demonstrating unprecedented discipline, solidarity, and bravery against brutal retaliation. Their courage forced racist viciousness into the open; journalists and their cameras then brought into living rooms the high-power water hoses turned on peaceful protesters, the grown men who spat on first-graders, the dogs who charged at protesters singing gospel hymns. The news brought a heightened appreciation of the possibility of making change from the bottom up. In contrast to the bitter liberal-versus-conservative national division in the 1980s and 1990s, the civil rights struggles seemed to galvanize, at least among the most articulate citizenry, broad majority approval for social change in the direction of greater democracy and equality. (There may have been a "silent majority" that did not approve.) While any individual battle might be won or lost, it seemed to supporters that their cause was unstoppable, so great was the groundswell of desire for the long-overdue racial equality and respect.

In fact, civil rights did not even unite southern African Americans; the conservative and the cautious adhered to a less challenging, more deferential approach (despite decades of evidence that it achieved little). Those who disapproved of the militants often came from an older generation made more careful by firsthand knowledge of the retaliatory power of white supremacy, while the new leaders were typically young. Civil rights was, at first, preeminently a black movement, but it was also the first of a series of youth movements that would transform American culture. Civil rights generated youth protest throughout the country, producing a political culture marked by antiauthoritarianism, direct action, and anger at the constraints of respectability. Particularly in the South, many whites from religious backgrounds were drawn into the movement through the student division of the YWCA, which was far more committed to interracial activity than the YMCA. The drama of the attack on segregation drew some northern and western young blacks and whites to the South to help, while others were inspired to contest inequality where they lived. Young whites emulated African American activists in many ways: they adopted the blue jeans that Student Nonviolent Coordinating Committee (SNCC) workers wore in identification with poor southern farmers and workers; their artistic sensibility was permanently revolutionized by black music—blues and rock and roll—and their images of heroism and virtue were modeled after the nonviolent resistance of SNCC volunteers who refused to run or defend themselves from beatings.

In the late 1950s, another kind of rebellion was developing, primarily among the more privileged whites: a cultural rebellion. Discovering and inventing unconventional art, music, and poetry; exploring a variety of intoxicants; and signaling defiance in the way they dressed, adherents of this new cultural revolution soon grew visible enough to draw mainstream media attention. The press created popular icons—"flower children" and "hippies"—whose values resembled those of the earlier 1950s beatnik rebels. The influence of this lifestyle dissent can be measured by how quickly it was picked up by commercial interests and sold back to a broader public: the new fashion included beards, long straight hair, psychedelic design, granny dresses, and beads. Handmade, patched, and embroidered clothing and jeans once bought at Sears Roebuck or Goodwill were soon being mass-produced in Hong Kong and sold in department stores. For its most zealous participants, counterculture iconoclasm and adventurousness meant such an extreme rejection of the work ethic, temperance, and discipline that it horrified many observers, including some in the movement. Excessive use of drugs, promiscuous sexuality, and irresponsibility were sometimes destructive to participants, some of whom later rebounded into conventionality. Women suffered particular exploitation, as the counterculture's gender ideology reaffirmed that of the conventional culture, but now with a twist, lauding "free" and "natural" heterosexual relations between women who were sexually open and "giving" and men who could not be tied down. Women were to be earth mothers, seeking fulfillment by looking after men and children, while guys needed freedom from marital or paternal responsibilities in order to find and express themselves.

This cultural rebellion had transformative potential and gave rise to some serious political challenges. When civil rights and the counterculture intersected on campuses, the result was a college students' movement for free speech that would ultimately create the New Left and women's liberation. The first major student revolt, at the University of California at Berkeley in 1964, arose in reaction to the administration's attempt to prevent students from recruiting civil rights volunteers on campus. This protest movement spread to campuses late in the 1960s throughout the U.S., producing a series of protests against in loco parentis rules that treated students like children.

Campus protests soon expanded to include national issues and nonstudents. Sensitized to injustice and convinced of the potential of grassroots activism by what they learned from civil rights, more and more Americans began to see the Vietnam War as immoral and undemocratic. In the name of stopping communism, the U.S. was defending a flagrantly corrupt regime that had canceled elections when it seemed likely to lose to a popular, nationalist liberation movement that promised land reform in the interests of the poor peasantry. The most powerful nation in the world was attacking a tiny nation that had demonstrated not the slightest aggression toward Americans. The U.S. employed some of the cruelest weapons and tactics yet developed: shooting down unarmed peasants because of fear that they might be supporting the liberation movement; bulldozing villages; spraying herbicides from planes to deprive the guerrilla fighters of their jungle cover; dropping napalm, a jellied gasoline antipersonnel weapon that stuck to the skin and burned people alive. There was not yet extensive censorship of the press, so Americans routinely witnessed these atrocities on the evening news. American soldiers of color and of the working class were killed and injured in disproportionate numbers. Hundreds of young men began resisting or dodging the draft while scores of soldiers deserted and defied orders. So widespread, vocal, and convincing were the protests at home, including several massive national demonstrations, that by its end the Vietnam War became the only war in U.S. history to be opposed by a majority of the population.

The Vietnamese revolution was part of a wave of nationalist struggles of Third World countries against Western imperial domination, and these also influenced American domestic politics. Many of these emerging nations and movements took socialist forms, as Third World nationalists observed that the introduction of capitalism increased inequality and impoverishment. But many of these newly independent countries fell under Soviet domination as the price of the aid they so desperately needed, and leading parts of the American New Left, already angry at the stultifying domestic culture of the cold war, neglected to subject Soviet control to the same critique. U.S. interventions against communism, both military and covert, had the ironic effect of making the New Left less critical of Soviet and Chinese communism than it might have been otherwise.

Before Vietnam, the Cuban revolution of 1959 had seized the developing New Left imagination. Cubans overthrew the Batista dictatorship and brought to power a group of daring reformers committed, at first, not only to economic justice but also to educational, cultural, and political democracy. Influential New Leftists, including many future feminists, traveled to Cuba in the 1960s, volunteering to work in the sugar harvests, and their enthusiasm for Cuba's valiant struggle led them to overestimate its independence from the U.S.S.R., just as the anti–Vietnam War movement romanticized Vietnam (and overlooked its lack of democracy). The New Left's increasing identification with anti-imperialist and nationalist struggles around the world caused it to subordinate its early emphasis on freedom and democracy.

In the late 1960s in other First and even Second (communist) World countries, anti-imperialism intensified student rebellions similar to those in the U.S. These movements were strengthened by two factors not present in America: connection with working-class-based socialist movements, organized into Labor, Social Democratic, and Communist Parties; and anger at U.S. world domination. In most of western Europe—notably England, France, Italy, Germany, and the Netherlands—and also in Mexico, Brazil, and Argentina, student activism energized traditional Left politics, supporting strikes and Left parties while interjecting the direct action and cultural radicalism characteristic of youth movements. American radicals applauded with equal enthusiasm dissent in eastern Europe as well, where students helped articulate mass grievances against government and communist party dictatorships. Struggles against the U.S. and Soviet states seemed of a piece to American New Leftists. In this context of international mobilization, American radicals associated civil rights struggles in the U.S. with anti-imperialism. Blacks and other nonwhite groups identified themselves as a Third World within the U.S., victims of internal colonialism. (Some feminist groups would argue that women were another colonized people.)

Activism spread throughout the U.S., creating civil rights movements among other racial/ethnic groups, including Chicanos, Asian Americans, Native Americans; movements to protect the environment; a movement for the rights of the disabled; and renewed labor struggles for a fair share of the prosperity. Among whites there soon arose a national student organization that was to become central to the white New Left, Students for a Democratic Society

(SDS), established in 1962. With a membership reaching about 100,000 at its peak in the late 1960s, and with many times that number of students—including high school students—who considered themselves a part of the movement, SDS changed the attitudes of a considerable part of a generation. New Leftists and counterculture activists created institutions that spread progressive ideas still further: radical bookstores, a few national magazines, and many local underground newspapers. These were produced by amateurs working in scruffy offices, offering critical perspectives on everything from U.S. foreign policy to the local police to the latest films. Many of these underground newspapers combined words and graphics in innovative ways, inspired in part by the street art of 1968 in France where the *beaux arts* students had considerable influence.

Although the movement (civil rights and the New Left) had no unified ideology—its members included anarchists, social democrats, Marxist-Leninists, black nationalists—it bequeathed identifiable legacies to feminism. Most important among these were anti-authoritarianism and irreverence. Favorite buttons and T-shirts read "Question Authority" and "Never Trust Anyone Over 30." Arrogant and disrespectful, yes, but also understandably rebellious. The movement's message was: look beneath formal legal and political rights to find other kinds of power, the power of wealth, of race, of violence.

Following this instruction, some women began in the mid-1960s to examine power relations in areas that the movement's male leaders had not considered relevant to radical politics. The women's preliminary digging uncovered a buried deposit of grievances about men's power over women within the movement. Women in civil rights and the New Left were on the whole less victimized, more respected, and less romanticized than they were in the mainstream culture or the counterculture. Despite women's passionate and disciplined work for social change, however, they remained far less visible and less powerful than the men who dominated the meetings and the press conferences. Women came into greater prominence wherever there was grassroots organizing, as in voter registration in the South and the SDS community projects in

northern cities. Throughout the civil rights and the student movements, women proved themselves typically the better organizers, better able than men to listen, to connect, to reach across class and even race lines, to empower the previously diffident, to persevere despite failure and lack of encouragement. Still, the frustrations and humiliations were galling. In every organization women were responsible for keeping records, producing leaflets, telephoning, cleaning offices, cooking, organizing social events, and catering to the egos of male leaders, while the men wrote manifestos, talked to the press, negotiated with officials, and made speeches. This division of labor did not arise from misogyny or acrimony. It was "natural" and had always been so, until it began to seem not natural at all.

THE RISE OF SECOND-WAVE FEMINISM

Although women's liberation had foremothers, the young feminists of the late 1960s did not usually know about this heritage because so little women's history had been written. Feminist historians have now made us aware that a continuing tradition of activism stretched from "first-wave" feminism, which culminated in winning the right to vote in 1920, to the birth of the "second wave" in 1968. Some women of unusual longevity bridged the two waves. Florence Luscomb, who had traveled the state of Massachusetts speaking for woman suffrage during World War I, also spoke for women's liberation in Boston in the early 1970s. Within many progressive social movements, even at the nadir of the conservative 1950s, there were discontented women agitating against sex discrimination and promoting female leadership. Within the Communist and Socialist Parties there had been women's caucuses and demands to revise classic socialist theory to include sex inequality. We meet a representative few of them in chapter 1: folksinger Melvina Reynolds, the women of the Jeannette Rankin Brigade. Some women spanned the older progressive causes and the new feminism—Ella Baker, Judy Collins, Ruby Dee, Eleanor Flexner, Fanny Lou Hamer, Flo Kennedy, Coretta Scott King, Gerda Lerner, Amy Swerdlow.

Liberal women had continued to be politically active between feminism's two waves. They were mainly Democrats but there were some Republicans, such as Oveta Culp Hobby, who became the first secretary of the Department of Health, Education and Welfare, established in 1953. In 1961 this women's political network persuaded President Kennedy, as payback for their support in the close election of 1960, to establish a Presidential Commission on the Status of Women. It was chaired by Eleanor Roosevelt, embodying continuity with first-wave feminism and the New Deal, and Women's Bureau head Esther Peterson served as vice-chair. Kennedy may have expected this commission to keep the women diverted and out of his hair. But the commission produced substantive recommendations for a legislative agenda and set in motion a continuing process. Its report, issued in 1963, called for equal pay for *comparable* work (understanding that equal pay for *equal* work would not be adequate because women so rarely did the same work as men), as well as child care services, paid maternity leave, and many other measures still not achieved. Determined not to let its momentum stall or its message reach only elite circles, the commission built a network among women's organizations, made special efforts to include black women, and got Kennedy to establish two ongoing federal committees. Most consequentially, it stimulated the creation of state women's commissions, created in every state by 1967. The network that formed through these commissions enabled the creation of the National Organization for Women (NOW) in 1966.

NOW's history has been often misinterpreted, especially by the radical women's liberationists, who denounced it, as the radicals of SNCC criticized their elders and the New Left criticized the Old Left, as stodgy and "bourgeois." At first NOW included more working-class and minority leadership than women's liberation did. Many of its leaders identified strongly with civil rights and defined NOW as pursuing civil rights for women. Former Old Leftist Betty Friedan and black lawyer and poet Pauli Murray were centrally involved in the East, while in the Midwest, labor union women like Dorothy Haener of the United Auto Workers and Addie Wyatt of the Amalgamated

Meatcutters were prime movers. NOW's first headquarters was provided by the UAW. NOW concentrated heavily on employment issues, reflecting its close ties to the U.S. Women's Bureau and the unions, and NOW's membership was composed largely of employed women. NOW refused to endorse reproductive rights, which the majority considered too controversial, but it rejected the idea that gender was immutable and called for "equitable sharing of responsibilities of home and children and of the economic burdens of their support." This position marked a decisive break with earlier women's rights agitation, which had primarily accepted the traditional division of labor—breadwinner husbands and housewives—as inevitable and desirable. And this position was to give rise to tremendous advances in feminist theory in the next decades.

NOW represented primarily adult professional women and a few male feminists, and at first it did not attempt to build a mass movement open to all women. Although only thirty women had attended its founding conference, and 300 its second conference, NOW demonstrated political savvy in creating the impression that it spoke for a mass power base. It had no central office of its own for three years— networking among a relatively small group did not require one. Its members used their professional and political skills to exert pressure on elected officials.

NOW concentrated on lobbying, using its ties to the few women in influential positions in government; its program focused on governmental action against sex discrimination. Its members met with the attorney general, the secretary of labor, the head of the Civil Service Commission. Its board of directors read like entries from a "Who's Who" of professional women and their male supporters. Its initial impetus was anger that the Equal Employment Opportunity Commission (EEOC) was not enforcing the sex-discrimination provisions of the Civil Rights Act of 1965, and it got immediate results: in 1967 President Johnson issued Executive Order 11375, prohibiting sex discrimination by federal contractors. In the same year NOW forced the EEOC to rule that sex-segregated want ads were discriminatory (although newspapers ignored this ruling with impunity for years). NOW's legal committee, composed of four high-powered Washington lawyers, three of them federal employees, brought suits against protective legislation that in the name of protecting women's fragility in fact kept them out of better jobs. (In arguing one case the five-foot, 100-pound lawyer picked up the equipment the company claimed was too heavy for women and carried it around with one hand as she argued to the jury.)

Women's liberation derided NOW's perspective and tactics as "liberal"—not in the 1990s pejorative sense, coined by the Right, of permissive, but in the 1960s sense, used by the Left, as legalistic and compromising. When a mass women's movement arose, it was not liberal but radical in the sense of seeking out the roots of problems and working for structural change at a level more fundamental than law. It wanted not just to redistribute wealth and power in the existing society, but to challenge the sources of male dominance: the private as well as the public, the psychological as well as the economic, the cultural as well as the legal. Given this radical agenda it was hard for women's liberation to become a player in the political process, and it tended to make purist and moralistic judgments of those who chose to work within the system.

The mass women's movement arose independently of NOW and the government commissions, and its members had a different style: they were younger, typically in their twenties, and less professional. Most importantly, it generated groups consisting of women only. The new women's liberation movement insisted that women needed a woman-only space in which they could explore their grievances and define their own agenda. They observed that women frequently censored not only what they said but even what they thought when men were around. Arriving directly from male-dominated, grassroots social-justice movements, these women longed for a space where they could talk freely with other women. First in Chicago, then in several other cities such as Gainesville, Florida; Chapel Hill, North Carolina; Washington, D.C.; and New York City, women's liberation groups formed in 1967 and 1968. At a 1968 antiwar demonstration in Washington organized by the Jeannette Rankin Brigade, 500 women gathered as a women's liberation counter-conference and then spread the movement to other towns and cities. In August 1968 twenty of them met in Sandy Springs, Maryland, to plan a larger conference. Everyone present was disturbed by the fact that they were all white. But identifying this problem did not mean they could solve it: when over 200 women from thirty-seven states and Canada met in Chicago at Thanksgiving, black women's groups were not represented, because they had not been invited or because they were not interested.

The first women's liberation groups were founded by veteran activists, but soon women with no previous movement experience joined. The decentralization of the movement was so great, despite the few early national conferences and women's frequent travel and relocation, that different geographic locations developed different agendas and organizational structures. In Iowa City, a university town, the movement began with college students and concentrated much of its energies on publishing a newspaper, *Ain't I a Woman?* In Gainesville, Florida, another university town, the movement originated in civil rights networks. In several large cities—Baltimore, Chicago, Boston, Los Angeles—single citywide organizations brought different groups together; in New York City an original group, New York Radical Women, gave birth to several smaller groups with divergent ideologies. Small-town feminists had to hang together despite their differences, while in big cities there was room to elaborate various political positions. Different cities had different ideological personalities: Washington, D.C., was best known for The Furies, a lesbian separatist group, while Chapel Hill, North Carolina, was noted for its socialist-feminist orientation.

The movement developed so widely and quickly that it is impossible to trace a chronology, impossible to say who led, what came first, who influenced whom. This lack of a clear narrative, and the sense that participants across great distances were making some of the same breakthroughs simultaneously, are characteristic of all mass social movements. In this case, though, we can outline some of the major political factions. We are identifying not the various theoretical positions in feminist intellectual debates today, but the theory that informed the practices of women's liberation groups in the early 1970s.

WOMEN'S LIBERATION DEVELOPS

The movement's characteristic form of development was consciousness-raising (CR), a form of structured discussion in which women connected their personal experiences to larger structures of gender. (See chapter 3 for a full discussion of CR.) These discussion groups, usually small, sprung up starting in 1968–70 throughout the country among women of all ages and social positions. They were simultaneously supportive and transformative. Women formed these groups by the hundreds, then by the thousands. In Cambridge/Boston where a core group offered to help other women form CR groups, a hundred *new* women attended weekly for several months. The mood was exhilarating. Women came to understand that many of their "personal" problems—insecurity about appearance and intelligence, exhaustion, conflicts with husbands and male employers—were not individual failings but a result of discrimination. The mood became even more electric as women began to create collective ways of challenging that discrimination. At first there was agitprop: spreading the word through leaflets, pamphlets, letters to newspapers; pasting stickers onto sexist advertisements; verbally protesting being called "girl" or "baby" or "chick"; hollering at guys who made vulgar proposals on the streets. Soon action groups supplemented and, in some cases, replaced CR groups. Women pressured employers to provide day care centers; publicized job and school discrimination; organized rape crisis hot lines; opened women's centers, schools, and credit unions; built unions for stewardesses and secretaries; agitated for women's studies courses at colleges; published journals and magazines.

Soon different groups formulated different theoretical/political stands. But the clarity and discreteness of these positions should not be exaggerated; there was cross-fertilization, none was sealed off from others, the borderlines and definitions shifted, and there were heated debates *within* tendencies. Liberal feminists were at first associated with NOW and similar groups, although these tended to merge with women's liberation by the end of the 1970s. Those who remained committed to a broad New Left agenda typically called themselves socialist feminists (to be distinguished from Marxist feminists, who remained convinced that Marxist theory could explain women's oppression and were not committed to an autonomous women's movement). Socialist feminists weighed issues of race and class equally with those of gender and tried to develop an integrated, holistic theory of society. Radical feminists, in contrast, prioritized sexual oppression, but by no means ignored other forms of domination. Our research suggests that the radical/socialist opposition was overstated, but small theoretical differences seemed very important at the time because the early feminists were in the process of developing new political theory, not yet making political alliances to achieve concrete objectives. A few separatists, often but not exclusively lesbians, attempted to create self-sustaining female communities and to withdraw as much as possible from contact with men. By the late 1970s, some women had become cultural feminists, celebrating women's specialness and difference from men and retreating from direct challenges to sexist institutions; they believed that change could come about through building new exemplary female communities. But despite this proliferation of ideological groupings, most members of women's liberation did not identify with any of these tendencies and considered themselves simply feminists, unmodified.

Racial/ethnic differences were more significant. Feminists of different racial/ethnic groups established independent organizations from the beginning and within those organizations created different feminisms: black, Chicana, Asian American, Native American. Feminists of color emphasized the problems with universalizing assumptions about women and with identifying gender as a category autonomous from race and class. But here too we found that these *theoretical* differences are sometimes overstated; and feminists of color were not more unanimous than white feminists—there were, for example, black liberal feminists, black socialist feminists, black radical feminists, black cultural feminists. These complexities do not negate the fact that feminists of color experienced racism within the women's movement. The majority of feminists, white women from middle-class backgrounds, were often oblivious to the lives of women from minority and working-class families. Feminists of color faced the additional problems that certain women's issues, such as reproductive rights, had been historically tainted by racism; and that feminist criticisms of men were experienced differently, often as betraying racial solidarity when the men were themselves victims of racism.

Lesbians sometimes created separate feminist groups, but the gay-straight conflict has also been exaggerated. Ironically, while some accused women's liberation of homophobia, other accused it of being a lesbian conspiracy. As lesbians became more open and vocal, they protested the heterosexual assumptions of straight feminists, but they also experienced discrimination from the male-dominated gay movement. For the most part lesbians continued to be active in women's liberation and made important contributions to feminist theory. Lesbians even led campaigns of primary concern to heterosexual women, such as campaigns for reproductive rights.

At the beginning of the movement, feminists tended to create multi-issue organizations, which in turn created committees to focus on single issues, such as day care, rape, or running a women's center. One of the fundamental tenets of early feminist theory was the interconnectedness of all aspects of women's oppression. As political sophistication grew and activists grasped the difficulties of making sweeping changes, feminists settled for piecemeal, fragmented activism. By the mid-1970s feminist politics often occurred in single-issue organizations focussed on, for example, reproductive rights, employment discrimination, health, domestic violence, female unions, women's studies. Single-issue politics de-emphasized theory, which reduced divisions; it had the advantage of making coalitions easier but the disadvantage of turning theory construction over to academics, who were usually divorced from activism. The coalitions and compromises necessitated by single-issue politics made the movement less radical and more practical. Single-issue politics also lessened the movement's coherence as its activists became specialized and professionalized.

ORGANIZATIONAL PRINCIPLES OF WOMEN'S LIBERATION

In sharp opposition to its liberal feminist sisters in NOW, women's liberation preferred radical decentralization. In addition to following New Left principles of direct democracy and anti-authoritarianism, these young feminists had their own woman-centered reasons for lack of interest in, even hostility toward, creating a large national organization. Women, whose voices had been silenced and whose actions had been directed by others, were loath to have anyone telling them what to think or do. They understood that central organization would produce principles, programs, and priorities they would be required to follow. They also sensed that a movement growing at such velocity could not be contained by central organizations, which would only inhibit creative growth. Without formal rules of membership, any group of women could declare themselves a women's liberation organization, start a newspaper or a women's center, issue a manifesto. The resulting diversity then made it all the harder to keep track of, let alone unify, the many groups.

Not only was there no formal structure bringing groups together, there was very little structure within groups, and this was, again, by choice. Feminists could dispense with Roberts' Rules of Order because the groups were small and the members usually knew each other well. But they were often also hostile in principle to formal procedures, which they saw as arbitrary and not organic. This attitude was part of the feminist critique of the public/private distinction, and it was a way of making the public sphere accessible to women who were traditionally more experienced with a personal, familial form of conversing. In small meetings, especially in the consciousness-raising groups that were the essence of women's liberation, the informal "rapping" style was nurturant, allowing women to speak intimately and risk self-exposure, and therefore to come up with rich new insights into the workings of male dominance. When there were large meetings and/or sharp disagreements, the sessions often became tediously long, unable to reach decisions, and even chaotic. As a result, small groups of women or strong-minded and charismatic individuals sometimes took charge, and others, exhausted by the long aimless discussions, grudgingly relinquished power to these unelected leaders.

Women's liberation faced a major dilemma with respect to leadership. Its search for direct democracy led the movement to revere the principle of "every woman a leader" and to imagine that collectives could speak with one voice. Consequently the movement empowered thousands of women who had never dreamt they could write a leaflet, speak in public, talk to the press, chair a meeting, assert unpopular points of view, or make risky suggestions. The emphasis on group leadership meant that many important statements were unsigned, written anonymously or collectively, or signed with first names only, indicating the degree to which theory and strategy were being developed democratically. But the bias against leadership hindered action, decision-making, and coherent communication beyond small groups. More problematically, the movement did create leaders, but they were frequently unacknowledged and almost always unaccountable because they were essentially self-appointed rather than chosen by the members. This led to widespread, sometimes intense resentment of leaders. The hostility, usually covert, sometimes escalated to stimulate open attacks, as women publicly criticized or "trashed" leaders in meetings. One result was that individuals who had worked hard and made personal sacrifices felt betrayed and embittered. Another was that women's liberation groups became vulnerable to takeovers by highly organized sectarian groups (mainly the Marxist-Leninist sects) or obstruction by disturbed individuals who could not be silenced. Perhaps the most deleterious result was that many women became reluctant to assert leadership and thus deprived the movement of needed talent. The leadership problem involved the movement's denial of internal inequalities, its refusal to recognize that some women were more articulate and self-confident; had more leisure time, connections, and access to power; or were simply more forceful personalities. These inequalities mainly derived, as the feminists' own analysis showed, from the class and race hierarchy of the larger society. This is an example of utopian hopes becoming wishful thinking: feminists so badly wanted equality that they pretended it was already here.

Despite decentralization and structurelessness, women's liberation created a shared culture, theory, and practice. In an era before e-mail, even before xeroxing, printed publications were vital and feminists spent a significant proportion of their energy, resources, and ingenuity producing them. Mimeographed pages stapled together into pamphlets were the common currency of the early years of the movement, and soon a few feminist publishing houses, such as KNOW in Pittsburgh, Lollipop Inc. in Durham, and the Feminist Press in New York, were printing and selling feminist writings for prices ranging from a nickel to a quarter. These were widely discussed, debated, and answered in further publications. Many documents in this book, including *The Politics of Housework* and *The Myth of the Vaginal Orgasm*, were published in this manner. By the mid-1970s over 500 feminist magazines and newspapers appeared throughout the country, such as *Women, A Journal of Liberation* from Baltimore, *It Ain't Me Babe* from the San Francisco Bay Area, *Off Our Backs* from Washington, D.C., *Everywoman* from Los Angeles. The male-dominated New Left underground press, like the New England Free Press in Boston or Liberation News Service, a left-wing news syndicate, also published a great deal of women's liberation news and position papers.

Unlike *Ms.*, a mass-circulation advertisement-supported liberal feminist magazine established in 1972, women's liberation publications struggled along without funds or paid staff, featuring not-quite-aligned layouts, sometimes poorly written pieces, and amateur poetry and drawings. Many articles were signed simply "Susan" or "Randy," or not signed at all, because the movement was hostile to the idea of intellectual private property. The papers sometimes forgot to print dates of publication, addresses, and subscription information. Women worked hard at producing these publications but, unfortunately, less hard at financing and distributing them, so many were irregularly published and short-lived. Nevertheless, it was in these homespun rags that you could find the most creative and cutting-edge theory and commentary.

WHAT WOMEN'S LIBERATION ACCOMPLISHED

Dear Sisters focuses on the activism of the early years of women's liberation, approximately 1968 to 1976. Although we try whenever possible to refer to the achievements that arose from these campaigns, most transformations only revealed themselves later. Social change, after all, happens slowly.

Judicial and legislative victories include the legalization of abortion in 1973, federal guidelines against coercive sterilization, rape shield laws that encourage more women to prosecute their attackers, affirmative action programs that aim to correct past discrimination—but not, however, the Equal Rights Amendment, which failed in 1982, just three states short of the required two-thirds. There are many equally important but less obvious accomplishments: not only legal, economic, and political gains, but also changes in the way people live, dress, dream of their future, and make a living. In fact, there are few areas of contemporary life untouched by feminism. As regards health care, for example, many physicians and hospitals have made major improvements in the treatment of women; about 50 percent of medical students are women; women successfully fought their exclusion from medical research; diseases affecting women, such as breast and ovarian cancer, now receive more funding thanks to women's efforts. Feminists insisted that violence against women, previously a well-kept secret, become a public political issue; made rape, incest, battering, and sexual harassment understood as crimes; and got public funding for shelters for battered women. These gains, realized in the 1980s and 1990s, are the fruits of struggles fought in the 1970s.

Feminist pressure generated substantial changes in education: curricula and textbooks have been rewritten to promote equal opportunity for girls, more women are admitted and funded in universities and professional schools, and a new and rich feminist scholarship in many disciplines has won recognition. Title IX, passed in 1972 to mandate equal access to college programs, has worked a revolution in sports. Consider the many women's records broken in track and field, the expanding number of athletic scholarships for women, professional women's basketball, and the massive popularity of girls' and women's soccer.

Campaigning to support families, feminists organized day care centers, developed standards and curricula for early childhood education, demanded day care funding from government and private employers, fought for parental leave from employers and a decent welfare system. They also struggled for new options for women in employment. They won greater access to traditionally male occupations, from construction to professions and business. They joined unions and fought to democratize them, and they succeeded in organizing previously nonunion workers such as secretaries, waitresses, hospital workers, and flight attendants. As the majority of American women increasingly need to work for wages throughout their lives, the feminist movement tried to educate men to share in housework and child raising. Although women still do the bulk of the housework and child rearing, it is common today to see men in the playgrounds, the supermarkets, and at the PTA meetings.

Feminism changed how women look and what is considered attractive, although the original feminist impulse toward simpler, more comfortable, and less overtly sexual clothing is being challenged by another generation of women at the turn of the century. As women's-liberation influence spread in the 1970s, more and more women refused to wear the constricting, uncomfortable clothes that were required in the 1950s—girdles, garter belts, and stockings; tight, flimsy, pointed, and high-heeled shoes; crinolines and cinch belts; tight short skirts. Women wearing pants, loose jackets, walking shoes, and no makeup began to feel attractive and to be recognized by others as attractive. By the 1980s, however, younger women began to feel that feminist beauty standards were repressive, even prudish, and developed a new, more playful, ornate, and multicultural fashion sensibility that may signal a "third wave" of feminism. Women's newfound passion for athletics has made a look of health and strength fashionable, sometimes to an oppressive degree as women feel coerced to reach a firm muscular, spandex thinness. At the same time, a conservative antifeminist backlash is also influencing fashion, trying to reestablish an allegedly lost femininity. The politics of feminism is being fought out on the fashion front.

Other aspects of the culture also reveal feminism's impact. Finally some older movie actresses, such as Susan Sarandon, Olympia Dukakis, and Meryl Streep, are recognized as desirable, and women entertainers in many media and art forms are rejecting simplistic, demeaning, and passive roles, despite the reemergence of misogynist and hypersexualized entertainments. Soap operas, sitcoms, even cop shows now feature plots in which lesbianism, abortion, rape, incest, and battering are portrayed from women's perspectives. In the fine arts, women's progress has been slower, illustrating the fallacy of assuming that the elite is less sexist than those of lesser privilege. The way we speak has been altered: new words have been coined— "sexist" and "Ms." and "gender"; many Americans are now self-conscious about using "he" to mean a human, and textbooks and even sacred texts are being rewritten in inclusive language. Women now expect to be called "women" instead of "ladies" or "girls."

Some of the biggest transformations are personal and familial, and they have been hotly contested. Indeed, even from a feminist perspective not all of them are positive. Women's relationships with other women are more publicly valued and celebrated and lesbianism is more accepted. People are marrying later and some are choosing not to marry. Most women today enter marriage or other romantic relationships with the expectation of equal partnership; since they don't always get this, they seem more willing to live as single people than to put up with domineering or abusive men. Conservatives argue that the growth of divorce, out-of-wedlock childbirth, and single motherhood is a sign of social deterioration, and certainly the growing economic inequality in the U.S. has rendered many women and especially single mothers and their children impoverished, depressed, and angry. But, feminists retort, is being poor in a destructive marriage really better than being poor on one's own? Even the growth of single motherhood reflects an element of women's choice: in different circumstances both poor and prosperous women are refusing to consider a bad marriage the price of motherhood, and are giving birth to or adopting children without husbands. More women think of marriage as only one possible option, aware that singleness and lesbianism are reasonable alternatives. Even women who do marry increasingly consider marriage only one aspect of life, supplementing motherhood and work. There is a growing sentiment that families come in a variety of forms.

By the mid-1970s an antifeminist backlash was able to command huge funding from right-wing corporate fortunes, fervent support from religious fundamentalists, and considerable media attention. The intensity of the reaction is a measure of how threatened conservatives were by popular backing for women's liberation and the rapid changes it brought about. Even with their billions of dollars, their hundreds of lobbyists and PR men, their foundations and magazines dishing out antifeminist misinformation, as compared to the puny amounts of money and volunteer labor available to women's liberation, the striking fact is that public opinion has not shifted much. Polls show overwhelming support for what feminism stands for: equal rights, respect, opportunity, and access for women.

That there is still a long way to go to reach sexual equality should not prevent us from recognizing what has been achieved. If there is disappointment, it is because women's liberation was so utopian, even apocalyptic, emerging as it did in an era of radical social movements and grand optimism. Unrealistic? Perhaps. But without utopian dreams, without anger, without reaching for the moon and expecting to get there by express, the movement would have achieved far less. In fact, without taking risks, feminists would never have been able to imagine lives of freedom and justice for women.

Feminism is by no means dead. Feminist groups continue to work on specific issues such as reproductive rights, rape, violence against women, sweatshops, sexism in the media, union organizing, and welfare rights. Nevertheless, the mass social movement called women's liberation did dissolve by the end of the 1970s. This is not a sign of failure. All social movements are short-lived because of the intense personal demands they make; few can sustain the level of energy that they require at their peak of activity. Moreover, as people age, most put more energy into family, employment, and personal life. Equally important, women's liberation could not survive outside the context of the other progressive social movements that nurtured hope and optimism about social change. As the Left declined, the right-wing backlash grew stronger. It did not convert many feminists to conservatism but it moved the mainstream far to the right. Given this change in mainstream politics, it is all the more striking that so few feminist gains have been rolled back and many have continued and even increased their momentum. Although the word "feminist" has become a pejorative term to some American women, most women (and most men as well) support a feminist program: equal education, equal pay, child care, freedom from harassment and violence, shared housework and child rearing, women's right to self-determination.

This book documents the relatively short period of maximum grassroots participation in the women's movement, from about 1968 to approximately 1977. We selected the documents, most of which have been abridged in order to keep this book reasonably short and reasonably priced, from among many hundreds more that we considered. Our choices reflect the range of views and activities of women's liberation and are not limited to our own opinions. Many of the pieces were written collectively or anonymously, and some were signed with pseudonyms. Some of the signed pieces had authors we were unable to track down. We selected pieces for their readability and accessibility, and we tried to create the mix that would present women's liberation most completely and accurately. We deposited most of the documents we collected in the Tamiment Library at New York University, where they are available to the public.

Dear Sisters is not organized as a chronological narrative, because of the simultaneous development of women's liberation in many different locations. We did not organize the book by specific issues or campaigns, because feminists across this large country focussed on so many different issues. Instead we organized the documents here into eight major areas—health, sexuality, reproductive rights, violence against women, family, education, work, and culture—with the understanding that not every document fits neatly into one of these, and that many overlap several categories. In addition, in order to convey the movement's understanding that all aspects of women's oppression are connected and its impulse toward changing the totality of women's lives, we constructed four chapters along different principles at the beginning of the book. They present women's liberation comprehensively: how the movement arose, its political influences, how it organized, and its theories.

I
Origins

1

A Movement Arises

The source of the women's liberation movement, sometimes called second-wave feminism, was the civil rights movement, just as the antislavery movement gave birth to the first-wave women's rights movement in the 1840s. In the 1950s and 1960s, thousands of feminist foremothers from all over the United States participated in the civil rights movement in the South, helping to register voters, working in Freedom Schools, and participating in campaigns to desegregate public facilities. From an understanding of racism and the struggle against it, a new generation of feminists learned organizing skills and eventually became a core group in the new women's movement. What they learned about racism helped them elaborate an analysis of sexism and institutionalized male dominance.

In 1964 Mary King wrote a paper for a conference of the Student Nonviolent Coordinating Committee (SNCC), the most militant interracial civil rights group of the time, on "how my growing perception of myself as a woman might affect the structure and program of SNCC," and Casey Hayden cosigned it. The two women had been reading Simone de Beauvoir's *The Second Sex* (a pioneering work of feminist theory published first in French and then in English in 1953) and the fiction of then-feminist and Leftist Doris Lessing, and had been discussing them with other women in SNCC. The paper received an overwhelmingly negative response at the conference. Nevertheless, a year later Hayden and King coauthored a second document and mailed it to forty civil rights and anti–Vietnam War women activists; it was subsequently published in *Liberation,* a pacifist magazine. This memo came to be regarded as the first expression of the need for a women's liberation movement, although the authors could not have imagined such a movement developing—a mere three years before it took off like wildfire.

Casey Hayden (formerly Sandra Cason, then married to Tom Hayden, an early leader of Students for a Democratic Society, a militant student anti–Vietnam War group) and Mary King (the product of six generations of ministers) came to political activism from southern white Protestant interracial activities, an important source of early feminism. Young women civil rights participants benefited from the leadership of older activists such as Ella Baker, Fannie Lou Hamer, and Unita Blackwell. But at the same time women were largely confined to secondary positions in the civil rights organizations and found themselves doing the "shit work"—typing, mimeographing, cleaning, and running errands—while men made the decisions and talked to the press. Soon some women, black and white, became alienated because of SNCC's shift away from nonviolence and toward an ideological, centralized, black nationalism, just as some men in the white New Left were drawn to ultra-revolutionary rhetoric.

Sex and Caste
CASEY HAYDEN AND MARY KING

1965

A Kind of Memo from Casey Hayden and Mary King to a number of other women in the peace and freedom movements.

• Sex and caste: There seem to be many parallels that can be drawn between treatment of Negroes and treatment of women in our society as a whole. But in particular, women we've talked to who work in the movement seem to be caught up in a common-law caste system that operates, sometimes subtly, forcing them to work around or outside hierarchical structures of power which may exclude them. Women seem to be placed in the same position of assumed subordination in personal situations too. It is a caste system which, at its worst, uses and exploits women.

This is complicated by several facts, among them:

1. The caste system is not institutionalized by law (women have the right to vote, to sue for divorce, etc.);
2. Women can't withdraw from the situation (à la nationalism) or overthrow it;
3. There are biological differences (even though those biological differences are usually discussed or accepted without taking present and future technology into account so we probably can't be sure what these differences mean). Many people who are very hip to the implications of the racial caste system, even people in the movement, don't seem to be able to see the sexual caste system and if the question is raised they respond with: "That's the way it's supposed to be. There are biological differences." Or with other statements which recall a white segregationist confronted with integration.

• Women and problems of work: The caste system perspective dictates the role assigned to women in the movement, and certainly even more to women outside the movement. Within the movement, questions arise in situations ranging from relationships of women organizers to men in the community, to who cleans the freedom house, to who holds leadership positions, to who does secretarial work, and who acts as spokesman for groups. Other problems arise between women with varying degrees of awareness of themselves as being as capable as men but held back from full participation, or between women who see themselves as needing more control of their work than other women demand. And there are problems with relationships between white women and black women.

• Institutions: Nearly everyone has real questions about those institutions which shape perspectives on men and women: marriage, child rearing patterns, women's (and men's) magazines, etc. People are beginning to think about and even to experiment with new forms in these areas.

• Men's reactions to the questions raised here: A very few men seem to feel, when they hear conversations involving these problems, that they have a right to be present and participate in them, since they are so deeply involved. At the same time, very few men can respond non-defensively, since the whole idea is either beyond their comprehension or threatens and exposes them. The usual response is laughter. That inability to see the whole issue as serious, as the strait-jacketing of both sexes and as societally determined, often shapes our own response so that we learn to think in their terms about ourselves and to feel silly, rather than trust our inner feelings. The problems we're listing here, and what others have said about them, are therefore largely drawn from conversations among women only—and that difficulty in establishing dialogue with men is a recurring theme among people we've talked to.

Objectively the chances seem nil that we could start a movement based on anything as distant to general American thought as a sex-caste system. Therefore, most of us will probably want to work full time on problems such as war, poverty, race. The very fact that the country can't face, much less deal with, the questions we're raising means that the movement is one place to look for some relief. Real efforts at dialogue within the movement and with whatever liberal groups, community women, or students might listen are justified. That is, all the problems between men and women and all the problems of women functioning in society as equal human beings are among the most basic that people face. We've talked in the movement about trying to build a society which would see basic human problems (which are not seen as private troubles) as public problems and would try to shape institutions to meet human needs rather than shaping people to meet the needs of those with power. To raise questions like those above illustrates very directly that society hasn't dealt with some of its deepest problems and opens discussion of why that is so. (In one sense, it is a radicalizing question that can take people beyond legalistic solutions into areas of personal and institutional change.)

We Don't Need the Men

MALVINA REYNOLDS

1958

2) We don't need the men,
   We don't need the men.
   We don't need to have 'em around,
   Except for now and then.
   They can come to see us when they have
   Tickets for the symphony.
   Otherwise they can stay at home and
   Play a game of pinochle.
   We don't care about them,
   They'll look cute in a bathing suit
   On a billboard in Newfoundland.

3) We don't need the men,
   We don't need the men.
   We don't need to have 'em around,
   Except for now and then.
   They can come to see us when they're
   Feeling pleasant and agreeable.
   Otherwise they can stay at home and
   Holler at the T.V. programs.
   We don't care about them,
   We can do without them,
   They'll look cute in a bathing suit
   On a billboard in Madagascar.

4) We don't need the men,
   We don't need the men.
   We don't need to have 'em around,
   Except for now and then.
   They can come to see us when they're
   All cleaned up with a suit on,
   Otherwise they can stay at home
   And (spoken) drop towels in they *own* bathroom.
   We don't care about them,
   We can do without them,
   They'll look cute in a bathing suit
   On a billboard in Tierra del Fuego.

An Appeal to Mothers, Black and White

MOTHERS' DRAFT RESISTANCE   1968

An Appeal
to
MOTHERS
Black and White

If you, as parent of a minor son, object
to his being taken from you and turned into a paid
killer, then oppose military conscription NOW,
before it is too late.

THE DRAFT IS:
        UNFAIR
        UNDEMOCRATIC
        UNCONSTITUTIONAL
        UNAMERICAN
              and
        IMMORAL

Refuse to cooperate with such an evil
system; stop accepting the
unacceptable.

If you do not stand for your son,
WHO WILL?

JOIN Mothers' Draft Resistance

The young men who oppose military
conscription, the Vietnam war, and killing
should not have to stand alone, for their principles
and ideals. We, as adults and parents, must stand
with them, and for them, and protest with them,
the illegal
and immoral acts which are being carried
out in our name, and in the name of our beloved
country.

Let us fill the courts with cases of
mothers refusing to give up their sons
to illegitimate authority, and our jails
with mothers, if need be.

EVERY DAY IS MOTHERS' DAY!
Mother's Day Demonstration

Groups like Mothers' Draft Resistance infuriated many young feminists. The budding new women's liberation movement wanted to act on women's issues and not merely to support men's resistance. Equally, they did not wish to pigeonhole women as mothers nor accept the self-sacrificing, passive, sentimental connotations of motherhood wielded as a traditional political symbol. This leaflet, jointly sponsored by Chicago and New York groups, called women to a counter-demonstration in Washington, D.C., against a Jeannette Rankin Brigade anti-Vietnam War action. That group, named for the first congresswoman, a pacifist who opposed World War I, represented a coalition between the Old Left-influenced Women Strike for Peace and religious and peace groups. Eighty-seven-year-old Jeannette Rankin herself marched, along with Coretta Scott King, folksinger Judy Collins, and other celebrities.

At this demonstration—the first public appearance of the new feminism—a group of younger women protested not only the war but also the motherhood discourse of the older women. The young feminists carried banners reading "DON'T CRY, RESIST!" and complained that "until women go beyond justifying themselves in terms of their wombs and breasts and housekeeping abilities, they will never be able to exert any political power." This event marks the first use of the slogan "Sisterhood is Powerful!" The demonstrators staged a funeral procession carrying a large dummy with a blank face, blonde curls, and a candle, lying on a bier festooned with curlers, garters, hairspray, and S & H Green Stamps. They were burying the old support-your-man, nice-girl version of womanhood.

Burial of Weeping Womanhood

RADICAL WOMEN'S GROUP

1968

You are joyfully invited to
attend the burial
of
WEEPING WOMANHOOD
who passed
with
a
sigh
to her Great Reward
this year of the lord
1968
after 3000 years of
bolstering the egos of the
warmakers
and
aiding the cause of war . . .

BURIAL

Arlington National Cemetery
Monday, January 15, 1968

Don't Bring Flowers . . .

Do be prepared to sacrifice your traditional female roles. You have refused to hanky-wave boys off to war with admonitions to save the American Mom and Apple Pie. You have resisted our roles of supportive girlfriends and tearful widows, receivers of "regretful" telegrams and worthless medals of honor. And now you must resist approaching Congress playing these same roles that are synonymous with powerlessness. We must not come as passive suppliants begging for favors, for power cooperates only with power. We must learn to fight the warmongers on their own terms, though they believe us capable only of rolling bandages. Until we have united into a force to be reckoned with, we will be patronized and ridiculed into total political ineffectiveness. So if you are really sincere about _ending_ this war, join us tonight and in the future.

Yet another stream contributing to the rise of women's liberation was the "homophile" movement that appeared in the U.S. in 1950, dedicated to seeking civil rights for homosexuals. But sexism within the homophile movement eventually led lesbians to separate from the major male-dominated gay organization, the Mattachine Society. In 1955 lesbians established their own organization, the Daughters of Bilitis, a name taken from a book of poetry by Sappho, an ancient Greek schoolteacher who lived on the isle of Lesbos and wrote romantic poems to her female student. Early DOB leaders liked the name because it sounded like any other women's lodge, thus protecting them from harassment—a vital consideration given the legacy of McCarthyism, which had persecuted gays as well as "Reds." When DOB initiated a monthly magazine, *The Ladder*, in 1956, the editor assured readers that a recent Supreme Court decision gave her the right to refuse to reveal subscribers' names to Congress.

In the 1960s the DOB grew closer to the embryonic feminist movement. That alliance was doubly productive: learning about lesbianism led heterosexual feminists to a deeper questioning of sexual norms, while the boldness of heterosexual feminists—who had not been closeted or socialized to hide—influenced lesbians toward being "out" and proud.

What Concrete Steps Can Be Taken to Further the Homophile Movement

SHIRLEY WILLER   1966

The important difference between the male and female homosexual is that the Lesbian is discriminated against not only because she is a Lesbian, but because she is a woman. Although the Lesbian occupies a "privileged" place among homosexuals, she occupies an under-privileged place in the world.

It is difficult for a woman to be accepted as a leader in any community or civic organization and the woman who does succeed in breaking down the barriers in recognition is usually greeted with a mixture of astonishment and sympathetic amusement. There are few women who desire to emulate Carrie Nation, chained to a fire hydrant and swinging a battle-axe—but the few women who achieve community, professional or civic leadership are compared to that image, sometimes rightfully so, since despite legal recognition of feminine equality, the road to public recognition for each woman leads across the battlefield.

Lesbians have agreed (with reservations) to join in common cause with the male homosexual—her role in society has been one of mediator between the male homosexual and society. The recent DOB Convention was such a gesture. The reason we were able to get the public officials there was because we are women, because we offered no threat. However, they did not bargain for what they got. They did not expect to be challenged on the issues of male homosexuality. In these ways we show our willingness to assist the male homosexual in seeking to alleviate the problems our society has inflicted on him.

There has been little evidence, however, that the male homosexual has any intention of making common cause with us. We suspect that should the male homosexual achieve his particular objectives in regard to his homosexuality he might possibly become a more adamant foe of women's rights than the heterosexual male has ever been.

The Lesbian's Other Identity
DEL MARTIN

In speaking to public audiences about the Lesbian, DOB spokeswomen have often alluded to the fact that she is first a human being, a woman second, and incidentally a Lesbian. DOB's program over the years, however, has lent itself almost exclusively to the Lesbian role—the problems these women face in employment, for instance, as Lesbians. But don't they also face employment discrimination just on the basis of being women? And wouldn't it also serve the purpose of DOB to join with other women's organizations in fighting against sex discrimination as it relates to women?

Lesbianism and Feminism
WILDA CHASE

Recently a Women's Liberation encounter group—a therapy-oriented group—appeared as guests at an open discussion meeting at the DOB. They explained how their group was formed in response to the ever-recurring confessions of women in the Movement that they feel "damaged" through their relationships with men, that their sense of *self* is diminished. They feel that the time has come for women to admit that they are being (have always been) short-changed in their relationships with men, and that their best course is to *give one another* the recognition and encouragement for the personal growth and fulfillment they are denied by men. Some of them feel intense hate and anger toward men for their refusal (or, as some believe, their natural incapacity) to return to women the self-recognition they *take* from women as a natural right.

It is ironic that feminists have always been accused of being lesbians. They are far from it. In fact, their *heterosexuality* is their problem.

Lesbians do have definite advantages over heterosexual women. Their less intimate contact with men gives them a margin of protection against the grossest forms of damage. They should guard against complacency, however. Like all female citizens who grow up and live in a male-dominated world, lesbians also have identity problems. They, too, are self-alienated to some degree. Furthermore, their political consciousness is much lower than that of the women in the Movement.

Lesbians may be psychically healthier than feminists, but their political IQ is generally disgracefully low. They have a lot to learn. They do have a vague notion that equal employment opportunity, equal educational opportunity, etc., somehow apply to them. But that is usually as far as they can go. One DOB member of the encounter meeting conceded that the abortion laws perhaps *should* be repealed. "It *is* possible—god forbid—that I could be raped," she said. That much occurred to her. She did not ask the larger question of why women should tolerate having male legislators make laws controlling the use of women's bodies.

Feminism irrelevant to lesbians? Snap out of it, sisters, and get with it! *Demand* your rights to your whole human dignity. *Demand* living conditions which will enable you to be fully, creatively *yourself,* not just a shadow of yourself. It is a characteristic of life that it pays no higher a price than you ask of it. Don't learn too late that you have priced yourself lower than life was prepared to pay.

To the Women of the Left
SDS WOMEN

1967

To the Women of the Left:

We have been meeting weekly for the last two months to discuss our colonial status in this society and to propound strategy and methods of attacking it. Our political awareness of our oppression has developed thru the last couple years as we sought to apply the principles of justice, equality, mutual respect and dignity which we learned from the Movement to the lives we lived as part of the Movement; only to come up against the solid wall of male chauvinism.

Women must not make the same mistake the blacks did at first of allowing others (whites in their case, men in ours) to define our issues, methods and goals. Only we can and must define the terms of our struggle. The time has come for us to take the initiative in organizing ourselves for our own liberation.

While we welcome inquiries and assistance from all concerned persons, this organization and its sister chapter now forming in N.Y. are open only to women.

1. As women are 51% of the population of this country, they must be proportionally represented on all levels of society rather than relegated to trivial functions that have been predetermined for them. Particularly they must be allowed to assume full participation in the decision-making processes and positions of our political, economic and social institutions.

2. We condemn the mass media for perpetuating the stereotype of women as always in an auxiliary position to men, being no more than mothers, wives or sexual objects. We specifically condemn the advertising concerns for creating the myths about women solely to profit from them as consumers. Furthermore, we call for a boycott of the thriving women's magazines, such as *McCalls, Good Housekeeping, Vogue* (etc., etc.) for romanticizing drudgery and promoting a false mystique of emancipation.

3. There must be total equality of opportunity for education, at all levels and in all fields. Women should be fully educated to their individual potential instead of being subtly persuaded that education is of little value to their long-range interests.

4. Equal employment opportunities must be enforced. This includes equal pay for equal work, no discrimination on the basis of women's childbearing functions, and open access to all jobs, particularly managerial and policy making positions.

5. The labor movement and all labor organizations, unions and groups must admit women on an equal basis to all executive and policy levels while encouraging women to assume leadership roles in their organizations. There must be a concerted effort to organize and unionize those low-paying, servile occupations in which women are primarily employed.

6. Women must have complete control of their own bodies. This means a) the dissemination of birth control information and devices, free of charge by the state, to all women regardless of age and marital status; b) the availability of a competent, inexpensive medical abortion for all women who so desire.

7. The structure of the family unit in our society must be reconsidered and the following institutional changes must be incorporated: a) a fundamental revamping of marriage, divorce and property laws and customs which cause an injustice to or a subjection of either sex; b) the equal sharing by husbands and wives of the responsibility for maintaining the home and raising the children; c) the creation of communal child care centers which would be staffed by women and men assuming equal responsibility and controlled by the adults and children involved in the center; d) the creation of non-profit-making food preparation centers conveniently located in all communities.

We recognize that women are often their own worst enemies because they have been trained to be prejudiced against themselves. We know that to become truly free, we must abdicate the superficial privilege which has been purposely substituted for equality and replace it with an equal share of responsibility for taking power in our society.

The New Left encompassed young people of many racial/ethnic groups, and every group experienced a feminist awakening, as women articulated both grievances and aspirations. Contrary to the common myth that women's liberation was only white, Asian American women, led by Chinese and Japanese Americans, began discussing their oppression and their vision of women's liberation in the early 1970s in both California and New York.

Definitions of what constitutes feminism need to reflect the diversity of ideological orientations and political experience. These women did not always identify as feminists, and remained primarily identified with an Asian American movement. The following description is from a 1989 article by Susie Ling, professor of Asian American Studies at Pasadena City College.

The Mountain Movers
SUSIE LING

In the summer of 1968, a campus group called Sansei Concern organized an "Are You Yellow?" conference at UCLA to discuss issues of "yellow power," identity, and the war in Vietnam. Sansei Concern would later change its name to "Oriental Concern" in an effort to incorporate other Asian ethnic groups. In 1969, the group changed its name once more to reflect its growing sophistication: Asian American Political Alliance. In November of 1968, Third World students went on strike at San Francisco State College, sending ripple effects to the Los Angeles area. Asian American Studies courses were introduced on several campuses in 1969. In the local communities, organizations such as Yellow Brotherhood, Japanese American Community Services—Asian Involvement (JACS-AI), Asian American Hardcore and the newspaper *Gidra* took root.

Women had been involved in each stage of the growing Asian American Movement. But women felt that they were restricted to subordinate roles of taking minutes, making coffee, typing, answering phones, and handling the mail. One woman described her frustration:

> I remember I wrote a poem once where I referred to myself as the toilet cleaner. I always found myself [at a community center] on the weekends cleaning the goddamn toilet. Literally [I was] the toilet cleaner.

Other women were frustrated with the kind of "subtle attitude that men had a right to women, sexually." One participant said that she became concerned about women's issues after working with "a lot of male chauvinist pigs. The guys were young and they were the most macho." The ensuing confrontations paralleled the break of the Women's Liberation Movement from the New Left.

The first voicings of dissatisfaction within the Asian American Movement occurred spontaneously. Women began to share their complaints in informal settings. Subsequently, the women began to assert themselves in larger group settings. Some of the confrontations were taken seriously, while others were not.

> I remember one meeting with thirty people or so. We all went around the room and introduced ourselves. This one guy said "My name is so-and-so and this is my wife; she has nothing to say." That really stuck in my mind. I and other women just exploded. That sort of focused what we had been feeling.

One particular incident in the early 1970s epitomizes the emotional frustration of the women:

> One of the women we were working with got beat up real bad by this guy—it was the second time that he had done that. Somehow it really struck a note. It was that she represented the blatant form of what a lot of us were feeling—this anger against chauvinism. We felt it had to stop. We got together with a few hours notice. We decided to teach him a lesson. Many of these women never had any physical violence experience before, [they had] never even been hit by their parents. But we decided to teach him a lesson and the only way was to kick his ass. Again, I really

stress that [for] the type of people involved, it wasn't a natural thing for us. But at the time, it really made sense.

> There were about fifteen to twenty women, so we went over to this guy's house. One of us summed it up as "Militarily, it may not have been a victory, but politically, it was." We had decided that we were going in there to teach him a political lesson, explain to him why we were doing this. But because these women were taught not to express anger, and we never express it physically, it took us so long to strike the first blow. It was really funny. We kept explaining on and on. We were just standing there. So finally one of the women went up to him and slugged him and then everybody jumped on him. It was really more of rolling around and that kind of stuff. But he got totally freaked out. More than if he actually got his ass kicked. We never thought it would happen that way. I felt great [afterwards]. It was such a different and radical thing to do that [it] was a profound experience. I'm not saying that this is a solution to male chauvinism. It was a spontaneous thing.

The women established consciousness-raising groups. The content and structure of several study and support groups differed. Some explored the personal dimensions of being Asian women in America:

> So we each had a day where we spoke about our lives. We'd all start crying. I remember it being really scary for people. In fact, some people dropped out of the group when they found out we were going to do this. It was so vulnerable to say some of the things we said to each other.

Another study group spent weekly meetings broadening their understanding of international and domestic political issues.

> I thought that was the overriding significance of the group, that we developed politically through it when we would have been very inhibited in a mixed setting. It was important to have this group, to have a safe environment.

Members of these groups supplemented their study and discussion with community activism. The women provided social services, made public presentations, wrote, taught, and organized politically on grassroots levels. Perhaps the most memorable activity was the sending of delegates to the Vancouver Indochinese Women's Conference in April of 1971. Delegates returned to Los Angeles and shared their experiences with activists who were not able to attend. One male summed up the encounter:

> When the sisters came back from Canada, there was this glow, this aura with them. I and other brothers felt that we really missed something. I wish like hell I could have gone.

Many of the women lived together in cooperatives or shared apartments. Friendships developed that largely remained important to the women in the ensuing years.

In April of 1969, seven Asian Americans pooled together one hundred dollars each to establish the monthly publication *Gidra,* which became the organ of the Asian American Movement in Los Angeles. In the very first issue, Dinora Gil wrote in "Yellow Prostitution":

> It is not enough that we must "kow tow" to the Yellow male ego, but we must do this by aping the Madison Avenue and Hollywood version of *White* femininity. All the peroxide, foam rubber, and scotch tape will not transform you into what you are not. Whether this is a conditioned desire to be white, or a desperate attempt to attain male-approval, it is nothing more than Yellow Prostitution.

Gidra continued to feature feminist voices. In its final issue, Mike Murase, a founder of the paper wrote:

> In 1971, we began publishing a series of issues focusing on specific themes beginning in January with the Women's Issue produced under the guidance of fifteen Asian women. Their editorial comment was clear and bold, "We as Asian women have united in opposition to this society which has reduced women to economic and

psychological servitude, and Third World women and men to racist, dehumanizing stereotypes." They emphatically rejected notions prevalent among some circles of women that men are the oppressors and stated their intention to "oppose the capitalist system, resist the racist images imposed on both ourselves and our brothers, and struggle with our brothers against male chauvinism [so that we can] join in constructing the definitions for self-determination in the revolutionary struggle."

Asian American Studies programs were established at UCLA and California State College, Long Beach, in 1969 following the massive Third World student strike at San Francisco State College and UC Berkeley the previous year. The strike shook the foundations of higher learning. At UCLA, the first "Asian Women in America" course was offered in the winter quarter of 1972 in the campus' experimental college system. The syllabus read:

> As Asian American women, our roles and position are in large part defined by American perceptions and stereotypes as well as remnants of East Asian cultures that have been carried to America. In this course, we hope to generate a new perspective applicable to other non-white women as well.

The course generated positive feedback and was taught again in spring 1973 and winter 1974, both times by a collective of staff, graduate, and undergraduate students. The instructors experimented with creative approaches. For example, they tried to foster community awareness by meeting once a week at off-campus locations such as the Asian Women's Center, the Senshin Buddhist Church, and the Pilipino Community Center. Some sessions also encouraged public participation. Team teaching was especially popular due to the lack of research materials on Asian American women and the stress on democratic participation in the progressive movement.

The collective approach to teaching was frowned upon by college administrators who refused to approve the course's transition to regular curriculum. At UCLA, one academic committee reported:

> There was very little substantive material related to the "problems of Asian American women," with the almost sole preoccupation of the students centering around the political aspects of "capitalist society." Incredible laxity was permitted in the use of phrases like "third world women" to describe Asian U.S. women. The subcommittee voted unanimously to recommend against the acceptance of this course.

It was not until 1976 that the course reentered the UCLA curriculum. The team teaching approach was exchanged in favor of the more traditional, one-professor structure.

One of the most obvious community needs in Los Angeles was child care:

> The women needed a child care center all day. Education was important, but at the same time, they couldn't find jobs such as bank telling because they had kids. They had to settle for jobs which they can bring kids to or have someone else watch their kids.

Nowhere was this more apparent than in Chinatown where many women worked in the garment industry.

In 1972, six women formed Little Friends Playgroup, which was based out of an apartment in Chinatown. The staff was mostly comprised of college-oriented women with education majors. The Little Friends Playgroup project worked in close conjunction with other Chinatown organizations such as Chinatown Teenpost, the Food Co-op, Asian American Tutorial Project and Chinatown Youth Council. The Little Friends Playgroup received government funding later and still exists today.

Women activists from universities and communities came together at the end of 1971 to plan for an Asian women's center that would serve as the focal point of community concerns. A proposal was written, submitted in the Department of Health, Education and Welfare, and approved. Funding began in July of 1972. Although the proposal was actually written for the drug abuse program, Asian Sisters, the women decided to creatively manage and stretch the federal monies so that other issues would also be addressed.

Under the guidance of a board and coordinating committee, five program areas were established:

1. education, to develop resources;
2. counseling;
3. child development or Little Friends Playgroup;
4. drug abuse, extending the Asian Sisters program; and
5. health, offering pregnancy counseling, birth control, and abortion referrals.

The Center was a major hub of the Asian American Movement in Los Angeles, serving many different functions. In 1976, the pressures of complex financial, personal, and organizational factors, as well as government cutbacks to social services, forced its closure. Miya Iwataki, director of the Center, pointed to its lasting accomplishments:

> This Center was the only fully federally funded program in which the staff analyzed past experiences of other funded programs to try to fully understand the pitfalls, the co-optation, the seemingly inevitable diversion from long-term, complete solutions. Federal funding was recognized for what it was—a bandaid to keep us quiet.
>
> But the Center recognized and addressed this problem. Not only was the funding stretched to its limit for needs other than those the government had stipulated, but programs that were really needed were attempted. Concrete material and people-power support was given to key Third World as well as Asian causes. We tried to test if federal funding could be used in a way that would benefit our people and not stifle work for radical social change.
>
> For so many of us, it was [also] an opportunity to test our leadership. It was a challenge to build and squeeze as much as we could out of a system that had been squeezing us for decades and even centuries.

The 1968 to 1976 period of the Asian American Women's Movement had two seemingly contradictory trends:

1. a rebellion against male chauvinism in the Asian Movement and with Asian culture and at the same time,

2. a strong allegiance and identity with the same Asian American Movement. The Asian women were very explicit about not wanting to be identified with what they perceived as an "anti-male" trend in the general feminist movement. The interviewees were emphatic about their rapport with men. To the question, "As an Asian American woman, do you consider yourself a "feminist"? women answered:

> [If you define it as] someone who believes in women's rights and equality, if that's the definition, then I believe in it. The media has portrayed feminism as the fight between men and women, that feminists are anti-male. If that's the definition you are using, then I don't believe in it. I think that men and women have to work together. Although women have to strive for equality, men also need education. We need to strive for equality for all.

> No, because I understand "feminism" to mean something negative. I'm not really sure what it means but it has a connotation of being anti-men. I don't agree with that kind of viewpoint.

The Asian perception of the white-dominated, middle class Women's Liberation Movement was generally negative. Not only were the media stereotypes of the Women's Movement as "anti-male" accepted, white women were also blanketly accused of being fascist. Even today, some Asian activists would not claim to be a "feminist" for fear of being associated with the general women's movement despite their strong interests in women's equality. In its own infancy and early development the Women's Movement was in fact not very sensitive to the issues of racial minorities and lower class women. Black, Chicano, Native American, and Asian Pacific women felt alienated and at times exploited.

The Asian women strongly identified themselves as a subset of the Asian American Movement to which they gave their primary allegiance.

Principles
NEW YORK RADICAL WOMEN   1968

We take the woman's side in everything.

We ask not if something is "reformist," "radical," "revolutionary," or "moral." We ask: is it good for women or bad for women?

We ask not if something is "political." We ask: is it effective? Does it get us closest to what we really want in the fastest way?

We define the best interests of women as the best interests of the poorest, most insulted, most despised, most abused woman on earth. Her lot, her suffering and abuse is the threat that men use against all of us to keep us in line. She is what all women fear being called, fear being treated as, and yet what we all really are in the eyes of men. She is Everywoman: ugly, dumb (dumb broad, dumb cunt), bitch, nag, hag, whore, fucking and breeding machine, mother of us all. Until Everywoman is free, no woman will be free. When her beauty and knowledge is revealed and seen, the new day will be at hand.

We are critical of all past ideology, literature and philosophy, products as they are of male supremacist culture. We are re-examining even our words—language itself.

We take as our source the hitherto unrecognized culture of women, a culture which from long experience of oppression developed an intense appreciation for life, a sensitivity to unspoken thoughts and the complexity of simple things, a powerful knowledge of human needs and feelings.

We regard our feelings as our most important source of political understanding.

We see the key to our liberation in our collective wisdom and our collective strength.

Bread and Roses, a large Boston organization, was typical of the socialist-feminist strain in women's liberation. With the term "socialist," these women signaled their conviction that the capitalist system itself generated brutal and destructive inequalities of class and race as well as sex, and required major public intervention in the interest of the majority. In practice, socialist feminists tended to emphasize class and race as much as gender and to define the enemy as a social/economic/political system of male supremacy rather than masculinity or male self-interest. In the 1970s, socialist and radical feminism seemed markedly different, but they actually differed only subtly. However, they both differed sharply from liberal feminism, usually represented by NOW, the National Organization for Women, which concentrated on seeking immediate legal and economic reform and did not dream of apocalyptic change.

In their outreach leaflet, written to be distributed at a pro-child-care demonstration in Boston, the Bread and Roses feminists defined themselves as refusing to "be realistic." By this they meant that, instead of accepting a share of power in the man's world, they insisted on changing the whole structure of society. In their outreach, Bread and Roses demonstrated a confidence that women could organize themselves; rather than inviting women to a meeting of their organization, they merely urged them to talk to their friends. In this perspective we see very clearly the difference between a movement and a formal organization, and women's liberation's commitment to decentralization. This snowballing, leaderless growth of the women's movement could only happen in a context of widespread activism and optimism about possibilities for social justice.

Outreach Leaflet
BREAD AND ROSES

1970

Sisters

We are living in a world that is not ours—"it's a man's world." We feel our lives being shaped by someone or something outside ourselves; because we are females we are expected to act in certain ways and do certain things whether or not it feels right to *us*. We have had to teach ourselves to turn off our real feelings and real desires—to be "realistic"—in other words, to accept the place we have been given in the world of men.

But it's no good—deep in our guts we know this. Cooking and cleaning and children have not given us the fulfillment the ladies' magazines promised even after we've followed all their recipes. Our most honest selves know there is more to it than being hung-up when our emotions fight against a casual sexual affair. Why have we always assumed it was *our* fault if the "new morality" wasn't satisfying us? What does it mean when men whistle at us on the street?

We are waking up angry and shocked, amazed that we didn't realize before. Women begin to name enemies: men, capitalism, families, neurosis, technology, etc. And in various ways we start trying to make changes. Some women—such as those who have expressed themselves in the platform of this march—look to the state and federal legislatures to give us the unrestricted humanity which has been denied us for so long. They have decided to "work within the system." In other words, they say, "Let us into the world you men live in. Give us your education and your jobs and your public positions. Free us with childcare programs designed in your offices." Is this really what we want? How about female generals in Vietnam? DO WE WANT EQUALITY IN THE MAN'S WORLD, OR DO WE WANT TO MAKE IT A NEW WORLD?

Women being ourselves and believing in ourselves, women finding the strength to live how we feel, *powerful* women, can lead the way to create a new kind of politics, a new life.

To join the Women's Liberation Movement, begin by talking with friends. Here are some words which might help to get started:

date-bait   community-controlled childcare centers
fathers   my boss   castrating woman   *Playboy*   rape
fashions   marriage   high school   abortions   doctors
pretending orgasm   masculinity   self-reliance

Consciousness-raising often brought with it the release of pent-up anger against men. But far from repudiating men, a charge often falsely applied to feminism, early women's liberation groups focused optimistically on changing men's behavior so as to nurture more egalitarian heterosexual relationships. This witty analysis of men's defenses helped women in their private struggles by demonstrating that their problems were shared.

Cocktales

1969

Here are some male reactions commonly heard when talking to men about women's liberation. They must be pointed out and exposed for what they are, so that they may no longer have the effect of keeping women's consciousness down.

THE LAUGH: Dismissing the issue without even discussing it. This puts all the burden of proof on you.

YOUR FAULT: It's your personal problem. Not a social, political one. "Something in your life must have twisted you so you hate men. See a psychiatrist." This is the technique of trying to isolate you.

WOMEN ARE "DIFFERENT": The separate-but-equal argument based upon biological data. "You're not inferior, just different. I love women." This technique uses physiology as proof positive of the validity of the status quo. Most oppressed groups in the world have some physiological argument tacked on to them.

WOMEN'S RIGHTS WERE WON 40 YEARS AGO: Recognizes the problem as a past one, but denies that it still exists.

THE MALE LIBERAL: "I'm all for it, but what about the children, etc." The technique works to agree that there's a "problem," then tries to steer you back to the traditional role by specific guilt manipulations.

THE SUPER-FEMINIST: Having accepted the issue superficially or actually, but still needs to one-up you. So he becomes the super-feminist, moralizing to you about how you haven't quite made it yet, etc., helping the little woman with her problem. This maintains control over the process and also intimidates the woman.

WOMEN DON'T WANT FREEDOM: The oppressor turns on the oppressed and blames her for her own oppression. Since one can always find Aunt Toms, scared women, etc., this argument can seem real if one does not distinguish between who is the victim and who is the perpetrator.

I'LL ACCEPT WOMEN'S FREEDOM IF . . . : Women will go to Vietnam, etc. This is a very intimidating tactic because it is a threat that if women want to free themselves the few privileges they have will be taken away from them.

SHE'S ONLY A FEMINIST BECAUSE SHE'S A BITCH WHO CAN'T GET A MAN: And you don't want to be like that, do you? Third person tactic used to persuade women that the worst thing that could happen is to lose their oppressors.

Black feminism developed along with white, but it captured far less media attention. African American women, often due to necessity, had a stronger tradition of honoring women's independence. Surveys of the early 1970s showed that black women were on average more feminist than whites in their attitudes toward specific issues such as day care, education, equal pay, and equal work.

Some women of color were worried about creating disunity or diverting political groups from the struggle for racial equality, just as some white women feared dividing antiwar or other social justice movements. From the beginning of second-wave feminism, there were black feminists who believed, however, that the struggle for sexual equality required articulating grievances and anger against men. Doris Wright, a member of the board of NOW, became one of the founders of the National Black Feminist Organization in 1973. Her work represented a particularly militant stream of black feminism, because such critiques of black male dominance evoked allegations of betrayal from many mainstream and radical black leaders.

Angry Notes from a Black Feminist
DORIS WRIGHT

1970

The Man to Sam may be Whitey, but the Man to women is any man.

As a Black woman, maybe you still believe that what the black man's putting down is somehow different from what Whitey has been propagating and diseasing the world with all these years. Up to now, you've thought that your situation in this society was very different from that of your white sister. In fact, you've never even considered her your "sister" at all. She was some alien enemy who belonged to the Arch-Oppressor, and who lived in enemy territory. Well, two minutes in the Movement will prove to you that when it comes to being a member of the female sex, we're all in the same bag. All you have to do is look around to see the evidence of what Whitey really thinks of our white sister, and how he's used and abused her for his purposes.

Only in a society where male-approved perversions of the kind that lead to violence and power struggles are discouraged—and where continual competitive combat with other human beings is not rewarded—will man stop viewing woman as just part of the "spoils" of his world. And, Black sister, that's all we are to the black man—part of the spoils that he now feels he deserves after all those years of "masculine" privation at the hands of Whitey. To someone whose identity is all caught up with his striving for middle class status, we represent yet another symbol of his success, of his having "made it."

The Age of the Pedestal is about to dawn for us, Black sisters.

They have also succeeded in intimidating some Black women into anxious remorse over the fact that when Sam ran out and left them with the brood they had the courage and the moral strength to become the family's breadwinner. Black women have proven over and over again that they are capable leaders, not only as necessary heads of families but out in the world as well. We should never allow Whitey or Sam to shame us on that score. Of course, we·can always ask Sam where his gang was when our grandmother and her mother before her was out scrubbing floors and getting laid by Whitey to keep their children alive. Yeah, we all know the story. They were busy being castrated by society, or something.

Additional to the injustices encountered right along, the Black woman has now to put up with a whole new set of inequities stemming from her contact with the so-called radical or socialist scoundrel. This is the guy who functions under the guise of Reformer and Redeemer and drains off the best of our female talents. Energies that should be spent in furthering woman's and thereby humanity's cause are caught up instead on another male ego trip by such foaming-at-the-mouth phonies as the Black Panthers, Young Lords, Weathermen, and other "social revolutionaries." Another load of screaming male chauvinists! Leave it to the Man to come up with the superficial cures for society's ills. He'll never admit that *he's* the world's sickness and his politics are just the symptoms. Why are the energies of beautiful Black sisters wasted on helping a set of rats on the bottom overthrow the rats on top?

Only after we change the way in which children are socialized so that the male child does not grow up obsessed by the need to prove until the day he dies, in a variety of ways, but ultimately through violence, that he's a "Man," can we think of taking the next step toward the creation of a humane, collective society.

> The Young Lords were a Puerto Rican youth group that, like the Black Panthers with whom they were often allied, provided community services such as free breakfasts for children in local churches, as well as protesting racism and raising consciousness about colonialism. Despite an occasional emphasis on weapons and a generally macho stance, again like the Black Panthers, the Young Lords' largely male leadership was forced by women in the organization to publish a strong feminist "Position Paper." In 1973 women from the Young Lords joined with women from black power groups to form the Third World Women's Alliance (see chapter 2), thus demonstrating their growing identification as part of a "Third World," including oppressed peoples of color within the U.S. as well as in underdeveloped nations.

Position Paper on Women
YOUNG LORDS PARTY

Puerto Rican, Black, and other Third World (colonized) woman are becoming more aware of their oppression in the past and today. They are suffering three different types of oppression under capitalism. First, they are oppressed as Puerto Ricans or Blacks. Second, they are oppressed as women. Third, they are oppressed by their own men.

In the past women were oppressed by several institutions, one of which was marriage. In Latin America and Puerto Rico, the man had a wife and another woman, called *la corteja*. This condition still exists today. The wife was there to be a homemaker, to have children and to maintain the family name and honor. She had to be sure to be a virgin and remain pure for the rest of their life, meaning she could never experience sexual pleasure. The wife had to have children in order to enhance the man's concept of virility and his position within the Puerto Rican society. *La corteja* became his sexual instrument. The man could have set her up in another household, paid her rent, bought her food, and paid her bills. He could have children with this woman. Both women had to be loyal to the men. Both sets of children grew up very confused and insecure.

Women have always been expected to be wives and mothers only. They are respected by the rest of the community for being good cooks, good housewives, good mothers, but never for being intelligent, strong, educated or militant. In the past, women were not educated, only the sons got an education and mothers were respected for the number of sons they had, not daughters. Daughters were worthless and the only thing they could do was marry early to get away from home. At home the role of the daughter was to be a nursemaid for the other children and kitchen help for her mother.

The daughter was guarded like a hawk by her father, brothers and uncles to keep her a virgin. In Latin America the people used *dueñas* or old lady watchdogs to guard the purity of the daughters. The husband must be sure that his new wife has never been touched by another man because that would ruin the "merchandise." When he marries her, her purpose is to have sons and keep his home but not to be a sexual partner.

Sex was a subject that was never discussed, and women were brainwashed into believing that the sex act was dirty and immoral, and its only function was for the making of children.

Puerto Rican and Black men are looked upon as rough, athletic and sexual, but not as intellectuals. Puerto Rican women are not expected to know anything except about the home, kitchen and bedroom. All that they are expected to do is look pretty and add a little humor. The Puerto Rican man sees himself as superior to his women, and his superiority, he feels, gives him license to do many things—curse, drink, use drugs, beat women and run around with many women. As a matter of fact these things are considered natural for a man to do and he must do them to be considered a man. A woman who curses, drinks and runs around with a lot of men is considered dirty scum, crazy, and a whore.

Today, Puerto Rican men are involved in a political movement. Yet the majority of their women are home taking care of the children. The Puerto Rican sister that involves herself is considered aggressive, castrating, hard and unwomanly, viewed by the brothers as sexually accessible because, what is is she doing outside of the home? The Puerto Rican man tries to limit the woman's role because he feels the double standard is threatened, insecure without it as a crutch.

Machismo has always been a very basic part of Latin American and Puerto Rican culture. Machismo is male chauvinism and more. He can do whatever he wants because his woman is an object with certain already defined roles—wife, mother and good woman.

Machismo means physical abuse, punishment and torture. A Puerto Rican man will beat his woman to keep her in place and show her who's boss. Most Puerto Rican men do not beat women publicly because in the eyes of other men that is a weak thing to do. So they usually wait until they're home. All the anger and violence of centuries of oppression which should be directed against the oppressor is directed at the Puerto Rican woman. The aggression is also directed at daughters. The daughters hear their fathers saying "the only way a woman is going to do anything or listen is by hitting her." The father applies this to the daughter, beating her so that she can learn *respeto*. The daughters

grow up with messed up attitudes about their role as women and about manhood. They grow to expect that men will always beat them.

Sexual fascists are very sick people. Their illness is caused in part by this system which mouths puritanical attitudes and laws and yet exploits the human body for profit.

Sexual fascism is tied closely to the double standard and machismo. It means that a man or a woman thinks of the opposite sex solely as sexual objects to be used for sexual gratification and then discarded. A sexual fascist does not consider people's feelings; all they see everywhere is a pussy or a dick. They will use any rap, especially political, to get sex.

Third World sisters are caught up in a complex situation. On one hand, we feel that genocide is being committed against our people. We know that Puerto Ricans will not be around on the face of the earth very long if Puerto Rican women are sterilized at the rate they are being sterilized now. The practice of sterilization in Puerto Rico goes back to the 1930s when doctors pushed it as the only means of contraception. In 1947–48, 7% of the women were sterilized; between 1953 and 1954, 4 out of every 25; and by 1956 the number had increased to about 1 out of 3 women. In many cases our sisters are told that their tubes are going to be "tied" but are never told that the "tying" is really "cutting" and that the tubes can never be "untied."

Part of this genocide is also the use of birth control pills which were tested for 15 years on Puerto Rican sisters before being sold on the market in the U.S. Even now many doctors feel that these pills cause cancer and death from blood clotting.

Abortions in hospitals that are butcher shops are little better than the illegal abortions our women used to get. The first abortion death in NYC under the new abortion law was Carmen Rodriguez, a Puerto Rican sister who died in Lincoln Hospital. Her abortion was legal but the conditions in the hospital were deadly.

On the other hand, we believe that abortions should be legal if they are community controlled, if they are safe, if our people are educated about the risks and if doctors do not sterilize our sisters while performing abortions. We realize that under capitalism our sisters and brothers cannot support large families and the more children we have the harder it is to support them. We say: change the system so that women can freely be allowed to have as many children as they want without suffering any consequences.

The impact of women's liberation on beauty standards and the fashion industry has been nothing short of immense. Just as nineteenth-century women rebelled against tight corsets, second-wave feminism chose uncomfortable and binding clothing as one of its earliest targets. Before the movement began, women had to wear skirts, nylon stockings held up by girdles or garter belts, and, of course, high heels in order to be respectable and to earn a living. "Stamp Out High Heels" was one of many expressions of rebellion against these conventions. By the end of the 1970s, women everywhere had won the right to wear pants in public, even to the office. Today's informal athletic look in women's clothes and shoes owes much to this feminist activism.

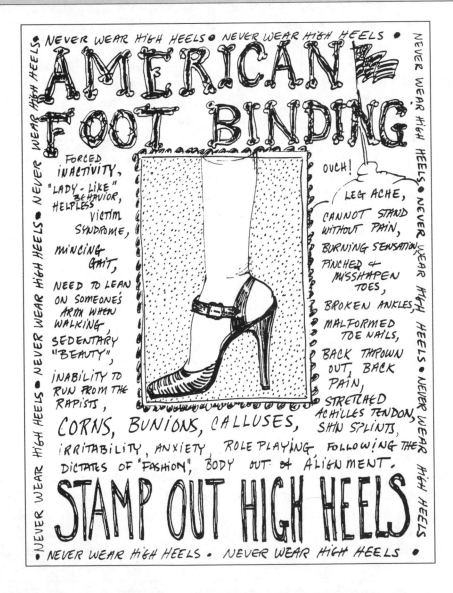

2

The New Left

Throughout the 1950s, 1960s, and 1970s the New Left raised issues that gripped millions of Americans, challenging racial inequality, militarism and interventionism, continuing poverty in the midst of affluence, environmental contamination, and a culture of conformity. Hundreds of thousands, mainly young people, became active participants in these movements for social justice. Readers in today's more conservative era can only understand feminism by placing it in the context of a more optimistic, daring, iconoclastic political culture.

Most accounts of second-wave feminism see it as a discrete movement rather than as part of the New Left. True, women's liberationists often broke from New Left organizations, but they also continued the New Left agenda. The two most important influences on the formation of women's liberation were civil rights and the anti–Vietnam War movement. Most of the early members of women's liberation owed the development of their political consciousness and their organizing experience to these movements, and the rapid spread of feminism was due in part to civil rights and antiwar networks.

Civil rights contributed to feminism both a rage at injustice and a vocabulary of concepts for understanding not just individual prejudice but structural discrimination, that is, how the entire workings of a society—its economy, culture, language, social relations, and political organization—enforce domination. Feminists also gained from civil rights a commitment to grassroots organizing, in which women particularly excelled, and which they considered as valuable as the marches, speeches, and confrontations that were more often led by men and covered by the media. The young feminists of the late 1960s and 1970s were inspired by many southern African American women leaders, often called "mamas" because they were already mature women when the struggle began.

The impact of the Vietnam War on a generation of young people in the 1960s and 1970s cannot be overstated. It became the most unpopular war in American history, opposed even by many mainstream politicians, as a result of the intensive and extensive antiwar movement. Protesters, outraged at the unprecedented brutality of American bombings, burnings, civilian casualties, and ecological destruction, much of it broadcast on television, forced the exposure of government dishonesty and permanently altered Americans' level of trust in government leaders. The contrast between U.S. policy in Vietnam (preventing elections, propping up corrupt leaders, and then getting rid of them when they no longer served U.S. geopolitical interests) and its theoretical commitment to democracy paralleled the hypocrisy involved in the toleration of disfranchisement and deprivation of human rights among African Americans in the South. Early feminists and other New Leftists not only opposed U.S. intervention in Vietnam, but were so angry that they supported, often uncritically, the opposition—the Vietnam National Liberation Front, called by the Americans the "Viet Cong." Many feminists admired and romanticized Vietnamese women who fought alongside men.

The Vietnam War also deepened feminist understanding of the mutually reinforcing relationship between militarism and racism/sexism: the armed forces used racist and sexist slurs to motivate soldiers and rewarded them with the privilege of sexual access to Vietnamese women. Wars always encourage prostitution and rape, and make soldiers feel entitled to treat women as spoils of war; in Vietnam the destruction of the countryside and of the peasant means of livelihood drove many women into sex work as a way to survive, and many thousands became rape casualties. At home, the war thus deepened feminist understanding of women's sexual victimization.

Histories of the New Left have suggested that feminism caused women to withdraw from the antiwar movement, but this was not actually the case. Rather, most feminists not only continued to participate and even lead antiwar activities, but they also helped educate many thousands of women about U.S. foreign policy. Moreover, they brought together the lessons of civil rights, antiwar, and women's liberation movements to develop a feminist critique of militarism and imperialism and their inverse connection to domestic policies that increased inequality at home. Some women, like the Catholic nurse–midwife Mary Moylan, took substantial risks in opposing the war. The antiwar movement began with petitions and demonstrations, but as the war escalated and legal measures proved futile, more dissenters began to use civil disobedience to protest what they considered crimes against humanity. Although few had Mary Moylan's courage in pouring blood on draft files, many applauded such militant actions.

Underground Woman
MARY MOYLAN   1970

There are two groups in the non-violent camp. One of those groups is straight pacifist; the other is much looser, and feels that somehow we have to continue to respect human life: and that's probably the only way we hew the pacifist line. The sort of public non-cooperation of pacifists bothers me; most pacifists I know would have told me to go take a walk in the park and smell the flowers, but it just didn't strike me as enough.

I have to laugh when I think about the Catonsville action. I don't regret it at all. I'm very content and happy I did it, but it was totally insane. The nine of us drove out to the Catonsville draft board offices around noon. It was a weekday, because we wanted to go when the board was open. Tom Lewis and I went in first, and he had a prepared speech to read to the clerks to reassure them that we were not going to wipe them out. Bureaucracy is fantastic: We walked in and nobody would look at us. Tom came up and started reading: "We are a group of clergymen and laymen concerned about the war." And nobody would look up, they were so busy writing. So we went through our scene—draft files were dumped into our baskets and the phones were taken care of so the clerks couldn't call for help until we had left the building. The clerks were very upset—one woman kept screaming about us taking *her* files, and she would have to protect *her* files. The other woman in the office was determined to make a phone call, so we went through a wrestling match. But we eventually made it out, and I guess they eventually called. The night before, we had cooked up some home-made napalm, so we put the files on the ground outside and stood around in a circle watching them burn. There were some people from the press there, and some of our people made statements. We stood there and we waited and we waited and we waited, and the people were watching us—the clerks from the second floor—and nobody knew what we were doing. Then a little cop on one of those three-wheel things came up and he stood there and watched us, and we thought, "My God, they're not going to arrest us; what are we going to do?" But eventually they came skidding into the parking lot and they arrested us, and we went through the arrest scene, with the FBI wandering in and out.

The establishment press constantly described us, after Catonsville, as "Catholic pacifists," and that's when I stopped believing the establishment press. I'm much too Irish to be a pacifist, and my relationship with the Roman Catholic Church has been off and on, to say the very least, for quite a while. Realizing that that was where I came from, the "Catholic" title bothered me less than the "pacifist" title. But it's even more difficult now because I have no relationship with the Catholic Church, nor do I want any. Everybody in the group, except George and me, was either a priest or a brother or a sister or an ex-one-or-the-other. So everyone assumed when they met me that I was an ex-nun. I've had a lot of problems in my life, but that wasn't one of them.

I suppose the political turning point in my life came while I was in Uganda. I was there when American planes were bombing the Congo, and we were very close to the Congo border. The planes came over and bombed two villages in Uganda (I don't know how the hell anyone figures out where the borders are). But it wasn't that; it was what the hell were American planes doing, piloted by Cubans, bombing the Congo when as far as I knew, the United Nations was the peace-keeping force in the Congo. Where the hell did the American planes come in?

I got involved with the women's movement about a year ago. I had heard about it and read about it and the women in Baltimore were forming a women's liberation group. I was in New York where there were all kinds of women's lib groups, so I got in on some of that. In my relations with men I was becoming more and more aware of the fact that they were chauvinists—I guess that's the nicest thing I can think of to say about them. It struck me that there were all these men running around trying to build a human society who couldn't relate to a woman as a human being. The man-woman relationship is a basic unit of society; even if we have communes or collectives, still men and women are going to be with each other. Unless we can deal with that, I feel that our attempts to relate to the Third World or to any other group of people are going to fail. I began to believe that SDS, before their split, would have their revolution, and I certainly wasn't going to stop them, but that we would just have to do it all over again because they were incapable of building a human society, in large part because they're incapable of dealing with women's liberation.

I think I'm really talking about freeing *people:* Men aren't proving anything about themselves as people in saying they've got muscles or that they can rape a woman; or that they're the brains and women are the heart; or that women have certain virtues, all of which are soft. Woman is compassionate, woman is this, that, and the other thing, and it's nice to have women around to help men out when they need compassion. I really feel that this is a pivotal issue, and for me it's just a gut reaction; I very definitely would only relate to brothers who, I felt, were trying to deal with the issue—and preferably, only to sisters. If I ever decided to go through Catonsville again, I would never act with men: It would be a women's action for me or I wouldn't act. The Vietnamese and Algerian women have provided me with a real inspiration.

I think men get into competition with each other, and I don't know what the hell everybody's trying to prove. We're all absurd when you come right down to it, but somehow all of us together add up to something that makes sense. And I don't think that any one person or any group of people makes any *more* sense; somehow it's a totality of making sense. The anarchism of the Movement with the very different groups operating makes sense. Out of all that is going to come a future that is a human society.

I have no problem with my own jail sentence. I'll be at the Women's Federal Reformatory at Alderson, West Virginia, and there's a whole bunch of sisters down there in that jail—sister criminals as a matter of fact. I think it will be interesting to see what the women's response will be to women's liberation and the whole Movement. I hate to make this confession, but I am really looking forward to two years of peace, two years of three meals a day, and a bed I can sleep in every night and count on. I don't know what their "solitary" or whatever they call it is like, but—two years: I can make it.

The idea of jail doesn't bother me that much; the idea of cooperating with the federal government in any way at all irritates the hell out of me. My alternatives are to go to jail, go aboveground with an assumed identity, stay underground, or leave the country. Any way I choose, the government is choosing for me. But what we're questioning is their right, and they lost that right because of the obscenity and insanity of their actions which are growing more and more obscene and insane.

Women Unite! Free the Panthers!

On Friday, May 1st, thousands of people will be in New Haven to demonstrate their support for 9 Black Panther Party men and women on trial there for trumped up charges of murder. The only real "crime" they have committed is understanding the oppression of black people in Amerika and being sensitive to their needs. The Panthers have begun to wage a struggle to liberate all oppressed people and to create a new society which would meet the needs of the people.

Free breakfast for children, free health clinics, and Liberation Schools—this, the day-to-day work of the Black Panthers has been the "crime" which has moved the repressive apparatus of this nation into high gear.

The attempt to smash the Panthers in New Haven and all over the country is part of the systematic attack against all people struggling for their liberation.

We as women have begun to identify our own oppression and understand its causes. We find it based in the same racist, exploitative system that oppresses blacks, browns and working class whites. We understand that this system has to be changed in order for anyone's liberation to be possible; that change occurs when masses of people collectively wage that struggle together. It is in our interest as women struggling for our own liberation, to ally ourselves with other forces fighting for freedom and self-determination.

We are calling upon women to join together in New Haven to demonstrate our solidarity with our Panther sisters and brothers. When the Panthers, when Women's Liberation, when the Vietnamese, when people all over the world begin to move, and move together, there are no repressive methods that can hold us back!!

Women's liberation revived the observance of International Women's Day, a holiday of socialist origins still celebrated in most countries of the world. In this leaflet for a 1970 International Women's Day demonstration, Boston's Bread and Roses rerouted the "freedom trail" commemorating the American Revolution to mark those places that symbolize women's continuing oppression. Its "Declaration of Women's Independence" drew on the Declaration of Independence and the 1848 Seneca Falls Declaration of Sentiments, the founding document of the women's rights movement. The Bread and Roses manifesto illustrates the breadth of women's liberation policy proposals and suggests that the women's movement was working toward a program of total social transformation, as opposed to one limited to privileged women's special interests.

Declaration of Women's Independence

BREAD AND ROSES   1970

Declaration of Women's Independence

WHEN IN THE COURSE OF HUMAN EVENTS, it becomes necessary for one sex to dissolve the political bonds which have connected them with another, and to assume among the powers of the earth the separate and equal station to which the laws of nature and of nature's God entitle them, a decent respect to the opinions of woman and mankind requires that they should declare the causes which impel them to the separation.

WE HOLD THESE TRUTHS TO BE SELF-EVIDENT: that all women and men are created equal and made unequal only by socialization:

that they are endowed by their creators with certain unalienable rights, which can be stolen from one group by another, but never given away:

that among these are life, liberty, and the pursuit of happiness:

that to secure these rights governments are instituted between men and women, deriving their just powers from the consent of the governed and their unjust powers from the oppression of the governed:

that whenever any form of government becomes destructive to the liberty of a sufficiently large group of people, be they a race, class, political group, or sex, it is the right of these people to alter or abolish it, and to institute new government, laying its foundation on such principles, and organizing its powers in such form, as to them shall seem most likely to effect their safety and happiness.

THE ECONOMY

Women must be enabled to participate in the economy on a basis of equality with men. We believe that the nature of work in our system is demeaning to human beings, and we do not want merely to upgrade women into the alienated jobs that men now hold. However, we refuse to do the low-grade, low-paid, and service work any more. Such jobs must be shared by men and women, as must housework be shared, and be recognized as legitimate work that deserves pay. We take it to be our right:

1. That all persons, including children, be assured a personal income commensurate with the cost of living and independent of their family status.

2. That all employers immediately be required to comply with the law of the land and pay equal wages for equal work.

3. An end to sex discrimination by job definition, which evades the law by defining all desirable jobs in such a way that only men can fill them. Secretarial and executive tasks should be shared between men and women; responsibility should be shared between doctor and nurse.

4. That all employers give priority to the hiring and promotion of women, with preferential hiring to women of races and classes that have been discriminated against. No men must be laid off to comply with this demand.

5. Childcare by men and women, during work hours, provided free by the employer, and controlled by workers and the community.

6. An end to discrimination against part-time or temporary workers, who are mostly female or minors: for example, equal fringe benefits and employment opportunities.

7. Maternity leave for both men and women, with guaranteed return and no loss of pay or seniority.

CONTROL OF OUR BODIES

Women should be able to control their own bodies, to have children if and when they want to, and to refrain from having children if they want to. This ultimately means an end to all laws governing birth control and abortion, with the exception of legal standards of health and safety. It also means that if proper health care is to be equally available to all women, we must have free medical care for all people. We consider these to be our rights:

1. Abortion, birth control devices, and pregnancy tests to be provided on demand to women of all ages, under safe conditions, at no cost.

2. Prenatal, maternity and postnatal care to be provided to all women at no cost. Women should be able to determine the manner and place in which they give birth.

3. Drastic increases in government funding of birth control research; research priorities to be determined by women, since it is their health which is at stake.

4. Higher safety standards for drug company research and regulation of their profits. An end to drug company imperialism in the form of testing unsafe drugs on third world women, and then charging exorbitant prices for them. No testing of dangerous drugs on mental patients, prisoners, or others whose lives are not their own.

5. Free, available and complete information about women's bodies, available to them as a right in all institutions.

6. An end to the double standard which puts prostitutes in jail and lets their clients go free.

7. An end to all forms of environmental abuses: particularly an immediate halt to those which have their most disastrous effects on women and children, such as Strontium 90 and DDT poisoning which poison mothers' milk.

8. While we think population control is essential, it must not be substituted for a sharing of the world's resources between rich and poor countries. Therefore, we want an end to the kind of population control, on the national and international levels, which concentrates on controlling the population of people of color.

THE FAMILY

The family unit should not be seen as the only economically and socially acceptable unit of society. Central to the liberation of women is the provision of alternatives to the present pattern of child-rearing and housekeeping, which results in each mother's bearing virtually the entire responsibility for her children and her home. Such alternatives would go far towards eliminating the untenable choice most women must make between bearing children and developing independent work. We therefore demand:

1. Free, community controlled 24 hour child-care centers, staffed equally by paid men and women, young and old.

2. Alternative forms of good, reasonably priced housing, including provisions for cooperative childcare, communal cooking, etc., for all people.

3. The establishment of a personal income for all persons, independent of familial status commensurate with the cost of living.

The state should not interfere in personal relationships. In this context we demand the abolition of all laws regulating marriage and divorce; the abolition of all laws regulating sexual behavior between consenting persons; the abolition of all laws regulating living arrangements, for instance, laws against cohabitation; and an end to the legal concept of illegitimacy. Children should have a choice of living arrangements with relatives, non-related adults, other children, and any combination of these possibilities. This means civil liberties for minors: they must not be legally penalized or prosecuted by their parents for choosing to live with other people, exercising their sexuality, or doing other things that offend their parents' sense of propriety. Any number of adults should be able to make legal contracts between themselves, other than marriage ceremonies, that will concern mutual responsibilities for each other and for children.

EDUCATION AND CULTURE

The educational system and the media in our country perpetuate undemocratic myths about the nature of women, working people, and black, brown, red and yellow people. They also deny these groups any knowledge of their own history. The media and educational system must be redesigned by the people whom they oppress, to express the past and to meet their needs for development in an atmosphere free from psychological oppression. With respect to women, these things are necessary:

1. An end to sexual tracking at all levels of the educational system. By this we mean not only courses specifically designed for each sex, but also the subtler forms of track-ing, such as encouraging boys to be smart and girls to be ladylike.

2. That all courses be thoroughly revamped by women to end the perpetuation of male supremacist myths.

3. That the facts about sex inequality be added as a topic to all school curricula, and that new courses be developed by women in their culture and history.

4. That vocational counselling in high schools and colleges be totally redesigned so as not to channel women into low status, low potential occupations.

5. That trade schools, vocational schools, colleges and graduate schools admit one-half women, with preferential treatment of women from races and classes that have been discriminated against.

6. An end to advertising which exploits women's bodies to sell products.

7. An end to sex-role stereotyping in the media.

Bread and Roses

Just as women were becoming critical of male chauvinism within the civil rights movement, so early feminists within the student movement challenged the male leadership's unwillingness to change its theory or practice in line with feminist critique. The relationship between feminists and the male-dominated New Left was intimate but also often angry, like an old couple who had bitter grievances against each other but were unable to break up.

SDS was the strongest and most visible New Left student organization. In 1967 it had approximately 200 chapters with more than 6,000 formal members; but it was in the nature of the New Left that membership was rarely formal and thousands of others who participated in meetings and demonstrations considered themselves part of "the movement." One historian estimates that 100,000 people considered themselves part of SDS in 1968.

Women who did not join the autonomous women's movement but remained in the New Left nevertheless attempted to move it in a feminist direction. Some feminists managed to get New Left organizations to adopt position papers on the oppression of women, but these did not usually translate into concrete action, and the male-dominated organizations continued to treat women's issues as marginal and secondary. By contrast the autonomous women's movement was breaking out of the confines of a conventional Left analysis in which class was always primary and the workplace was always the fundamental arena of struggle. New-born feminists were beginning to challenge their "brothers." In 1968 budding feminists in SDS disrupted the annual national convention to protest the dominant male elitism, posturing, and exclusion of women. The author of this article, Susan Sutheim, was both a reporter for *The Guardian*, a Left weekly paper established in 1948, and a feminist. Her dual loyalties are visible in her shift from a third-person to a first-person voice as she tells the story.

Women Shake Up SDS Session

SUSAN SUTHEIM   1968

East Lansing, Mich.

At 2 p.m. Thursday, June 13, the bullshit on the plenary session floor of the Students for a Democratic Society (SDS) national convention was, as usual, flying thick and fast, when seven women carrying large placards entered the back of the hall and made their way to the speaker's platform.

The signs identified the group as Karl Theory, Max Praxis, Stu W. Alliance and Ben Bullshit, some of the leading theoreticians and allegedly "elitist" leadership of SDS, followed by three people who just couldn't keep up with them—Girlfriend, Chick and Joe Chapter.

As they reached the stage, the lights went out and dozens of women scattered around the room took up the eerie, high pitched wail of the Algerian women (learned from the film "The Battle of Algiers"). As the cry died down, three women seized the floor microphones and began to read antiphonally, trying to communicate to the convention delegates their feelings about elitism, male chauvinism,

SDS rhetoric and the arrogance of many movement people.

But we women were fighting history: objective conditions on the convention floor were not open to our criticism, couched as it was in the form of a dramatic disruption. To our amazement and dismay, a group of women catcalled and hooted (as did many men) and effectively prevented us from reading our statement. The feeling in the room was, well, those women have done their little silly thing again—exactly the reaction we had hoped not to provoke.

We had been carried away by the excitement of a series of women's liberation workshops—seven in all—that met from Tuesday afternoon through Wednesday night. The quality of political exchange (superior to many other workshop sessions, and superior by far to the plenary sessions) and the nonelitist, collectively responsible way we had learned to work with each other had impressed us all.

In spite of our mutual responsibility to each other as women, however, we made serious mistakes when we attempted to deal with the convention as a whole. Our workshop discussions had centered in on the themes of SDS's tendency to produce elitist leadership; our feeling of exclusion from political debate, particularly in large groups (e.g., the plenary sessions and workshops of the convention); and our inability to express ourselves through the accepted forms (basically male in style) of rhetoric, charisma and assertiveness. We clearly agreed that our concern with elitism, exclusion and being stifled was not only a women's concern: many men at the convention failed to participate in floor debate and workshops, and must have felt as frustrated as we did.

We decided to act, rather than present another paper resolution that would be ritualistically endorsed and then ignored, and decided on guerrilla theater. But we were too optimistic about our ability to communicate through that form. Several such disruptions had already occurred, and people were immune to the shock. Our action was expected (rumors had been flying) and thus was no surprise. And people are still very uptight about the whole subject we have mistakenly allowed to be labeled "male chauvinism" and reacted, naturally, in a very uptight manner.

Our worst mistake, though, was that we acted out the very things we were trying to speak against: elitism and arrogance. A women's group which addresses itself to general human problems ("male chauvinism," for instance, oppresses men as well as women) while excluding one set of humans (men) is inherently elitist. Furthermore, we had involved only part of the women at the convention—elitist again, though by default, not intentionally. And we had the presumptuousness to expect everyone else to be quiet and listen to what we thought was a very important message about how we'd learned to work together in a nonelitist, nonarrogant, nonrhetoric-laden manner: how we'd made an alternative to the tendencies within SDS we deplored.

Many of us in women's groups did a lot of talking with men about why our action was such a fiasco, about why we had excluded men from our meetings (most women feel intimidated by the presence of men until they've been through several meetings with women alone), about what, in fact, we discussed at those meetings. We learned some valuable things. First, we learned that a lot of men felt left out; they figured we must be talking about things that were important to them as well as to us (true, and it was what we had also been saying).

A number of women also feel now that they want to invite men to participate in their meetings, to talk not only about the straw man of male chauvinism (women, we realized long ago, are some of the biggest male chauvinists around) but to talk about their movement, about politics, about the issues that concern us all as brothers and sisters in a struggle for human liberation.

Some New Left groups shared women's liberation's spirit of irreverence toward old verities, as in this advertisement for the anti-authoritarian New Left magazine, *Radical America*. By the early 1970s, some New Left groups also came to support women's liberation and to incorporate feminist ideas. Others, such as SDS and its spin-off Marxist–Leninist groups, did not rise to the challenge. Feminists grew more frustrated and angry as these retrograde groups refused to rethink matters of family, sexuality, and reproduction in the light of male power. In the letter to the editor on the next page, which the leading national Left newspaper of the time, *The Guardian*, refused to publish, rock critic and antiwar activist Ellen Willis lays out the theoretical claim that you need a theory of dual systems, capitalism and patriarchy, to understand women's oppression.

Brochure
RADICAL AMERICA

Letter to the Left

ELLEN WILLIS

You say, "the basic misperception is that our enemy is man, not capitalism." I say, the basic misperception is the facile identification of "the system" with "capitalism." In reality, the American system consists of two interdependent but distinct parts—the capitalist state and the patriarchal family.

The social organization for the production of commodities is the property system, in this case the capitalist state. The social organization for the production of new human beings is the family system. And within the family system, men function as a ruling class, women as an exploited class. Historically, women and their children have been the property of men (until recently, quite literally, even in "advanced" countries). The mistake many radicals make is to assume that the family is simply part of the cultural superstructure of capitalism, while both capitalism and the family system make up the material substructure of society. It is difficult to see this because capitalism is so pervasive and powerful compared to the family, which is small, weak, and has far less influence on the larger economic system than vice versa. But it is important for women to recognize and deal with the exploited position in the family system for it is primarily in terms of the family system that we are oppressed *as women*. If you really *think* about our exploitation under capitalism—as cheap labor and as consumers—you will see that our position in the family system is at the root.

Our position here is exactly analogous to the black power position, with male radicals playing the part of white liberals. Blacks answered "We can't work together because you don't understand what it is to be black; because you've grown up in a racist society, your behavior toward us is bound to be racist whether you know it or not and whether you mean it or not; your ideas about how to help us are too often self-serving and patronizing; besides, part of our liberation is in thinking for ourselves and working for ourselves, not accepting the domination of the white man in still another area of our lives. If you as whites want to work on eliminating your own racism, if you want to support our battle for liberation, fine. If we decide that we have certain common interests with white activists and can form alliances with white organizations, fine. But we want to make the decisions in our own movement." Substitute man-woman for black-white and that's where I stand. With one important exception: while white liberals and radicals always understood the importance of the black liberation struggle, even if their efforts in the blacks' behalf were often misguided, radical men simply do not understand the importance of our struggle. Except for a hip vanguard movement, men have tended to dismiss the woman's movement as "just chicks with personal hangups," to insist that men and women are equally oppressed, though maybe in different ways, or to minimize the extent and significance of male chauvinism ("just a failure of communication"). All around me I see men who consider themselves dedicated revolutionaries, yet exploit their wives and girl friends shamefully without ever noticing a contradiction.

Sincerely, Ellen Willis

Some women became so fed up with the male-dominated Left that they seceded entirely. Speaking for many, poet and former TV star Robin Morgan angrily denounced men's dominating and exploitive relationships with women, not only in the Left but also in the counterculture. Morgan's anger derives from the kind of sense of betrayal typical of a divorce because she had felt so much a part of the left and had such high expectations of it. Her connection to the left is shown in her numerous insider references to groups, individuals, and events too numerous for the editors to explain to current readers. In fact, Morgan's "farewell address" to the Left was published in the Left underground New York newspaper *The Rat*, just after it was taken over by a women's liberation group.

But while Robin Morgan was saying goodbye, many other feminists continued to feel part of the Left even as they fought with it, as in so many families. The leaflet for a Cambridge women's demonstration against the U.S. invasion of Cambodia in 1970 (page 59) is remarkable in its contrast to the Jeannette Rankin Brigade demonstration (page 24) held just two years earlier: now there is no mention of motherhood as a justification of women's political action. At the bottom of the leaflet we see evidence of the very strong influence of rock music on young women as well as men, although most of the groups were heavily male and even misogynist.

Sisters in Struggle 1970

Goodbye to All That

ROBIN MORGAN

So, *Rat* has been liberated, for this week, at least. Next week? If the men return to reinstate the porny photos, the sexist comic strips, the "nudie-chickie" covers (along with their patronizing rhetoric about being in favor of Women's Liberation)—if this happens, our alternatives are clear. *Rat* must be taken over permanently by women—or *Rat* must be destroyed.

Why *Rat?* Why not *EVO* or even the obvious new pornzines (Mafia-distributed alongside the human pornography of prostitution)? First, they'll get theirs—but it won't be a takeover which is reserved for something at least *worth* taking over. Nor should they be censored. They should just be helped not to exist—by any means necessary. But *Rat*, which has always tried to be a really radical *cum* life-style paper—that's another matter. It's the liberal co-optive masks on the face of sexist hate and fear, worn by real nice guys we all know and like, right? We have met the enemy and he's our friend. And dangerous. "What the hell, let the chicks do an issue; maybe it'll satisfy 'em for a while, it's a good controversy, and it'll sell papers"—runs an unheard conversation that I'm sure took place at some point last week.

And that's what I wanted to write about—the friends, brothers, lovers in the counterfeit male-dominated Left. The good guys who think they know what "Women's Lib," as they so chummily call it, is all about—and who then proceed to degrade and destroy women by almost everything they say and do: The cover on the last issue of *Rat* (front and back). The token "pussy power" or "clit militancy" articles. The snide descriptions of women staffers on the masthead. The little jokes, the personal ads, the smile, the snarl. No more, brothers. No more well-meaning ignorance, no more co-optation, no more assuming that this thing we're all fighting for is the same: one revolution under *man*, with liberty and justice for all. No more.

Let's run it down. White males are most responsible for the destruction of human life and environment on the planet today. Yet who is controlling the supposed revolution to change all that? White males (yes, yes, even with their pasty fingers back in black and brown pies again). It just could make one a bit uneasy. It seems obvious that a legitimate revolution must be led by, *made* by those who have been most oppressed: black, brown, and white *women*—with men relating to that the best they can. A genuine Left doesn't consider anyone's suffering irrelevant, or titillating; nor does it function as a microcosm of capitalist economy, with men competing for power and status at the top, and women doing all the work at the bottom (and functioning as objectified prizes or "coin" as well). Goodbye to all that.

Run it all the way down.

Goodbye to the male-dominated peace movement, where sweet old Uncle Dave can say with impunity to a woman on the staff of *Liberation*, "The trouble with you is you're an aggressive woman."

Goodbye to the "straight" male-dominated Left: to PL who will allow that some workers are women but won't see all women (say, housewives) as workers (just like the System itself); to all the old Leftover parties who offer their "Women's Liberation caucuses" to us as if that were not a contradiction in terms; to the individual anti-leadership leaders who hand-pick certain women to be leaders and then relate only to them, either in the male Left or in Women's Liberation—bringing their hang-ups about power-dominance and manipulation to everything they touch.

Goodbye to the Weather Vain, with the Stanley Kowalski image and theory of free sexuality but practice of sex on demand for males. "Left Out!"—not Right On to the Weather Sisters who, and they know better—they know, reject their own radical feminism for that last desperate grab at male approval that we all know so well, for claiming that the *machismo* style and the gratuitous violence is their own style by "free choice" and for believing that this is the way for a woman to make her revolution . . . all the while, oh my sister, not meeting my eyes because Weather Men chose Manson as their—and your—Hero. (Honest, at least . . . since Manson is the only logical extreme of the normal American male's fantasy [whether he is Dick Nixon or Mark Rudd]: master of a harem, women to do all the shit-work, from raising babies and cooking and hustling to killing people on order.) Goodbye to all that shit that sets women apart from women; shit that covers the face of any Weatherwoman which is the face of any Manson slave which is the face of Sharon Tate which is the face of Mary Jo Kopechne which is the face of Beulah Saunders which is the face of me which is the face of Pat Nixon which is the face of Pat Swinton. *In the dark we are all the same*—and you better believe it; we're in the dark, baby. Remember the old joke: Know what they call a black man with a Ph.D.? A nigger. Variation: Know what they call a Weatherwoman? A heavy cunt. Know what they call a Hip Revolutionary Woman? A groovy cunt. Know what they call a radical militant feminist? A crazy cunt. Amerika is a land of free choice—take your pick of titles. Left Out, my Sister—don't you see? Goodbye to the illusion of strength when you run hand in hand with your oppressors; goodbye to the dream that being in the leadership collective will get you anything but gonorrhea.

Goodbye to RYM II, as well, and all the other RYMs—not that the Sisters there didn't pull a cool number by seizing control, but because they let the men back in after only *a day or so* of self-criticism on male chauvinism. (And goodbye to the inaccurate blanket use of that phrase, for that matter: male chauvinism is an *attitude*—male supremacy is the *objective reality, the fact*.) Goodbye to the Conspiracy who, when lunching with fellow sexist bastards Norman Mailer and Terry Southern in a bunny-type club in Chicago, found Judge Hoffman at the neighboring table—no surprise: *in the light they are all the same.*

Goodbye to Hip Culture and the so-called Sexual Revolution, which has functioned toward women's freedom as did the Reconstruction toward former slaves—reinstituted oppression by another name. Goodbye to the assumption that Hugh Romney is safe in his "cultural revolution," safe enough to refer to "our women, who make all our clothes" without somebody not forgiving that. Goodbye to the arro-gance of power indeed that lets Czar Stan Freeman of the Electric Circus sleep without fear at night, or permits Toni Ungerer to walk unafraid in the street after executing the drawings for the Circus advertising campaign against women. Goodbye to the idea that Hugh Hefner is groovy 'cause he lets Conspirators come to parties at the Mansion—goodbye to Hefner's dream of a ripe old age. Goodbye to Tuli and the Fugs and all the boys in the front room—who always knew they hated the women they loved. Goodbye to the notion that good ol' Abbie is any different from any other up and coming movie star (like, say Cliff Robertson) who ditches the first wife and kids, good enough for the old days but awkward once you're Making It. Goodbye to his hypocritical double standard that reeks through all the tattered charm. Goodbye to lovely pro–Women's Liberation Paul Krassner, with all his astonished anger that women have lost their sense of humor "on this issue" and don't laugh anymore at little funnies that degrade and hurt them; farewell to the memory of his "Instant Pussy" aerosol-can poster, to his column for *Cavalier*, to his dream of a Rape-In against legislators' wives, to his Scapegoats and Realist Nuns and cute anecdotes about the little daughter he sees as often as any proper divorced Scarsdale middle-aged (38) father; goodbye forever to the notion that he is my brother who, like Paul, buys a prostitute for the night as a birthday gift for a male friend, or who, like Paul, reels off the names in alphabetical order of people in the Women's Movement he has fucked, reels off names in the best locker room tradition—as proof that *he's* no sexist oppressor.

Let it all hang out. Let it seem bitchy, catty, dykey, frustrated, crazy, Solanisesque, nutty, frigid, ridiculous, bitter, embarrassing, man-hating, libelous, pure, unfair, envious, intuitive, low-down, stupid, petty, liberating. WE ARE THE WOMEN THAT MEN HAVE WARNED US ABOUT.

And let's put one lie to rest for all time: the lie that men are oppressed too, by sexism—the lie that there can be such a thing as "men's liberation groups." Oppression is something that one group of people commits against another group specifically because of a "threatening" characteristic shared by this latter group—skin color or sex or age, etc. The oppressors are indeed *fucked up* by being masters (racism hurts whites, sexual stereotypes are harmful to men) but those masters are not *oppressed*. Any master has the alternative of divesting himself of sexism or racism—the oppressed have no alternative—for they have no power—but to fight. In the long run, Women's Liberation will of course free men—but in the short run it's going to *cost* men a lot of privilege, which no one gives up willingly or easily. Sexism is *not* the fault of women—kill your fathers, not your mothers.

Run it down. Goodbye to a beautiful new ecology movement that could fight to save us all if it would stop tripping off women as earth-mother types or frontier chicks, if it would *right now* cede leadership to those who have *not* polluted the planet because that action implies power and women haven't had any power in about 5,000 years, cede leadership to those whose brains are as tough and clear as any man's but whose bodies are also unavoidably aware of the locked-in relationship between humans and their biosphere—the earth, the tides, the atmosphere, the moon. Ecology is no big *shtick* if you're a woman—it's always been there.

Goodbye to the complicity inherent in the Berkeley Tribesmen being part publishers of Trashman Comics; goodbye, for that matter, to the reasoning that finds whoremaster Trashman a fitting model, however comic-strip far out, for a revolutionary man—somehow related to the same Supermale reasoning that permits the first statement on Women's Liberation and male chauvinism that came out of the Black Panther Party to be made *by a man*, talkin' a whole lot 'bout how the Sisters should speak up for themselves. Such ignorance and arrogance ill befits a revolutionary.

We know how racism is worked deep into the unconscious by our System—the same way sexism is, as it appears in the very name of The Young Lords. What are you if you're a "macho woman"—a female Lord? Or, god forbid, a Young Lady? Change it, change it to The Young Gentry if you must, or never assume that the name itself is innocent of pain, of oppression.

Theory and practice—and the light years between them. "Do it!" says Jerry Rubin in *Rat*'s last issue—but he doesn't, or every *Rat* reader would have known the pictured face next to his article as well as they know his own much-photographed face; it was Nancy Kurshan, the power behind the clown.

Goodbye to the New Nation and Earth People's Park, for that matter, conceived by men, announced by men, led by men—doomed before its birth by the rotting seeds of male supremacy which are to be transplanted in fresh soil. Was it my brother who listed human beings among the *objects* which would be easily available after the Revolution: "Free grass, free food, free women, free acid, free clothes, etc."? Was it my brother who wrote "Fuck your women till they can't stand up" and said that groupies were liberated chicks 'cause they dug a tit-shake instead of a handshake? The epitome of female exclusionism—"men will make the Revolution—and their chicks." Not my brother, no. Not my revolution. Not one breath of support for the new counterfeit Christ—John Sinclair. Just one less to worry about for ten years. I did not choose my enemy for my brother.

Goodbye, goodbye. The hell with the simplistic notion that automatic freedom for women—or non-white peoples—will come about ZAP! with the advent of a socialist revolution. Bullshit. Two evils pre-date capitalism and have been clearly able to survive and post-date socialism: sexism and racism. Women were the first property when the Primary Contradiction occurred: when one half of the human species decided to subjugate the other half, because it was "different," alien, the Other. From there it was an easy step to extend the Other to someone of different skin shade, different height or weight or language—or strength to resist. Goodbye to those simple-minded optimistic dreams of socialist equality all our good socialist brothers want us to believe. How liberal a politics that is! How much further we will have to go to create those profound changes that would give birth to a genderless society. *Profound*, Sister. Beyond what is male or female. Beyond standards we all adhere to now without daring to examine them as male-created, male-dominated, male-fucked-up, and in male self-interest. *Beyond all known standards,* especially those easily articulated revolutionary ones we all rhetorically invoke. Beyond, to a species with a new name, that would not dare define itself as Man.

I once said, "I'm a revolutionary, not just a woman," and knew my own lie even as I said the words. The pity of that statement's eagerness to be acceptable to those whose revolutionary zeal no one would question, i.e., any male supremacist in the counterleft. But to become a true revolutionary one must first become one of the oppressed (not organize or educate or manipulate them, but become one of them)—or realize that you *are* one of them already. No woman wants that. Because that realization is humiliating, it hurts. It hurts to understand that at Woodstock or Altamont a woman could be declared uptight or a poor sport if she didn't want to be raped. It hurts to learn that the Sisters still in male-Left captivity are putting down the crazy feminists to make themselves look okay and unthreatening to our mutual oppressors. It hurts to be pawns in those games. It hurts to try and change *each day of your life right now*—not in talk, not "in your head," and not only conveniently "out there" in the Third World (half of which is women) or the black and brown communities (half of which are women) but in your own home, kitchen, bed. No getting away, no matter how else you are oppressed, from the primary oppression of being female in a patriarchal world. It hurts to hear that the Sisters in the Gay Liberation Front, too, have to struggle continually against the male chauvinism of their gay brothers. It hurts that Jane Alpert was cheered when rapping about imperialism, racism, the Third World, and All Those Safe Topics but hissed and booed by a Movement crowd of men who wanted none of it when she began to talk of Women's Liberation. The backlash is upon us.

They tell us the alternative is to hang in there and "struggle," to confront male domination in the counterleft, to fight beside or behind or beneath our brothers—to show 'em we're just as tough, just as revolushonnery, just as whatever-image-they-now-want-of-us-as-once-they-wanted-us-to-be-feminine-and-keep-the-home-fire-burning. They will bestow titular leadership on our grateful shoulders, whether it's being a token woman on the Movement Speakers Bureau Advisory Board, or being a Conspiracy groupie or one of the "respectable" chain-swinging Motor City Nine. Sisters all, with only one real

alternative: to seize our own power into our own hands, all women, separate and together, and make the Revolution the way it must be made—no priorities this time, no suffering group told to wait until after.

It is the job of revolutionary feminists to build an ever stronger Independent Women's Liberation Movement, so that the Sisters in counterfeit captivity will have somewhere to turn, to use their power and rage and beauty and coolness in their own behalf for once, on their own terms, on their own issues, in their own style—whatever that may be. Not for us in Women's Liberation to hassle them and confront them the way men do, nor to blame them—or ourselves—for what any of us are: an oppressed people, but a people raising our consciousness toward something that is the other side of anger, something bright and smooth and cool, like action unlike anything yet contemplated or carried out. It is for us to survive (something the white male radical has the luxury of never really worrying about, what with all his options), to talk, to plan, to be patient, to welcome new fugitives from the counterfeit Left with no arrogance but only humility and delight, to plan, to push—to strike.

There is something every woman wears around her neck on a thin chain of fear—an amulet of madness. For each of us, there exists somewhere a moment of insult so intense that she will reach up and rip the amulet off, even if the chain tears at the flesh of her neck. And the last protection from seeing the truth will be gone. Do you think, tugging furtively every day at the chain and going nicely insane as I am, that I can be concerned with the puerile squabbles of a counterfeit Left that laughs at my pain? Do you think such a concern is noticeable when set alongside the suffering of more than half the human species for the past 5,000 years—due to a whim of the other half? No, no, no, goodbye to all that.

Women are Something Else. This time we're going to kick out all the jams, and the boys will just have to hustle to keep up, or else drop out and openly join the power structure of which they are already the illegitimate sons. Any man who claims he is serious about wanting to divest himself of cock privilege should trip on this: all male leadership out of the Left is the only way; and it's going to happen, whether through men stepping down, or through women seizing the helm. It's up to the "brothers"—after all, sexism is their concern, not ours: we're too busy getting ourselves together to have to deal with their bigotry. So they'll have to make up their own minds as to whether they will be divested of just cock privilege or—what the hell, why not say it, *say* it?—divested of cocks. How deep the fear of that loss must be, that it can be suppressed only by the building of empires and the waging of genocidal wars!

Goodbye, goodbye forever, counterfeit Left, counterfeit, male-dominated cracked-glass mirror reflection of the Amerikan Nightmare. Women are the real left. We are rising, powerful in our unclean bodies; bright glowing mad in our inferior brains; wild hair flying, wild eyes staring, wild voices keening: undaunted by blood we who hemorrhage every twenty-eight days; laughing at our own beauty we who have lost our sense of humor; mourning for all each precious one of us might have been in this one living time-place had she not been born a woman; stuffing fingers into our mouths to stop the screams of fear and hate and pity for men we have loved and love still; tears in our eyes and bitterness in our mouths for children we couldn't have, or couldn't *not* have, or didn't want, or didn't want *yet*, or wanted and had in this place and this time of horror. We are rising with a fury older and potentially greater than any force in history, and this time we will be free or no one will survive. POWER TO ALL THE PEOPLE OR TO NONE. All the way down, this time.

Free Kathleen Clever!

Free Anita Hoffman!

Free Bernadine Dohrn!

Free Donna Malone!

Free Ruth Ann Miller!

Free Leni Sinclair!

Free Jane Alpert!

Free Gumbo!

Free Bonnie Cohen!

Free Judy Lampe!

Free Kim Agnew!

Free Holly Krassner!

Free Lois Hart!

Free Alice Embree!

Free Nancy Kurshan!

Free Lynn Phillips!

Free Dinky Forman!

Free Sharon Krebs!

Free Iris Luciano!

Free Robin Morgan!

FREE VALERIE SOLANIS!

FREE OUR SISTERS!   FREE OURSELVES!

Although most feminists continued not only to care about but to act for civil rights, against the Vietnam War, for recognition of Cuba, for freedom and independence in Africa, and other causes not confined solely to women's interests, they increasingly preferred to participate as members of autonomous women's groups, as illustrated by the two graphics below. Out of the Chicago Women's Liberation Union (see chapter 3) grew the Chicago Women's Graphics Collective, which produced nationally circulated silk-screened color posters, many focused on the Vietnam War and other anti-imperialist struggles. (One of its most well known took the classic yellow diamond-shaped street sign, "Men Working," and altered it to read, "Women Working.") In Boston, Bread and Roses was an active group in the antiwar movement, and most demonstrations there featured a Bread and Roses speaker. The leaflet protesting the U.S. invasion of Cambodia in 1970 was a typical women's liberation production, with no pretense at looking professional, etched directly onto a mimeograph stencil in this era before photocopying became affordable.

Unite to Win
CHICAGO WOMEN'S GRAPHICS COLLECTIVE

Are You PISSED Off About The "NEW" War In Cambodia?

¡WOMEN!

"If, when the chips are down, the U.S. acts like a pitiful helpless giant..."

(The U.S. is a giant. It is very powerful because it has always been willing to rob and murder people to stay on top.) It invaded Vietnam and now Cambodia.

"... the forces of totalitarianism and anarchy..."

(People fighting for freedom here and throughout the world are called many names by the people who want to destroy them. Don't listen to them. Look around!)

"... will threaten free nations and free institutions throughout the world." NIXON

(All along Nixon has said that american troops were in south east asia to protect peoples "freedom". All along the U.S. has been murdering people fighting for their freedom. But these people are winning. In the U.S. people are fighting for freedom too. Black people have never been fooled by the giant. Now white people are beginning to join the people of the world to bring down the giant. Women have always been put down and kept from fighting for their freedom, and...

WE ARE PISSED OFF !!!

Join us in a demonstration (for women) against the Cambodian Invasion by U.S. troops... Cambridge Common, 4:30 Thursday

Feminists have been criticized for being humorless, a reputation that, if true, would not be surprising considering how often women have been the butt of jokes. In fact, women's liberation was rich with humor, including self-critical humor. Feminists deserve a lot of the credit for exposing and criticizing doctrinaire, jargony, and moralistic Left thinking, which critics named "politically correct," or PC, a pejorative. (It is important to remember that the concept of PC came from the democratic New Left's criticisms of dogmatism.)

By the early 1970s, SDS and the whole white student Left began to fragment, frustrated that peaceful protest was not ending the Vietnam War's heavy human and environmental casualties caused by bombing and chemical warfare. Some SDS members joined the "Weathermen" sect, which indulged in ultra-revolutionary rhetoric and called for armed struggle; others joined small sectarian parties whose members often took proletarian jobs and tried to organize the working class.

One of these sectarian groups, the Trotskyist Socialist Workers' Party (SWP), responded to the growing power of women's liberation by attempting to infiltrate and recruit from within it. Because the women's movement was committed to being open, welcoming to all, and democratic, the SWP was sometimes able to take over and destroy women's organizations by driving away independent-minded members repelled by the group's endless speechifying and dogmatism. This parody, a spurious letter from an organization entitled "WUNTRAC," takes aim at the SWP and similar sectarian organizations. Virtually every phrase and name in this leaflet satirizes some real people or rhetoric.

Even when feminists criticized the sexual sexism of the male Left, they often did so in a lighthearted vein, as in the following cartoon which reverses conventional male ogling.

WUNTRAC

WOMEN UNITED FOR NEEDLESS TROTSKYIST RHETORIC ACTION COALITION
36 W. 22 St., New York, N.Y. 10010

Endorsers (partial listing)

Ms. Richard M. Nixon,
   LAC Ladylike Action Coalition
Norman Mailer, MCP Contingent
Lucy Van Pelt, Fussbudget Contingent
Betty Friedan, NWPC National
   Women's Politico-Capitalists
Female Liberation
   Death Valley, Ca.
   The Vatican Peystown, Neb.
Jane Fonda, SADSAC Sons And
   Daughters of Stars Action
   Coalition
Jeanette MacDonald Rankin File
Planned Parenthood World Copulation,
   Intercourse, Pa.
Young Socialites Anonymous
Young Socialites for Woodhull &
   Douglas
SMAC Sado-Masochists Action
   Coalition
Florence Licecomb, Votes for
   Women Contingent
Polygrumists vs. Utah
Jilly Bean Queen, Tennis-Happy
   Women's Action Coalition
   (THWAC)
Trotwoman & Robinett
Gloria Stardom, YACYAC Young
   Anti-Capitalist Youth Action
   Conlition Fundraising Comm.
Nilitant Supporters Contingent
Dr. Rose Franzblubber
Snow White, Third World Women's
   Contingent
Gwumpy, Dopey & Sweepy, United
   Mine Workers Dwarf Caucus
M.C Barber
J. Edgar Hoover, Government
   Agents Contingent
Yoghurt Cultural Society
Joe Hamath, QUARTERBAC
HAC Hell's Angels Contingent
Leath Valley N.O.W.
Peystown N.O.W.
Vatican N.O.W.
Stay Loose Action Coalition
   (SLAC)

BUILD MASS RHETORIC ACTION COALITION!

Over _____ women from _____
   number over 10   number under 50
states came together on Nov. 20 in Washington, D.C., and San
Francisco for the first national WONAAC-sponsored mass mini-march
round the following demand, "Repeal All Anti-Abortion Laws." The
demonstration sparked much controversy for two blocks in each
direction, and resulted in the sale of more than _____
                                                   number over 5
subscriptions to the <u>Nilitant</u>, the largest number ever sold on
that date at a national abortion march. But in spite of this
overwhelming response, our success has been questioned by
hypercritical Utopian feminists on the ultra-left.

Our opponents in the so-called Women's Liberation Movement —
the Hopelessly Utopian Feminists (HUF) — have argued that the
Nov. 20 mini-march failed to win mass support for the following
reasons:
1. These "women" incorrectly claim that WONAAC could not mount
an effective militant campaign without the support of the
following women's liberation groups:

HUF	Rooftop Feminists
National Livingroom Feminists (NLF)	Closet Feminists
Suburban Women (Bedroom Feminists)	Cloakroom Feminists
Militant Food Coop (Pantry Feminists)	Lavatorical Feminists
WISEGAYS	Women's Ultra-Left Front
Back Porch Feminists	(WULF)

This is nonsense. While a handful of anti-mass-action
feminists may withhold support from politically correct actions
such as Nov. 20, indications are that their numbers will be more
than adequately replaced by the mounting enthusiasm of
committed revolutionary feminist men who make up the
overwhelming majority of the SWP-YSA.
2. These hypercritical reactionaries further argue that the
single-issue focus of our mini-march, Repeal All Anti-Abortion
Laws, was "too narrow." The absurdity of this argument is
immediately apparent. No explanation is necessary. Our

explanation is, of course, that in order to effectively mobilize insurgent reformist forces, a mass action coalition must build only one overwhelming sentiment at a time.

3. Our so-called feminist opponents contend that there was no clear target for our Nov. 20 marches, since no national institution can actually effect the repeal of state laws. This shows how little these women understand our strategy for a mass revolution. If anyone in Washington (or, God help us, San Francisco) had been able to meet our demand, it might have been met (!), thus setting back our efforts to build mass frustration. We must seek increasingly vague targets and hopeless demands.

4. The utopian argument is that women reject passive tactics such as including one's body in a "faceless mob." They ignore the obvious fact that the overwhelming majority of female activists at the WONAAC marches were members of YSA and SWP, whose uniformly short haircuts make their faces perfectly visible. Besides, these female activists contributed much more than their bodies. The bus fare alone was $10 per person.

5. The HUF women are indignantly crying "manipulation" at our vanguard attempts to organize them into a militant revolutionary cadre. Clearly, this is blatant red-baiting, just as the attacks on SWP-YSA by the C.P., the Maoists, the so-called "real Trotskyists," and other ultra-lefts are blatant red-baiting.

6. The hypercritics also charge that the media is tired of our pseudo-reformist marches. They attempt to support this statement by pointing out that marches built by NPAC, YACYAC, WONAAC, JUMPINGJAC, BRICABRAC, BIVOUAC, SMAC and other independent action coalitions look alike, sound alike, and may have interlocking directorates. This is the reason, they charge, that mass media coverage has shrunk in recent progressive demonstrations. In the spirit of honest self-criticism, we concede that coverage by the Republico-Democratic media organs such as the N.Y. Times and the NBC-CBS-ABC TV networks does fall short of our requirements. We therefore call for the formation of a Mass Independent Media Action Coalition (MIMAC) around the following demand: Cover Mass Marches on Demand!

It is not necessary to explain that these arguments are all fallacious. The correct reason that the Nov. 20 marches failed to bring masses of women into the streets is that the Ultra-Reformist National Organization for Women counter-productively scheduled its exclusionary fall-offensive board meeting for the same date. Thus, over 8 women from 14 states were divisively sidetracked to Atlanta.

In response to the overwhelming need for unity in the mass women's auxiliary to the revolutionary socialist movement, preparations are well underway for a mass action coalition formed around a single issue: End Single Issue Coalitions! This historic union of militant forces, Women United for Needless Trotskyist Rhetoric Action Coalition (WUNTRAC), is calling for a broad-based four-day conference to call for a militant activist campaign to build a militant activist mass demonstration on Feb. 30 in Death Valley, Ca. Funds are urgently needed.

CLIP AND MAIL TO WUNTRAC, 36 W. 22 St. NYC 10010 Make checks payable to WUNTRAC.

Name _____ Address _____

Zip _____ Phone _____

Organization _____

_____ I want to help build your staff salaries.

_____ I want to be hustled for Feb. 30.

_____ Enclosed is $175.30 for covered wagon transportation to Death Valley for the Feb. 30 mass action.

Please sign my name to your letters without my permission.

Cartoon and Letter Criticizing Sexist Cartoon

FRAN ROMINSKI, NAOMI WEISSTEIN

Open letter to NATIONAL GUARDIAN

Dear people:

The enclosed cartoon is our response to your printing of the LNS cartoon which juxtaposed the virile, potent, aggressive movement—male—against the fawning, prissy, decadent system—female.

We are all awaiting your next printing of a movement versus the system cartoon. We are fully expecting it will be something along the lines of a crowd of lily white, fine citizens—the movement—hanging a stupid, black, kinky-haired, ape-like nigger—the system.

May the revolution blow your minds. Your politics and passion both need an upheaval.

> Fran Rominski
> for Chicago Women's
> Liberation Writing Group

Gay liberation, like women's liberation, arose from the Left. The first public male and female gay rights organizations were organized in the 1950s by leftists. Just as women's liberation was bound up in a love/hate relationship with the New Left, so was gay liberation. The Old Left and civil rights organizations, among both whites and people of color, had been homophobic, and some specifically excluded gays. In response, starting in 1969, gay activists both struggled for recognition within the Left and created an autonomous movement. Betty Friedan, speaking for a sector of the National Organization for Women (NOW), expressed this homophobia, fearing that feminism would be stigmatized as lesbian, a "lavender menace." NOW, however, soon rejected these views. The women's liberation stream of the movement was, by contrast, relatively free of homophobia and usually considered gay liberation a fundamental part of the feminist program.

This platform shows the Left origins of gay rights. Like the Bread and Roses Declaration of Women's Independence, it focussed not only on gay issues but also on building an all-inclusive Left. Gay liberation, although typically portrayed as exclusively white, contained many people of color at its beginnings. At this time they identified with anti-imperialist struggles in Africa, Asia, and Latin America, and considered themselves "Third World" people within the U.S.

Platform
THIRD WORLD GAY REVOLUTION 1970

Our straight sisters and brothers must recognize and support that we, third world gay women and men, are equal in every way within the revolutionary ranks . . .

We want the right of self-determination for all third world and gay people, as well as control of the destinies of communities.

We want the right of self-determination over the use of our bodies: The right to be gay, anytime, anyplace; the right to free physiological change and modification of sex on demand; the right to free dress and adornment.

We want liberation for all women: We want free and safe birth control information and devices on demand. We want free 24 hour child care centers controlled by those who need and use them. We want a redefinition of education and motivation (especially for third world women) towards broader educational opportunities without limitations because of sex. We want truthful teaching of women's history. We want an end to hiring practices which make women and national minorities

1. a readily available source of cheap labor
2. confined to mind-rotting jobs under the worst conditions.

We want full protection of the law and social sanction for all human sexual self-expression and pleasure between consenting persons, including youth. We believe that current laws are oppressive to third world people, gay people, and the masses. Such laws expose the inequalities of capitalism, which can only exist in a state where there are oppressed people or groups. This must end.

We want the abolition of the institution of the bourgeois nuclear family.

We believe that the bourgeois nuclear family perpetuates the false categories of homosexuality and heterosexuality by creating sex roles, sex definitions, and sexual exploitation.

We want all third world and gay men to be exempt from compulsory military service in the imperialist army. We want an end to military oppression both at home and abroad.

We want an end to all institutional religions because they aid in genocide by teaching superstition and hatred of third world people, homosexuals and women. We want a guarantee of freedom to express natural spirituality.

We demand *immediate* non discriminatory open admission/membership for radical homosexuals into all left wing revolutionary groups and organizations and the right to caucus.

The feminism of women of color was also influenced by the Left. Women of color from civil rights movements felt a need to separate themselves doubly—from the male-dominated liberation movements and from the white-dominated women's movement—even as they continued to be a part of the New Left. For these women, class was as fundamental as race in their alienation from the white women's movement. The Third World Women's Alliance, based in New York City, published a newsletter, *Triple Jeopardy*, referring to their threefold oppression—as women, as people of color, and as members of the Third World.

Statement
THIRD WORLD WOMEN'S ALLIANCE

1968

The Third World Women's Alliance started about December, 1968. Within SNCC (Student Nonviolent Coordinating Committee) a Black women's liberation committee was established and a number of women who had been meeting over a period of a few months decided that we would be drawing in women from other organizations, and that we would be attracting welfare mothers, community workers, and campus radicals—so we decided to change the name to the Black Women's Alliance. As of now, the organization is independent of SNCC and at the same time SNCC has decided to retain its women's caucus.

We decided to form a Black women's organization for many reasons. One was and still is, the widespread myth and concept in the Black community of the matriarchy. We stated that the concept of the matriarchy was a myth and that it has never existed. Our position would be to expose this myth. There was also the widespread concept that by some miracle the oppression of slavery for the Black woman was not as degrading, not as horrifying, not as barbaric. However, we state that in any society where men are not yet free, women are less free because we are further enslaved by our sex.

Now we noticed another interesting thing. And that is, that with the rise of Black nationalism and the rejection of white middle class norms and values, that this rejection of whiteness—white cultures, white norms and values—took a different turn when it came to the Black woman. That is, Black men defined the role of black women in the movement. They stated that our role was a supportive one; others stated that we must become breeders and provide an army; still others stated that we had kotex power or pussy

power. We opposed these concepts also stating that a true revolutionary movement enhances the status of women.

Now one of the changes that have taken place in the organization, is that we recognize the need for Third World solidarity. That is, we could not express support for Asia, Africa and Latin America and at the same time, ignore non-Black Third World sisters in this country. We found that we would be much more effective and unified by becoming a Third World Women's organization. So our group is opened to all Third World sisters because our oppression is basically caused by the same factors and our enemy is the same. The name of the organization has been changed to reflect this new awareness and composition of the group—THIRD WORLD WOMEN'S ALLIANCE.

Some women in the movement cannot understand why we exclude whites from our meetings and program. The argument that we are all equally oppressed as women and should unite as one big family to confront the system is as artificial as the argument that Third World women should be fighting on only one front.

And to the white women's liberation groups we say . . . until you can deal with your own racism and until you can deal with your OWN poor white sisters, you will never be a liberation movement and you cannot expect to unite with Third World peoples in a common struggle.

Most white women involved in liberation groups come from a middle-class and student thing. They don't address themselves to the problems of poor and working class women, so there is no way in the world they would be speaking for Third World women. There are serious questions that white women must address themselves to. They call for equality. We answer, equal to what? Equal to white men in their power and ability to oppress Third World people??

It is difficult for Third World women to address themselves to the petty problems of who is going to take out the garbage, when there isn't enough food in the house for anything to be thrown away. Fighting for the day-to-day existence of a family and as humans is the struggle of the Third World woman. We are speaking of oppression, we don't need reforms that will put white women into a position to oppress women of color or OUR MEN in much the same way as white men have been doing for centuries. We need changes in the system and attitudes of people that will guarantee the right to live free from hunger, poverty, and racism. Revolution and not reform is the answer.

3

New Organizational Forms

Consciousness raising (CR) was the major new organizational form, theory of knowledge, and research tool of the women's liberation movement. CR operated on two assumptions: 1) that women were the experts on their own experience—as opposed to professionals such as doctors, psychologists, and religious leaders, usually male, many of whom had believed that they knew what was best for women; and 2) that feminist theory could only arise from the daily lives of women.

CR was usually practiced in small groups because it depended on encouraging every member to participate fully, reflecting the strong emphasis on democracy in the early women's liberation movement. Feminist CR fused analysis, insight, and action. Different women's groups used different CR systems, some more supportive and some more challenging to participants. CR often created emotional and political cohesiveness, but sometimes, especially if women came from different class and racial backgrounds, the process tended to alienate and silence those in the minority.

The CR form was appropriated for therapeutic purposes by support groups—from the disabled to Wall Street executives—and by commercial enterprises, but most of these appropriations neglect the core content of CR. The common denominator in early feminist CR was that women shared experiences in order collectively to analyze how male dominance worked and how it could be changed.

Although there are subtle differences in the two selections below (which would have been important to participants at the time), they also share a basic perspective. Both Pam Parker Allen and the leaders of the Gainesville group were active in the civil rights movement, an experience which shaped that perspective.

The Small Group Process
PAMELA PARKER ALLEN
1969

We have chosen to analyze the group process because we need to have an understanding of what the group structure can and cannot do. In addition we need to analyze our abilities and weaknesses as women. What we found is that it is not easy for us to utilize group processes: processes which we call opening up, sharing, analyzing, and abstracting. We know very well how to open up, that is, talk about our problems; we do it all the time with friends. Some of us have learned to go further and share our experiences with the aim of giving others a perspective on their situations. Fewer of us know how to conceptualize and to generalize from experiences the common rules governing our behavior; and almost none of us knows how to think theoretically.

This is a very individual need: the need for a woman to open up and talk about her feelings about herself and her life; about why she came to a woman's group. This opening up is a reaching out to find human contact. It is important because there are times when we feel alone and confused and we need to open up about who we are and what our problems are. We need to know that someone understands our feelings, our confusion.

The group offers women a place where the response will be positive. "Yes, we know." "Yes, we understand." It is not so much the words that are said in response that are important; rather it is the fact that someone listens and does not ridicule; someone listens and accepts a woman's description of her life. There is the reinforcement that comes from knowing that other women know of what you are speaking; that you are not alone.

Not only do we respond with recognition to someone's account, but we add from our own histories as well, building a collage of similar experiences from all women present. The intention here is to arrive at an understanding of the social condition of women by pooling descriptions of the forms oppression has taken in each individual's life. Revealing these particulars may be very painful, but the reason for dredging these problems up is not only for the therapeutic value of opening up hidden areas. Through experiencing the common discussion comes the understanding that many of the situations described are not personal at all, and are not based on individual inadequacies, but rather have a root in the social order.

The sharing occasions have showed us that the solutions to our problems will be found in joining with other women, because the basis of many of our problems is our status as women. It was not only sharing the stories of our childhood, school, marriage and work experiences which led us to this realization. It was as much the positive feelings, the warmth and comradeship of the small group which reinforced the conviction that it is with other women both now and in the future that solutions will be found. The old stereotypes that women can't work together and don't like one another are shown to be false in practice.

After sharing, we *know* that women suffer at the hands of a male supremacist society, and that this male supremacy intrudes into every sphere of our existence, controlling the ways we are allowed to make our living and the ways in which we find fulfillment in personal relationships. We know that our most secret, our most private problems have a basis in the way women are treated, in the way they are taught to act, in the way women are allowed to live. Isolation turns frustration into self-doubt; but joining together gives women perspective that can lead to action. Through sharing they can see that they have been lied to, and begin to look critically at a society which so narrowly defines the roles they may play.

A third stage now takes place in the group: the experience of analyzing the reasons for and causes of the oppression of women. It is a new way of looking at women's condition: the development of concepts which attempt to define not only the why's and how's of our oppression but possible ways of fighting that oppression. Because the analysis takes place *after* the sharing of individual examples of oppression, it is based on a female understanding of the reality of women's condition.

It is our feeling that this period is important because it is the beginning of transcendence for women. Having gained a perspective on our lives through the sharing process, we now begin to look at women's predicament with some objectivity: This new approach is difficult for many of us, as our lives as women exist predominantly in the realm of immanence and subjectivity; we perform functions, but seldom get on top of a situation to understand how something works and why. This is a new and difficult procedure to learn.

The group is a first step in transcending isolation. Here sometimes for the first time in her life a woman is allowed an identity independent of a man's. She is being allowed to function intellectually as a thinker rather than as a sex object, servant, or mother. In short, the group establishes the social worth of the women present, a necessity if women are to take themselves seriously.

We have had to face realistically the inability of many of us to think conceptually. This inability comes from being encouraged to stay in the private sphere and to relate to people on personal levels even when working. We are training ourselves to get out from under our subjective responses and look at our reality in new ways. Although this is not easy for us, we see the absolute necessity of analysis, for our oppression takes both obvious and subtle forms which vary depending on our class and educational status. The complexity of women's situations necessitates that we bring information outside of our individual experiences to bear on our analysis of women's oppression. This is the period when questions can be asked about how the entire society functions. This is the period when books and other documentation become crucial. We have found that the writings coming out of the women's movement have been most valuable in helping us work out our analysis.

It is our contention, however, that this period of analysis belongs *after* the opening up and sharing experiences, for concepts, we find, must answer the questions which come from our problems as women. It is not in our interest to fit experiences into preconceived theory, especially one devised by men. This is not only because we must suspect all male thinking, as being male supremacist, but also because we must teach ourselves to think independently. Our thinking must grow out of an understanding of our condition as women if it is to answer our needs as women.

A synthesis of the analysis is necessary, and at some point decisions must be made as to priorities in problems and approach. However, before this can happen, a certain distance must exist between us and our concerns. We call this abstracting experience free space. When we remove ourselves from immediate necessity, we are able to take the concepts and analysis we have developed and discuss abstract theory. We are able to look at the totality of the nature of our condition, utilizing the concepts we have formulated from discussions of the many forms our oppression takes. Further, we begin to build (and to some extent, experience) a vision of our human potential.

We are only beginning to experience free space, abstracting, now that we have a year of opening up, sharing, and analyzing behind us. We are beginning to see how different institutions fulfill or prevent the fulfillment of human needs, how they work together, and how they must be changed. We are beginning to gain an overview of what type of women's movement will be necessary to change the institutions that oppress women. Specifically, we have begun to have a clear understanding of what role the small group can and cannot play in this social revolution. It is clear to us that the small group is neither an action-oriented political group in and of itself, nor is it an alternative family unit. Rather it is a place where we can rise above our particular necessities. We are members of humanity looking at the human condition rather than only our personal predicaments. We think this is where ideology can develop. And out of this emerging ideology will come a program grounded in a solid understanding of women's condition which will have its roots, but not its totality, in our own experience. Intellectually this is the most exciting stage. It is a joy to learn to think, to begin to comprehend what is happening to us. Ideas are experi-

ences in themselves, freeing, joyous experiences which give us the framework for formulating proposals for action.

This process for understanding experiences does not occur easily, and cannot occur if the demands for opening up and sharing are so great that there is no room for working the experience into concepts and then into theory. Women who are unable to receive enough ego support through the opening up and sharing process may fear abstraction because they think it is alienating them from themselves. This has happened with us and has led us to think that a certain amount of self-acceptance is necessary before a group can experience free space. The opening up experience is necessary, but in and of itself cannot give women a full understanding of their problems. But if opening up is what a particular woman continues to need, she should not be prevented from having it. However, it may be that it should take place outside the group; in therapy, for example.

It is not only women who cannot talk about anything but their subjective situations who can be detrimental to the group process. As destructive are the women who refuse to deal with the forms oppression takes in their personal lives and instead demand that the group begin its approach to the problems of women on the level of analysis. Invariably, we find that the women who have an over-all answer to the problems of women but refuse to confront the everyday examples of male supremacy in intimate male-female relationships either come from male-dominated political organizations or live with men who do.

The total group process is not therapy, because we try to find the social causes for our experiences and the possible programs for changing these. But the therapeutic experience of momentarily relieving the individual of all responsibility for her situation does occur and is necessary if women are to be free to act.

An ideology will develop for a women's movement, but it can and must develop from the people who make up that movement. It is important that the women's movement include as many women as possible so that the total condition of all women can be understood and included in our ideology.

What We Do at Meetings
GAINESVILLE WOMEN'S LIBERATION

Only women can come to our meetings. We feel that we women need to get together by ourselves and talk honestly. Most of us feel there are things we want to say about our situation that would be dangerous or embarrassing at this time to say in front of men, or that would require a lot of time to explain to men. Until we have the strength to say everything we need and want to say to men and not get clobbered for it, we must keep some things secret. We want to build good relationships among women, not only to win our struggle against male supremacy but for their own sake. It is impossible to build trust among women when there are men around.

Also, men tend to take over meetings. We think women know more about women than men do, and we can best analyze our situation and decide our course of action OURSELVES. We can, of course, ask men to join in special discussions or actions if WE decide WE want to. But we must have unity among ourselves FIRST.

WHAT WE HEAR AND SAY IN ALL MEETINGS IS CONFIDENTIAL! If it gets back to our men and/or bosses, we could get in trouble. We do not tell men anything that goes on at our meetings unless the group decides on something we want all to tell. That does not mean we can't talk with a man about some of the topics we discuss. We certainly do want to talk to him about doing half the housework! But we don't tell him the source of our comments. WE MUST NOT GIVE OUT ANY INFORMATION THAT CAN HARM OTHER WOMEN OR OUR MOVEMENT.

And even when we are talking to other women who are not in our group, we are careful not to identify who said what in any way, even though we might want to tell what we talked about. We also never talk to the news media about our group or our movement without first getting the o.k. of the group. Whether we say anything, and the gist of what we say, must be a group decision.

One of the groups uses the first half hour of the meeting for everybody to tell what made them happy or unhappy during the week. We found that our meetings usually began informally that way, anyway. So we decided if we went around the room, everybody would get to hear what everybody else had to say. From what makes us happy, we learn how we want things to be. From what makes us unhappy, we learn what we want to change. Sometimes someone tells something that we decide to take action on or that we will want to discuss in detail at another meeting.

The meeting centers, however, around a question that each woman can answer by giving her own experiences. Sometimes we decide on a question that has been used successfully in other groups, but most often we think up our own. The question often is a group of questions. They ask how we feel about something, not just what happened. One question that has been used a lot is: Which do/did you prefer, a boy, a girl, or no children? Why? How do/did you feel when someone else said which they wanted? Why?

Good questions often come from women who are in the middle of a problem. The danger in using these immediate experiences for questions is that the meeting can fall into advice giving. We assume that we need to do a whole lot more than give advice, so the group is responsible to see that the question gets phrased in such a way that everybody starts thinking about their own similar experiences and looks for the common root of the problem.

In answering the question we sit in a circle (of sorts) and go around the room. Each woman answers the question from her personal experiences, instead of what she read in a book somewhere, or what she heard somebody else say about it.

THIS IS HOW WE GET TO THE TRUTH. So many lies have been written and spoken about women that we look to ourselves to find out what is really true about us. We try to discover what we really think and feel in our group instead of what we know we're expected to think and feel.

WE WOMEN ARE THE EXPERTS ON WOMEN. Telling it like it is may be the most difficult action of our movement. It is an act of great courage and an act of faith in our sisters and in the success of our movement.

We go around the room answering the question because it helps us keep to the point. Instead of discussing a number of things superficially, we are able to go deeply into and understand a specific issue. As each woman takes her turn in answering the question, she automatically brings the discussion back to the topic.

Also, we've found that every woman usually talks if the going around the room method is used. Women who are reluctant to talk in a group feel more responsibility to contribute their own experiences and don't resent the women who talk a lot as much, and talkative women don't resent other women for not contributing their experiences. Although this method puts a check on those women who talk too much if they have the opportunity to do so, we must recognize that each woman needs to "be herself." This method lessens the temptation to attack those who talk a lot by accusing them of dominating the meeting, and of attacking those who talk very little by accusing them of not contributing enough.

It should be understood that no woman is expected to tell EVERYTHING about her life. There are some things that each of us does not want to disclose to the group at this time. We do expect that each woman tell the truth about what she does talk about, however.

Decisions about this and other things in our group are as democratic as we know how to make them. If we vote on something, those who are in the minority have a chance to reconsider their vote and decide whether or not to go along with the majority or whether to stop the group from doing what it has voted to do.

Our meetings are often spirited as we women let ourselves go in search of some answers. Many of us are so used to seeing and being quiet and "nice" women that sometimes it can be a bit surprising when we get caught up in a meeting where the natural, noisy, robust, free side of ourselves comes out strongly. This part of us, which as women most of us have never been allowed to show, should not be put down. After awhile we begin to like it in ourselves and in other women as much as we like the gentle, tender side.

It can be frightening when the desperation, anger, and impatience that begins when we stop blaming ourselves and start seeing things as they really are comes through when we talk. When we finally see some hope after all these years, we sometimes are very intense. We feel like everything in our life depends on what we're doing in the group. We live in a world that is trying hard to be "cool," and we're not used to the expression of feelings that sometimes come out, especially in the presence of other women. We also tend to think that our feelings are personal, and group sharing of group feelings is a new experience.

Arguing a point does not necessarily equal hostility if we realize that each person's comments must be heard with a clear mind and evaluated on its own merits. That is, no one is either right or wrong all the time. No matter how many times a woman has been right or wrong in past discussions, her observations and understanding THIS TIME is what matters.

We don't dismiss women who seem to have a different experience than the majority as being "an exception." We are not trying to agree that we all felt the same way or did the same thing in a given situation. Often two or more different actions or feelings are what we call "contradictions." What we mean is, two or more different experiences which seem to be opposite and unrelated to each other.

Contradictions are important because they divide women. At the root of each is the discovery that, with things the way they are, we're "damned if we do and damned if we don't." For example, at one meeting we answered a question dealing with how we felt about our mothers. Most of the group said they hated their mothers for not letting them date early, wear make-up, etc. One woman said she hated her mother because she had pushed her into wearing make-up and dating at a very young age. Instead of saying the woman who had the opposite experience of everyone else in the group was "wrong" or was "an exception" that didn't count, we talked further and figured out that mothers on both sides of this contradiction (early dating vs. late dating) were only trying to do what they thought was best for their daughters. That is, they wanted their daughters to make a good marriage—they just had two different ways of going about it. As it turned out, their daughters hated them either way. The immediate result of this discussion was that many of us began to understand and therefore stop hating our mothers, thus cutting down one division among women.

As an example, let's say the group was talking about playing dumb with men. Some women play dumb a lot as a means of trying to get what they want, even though it doesn't always work. Others don't play dumb and don't suffer the humiliation, but often don't get what they want and even may get punished. So both ways are presently about equal and we're damned either way. However, one side is ultimately better than the other. We women should not have to play dumb, and we don't want to in the new society we are working for. However, the group may decide that it is o.k. to play dumb for the time being because we don't have enough power yet to stop playing dumb. Or, it may decide that the time has come to take a GROUP stand against playing dumb. In order to change this bad situation, we must figure out why we have to play dumb so we will know what conditions have to be changed before we can stop.

When we talk about our problems as women, we are often accused of doing "therapy" in our group. The very word "therapy" is wrong because it assumes that there is something wrong with women and that there is a cure, or something a woman can do for herself to solve her problems. We women don't NEED therapy. We are messed over, not messed up. We need to change what causes our problems, not just adjust to those bad conditions. One of the first things that we discover in the group is that personal problems are really political problems. That is, there is no way out by ourselves. We need collective action for a collective solution.

This is not to deny that these sessions make us feel better about ourselves. When we hear other women have the same problems we say, "Wow! It's not my fault. There's nothing wrong with ME."

The women's liberation movement showed its New Left roots in its commitment to direct, participatory democracy and its suspicion of formal procedural rules, elected offices, and leadership. The New Left questioned whether the U.S. was truly a democracy, observing how few people vote, how wealthy interest groups exerted a disproportionate influence on the system, who can afford to run for office, what they support once in office, how people of color and white women are excluded from the political process, the way the political process becomes so obscure to ordinary people that they tune out and become passive objects rather than subjects of government. Participatory, direct democracy attempts to restore political subjectivity to citizens, insisting that they contribute actively to decision-making, as opposed to merely voting for representatives. Women's liberation groups typically had no formal criteria for membership, and anyone who dropped in became a member. There were neither dues nor officers, and people volunteered for committees by putting their names on sign-up sheets. The suspicion of leaders could be extreme: all ideas were considered to have come from the group, and many leaflets and pamphlets were published without individual names or were signed with pseudonyms.

This model can work well in small groups with people of similar backgrounds and belief systems. But in larger organizations, the lack of formal procedures can make it harder for some members to have any voice and harder to resolve conflict. Because there were no elected or mutually agreed-upon leaders, particularly charismatic, articulate, or well-connected individuals would become informally more influential than others, or might be sought out as spokeswomen by the media. These "heavies," as they were sometimes called, often provoked resentment from others in the group and might find themselves the targets of snide remarks and open hostility.

Such problems gave rise to Jo Freeman's 1970 critique. A civil rights veteran, member of one of the earliest women's liberation groups, founded in 1967 in Chicago, and later founder and editor of a national feminist newsletter, the *Voice of Women's Liberation Movement,* Freeman observed that direct democracy with its lack of officers and structure could actually impede democratic development. She offers two primary arguments: first, that all groups naturally give rise to structures and leaders, and that when leadership is informal rather than formal it can become irresponsible, without accountability to membership; second, that structurelessness often cripples groups and prevents political action.

The Tyranny of Structurelessness
JO FREEMAN

1970

During the years in which the women's liberation movement has been taking shape, a great emphasis has been placed on what are called leaderless, structureless groups as the main form of the movement. The source of this idea was a natural reaction against the overstructured society in which most of us found ourselves, the inevitable control this gave others over our lives, and the continual elitism of the Left and similar groups among those who were supposedly fighting this over-structuredness.

The idea of structurelessness, however, has moved from a healthy counter to these tendencies to becoming a goddess in its own right. The idea is as little examined as the term is much used, but it has become an intrinsic and unquestioned part of women's liberation ideology. For the early development of the movement this did not much matter. It early defined its main method as consciousness-raising, and the structureless rap group was an excellent means to this end. Its looseness and informality encouraged participation in discussion and the often supportive atmosphere elicited personal insight. If nothing more concrete than personal insight ever resulted from these groups, that did not much matter, because their purpose did not really extend beyond this.

FORMAL AND INFORMAL STRUCTURES

Contrary to what we would like to believe, there is no such thing as a structureless group. Any group of people of whatever nature coming together for any length of time, for any purpose, will inevitably structure itself in some fashion. The structure may be flexible, it may vary over time, it may evenly or unevenly distribute tasks, power and resources over the members of the group. But it will be formed regardless of the abilities, personalities and intentions of the people involved. The idea becomes a smokescreen for the strong or the lucky to establish unquestioned hegemony over others. This hegemony can easily be established because the idea of structurelessness does not prevent the formation of informal structures, but only formal ones. Similarly, laissez-faire philosophy did not prevent the economically powerful from establishing control over wages, prices and distribution of goods; it only prevented the government from doing so. Thus structurelessness becomes a way of masking power, and within the women's movement it is usually most strongly advocated by those who are the most powerful (whether they are conscious of their power or not).

For everyone to have the opportunity to be involved in a given group and to participate in its activities the structure must be explicit, not implicit. The rules of decision-making must be open and available to everyone, and this can only happen if they are formalized. This is not to say that formalization of a group structure will destroy the informal structure. It usually doesn't. But it does hinder the informal structure from having predominant control and makes available some means of attacking it.

An elite refers to a small group of people who have power over a larger group of which they are part, usually without direct responsibility to that larger group, and often without their knowledge or consent. A person becomes an elitist by being part of, or advocating, the rule by such a small group, whether or not that individual is well-known or not known at all. Notoriety is not a definition of an elitist. The most insidious elites are usually run by people not known to the larger public at all. Intelligent elitists are usually smart enough not to allow themselves to become well-known. When they become known, they are watched, and the mask over their power is no longer firmly lodged.

Because elites are informal does not mean they are invisible. At any small group meeting anyone with a sharp eye and an acute ear can tell who is influencing whom. The members of a friendship group will relate more to each other than to other people. They listen more attentively and interrupt less. They repeat each other's points and give in amiably. The outs they tend to ignore or grapple with. The outs' approval is not necessary for making a decision; however it is necessary for the outs to stay on good terms with the ins. Of course, the lines are not as sharp as I have drawn them. They are nuances of interaction, not pre-written scripts. But they are discernible, and they do have their effect. Once one knows with whom it is important to check before a decision is made, and whose approval is the stamp of acceptance, one knows who is running things.

When informal elites are combined with a myth of structurelessness, there can be no attempt to put limits on the use of power. It becomes capricious.

This has two potentially negative consequences of which we should be aware. The first is that the informal structure of decision-making will be like a sorority: one in which people listen to others because they like them, not because they say significant things. As long as the movement does not do significant things this does not much matter. But if its development is not to be arrested at this preliminary stage, it will have to alter this trend. The second is that informal structures have no obligation to be responsible to the group at large. Their power was not given to them; it cannot be taken away. Their influence is not based on what they do for the group; therefore they cannot be directly influenced by the group. This does not necessarily make informal structures irresponsible. Those who are concerned with maintaining their influence will usually try to be responsible. The group simply cannot compel such responsibility; it is dependent on the interests of the elite.

THE STAR SYSTEM

The idea of structurelessness has created the star system. We live in a society which expects political groups to make decisions and to select people to articulate those decisions to the public at large. The press and the public do not know how to listen seriously to individual women as women; they want to know how the group feels. Only three techniques have ever been developed for establishing mass group opinion: the vote or referendum, the public opinion survey questionnaire and the selection of group spokespeople at an appropriate meeting. The women's liberation movement has used none of these to communicate with the public. Neither the movement as a whole nor most of the multitudinous groups within it have established a means of explaining their position on various issues. But the public is conditioned to look for spokespeople.

While it has consciously not chosen spokespeople, the movement has thrown up many women who have caught the public eye for varying reasons. These women represent no particular group or established opinion; they know this and usually say so. But because there are no official spokespeople nor any decision-making body the press can interview when it wants to know the movement's position on a subject, these women are perceived as the spokespeople. Thus, whether they want to or not, whether the movement likes it or not, women of public note are put in the role of spokespeople by default.

POLITICAL IMPOTENCE

Unstructured groups may be very effective in getting women to talk about their lives; they aren't very good for getting things done. Unless their mode of operation changes, groups flounder at the point where people tire of just talking and want to do something more. Because the larger movement in most cities is as unstructured as individual rap groups, it is not much more effective than the separate groups at specific tasks. The informal structure is rarely together enough or in touch enough with the people to be able to operate effectively. So the movement generates much emotion and few results. Unfortunately, the consequences of all this motion are not as innocuous as the results, and their victim is the movement itself.

Since the movement at large is just as unstructured as most of its constituent groups, it is similarly susceptible to indirect influence. But the phenomenon manifests itself differently. On a local level most groups can operate autonomously, but the only groups that can organize a national activity are nationally organized groups. Thus, it is often the structured feminist organizations that provide national directions for feminist activities, and this direction is determined by the priorities of these organizations. Such groups as the National Organization of Women and Women's Equality Action League and some Left women's caucuses are simply the only organizations capable of mounting a national campaign. The multitude of unstructured women's liberation groups can choose to support or not support the national campaigns, but are incapable of mounting their own. Thus their members become the troops under the leadership of the structured organizations. They don't even have a way of deciding what the priorities are.

As long as the women's liberation movement stays dedicated to a form of organization which stresses small, inactive discussion groups among friends, the worst problems of unstructuredness will not be felt. But this style of organization has its limits; it is politically inefficacious, exclusive and discriminatory against those women who are not or cannot be tied into the friendship networks.

PRINCIPLES OF DEMOCRATIC STRUCTURING

Once the movement no longer clings tenaciously to the ideology of structurelessness, it will be free to develop those forms of organisation best suited to its healthy functioning. This does not mean that we should go to the other extreme and blindly imitate the traditional forms of organisation. But neither should we blindly reject them all. Some traditional techniques will prove useful, albeit not perfect; some will give us insights into what we should not do to obtain certain ends with minimal costs to the individuals in the movement. Mostly, we will have to experiment with different kinds of structuring and develop a variety of techniques to use for different situations. The lot system is one such idea which has emerged from the movement. It is not applicable to all situations, but it is useful, in some. Other ideas for structuring are needed. But before we can proceed to experiment intelligently, we must accept the idea that there is nothing inherently bad about structure itself—only its excessive use.

What Men Can Do for Women's Liberation

GAINESVILLE WOMEN'S LIBERATION   1970

At the center of the Women's Liberation Movement is a demand that men change the way they have been acting towards women for centuries. Because of its central importance to the movement, the Women's Liberation groups in Gainesville focused on the question "What can men do now for women's liberation?" and agreed on the following answers. Although a list of this sort is never complete, we think that this one has a great immediate value for people who want to start now to end male domination.

Set up a day-care center at the shop or place of work so that more women can be free to work.

Exercise no job discrimination toward women at any level (whether this be done officially or personally).

Refuse to work where women aren't given equal pay and let the employer know how you feel about it.

Have as much confidence in a woman doctor as you would a man. If she's a woman and has made it, you can be sure that she is qualified.

Encourage other men to do what has been considered "women's work" in the past.

If your wife wants to keep her own name or doesn't want to wear a wedding band, view this not as a rejection, but as an indication of her desire to enter into a fully adult and equal relationship. She is with you by choice, not compulsion.

If you can't cook, learn.

Share in all the housework without being asked, not just the occasional jobs like painting the kitchen or fixing a leaky pipe.

You helped conceive the children, so share in their upbringing. That includes babysitting, diaper-changing, feeding, dressing, and everything on an equal basis with your wife.

Fathers should provide a model for their children that is not male supremacist. Break with standard house-keeping patterns. Encourage children of both sexes to help equally with chores when it's chore time. Don't laugh at boys if they show an interest in cooking or washing dishes (many do) or little girls if they want to learn to build things.

Don't buy your son educational toys and your daughter a doll.

Push your high school to make home economics and industrial arts compulsory for boys and girls. Boys need cooking skills as much as girls need mechanical know-how.

Push your school principals and guidance counselors to allow girls to attend high school while pregnant and afterwards.

Stop punishing girls who don't play dumb.

Don't say one thing among your men friends and another to a woman. A woman cannot correct you or challenge the inaccuracies of your thinking if she doesn't know what it is you really *are* thinking. And even though it is not easy to challenge all the ideas that your male friends have held and benefited from for centuries, it is a necessity in changing the ideas of the whole society.

Don't descend to man talk in which women are talked about as if they were animals. "My chick," "I screwed the pig," etc. Insist that other men stop talking this way.

Listen to a woman's ideas. Hers are as good as a man's or better.

Don't ask a woman to pay for everything with sex.

Stop being patronizing. See a woman for what she is. Don't trap her and yourself by acting like she's beneath you.

Provide babysitting and transportation for WL meetings.

Don't say you believe in women's liberation and then take advantage of a woman. Don't use women's liberation as a weapon to get out of doing things or to take liberties. ("You're liberated now so you can carry your own groceries." "You're an equal now so I can hit you.")

Don't be super critical of a woman's behavior because she is in Women's Liberation. Don't expect her to act like a liberated woman until you become a liberated man.

Don't try and make points with women by bragging what a non–male supremacist you are. Admit your chauvinism so we can try and help you get out of it.

Don't make jokes about WL. It's a serious thing. Women die from male supremacy every year.

The first national convention of *El Partido de la Raza Unida* (Party of the People United) took place in 1970 in El Paso, and from the beginning it defied stereotypes about Chicanos (people of Mexican descent), including the assumption that all Latino culture is patriarchal and ultra-Catholic. More than 40 percent of the delegates were women, and six of the eighteen state delegations were chaired by women. This overwhelmingly Catholic meeting nevertheless endorsed the repeal of all antiabortion laws.

Chicanas had formed a caucus, an organizational form that feminists often used in male-dominated groups as a means of building women's solidarity and power. This caucus adopted a remarkably wide-ranging platform, including both issues specific to the Chicano community, such as the provision of interpreters, and matters of the most universal concern, such as child care.

Women of *La Raza* Unite!

1972

We, as *Chicanas*, are a vital part of the *Chicano* community. (We are workers, unemployed women, welfare recipients, housewives, students.) Therefore, we demand that we be heard and that the following resolutions be accepted.

Be it resolved that we, as *Chicanas*, will promote *la hermanidad* [sisterhood] concept in organizing *Chicanas*. As *hermanas*, we have a responsibility to help each other in problems that are common to all of us. We recognize that the oldest example of divide-and-conquer has been to pro-

mote competition and envy among our men and especially women. Therefore, in order to reduce rivalry, we must disseminate our knowledge and develop strong communications.

Be it also resolved, that we as *Raza* must not condone, accept, or transfer the oppression of *La Chicana*.

That all *La Raza* literature should include *Chicana* written articles, poems, and other writings to relate the *Chicana* perspective in the *Chicano* movement.

That *Chicanas* be represented in all levels of *La Raza*

Unida party and be run as candidates in all general, primary, and local elections.

JOBS

Whereas the Chicana on the job is subject to unbearable inhumane conditions, be it resolved that:

Chicanas receive equal pay for equal work; working conditions, particularly in the garment-factory sweatshops, be improved; Chicanas join unions and hold leadership positions within these unions; Chicanas be given the opportunity for promotions and be given free training to improve skills; there be maternity leaves with pay.

PROSTITUTION

Whereas prostitution is used by a corrupt few to reap profits for themselves with no human consideration for the needs of mujeres, and whereas prostitutes are victims of an exploitative economic system and are not criminals, and whereas legalized prostitution is used as a means of employing poor women who are on welfare, be it resolved that:

1. those who reap profits from prostitution be given heavy prison sentences and be made to pay large fines;
2. that mujeres who are forced to prostitution not be condemned to serve prison sentences;
3. that prostitution not be legalized.

ABORTIONS

Whereas we, as Chicanas, have been subjected to illegal, dehumanizing, and unsafe abortions, let it be resolved that we endorse legalized medical abortions in order to protect the human right of self-determination. Be it also resolved that Chicanas are to control the process to its completion. In addition, we feel that the sterilization process must never be administered without full knowledge and consent of the individual involved.

COMMUNITY-CONTROLLED CLINICS

We resolve that more Chicano clinics (self-supporting) be implemented to service the Chicano community:

1. for education about medical services available (birth control, abortion, etc.);
2. as a tool for further education of Chicana personnel into medical areas, returning to the barrios;
3. as political education for our people in view of the contracting bandaid programs now in existence.

CHILD-CARE CENTERS

In order that women may leave their children in the hands of someone they trust and know will understand the cultural ways of their children, be it resolved that Raza child-care programs be established in nuestros barrios. This will allow time for women to become involved in the solving of our Chicano problems and time to solve some of their own personal problems. In order that she will not be deceived by these programs, be it further resolved that these programs should be run and controlled by nuestra raza.

DRUGS

Whereas drug administration and drug abuse is a big problem among our people, and whereas Chicanos and Chicanas are not presently adequately represented in drug-education programs, be it resolved that: this conference go on record as advising all local public health and public schools and La Raza that the possession of marijuana must be decriminalized; and that a study on Chicanas in prison on drug-abuse charges be made as soon as possible; and that Chicanos and Chicanas who are bilingual and relate to La Raza must be employed on a parity basis in all drug-abuse programs.

EDUCATION

Whereas we resolve that legislation concerning sex discrimination in education be supported and carried out by the Chicano community, we further resolve that a legislative clearinghouse be established to disseminate information pertaining to Chicanas.

That Chicana classes educating the Chicana, Chicano, and community in educational growth together be implemented on all campuses. That these classes be established, controlled, and taught by Chicanas. The classes should deal with existing problems faced by the *Chicana* as a wife, mother, worker, and as a member of *La Raza,* and historical research should also be done by the classes into the discrimination against *Chicana* women.

RESEARCH

Whereas we resolve that research information be gathered and disseminated on the *Chicana* in the following areas: (1) health, education, and welfare, (2) labor, (3) women's rights, (4) funding sources.

INTERPRETERS

Whereas many *La Raza* women do not speak English, and *whereas* this poses a problem in their support of their minor children, be it resolved that juvenile justice courts be petitioned to provide interpreters for Spanish-speaking mothers, and be it further resolved that *Chicanos* form a committee to offer time and moral support to mothers and children who have juvenile justice court actions.

VIETNAM

Whereas the Vietnam war has victimized and perpetuated the genocide of *La Raza,* and has been used as a vehicle of division within our community and *familia,* be it resolved that we as *Chicanas* demand an immediate halt to the bombing and a withdrawal from Vietnam.

Women's liberation gave rise to a variety of woman-owned and woman-operated enterprises, from baby-sitting cooperatives to credit unions. In the early years of the movement these operated on the ultra-democratic principles characteristic of the 1960s: the businesses were nonprofit, everyone was encouraged to learn all the skills, and there were few if any wage differentials. The enterprises were often run with collective decision-making, and they sought above all to serve and empower women. Later, more conventionally organized women's for-profit businesses flourished, but the ground was broken by these earlier, more democratic and feminist initiatives. Between 1977 and 1992, the number of woman-owned businesses in the U.S. expanded by 15 percent a year, until women's share constituted one-third of all businesses. This positive trend does not, however, necessarily lead to economic equality: Situated primarily in the retail or service trades, women's firms tend to be much smaller than men's; about 50 percent were home-based; 40 percent had before-tax profits of less than $10,000, and 25 percent reported before-tax losses. Only 1 percent had before-tax profits of $100,000 or more.

The following selections offer feminist critical analyses of two projects: a professional journalist's account of a women's restaurant and an evaluation of a women's school by the group that ran it. Both illustrate a constructive feminist practice of engaging in self-criticism in order to learn and to help others benefit from experience.

You Are Where You Eat
LAURA SHAPIRO

1975

It used to be that anything with the word "women's" attached to it was self-explanatory and limited by common understanding, e.g. women's magazine (*Good Housekeeping*), women's candidate (John Lindsay) or women's complaint (cramps). Now that women themselves can create and define what's to be their own we have hundreds more—women's television show, bookstore, bank, center, school, bar, tour, religion, art and music—but the category itself has become a problem. What do we mean by "women's"? Even using the word "feminist" instead is now just a back route to the same question, eliminating only Phyllis Schlafly and others on the slave circuit. Cambridge has a number of "women's" places and organizations and one that's recently emerged from a dark struggle to define the term is Bread and Roses, the women's restaurant at 134 Hampshire Street.

A year ago this month a group of women began to rehabilitate what Pat Hynes, one of the restaurant's founders, called "A horrible old bar, violent, and full of dirty alcoholics—it was a male bar, in the worst sense." At that time Pat had just left a job with the campus ministry at Northeastern, where she had opened a women's center and organized a conference on women in higher education. Pat and a few other women she worked with at Northeastern spent five months revamping the place and trying to get the smell of stale beer out. The labor force was female, as much as possible. They couldn't find any local women who are licensed electricians or plumbers, it turned out, and tax accountants seem to be male too. But women did nearly everything else, whether or not they knew how, and found the newness and difficulty exhilarating.

"I felt stretched and broadened as never before," Gill Gane, co-founder of the restaurant, said. She's a South African who came to this country seven years ago and has been writing and teaching. "We were going into areas women never went into before, dealing with inspectors, licensing, going to restaurant auctions, physically working on getting the place together." Ann Kendall, one of the board members, a Cambridge woman active in NOW, called it "a women's barn-raising."

Meanwhile they were raising money through a series of small dinner parties, and by December they had about $20,000 and were ready to start. The first event was an open house for 300 women who brought plants, plates and anything else they could give. From the beginning it was meant to be more than a restaurant. Bi-weekly art exhibits are held there, a variety of presentations and entertainments are given by women on Sunday nights, and in place of receiving tips money is collected for feminist causes.

"Having it be a restaurant keeps us going, but that's not at all our main purpose," Pat told me. "We've been persistent and aggressive about making it a women's place. Women from the Women's Community Health Center, the Feminist Credit Union, New Words (the bookstore)—they meet there, they have dinner, they stay and talk. And one of our purposes is to have it used that way. It's a cultural institution."

"We wanted it to be a super comfortable place," Gloria Bernheim, the other board member, added. "Especially—and this was a very high priority—a place where women coming in alone can be comfortable."

The food is woman-identified too. "I feel that vegetarian eating and cooking is a lot closer to feminism than meat-eating," Pat remarked. "Meat-eating is like cannibalism. That's the way men see women, in the terms that apply to meat. Or as chicks." The menu stresses vegetarian, low-priced dinners, all with fresh produce. Occasionally they serve chicken or fish, but never beef, and in this way too they're able to keep the prices between $1.75 and $3.50.

After a big rush right in the beginning they settled into a steadily good, small business of between 50 and 100 customers a night. *Gourmet Magazine* has even written to them ("Dear Sirs . . .") with a reader's request for their recipe for bread. Five women work full-time at the restaurant, and three or four are employed part-time. Everyone gets the same salary ($3 an hour) and the work is rotated so that no one is stuck with the worst of it. "It was important not to be a capitalist business," stressed Gill. "That meant not to have alienating labor, or to be exploitative, to depend on tips or be servile waitresses. We wanted it to be a good work situation."

And it was a good work situation, as so many enterprises built by what Ann Kendall called "loving consensus" are—at least in the beginning. "We learned that loving consensus isn't enough." Ann reflected, "Nobody had any notion that we'd turn into 'the workers' and 'the bosses.' Can you be people, and have a business too?" The problem started with a 19-year-old employee who was a lesbian feminist, but she was in fact only a catalyst for the unavoidable and explosive question: what about men? And its corollary, what about straight women? Women who came to the restaurant with men increasingly were made to feel conspicuous and unwelcome, groups with men had to wait longer to be seated, and after a while any woman who didn't look the way a lesbian feminist ought to look was treated as an intruder. The restaurant is small and intimate enough so that one person is able to dramatically alter the atmosphere. Finally a group of women who work nearby and had eaten frequently in the restaurant called Pat to tell her they simply wouldn't go there anymore.

Most of the staff and the two board members had assumed that men would be coming to the restaurant, and while their priority was to make it a place where all women felt at home and comfortable, none of them wanted to discourage men or heterosexual couples or straight women. As Ann pointed out, "If you're rude to women with men, then you're trashing women." There were long meetings and endless discussions but the atmosphere grew more and more unpleasant at the restaurant until Pat took it upon herself to fire the employee. Two others quit in protest, leafletted one night in front of the restaurant, and suddenly the mental trauma was not just lesbian exclusivity but labor relations—the right to hire and fire.

More meetings. Not only the staff, the two board members, and women who had helped financially, but many who just felt involved because they were women joined the controversy. Some believed in worker control, some in worker plus customer control, others in consensus control but with ultimate power in the hands of Pat, Gill and the board. Since ultimate power was in fact in the founders' hands already and Pat especially believed it belonged there, the last position prevailed. (Gill found this unacceptable, and has resigned.)

Pat is firm that women shouldn't be identified by sexual preference. "Being a feminist transcends it—I feel that's the deepest message of feminism," she said.

When I went to the restaurant a few weeks ago, accordingly, I ran into none of the lesbian evil-eye I had been told to expect by friends who'd eaten there in earlier months. It was an utterly calm, accepting and refreshing place to be; and remarkably different from any other place I can think of. Sometimes in a "women's" center or bar you feel just as much on display and as vulnerable as you would if you strolled into Locke-Ober's alone on a Saturday night, but Bread and Roses has a distinctly it's-all-right-to-be-a-woman atmosphere. And the handful of men sitting around looked comfortable too. (We had very good salads, by the way, lots of lentils and an excellent nut pate.)

That ambiance makes a good enough definition of a "women's restaurant" for me, but it won't long satisfy the people who work there or who put money into it. Pat comes across as one of the most clearheaded, sensitive and mature women I've ever met, as well as an enormously sympathetic feminist, and so her thoughts regarding the restaurant will probably be the right ones. But what if she weren't? Perhaps even a feminist business shouldn't depend on individual morality.

The problem is not who gets the profits—the restaurant will channel them into various feminist projects and hopes eventually to set up a trust fund—or even who gets the power, since formulas can be developed for sharing that too. Organization itself is what's vital: open, unmysterious, and run with by-laws, not impressionism. No matter how much of a women's and workers' paradise you want, you can only get there with the usual faceless business practices: expecting the worst of everyone and setting up a system that can handle it. If feminists can do it with rigorous honesty and justice as well as purity, goodness and mercy, then they're better than anybody. I wouldn't mind believing that.

Analysis of Chicago Women's Liberation School
CHICAGO WOMEN'S LIBERATION UNION

"What we don't know we must learn; what we do know, we should teach each other."

Women in Chicago are learning to tell a distributor from a carburetor, the clitoris from the vulva, good healthy food for survival from the plastic, often poisonous variety being sold off the shelves in supermarkets. Women are learning—or relearning—the theories of Marxism from a feminist perspective, how to get a divorce without a lawyer, how we can move with freedom and joy—together. And we're learning why we never learned any or all of these things in the course of our lives.

These revelations are all a part of the Liberation School for Women, a project of the Chicago Women's Liberation Union, a city-wide organization of radical women made up of chapter (either neighborhood, campus, or interest group) and work-groups, whose basic political principles are anti-racism, anti-sexism, anti-capitalism, and anti-imperialism.

Planning for the School began in the fall of 1970 when a group of women from CWLU wanted to develop a program to respond to some of the needs of the women's movement in Chicago. The first was to bring more women in contact with the ideas of women's liberation through a source other than the established media, giving these newly interested women an overview of the movement and their own possible role within it. The second was the need for political education for the members of the Union and women in the women's movement in general: we saw the School as a place to develop our analysis and strategy as well as to do research. Thirdly, the School was intended to provide an opportunity to learn skills, both those which are necessary for survival but have been considered out of the sphere of the "woman's role" and/or those which are essential to build our movement.

The response has been fantastic. Since the first six-week session began in February, 1971, we have grown steadily through three sessions, both in terms of the number of classes offered and the total number of women involved: we began with eight classes in which 120 women enrolled; this term we have 20 classes and over 220 women enrolled.

Specifically, in the three areas mentioned earlier, how well have we succeeded?

The women who have taken introductory classes have been largely white, young and middleclass, many of them mothers with young children. They have been helped to come to the School through a policy of co-operative childcare run by the workgroup. At first we began by trying to pay for sitters collectively; now we have a system whereby everyone taking a class is asked to volunteer to sit on the evenings she is free. Women who need sitters are given the master list and can call anyone up to three times.

We have not been able to find such an easy way, however, to help and encourage women who are not "school oriented" and/or those for whom study or school is a luxury they cannot afford. Many of the women who feel excluded by the women's movement as a whole, such as poor and working class women, have so far not been reached by the School. We are trying to deal with this problem by offering neighborhood extension courses outside the central location of the School, which is at a church in a largely young, white, middle-class, student or ex-student section of the city. We have already offered most of the introductory courses as extension classes in various communities, and we are planning to expand the idea as an organising tool around job oppression, probably beginning with a course for secretaries in the "Loop" or business district of the city.

Similarly the School *has* offered a place to do serious study on questions relevant to the women's movement. It shows a new, woman-controlled, approach to women's studies which we hope will provide a model for other institutions.

Another problem has been that not all students are serious—they seem unwilling to put in the time and reading necessary to make a class really worthwhile. This may be an attitude retained from student days in straight schools when the object of classes was too often to do as little as possible while still making the grades. We see it too as reflecting on the way in which we have been taught not to take ourselves or our activities seriously.

As far as the third need is concerned, the School *has* provided a place to learn skills. Some of the classes in this category, many of which also function as introductory classes, have been auto-repair, fix-it, silk screening, photography, and prepared childbirth. The main criticism here has been that many such classes have concentrated on teaching the skill to the exclusion of any personal exchange among the students. Also, there has been the danger that in skills classes the political rationale behind the classes and behind the School as a whole has not been discussed.

The more we can connect the work of the School with other organising projects the more valuable it becomes.

The interrelationship of the School and the Union could be seen perhaps in a projection for the future which could possibly be one that made as a condition of membership in CWLU that members take at least one class a year in the School. This would ensure that the membership was dealing with political questions, reading, and being serious about its commitment.

We hope to see participation in the School become a springboard for students to a deeper commitment for social change, a deeper commitment to the movement and to the CWLU as part of that movement. We feel that we must involve each class in some kind of action project. One model might be to involve people in the Women and Their Bodies classes in pregnancy testing or abortion counselling; another may stem from the Prepared Childbirth course, which offers a service otherwise unavailable to many women, raises consciousness about our oppression within the health care system and our lack of control over our own bodies, and offers the possibility of direct action closely related to the course content. In this case, the women in the class plan to demand that various clinics and hospitals start offering prepared childbirth courses. With this kind of action, the Liberation School will not be co-opted by institutions representing ways of life to which we are opposed but rather will challenge such institutions in meaningful ways.

Our goal is to create positive dissatisfaction in the participants in the Liberation School, a realization of the dissatisfaction many women feel with their lives, not a dissatisfaction which grows silently within each isolated woman and sours her life, but one which leads her to question her situation, to challenge it, to grow with other women to an understanding that sisterhood is powerful.

4

Feminist Theory

One of the major "theoretical" contributions of women's liberation was to challenge the very meaning of "theory." Rejecting a high-faluting academic and philosophical form of theorizing, feminists began to develop and write theory in new ways. The following examples illustrate irreverent forms through which feminists developed theory. Norma Allen created a brief illustrated booklet to discuss what we now call gender, and Jayne West wrote a humorous/dead serious quiz.

What Is a Woman?
NORMA ALLEN

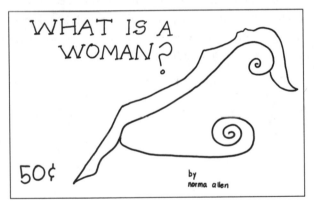

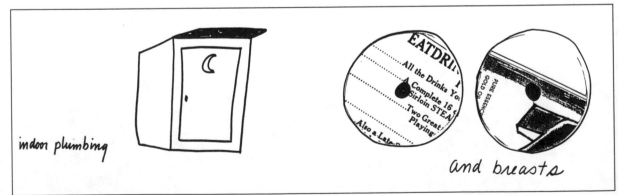

give milk to children and

 Women also have brains...

 which are being STIFLED AND SMOTHERED because

 Society doesn't need them.  WHY?

Woman are necessary to keep the military-industrial complex going.  New York Stock Exchange

because we live in a CAPITALIST Economy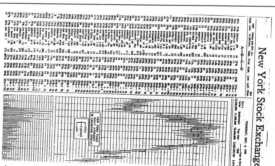

in which women are only

TO SCREW,

to consume,

TO MAKE SONS,

To serve mankind.

WOMEN ARE 20th century SLAVES.

But women today are well-off. They have washers, dryers, vacuum cleaners, station wagons, Mr. Clean, electric mixers, permanent press, P.T.A., instant mashed potatoes, hair spray, college degrees, joint checking accounts, teflon, Y.W.C.A., charm schools, frozen foods, pants suits, etc.

But they don't have POWER over their own lives—

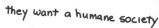

women
want
more
than
EQUALITY
with
men—

they want a humane society

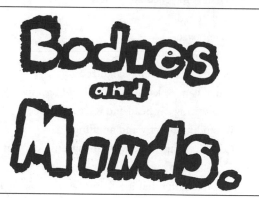

where
women
can
have
the
freedom
of
their

Bodies and Minds.

for more copies
and further
information write:
Washington D.C. Women's
    liberation
Box 13098
  T Street Station
Washington, D.C.
      20009

Are Men Really the Enemy?

JAYNE WEST

AN EXAMINATION

Please use a No. 2 lead pencil when taking this test. Look only at your own paper except in an emergency. No talking, gum chewing, swearing, or primping during the test. In case of fire or nuclear attack, the above rules will be suspended. You are now ready to begin. Don't. We'll tell you when to start. You may begin in exactly a few minutes.

TRUE OR FALSE

1. ___ Woman's work is never done.
2. ___ You can't tell a book by its cover.
3. ___ Housework can be fun.
4. ___ Women make the best mothers.
5. ___ A female dog is referred to as a bitch.
6. ___ One of the more degrading terms that can be applied to a man is "son of a bitch."
7. ___ The discovery that she is castrated is a turning point in a girl's life. (Freud)
8. ___ Life is a bowl of cherries.
9. ___ A little loving goes a long way.
10. ___ The ten most wanted men are men.
11. ___ The opposite of a tomboy is sissy.
12. ___ Beauty is as beauty does.
13. ___ Intelligent women are often ugly.
14. ___ The best chefs in the world are men.
15. ___ A girl should find out what a man's interests are and learn about them so as to have more pleasant conversations with him.
16. ___ I can do a pushup.
17. ___ When the blank says check one M_. F_. I do so without hesitation or contemplation.
18. ___ Some of the finest athletes in the world are women.
19. ___ Sen. Margaret Chase Smith could have been President if she had only remained in the race.
20. ___ Women when angered are capable of extreme forms of violence and insanity.
21. ___ I find it very convenient to carry a purse since I haven't any pockets.
22. ___ The way to a man's heart is through his stomach.
23. ___ *Flighty* is often used when referring to men.
24. ___ A permanent isn't really.
25. ___ Gentlemen prefer blondes.
26. ___ I think that it was certainly necessary that the Mormons had many wives.
27. ___ I often envy the convenience men enjoy in regard to urination.
28. ___ Women are made not born.

MULTIPLE CHOICE

1. Most rapes are committed by
   A. women
   B. children
   C. men (perverts)
   D. I am unable to distinguish rape from ordinary sexual relations.
2. When I am yelled at on the street I am
   A. flattered
   B. annoyed
   C. astonished
   D. sure I have been recognized
3. When I am yelled at on the street I respond by
   A. lowering my head and walking quicker
   B. smiling sweetly and nodding
   C. addressing myself to the specific content of the yeller and applying it appropriately
   D. pretending that it was not I who was yelled at and that I am not in that place and that he is not real and I am not real and thus simply extracting myself from the situation.
4. Which of these things do you prefer to be called?
   A. lady
   B. woman
   C. female
   D. girl
   E. none of the above
5. The reason I keep my legs together when sitting is
   A. some of my underwear has holes in it

B. my legs get cold if I don't

C. my mother always told me to and it's a hard to break habit

D. I like to keep my privates private.

6. When I was a little girl I wanted to be a
   A. nurse
   B. cowgirl
   C. teacher
   D. secretary
   E. boy

7. If I had a baby girl, I would be
   A. disappointed
   B. I wouldn't care as long as it was healthy
   C. burdened
   D. quite annoyed with the Pill

8. When I play games or sports with a man
   A. I let him win
   B. he always beats me
   C. I try to be athletic and healthy so he will play with me again
   D. I just play the best I can and don't worry about the outcome

9. Which of the following things can a man do better than a woman?
   A. cook
   B. sew
   C. masturbate
   D. all of the above

10. If I could do away with anything I wanted, the first thing I would do away with is
   A. the family
   B. the state
   C. private property
   D. menstrual periods
   E. all the above

DRAW A MAN

FILL THE BLANK

1. _____ is never _____ .

2. Make a list of famous women who are not known by Mrs. _____ .

3. My most embarrassing moment was when _____
_____ .

4. My least embarrassing moment was when _____
_____ .

5. In the Orthodox Jewish worship it is said by men: "Thank God that I was not born a _____ ."

MATCHING

A. shorts
B. panties
C. bachelor
D. old maid
E. sissy
F. tomboy
G. three
H. unlimited
I. playboy
J. compassionate
K. whining

1. boy or girl who plays like a girl
2. unmarried woman
3. woman who is somewhat free sexually
4. men's underwear
5. unmarried man
6. women's underwear
7. man who is free sexually
8. number of dribbles allowed in girl's basketball
9. man who sheds tears
10. woman who sheds tears
11. boy who plays like a girl

ESSAY

1. Discuss the variations in tone possible when asking a male druggist this question: "Do you have Tampax Super?"

2. Discuss the population distribution along sexual lines were parents able to determine the sex of their offspring.

3. Discuss your motive for taking this test.

4. Discuss how a woman can have her cake and eat it too.

5. Discuss anything you want.

6. Erase all marks from this paper (except your responses) and pass the paper up to the person to your left. If there is no one on your left, walk to the center aisle and place your paper on the floor and sit upon it. Anyone doing anything that strange is certain to be noticed and helped.

GOOD LUCK! YOU HAVE BEEN A GOOD TESTER AND THAT IS NOT NOTHING

Redstockings, a New York City group with branches in Florida and California, formed in January 1969, was influential in the development of radical feminist theory. Its name referred to "bluestockings," the eighteenth-century British pejorative term for brainy women. Radical feminists saw women's oppression as fundamental, a form of inequality and domination that underlay virtually all human society. Influenced, as their name also suggests, by the Marxist tradition, Redstockings took class analysis a step further and extended it to relations between men and women, arguing that all men benefit from women's subordination and that conflict between the sexes was political. It followed from their class analysis that women as a class could exercise political power. Their position did not reject traditional class analysis and they were aware of the great inequalities among women, as this early manifesto showed, but they also understood that "sisterhood was powerful." In contrast to versions of feminist theory that emphasize women's victimization, Redstockings rejected interpretations that blamed women's oppression on women's own inadequacies (an expansion of this "pro-woman" argument can be found in Ellen Willis's article in chapter 12).

Manifesto
REDSTOCKINGS

1969

1: After centuries of individual and preliminary political struggle, women are uniting to achieve their final liberation from male supremacy. Redstockings is dedicated to building this unity and winning our freedom.

2: Women are an oppressed class. Our oppression is total, affecting every facet of our lives. We are exploited as sex objects, breeders, domestic servants, and cheap labor. We are considered inferior beings, whose only purpose is to enhance men's lives. Our humanity is denied. Our prescribed behavior is enforced by the threat of physical violence.

Because we have lived so intimately with our oppressors, in isolation from each other, we have been kept from seeing our personal suffering as a political condition. This creates the illusion that a woman's relationship with her man is a matter of interplay between two unique personalities, and can be worked out individually. In reality, every such relationship is a *class* relationship, and the conflicts between individual men and women are *political* conflicts that can only be solved collectively.

3: We identify the agents of our oppression as men. Male supremacy is the oldest, most basic form of domination. All other forms of exploitation and oppression (racism, capitalism, imperialism, etc.) are extensions of male supremacy: men dominate women, a few men dominate the rest. All power structures throughout history have been male-dominated and male-oriented. Men have controlled all political, economic and cultural institutions and backed up this control with physical force. They have used their power to keep women in an inferior position. *All men* receive economic, sexual, and psychological benefits from male supremacy. *All men* have oppressed women.

4: Attempts have been made to shift the burden of responsibility from men to institutions or to women themselves. We condemn these arguments as evasions. Institutions alone do not oppress; they are merely tools of the oppressor. To blame institutions implies that men and women are equally victimized, obscures the fact that men benefit from the subordination of women, and gives men the excuse that they are forced to be oppressors. On the contrary, any man is free to renounce his superior position provided that he is willing to be treated like a woman by other men.

We also reject the idea that women consent to or are to blame for their own oppression. Women's submission is not the result of brainwashing, stupidity, or mental illness but of continual, daily pressure from men. We do not need to change ourselves, but to change men.

The most slanderous evasion of all is that women can oppress men. The basis for this illusion is the isolation of individual relationships from their political context and the tendency of men to see any legitimate challenge to their privileges as persecution.

5: We regard our personal experience, and our feelings about that experience, as the basis for an analysis of our common situation. We cannot rely on existing ideologies as they are all products of male supremacist culture. We question every generalization and accept none that are not confirmed by our experience.

Our chief task at present is to develop female class consciousness through sharing experience and publicly exposing the sexist foundation of all our institutions. Consciousness-raising is not "therapy," which implies the existence of individual solutions and falsely assumes that the male-female relationship is purely personal, but the only method by which we can ensure that our program for liberation is based on the concrete realities of our lives.

The first requirement for raising class consciousness is honesty, in private and in public, with ourselves and other women.

6: We identify with all women. We define our best interest as that of the poorest, most brutally exploited woman.

We repudiate all economic, racial, educational or status privileges that divide us from other women. We are determined to recognize and eliminate any prejudices we may hold against other women.

We are committed to achieving internal democracy. We will do whatever is necessary to ensure that every woman in our movement has an equal chance to participate, assume responsibility, and develop her political potential.

7: We call on all our sisters to unite with us in struggle.

We call on all men to give up their male privileges and support women's liberation in the interest of our humanity and their own.

In fighting for our liberation we will always take the side of women against their oppressors. We will not ask what is "revolutionary" or "reformist," only what is good for women.

The time for individual skirmishes has passed. This time we are going all the way.

Another radical feminist New York group, The Feminists, was influential despite its small size because it wrote a great deal in a militant, provocative style. The Feminists differed from the Redstockings in emphasizing certain institutions as oppressive to women, particularly marriage, love, and sex. They limited the number of married women allowed to join their group, assuming that marriage weakened women's commitment to feminism. Less conscious about racism than many other groups, the feminists did, however, emphasize class inequality and enforce strict rules designed to ensure that every member of the group participated equally. Ironically, despite this commitment to egalitarianism, the group had one acknowledged leader, Ti-Grace Atkinson. Her discussion of love assumes heterosexuality and, therefore, love between unequals. This was typical of most feminists at this time, but Atkinson is also critical of heterosexuality, insisting that heterosexual love is pervaded by inequalities of power, an important insight, however overstated and unnuanced.

Radical Feminism and Love
TI-GRACE ATKINSON

1969

I propose that the phenomenon of love is the psychological pivot in the persecution of women. Because the internalization of coercion must play such a key functional part in the oppression of women due to their numbers alone, and

because of the striking grotesqueness of the one-to-one political units "pairing" the oppressor and the oppressed, the hostile and the powerless, and thereby severing the oppressed from any kind of political aid, it is not difficult to conclude that women by definition must exist in a special psycho-pathological state of fantasy both in reference to themselves and to their manner of relating to their counter-class. This pathological condition, considered the most desirable state for any woman to find herself in, is what we know as the phenomenon of love.

Because radical feminists consider the dynamics of their oppression the focal point of their analysis, it was obvious that some theory of "attraction" would be needed. Why do women, even feminists, consort with the enemy? For sex? Very few women over 30 say that; that's the male-role reason. What nearly all women mutter in response to this is: for love.

There has been very little analytic work done on the notion of "love." This is remarkable, considering the importance of it in ethics and political philosophy. Philosophers usually skirt it or brush it aside by claiming it's irreducible or irrational. Or they smile and claim it's the *sine qua non*. All these things may be true and are clues to the political significance of "love": it's basic; it's against individual human interest; a great deal rests upon it.

Any theory of attraction could begin with the definition of the verb to attract: the exertion of a force such as magnetism to draw a person or thing, and susceptibility in the thing drawn. Magnetism is caused by friction or conflict, and the primary relationship between men and women of class confrontation or conflict certainly suffices for the cause of magnetism. Usually the magnetized moves towards the magnet in response to the magnet's power, otherwise the magnetized is immobile.

The woman is drawn to—attracted by—desirous of—*in* love *with*—the man. She is power*less,* he is power*ful.* The woman is instinctively trying to recoup her definitional and political losses by fusing with the enemy. "Love" is the woman's pitiful deluded attempt to attain the human: by fusing; she hopes to blur the male/female role dichotomy,

and that a new division of the human class might prove more equitable: she counts on the illusion she has spun out of herself in order to be able to accept the fusion, to be transferred to the whole and, thus, that the new man will be garbed now equally in her original illusion. Unfortunately, magnetism depends upon inequity: as long as the inequity stands, the fusion may hold (everything else relevant remaining the same); if the inequity changes, the fusion and the magnetism fall with the inequity. A woman can unite with a man as long as she is a woman, i.e., subordinate, and no longer. There's no such thing as a "loving" way out of the feminist dilemma: that it is as a *woman* that women are oppressed, and that in order to be free she must shed what keeps her secure.

The main difficulty [is] understanding the shift from the woman desiring an alliance with the power*ful* to the woman being *in love with* the man. It's clear that love has to do with some transitional or relational factor. But from what to what? It is a psychological state the woman feels she must enter into. But why, exactly? She is going from the political, the power*less* identification, to the individual, one-to-one unit. She is disarming herself to go into the enemy camp. Is love a kind of hysterical state, a *mind*less state therefore a *pain*less state, into which women retreat when the contradiction between the last shreds of their human survival and the everyday contingencies of being a woman becomes most acute?

Is love a kind of frenzy, or something like a Buddhist immolation, to unite with the One? The love women feel for men is most akin to religious love.

But hysteria might be a more useful paradigm for us since it's limited almost exclusively to women (the word "hysterical" derives from the Greek word for "uterus") and the condition is marked by certain characteristics strikingly similar to those of "love": anxiety converted into functional symptoms of illness, amnesia, fugue, multiple personality.

It is often assumed that black feminism arose later than white feminism, that black feminism was a version of white feminism adapted to the black community. But in fact black feminism has its own autonomous roots and it was part of women's liberation from its beginnings. Black feminists' concerns, emphases, and actions differed sometimes from those of whites but they shared an appreciation of women's daily strengths, a deep anger at male supremacy, and a critique of liberation movements that subordinated women. The Mount Vernon/New Rochelle group, also called "The Damned," that generated this "Historical and Critical Essay" was multiclass and multigenerational, unlike many white groups.

The essay denounced not only the white power structure but also those blacks who had accommodated to it. This group called for reproductive choice for black women (see also a letter from this group in chapter 6), but also affirmed black women's power as mothers, a theme found frequently in black feminism. Above all, the group emphasized that black women need to study and theorize. They wrote a great deal, but their writings have been largely overlooked.

A Historical and Critical Essay for Black Women
PATRICIA HADEN, DONNA MIDDLETON, AND PATRICIA ROBINSON   1969–70

It is time for the black woman to take a look at herself, not just individually and collectively, but historically, if she is to avoid sabotaging and delaying the black revolution. Taking a look at yourself is not simply good tactics; it is absolutely necessary at this time in the black movement when even black radical males are still so insecure about their identity and so full of revolutionary phantasies that they cannot reach out to the black woman in revolutionary love—to urge us to begin to liberate ourselves, to tell us the truth: "Black women, you are the most pressed down of us all. Rise up or we as black men can never be free!"

No black man can or should even think he can liberate us. Black men do not have our economic, social, biologic, and historic outlook. We are placed by those who have historically formed and manipulated the values in this society— white males—at the very bottom of all these perspectives. There is so much scorn and fear of WOMEN, ANIMAL and BLACK in this Western culture, and since we are all three, we are simply kept out of history. Except for certain "house women," history is made only by males. The word ANIMAL is used by most males to mean a hated and despicable condition, and anything that is hated is simultaneously feared. Black women get put down as "bitch dogs" and "pussies" by Western white and black men, especially those who so smugly overestimate their brain power flying from campus to campus rapping about reason and SOUL. Their heads blow out this intellectual and educated *spiel* on white and black power. They back it up, like males have always done down through written history, with Gods in their own image. What a come down it is to these males that they so often have to slip away from Harlem and Wall Street—to take "a crap." And how they struggle against the fact that, like so many animals, they are born of the female and from the moment of their leaving our dark wombs, they, like all animals, begin to die! Yet we black women in our deepest humanity love and need black men, so we hesitate to revolt against them and go for ourselves.

If we black women get a few of the goodies and we have bought all that jive put down on us by our field nigger families, who all our lifetime pushed and hustled to be just simple house niggers, our anger and frustration go underground. We don't dare to endanger what we have been conditioned to accept as making it—a little glass house full of TV crap. We become nervous-nagging-narrow-minded murderers of ourselves and our children. We turn our madness and frustrations into other channels against other black women and against our oppressed white sisters. We even trip out on some. We psych out on sex with some cat that is as hung-up as we are. They got the nerve to break into the bag of cleanliness, godliness, and "I'm better than you are, baby?"

If we are poor black women, one night in the streets we explode. That small razor cupped in our fingers slashes his hated black face, that face that reflects our own. We look at him and see ourselves for what we really are—traitors to ourselves as poor black women and traitors to him, our street-brother, because we let him get to where he's at now—not a man just a jive-time turkey. We did not confront him long ago because our minds were not "wrapped." But now we can hear, see, feel our mistakes through his actions against us, toward his children and his mother. Now he's going to try to prove himself a man—"walk that walk; talk that talk." He's still hanging on to his jive thing. He bops on the corner and raps that he's straight. "I'm coming to my people!" He's still out there *fucking* with his drugs and talking shit. We lunge and sink our knife deep into his chest to blot out this awful truth. His blood oozes and stops while ours gushes from between our legs. Nothing gets born. We just end up murderers of the future of our people.

Black women in the United States are so systematically left out of this society that we do not have an important part in producing the products bought and sold in this economy. We are civil servants, domestic servants, and servants to our families. We have no Gods in our own image, even though South American women, through Catholicism, have the Black Madonna. We are separated from black men in the same way that white women have been separated from white men. But we are even less valued by white and black males because we are not white. The American Dream is white and male when examined symbolically. We are the exact opposite—black and female and therefore carry the stigma, almost religious in nature, of the spurned and scorned and feared outcast.

The Western world was built on much more than colonialism and imperialism. It was also built on a split in the minds of men that thoroughly separated male from female as well as the body from the mind. This mind-blowing phenomenon caused all things having to do with the animal body to be repressed unconsciously. It is a fact of the psyche that repressed feelings, like oppressed peoples, do not stay repressed. Repressed feelings, like living energy,

struggle against the force of repression to rise to consciousness. Repression of feelings, which we have learned through the conditioning of myths, is unacceptable, is a constant struggle.

Men's own feminine nature, inherent in their bisexuality, was denied by them. This mental split enabled the male to deny the fact that he was an animal, to struggle against the darkness and toward the light, and to lessen the fact of his dependence on women for his nourishment before and after birth.

Most important, he could deny his dependence on women for his very birth and life. He could now ripple his large muscles and dream of soaring one day to the heavens, where he could be in charge and therefore be worshiped as the God of Light and the Heavens and Apollo. The woman's body, which receives, hosts, and gives forth the future of the species, is inherently powerful. Her body and power had to be overthrown and suppressed when the male felt overwhelmed by this power and responded with the desperate need to take power from the woman. His desperate need became a living force in his use of external power over others and in the repression of his own soft femininity.

Some thousands of years ago, the female was considered the Goddess of the Universe from which heaven and earth sprang. Certainly this myth conforms to basic reality—out of one comes two. The female births both the male and the female. The Adam and Eve myth that has for so long been an important part of black women's education through our part-time father—the Negro minister—and our devoutly religious black mothers, turns this basic reality on its head and into its opposite. The male gives birth through the magical intervention of an all-powerful male God. The rib of Adam is plucked out and made into woman by this powerful medicine man who resembles in action the African and Asian tribal priest. Indeed, this is a powerful myth, for it grants the role of man in human creation while at the same time utterly denying woman's role. Deep down we black women still believe this clever religious tale that puts us out of creation. The fact that we do exposes our terrible dependence on outside authority and our fear of trusting and thinking for ourselves.

Today in the time of the cities, cybernetics, nuclear power, and space exploration, white men have developed a man-made body, the self-regulating machine. It can operate a whole series of machines and adjust itself much as our human brain is able to readjust to the needs of our body and to operate the human body. It can also do the mental and physical work of men's bodies. At last man has done away with the practical need for his own human form. Now he must turn his attention to the danger the woman's body has always posed to his rule. He struggles to perfect artificial insemination and a machine host for the human fetus. He concerns himself with the biological control of reproduction of the species. Those white males who rule the free world (capitalist world) understand that if they are to keep their rule over women and so-called lesser men, they must stop being dependent on their bodies and must perfect machines which they can control absolutely.

Historical and political understanding of ourselves and our actual place in the American Dream is more important at this time than the gun. We black women look at our backwardness, our colossal ignorance and political confusion, and want to give up. We do not like ourselves or each other. Our contradictory feelings about our black brothers, who seem simultaneously to move forward and backward, are increased by their continual cautioning that we must not move on our own or we will divide the movement. About all that we will mess up will be their black study, black power, cultural nationalism hustle. Forget black capitalism, because when the master offers you his thing, you know it's over! There have been other movements in history when revolutionary males have appeared conservative, opportunistic, or just "stopped at the pass," and revolutionary women have always forged ahead of the males at this time to take the revolution to a deeper stage.

Black revolutionary women are going to be able to smash the last myths and illusions on which all the jive-male oppressive power depends. We are not alone anymore. This country no longer holds one well-armed united majority against an unarmed minority. There is a whole bunch of brown and yellow poor folks out there in the world that the ruling middle-class of this country have used and abused, stolen from and sold their shoddy goods to at way-out prices. They are fighting back now, taking over those U.S. companies that sucked their people and their land. They are putting out the United States Army and capitalist investors as they did in China and Cuba.

It is important for black women to remind themselves occasionally that no black man gets born unless we permit it—even after we open our legs. That is the first, simple step to understanding the power that we have. The second is that all children belong to the women because only we know who the mother is. As to who the father is—well, we can decide that, too—any man we choose to say it is, and that neither the child nor MAN was made by God.

Third, we are going to have to put ourselves back to school, do our own research and analysis. We are going to have to argue with and teach one another, grow to respect and love one another. There are a lot of black chicks, field niggers wanting to be house niggers, who will fight very hard to keep this decaying system because of the few, petty privileges it gives them over poor black women. We will be disappointed to lose some house women who will have to revert to their class and who will go with the master, like they did during slavery. Finally, we are going to have to give the brothers a helping hand here and there because they will be uptight, not only with the enemy but with us. But at the same time we've got to do our own thing and get our own minds together.

All revolutionaries, regardless of sex, are the smashers of myths and the destroyers of illusion. They have always died and lived again to build new myths. They dare to dream of a utopia, a new kind of synthesis and equilibrium.

In certain cities—notably Cambridge/Boston, Chicago, New Haven, Minneapolis/St. Paul, and Seattle—women's liberation groups developed a socialist feminist approach. A strong tendency within women's liberation, socialist feminism has been neglected in the popular understanding of 1970s feminism—because socialism itself became an increasingly marginalized idea in the U.S. after the decline of the New Left, because socialist feminists focussed more on organizing and less on writing theory, and because radical feminism flourished in New York, the media capital of the U.S.

Socialist feminists differed from radical feminists in arguing that several forms of domination—sexism, racism, capitalism, imperialism—could in different contexts be of equal importance. Because of their class and race consciousness, socialist feminists concentrated on organizing working-class women, agitating for day care centers, and supporting anti-war and anti-imperialist movements. In fact, socialist feminists shared a great deal with radical feminists: a commitment to an autonomous women's movement and to consciousness-raising as a means of developing theory and an analysis of how men benefited from sexism. Both women's liberation tendencies engaged in activism about reproductive rights, sexual harassment and violence against women, and sexism in the media, and both created alternative women's institutions such as women's centers, schools, restaurants, clinics, and bookstores. Socialist feminists, however, less often rejected the Left and more often attempted to transform its theory and practice so as to include women's liberation in its core. (Socialist feminists should not be confused with Marxist feminists, who attempted to insert feminist ideas into the existing body of Marxist theory and often tried to recruit women into their male-dominated political parties.)

The Chicago Women's Liberation Union was one of the biggest, most active, and longest-lasting socialist-feminist groups. It conducted a wide range of projects, such as a poster-making group, a rock band, secretarial organizing, and day care organizing.

Socialist Feminism
CHICAGO WOMEN'S LIBERATION UNION   1972

We choose to identify ourselves with the heritage and future of feminism and socialism in our struggle for revolution.

From feminism we have come to understand an institutionalized system of oppression based on the domination of men over women: sexism. Its contradictions are based on the hostile social relations set into force by this domination. This antagonism can be mediated by the culture and the flexibility of the social institutions so that in certain times and places it seems to be a stable relationship. But the antagonisms cannot be eliminated and will break out to the surface until there is no longer a system of domination.

But we share a particular conception of feminism that is socialist. It is one that focuses on how power has been denied women because of their class position. We see capitalism as an institutionalized form of oppression based on profit for private owners of publicly-worked-for wealth. It

sets into motion hostile social relations in classes. Those classes too have their relations mediated through the culture and institutions. Thus alliances and divisions appear within and between classes at times clouding the intensity or clarity of their contradiction. But the basic hostile nature of class relations will be present until there is no longer a minority owning the productive resources and getting wealthy from the paid and unpaid labor of the rest.

We share the socialist vision of a humanist world made possible through a redistribution of wealth and an end to the distinction between the ruling class and those who are ruled.

The following would be *among* the things we envision in the new order, part of everyday life for all people:

- free, humane, competent medical care with an emphasis on preventive medicine, under the service of community organizations

- people's control over their own bodies—i.e., access to safe, free birth control, abortion, sterilization, free from coercion or social stigma
- attractive, comfortable housing designed to allow for private and collective living
- varied, nutritious, abundant diet
- social respect for the work people do, understanding that all jobs can be made socially necessary and important
- democratic councils through which all people control the decisions which most directly affect their lives on the job, in the home, and community
- scientific resources geared toward the improvement of life for all, rather than conquest and destruction through military and police aggression
- varied, quality consumer products to meet our needs
- an end of housework as private, unpaid labor
- redefinition of jobs, with adequate training to prepare people for jobs of their choice; rotation of jobs to meet the life cycle needs of those working at them, as well as those receiving the services.
- political and civil liberties which would encourage the participation of all people in the political life of the country
- disarming of and community control of police
- social responsibility for the raising of children and free client-controlled childcare available on a 24-hour basis to accommodate the needs of those who use it and work in it
- free, public quality education integrated with work and community activities for people of all ages
- freedom to define social and sexual relationships
- a popular culture which enhances rather than degrades one's self respect and respect for others
- support for internal development and self-determination for countries around the world

We find it futile to argue which is more primary—capitalism or sexism. We are oppressed by both. As they are systems united against our interests, so our struggle is against both. This understanding implies more than women's cau-

ses in a "movement" organization. What we as socialist feminists need are organizations which can work for our particular vision, our self-interest in a way that will guarantee the combined fight against sexism and capitalism. At times this will mean independent organizations, at other times joint activity recognizing specific situations and general conditions.

As socialist feminists we have an analysis of who has power and who does not, the basis for that power and our potential as women to gain power.

The focus on power is an institutional focus, one that examines the structure of existing institutions and determines who, specifically, has power and how that power is used to oppress women. This includes understanding the interrelation between the economic sector and the social institutions which reinforce ruling class control. The family, church, schools and government priorities which oppress us reflect and reinforce this control. These are reflected in and are served by the dominant ideology, a cultural dominance which controls our everyday private lives.

Women are for liberation not just for abstract reasons and a sense of what is "correct" for women, or because they will be the "wave of the future." They are attracted because we present a picture of reality that they also know, as well as hold out a vision that they wish to share. But talking of such a reality is not sufficient. If we are going to be a movement of all women, we must be able to serve our own self-interest. Unable to fully offer alternatives for women ourselves, we must be able to hold out the realistic promise of obtaining some of these alternatives through struggles which can be won.

We emphasize self-interest because we feel that recently the movement has gotten far away from thinking about it or what moves women to act, or what moves us to act. Idealism alone now guides us abstractly. We argue it, we live it, we see it. But we cannot always count on it. We raise the subject of self-interest to insure that we really are speaking to women's needs.

Decisions about what reforms to fight for and how, must be made on the basis of the following three criteria:

1. WILL THE REFORM MATERIALLY IMPROVE WOMEN'S LIVES? Whatever our priorities, we must focus on meeting our immediate needs. While we believe that sexist capitalism cannot implement all of the reforms we are for, it is possible to use its own rules against itself. That is, we can force change through pressure. Thus, our strategy is quite different from that of raising maximalist demands—demanding something that can't be done under capitalism in order to prove that capitalism is bad. Many reforms are really beneficial to us, can be won and build our confidence. Nevertheless, the reform itself is not the only end. We also are oppressed by our lack of power to control that reform.

2. WILL THE STRUGGLE FOR THE REFORM GIVE WOMEN A SENSE OF THEIR OWN POWER? We need to struggle around issues where success is obviously *our* victory rather than a gift from those in power. Our struggle for reforms must build our movement. Our movement's strength can only be sustained through organizations. Through organizations, individual women can collectively have a sense of their power. Otherwise, even when we win, we don't know it or can't claim it. (Who forced troop withdrawals in Indochina—the President or the movement? Who forced abortion law reform in New York—the state legislature or the women's movement?)

3. WILL THE REFORM ALTER EXISTING RELATIONS OF POWER? We want not only concrete improvements but the right to decide on those improvements and priorities. We want power restructured, wealth redistributed, and an end to exploitation.

We want to emphasize the need for a multi-level approach to women's liberation. Having such an approach, we can avoid some of the pitfalls of dogmatic sectarianism about the correctness of a single issue or program. We must be open and encourage alternatives. The need for a coherent strategy which encompasses education, service and action—but mixes them consciously—cannot be emphasized too much. There are some moments when an issue is ripe and other times when it is important, but will not move women, cannot be won and does not speak to women's felt needs.

But we cannot degenerate into a vague pluralism that says any effort is as good as any other effort. We can be anti-sectarian, encourage a variety of approaches and know that we must move to many approaches and reach the many aspects of our lives as women. At the same time, we can follow a coherent strategy to set priorities for immediate work that we think is important. Of course, the test of tolerance and sectarianism is in reality. We must see how we are perceived, received and grow. Reality is a good cure.

We welcome almost any activity that works for women. At this time, however, we wish to emphasize the importance of all three criteria mentioned earlier: improving women's lives, giving women a sense of their power, and altering relations of power. The three criteria should be applied to any proposed activity.

On the abortion issue, for example, the socialist feminist approach is different from seeking only legislative change.

Our approach is broader than a "write your senator" campaign. It means, for example, finding out and publicizing the church groups lobbying against abortion and challenging their tax-exempt status for lobbying. It also means finding out what corporate executives are on those church boards and launching consumer action against them and their businesses for their support of the church's lobby.

A major trend in the current women's movement is to organize counter-institutional projects to directly meet the needs of women. Counter-institutions can do a number of things. They can help to raise the expectations of women who use and staff the institutions as to what is possible. They can provide services which meet the needs of women now. They can demonstrate that the problems addressed are social in nature and in solution. They convey to the broad constituencies we seek to address that we have positive programs to offer for solving the problems we draw attention to, and that we are not simply negative in orientation. In contrast to consciousness-raising, such programs dispel the specter of endless problems without apparent solutions.

For example, a feminist-sponsored health center provides a needed service that materially improves our immediate condition. It demonstrates that women acting together can change some of their circumstances. It can contribute to building an organized base of power among women ready to fight on an ongoing basis for their rights.

However, counter-institutions have some limitations. They may foster false optimism about change by indicating that problems can be solved in the spaces between existing institutions. Such programs could take up all the time of more than all of us involved in the present movement and never meet all the needs. Such activities cannot alter the power relations if they make no demands on those in power.

We argue the importance of combining counter-institutions with direct action organizing to build on the strengths of each. Such organizing focuses demands on social institutions, thus countering the conclusion that society is unchangeable. It also counters an over-optimism about the potential of self-help to change women's lives by pressing the point that significant changes can be made for all women only through far-reaching changes in power relations. The most useful role of the counter-institutional projects is providing a vision for an alternative and at the same time demonstrating the need for demanding change from those in power.

A PROJECT SHOULD BE CHOSEN SO THAT IT:

- moves women into direct action and groups where they can evaluate their efforts (e.g. ongoing organizations)
- can identify specifically what institutions and who within those institutions exercises control over the issue and has the power to make reforms in response to pressure
- identifies what a victory would be

THE PROJECT SHOULD:

- be broken into parts and fought as reforms that can conceivably be won
- provide step-by-step activity for involvement

Here is an example of how some of us developed one project—fighting for child care with the Action Committee for Decent Childcare.

We had decided that a struggle for free, 24-hour, client-controlled childcare would meet our ideological criteria. However, this position, as an initial statement of our goals, had an immediate weakness. Raising this demand before we had an organization alienated us from even the women who later became our strongest allies. Our vision seemed so wild-eyed, so far from the existing situation, that it appeared completely unrealistic. Once we won some specific demands, raising these same ideals became more rational and acceptable because the possibility was real—women began to gain a sense of their own power.

It should be pointed out that we had decided to form a mass organization. We were attempting to reach a different group of women from those already in the Chicago Women's Liberation Union. We felt that women who worked with the Action Committee for Decent Childcare would, at some point, become interested in joining CWLU. Such women would probably never join a women's liberation organization without some intermediate alternative. But whether or not they joined CWLU, the movement's ideas and strength would grow with this mass form.

A second problem we faced was [that] the very women we hoped to involve (those with young children) were among the least likely to ever be active in any kind of social movement. They simply don't have the time (because they don't have childcare), are less mobile, and don't think of themselves as active community members.

We spent three months gathering information about every aspect of the issue of childcare and considering all of the alternatives for vying for power. After the initial period, research was used to serve actions. We immediately eliminated the federal level since it is too remote to attack without a national organization to force some change. However, in instances where local offices really have power they might be appropriate targets. State and local agencies (and perhaps a few federal branches with responsibility for implementing guidelines or overseeing state and local programs) appeared to be easier and more successful targets.

With the state level dominated by Republicans and the local level by Democrats (as is often the case) we also considered ways to play one off against the other.

We considered institutional targets such as: colleges—students and staff; churches—parishioners and local communities; industry—employees. Each had some limitations as an initial project. For colleges, this seemed to be a more localized struggle where we would need to engage in campus organizing from the beginning and where we did not have an initial base. For churches there seemed to be some interest but most could not move ahead because of licensing laws in the city. For industry, we focused on developing contacts within unionized plants, for the union is the agent of the employees and had no reason to trust us before we had developed a real organization. We also considered welfare but here, too, we did not have the initial base for our first project.

After examining each of the above areas with the continual question of what we could do to meet women's real needs, give women a sense of their power and alter power relations, we decided on an initial strategy. Given the funding situation, we focused on licensing, an equally great problem, but one that was more manageable. Existing licensing laws prevented centers from opening rather than encouraging new centers.

Women became involved because of their need for childcare. Day care operators joined because we could provide services, communication and expose their problems with the city government in order to win real changes. This meant they took risks of retaliation by the city (any center can be closed down by using the arbitrary licensing laws against them) until enough operators were involved and singling out any one individual became difficult. Those who were vulnerable had parents organized for protection (with community hearings, tours for the press of beautiful centers about to be closed down for lack of political pull).

Although initially we believed our constituency would be all white (this was our base in the beginning), we very successfully developed a black and white organization on the basis of self-interest. In a black area, women demanded the creation of childcare centers, because there were none.

In an adjoining white area, women demanded that the few existing centers not be closed down. Once united, other common issues were raised.

We discovered that a few initial victories are extremely important for self-confidence. A reputation that you can win brings others into the organization. In one year, the Action Committee for Decent Childcare:

1. forced the city to undertake a complete review of all licensing procedures.
2. forced the Department of Human Resources to end closed-door meetings on childcare.
3. sponsored the first public meeting with the Department of Human Resources in August 1971 on day care licensing problems.
4. forced the city to set up a committee under Murrell Syler, Director of Childcare Services in the Mayor's Office, to review licensing (ACDC had half of the members on that committee).
5. wrote an analysis of the current codes, with recommendations for change that were used as the basis for the new licensing codes.
6. sponsored a series of community meetings in Hyde Park, the Southwest side, and the North side areas to which state representatives, senators, and aldermen were invited to present their positions on day care and to pledge support for specific proposals.
7. started moving toward community control of childcare.
8. made existing childcare groups more active in pressing for changes.

COUNTER-CULTURE

The women's movement has brought forth a women's culture with the development of women's poetry, music, art, history, women's centers in the cultural realm, and more practically oriented skills such as auto repair and karate. This culture has provided a place for our creativity to be expressed and enabled us to have more independence and self-confidence in areas where we have been denied knowledge and opportunity for expression in the past.

In addition, it has helped change many women's lives.

By providing an example of our vision, women's culture has helped develop a consciousness of how things could and should be better (which helps us understand how we are oppressed now).

At the same time, feelings of frustration and isolation among other things have led many women to seek only cultural alternatives—personal lifestyles of liberation. Many women have chosen to commit themselves entirely to development of a counter culture, dissociating themselves from any action or organizations and frequently moving from the city to the country. For its personal usefulness, we do not argue against it for those who can. But because of its limitation, we challenge this as a political program.

As socialist feminists, we are helping build an extended women's culture but also believe that it should be available for all women. This will fully be possible only if we challenge institutions which have power over us so that we might make it available to all. Our culture should be built into the kind of society for which we are fighting. Currently, our culture is only available to a small minority of women. Women must join together to struggle for power in order to bring about our vision for all women.

The Fourth World Manifesto was an early expression of what later came to be called cultural feminism. In the logic of this manifesto, women constituted a Fourth World, just as the capitalist countries had been called the First World, the Communist bloc the Second World, and the underdeveloped countries the Third World. The manifesto was written by a Detroit women's liberation group during the Vietnam War, to protest a meeting between North American women and the communist North Vietnam official women's organization that excluded the autonomous women's movement. The author, speaking for her group, took this opportunity to conceptualize women's oppression as a form of imperialism, subjugating the female body. Building on a notion of male and female cultures, as opposites, her theory assumes that maleness is an essential and fixed quality in men, across all cultures, in all times. In this theory, male culture is responsible for the world's evils, while female culture has developed out of subordination and resistance. In contrast to the conventional view of the female in the negative—as a lack rather than a presence—this manifesto affirms femaleness and women's culture as a positive and powerful international force.

Fourth World Manifesto
BARBARA BURRIS AND OTHERS

1971

At one time in the process of the cultures women did almost everything and men did nothing but hunt and make weapons and war. As men had free time due to women's performing all the drudge work for them (as slave labor really) they began to develop skills in certain things. As a skill developed women were no longer allowed to perform the task and it was passed on from father to son. As specialization increased women had more of the skills and trades taken away from them and were left only with the drudge chores of cleaning, washing, cooking, "raising" children, etc.

The female soul, suppressed and most often stereotyped in male art, is defined by negative comparisons to the male. The eternal feminine is seen as a passive, earth to be molded and formed, mysterious, unthinking, emotional, subjective, intuitive, practical, unimaginative, unspiritual, worldly, evil, lustful, super sexual, virginal, forever waiting, pain-enduring, self-sacrificing, calculating, narcissistic, contradictory, helpless, quivering mass of flesh.

The fact that women live under the power of belief in these characterizations causes a certain outlook which molds the female culture. Woman's position in society, her economic and psychological dependence, reinforce the female stereotypes. Because of the belief in these attributes and woman's position in society, not because of our inherent "female nature," women's concepts of the world are much different from men's.

Almost everything that has been defined as a male view of the world has its opposite in a female view. Because of the child-raising role and the emphasis on personal relationships women have a more personal, subjective view of things. Because of our subjection, women have a more fatalistic, passive view of the world. We are more in touch with our emotions and often find it necessary to use emotions in manipulating men. Through the imposition of a servant status on women the female culture has elaborated a whole servile ethic of "self-sacrifice." Self-sacrifice—as the major ethic of the female culture—has been one of the most effective psychological blocks to women's open rebellion and demand for self-determination. It has also been a major tool of male manipulation of females.

The institutions of a people are an essential part of their culture. The major institutions of every culture are the same—the family, religion, government, army and economy. Men and women have a completely different relationship to the institutions of "their" culture. In fact there are two cultures being hidden by the appearance of one culture under one set of institutions.

Women are excluded, except sometimes in token numbers and in the lowest working ranks, from participation in government, the army and religion. There are basically two economic institutions of a society—the substructure or family and the superstructure or outside world of work. Women are limited to an economic dependence in "their" caste work in the family. In work outside the family, women are caste laborers in the lowest paid drudge work. Women are kept from management or decision making in work outside the home.

Though it appears that both men and women live together within the institutions of a society, men really define and control the institutions while women live under their rule. The gov't, army, religion, economy and family are institutions of the male culture's colonial rule of the female.

A FEMALE CULTURE EXISTS. IT IS A CULTURE THAT IS SUBORDINATED AND UNDER MALE CULTURE'S COLONIAL, IMPERIALIST RULE ALL OVER THE WORLD. UNDERNEATH THE SURFACE OF EVERY NATIONAL, ETHNIC, OR RACIAL CULTURE IS THE SPLIT BETWEEN THE TWO PRIMARY CULTURES OF THE WORLD—THE FEMALE CULTURE AND THE MALE CULTURE.

National cultures vary greatly according to the degree of the suppression of the female culture. The veil and seclusion of women and their almost total segregation in Arab culture makes for differences between them and, for example, Sweden. A Swedish woman may not be able to tolerate the suppressed life of Arab women but she also, if she is sensitive, may not be able to tolerate her suppression as a female in Sweden. Crossing national boundaries often awakens a woman's understanding of her position in society. We cannot, like James Baldwin, even temporarily escape to Paris or another country from our caste role. It is everywhere—there is no place to escape.

The repression of female culture is only a question of degree all over the world—the underlying reality is basically the same—the denial of self-determination for women. Women traveling to a foreign country can readily communicate and understand other women in that country because female work and roles (culture) are basically the same all over the world. But it too often happens that women falsely identify with "their" country's dominant male culture and so cannot communicate with their sisters in subjection in other lands or in other races. This female identification with male cultural supremacy must be overcome if the Women's Movement is to be a truly liberating force.

Only the suppressed female culture in all races, in all lands, can be proud of the female principle. For females need not prove their "manhood" as they can never be males or a part of the dominant male world culture. Therefore women will be forced—by the very fact of being female—to defend and raise the banner of the female principle.

All of the female culture traits are defined as negatives by the dominant world male culture. We do not believe them to be so (except all those that keep us subservient such as passivity, self-sacrifice etc.).

We are proud of the female culture of emotion, intuition, love, personal relationships etc., as the most essential human characteristics. It is our male colonizers—it is the male culture—who have defined essential humanity out of their identity and who are "culturally deprived."

We are also proud as females of our heritage of known and unknown resisters to male colonial domination and values.

We are proud of the female principle and will not deny it to gain our freedom.

It is only by asserting the long suppressed and ridiculed female principle that a truly human society will come about. For the split between the male and the female will only be bridged and a fully human identity developed—encompassing all human characteristics into each person which were previously split up into male and female—when the female principle and culture is no longer suppressed and male domination is ended forever.

We identify with all women of all races, classes and countries all over the world. The female culture is the Fourth World.

Feminism has long been engaged in a struggle with male-dominated religion, but frequently the struggle took place within a religious framework. The foremother of today's religious feminists was Elizabeth Cady Stanton, whose controversial *Woman's Bible* (published in the late 1890s) offered a learned critique of what she considered patriarchy's distortion of true Christian teachings. In 1968, Catholic theologian Mary Daly renewed the critique with her *The Church and the Second Sex,* and a rich movement soon followed, in Catholicism, Protestantism, and Judaism. Some religion-based organizations such as the YWCA nurtured incipient feminism in the 1960s, and soon religious feminism gave rise to both feminist theology and demands for changes in hierarchies and practices. Womanist theology calls for an androgynous view of God and Jesus, gender-neutral language in liturgy, and ceremonies that address women's unique experiences, such as childbirth. Religious feminists have researched and rewritten church histories to document the earlier prominence of women in religious institutions and texts. They have agitated for the inclusion of women as ministers, priests, and rabbis, and in leadership positions.

As a result, religion became an arena of considerable feminist success. More women are in the pulpit than ever before: women are nearly 15 percent of Episcopalian clergy and 45 percent of newly ordained Reform rabbis. Some of the largest divinity schools now enroll more than 22 percent women, curricula in these schools have been reshaped to include women, and many religious services now use androgynous language. The following selection is excerpted from a sermon given in 1970 at a University of Chicago chapel.

You Are Not My God, Jehovah!
REV. PEGGY WAY

1970

YOU ARE NOT MY GOD, JEHOVAH!

I will not *bow down* before a god who has men pray: I thank the Lord that Thou has not created me a woman . . . I will not *worship* a god who only trusts his priesthood and his power and his prophecy to men . . . I will not *serve* a god for whom woman *was* unclean for twice as long when she bore a girl child . . . or a god for whom a woman's mission is to listen and a man's mission to speak.

YOU ARE NOT MY GOD, JEHOVAH! Let us look into these things . . .

The human spirit is to be a soaring one . . . which stands on the abyss but yet affirms . . . which is so deeply rooted it is free . . . which chooses to what or Whom its bondage is to be . . .

WHAT AM I TO DO WITH A GOD WHO ONLY KNOWS OF WOMEN AS HARLOTS OR VIRGINS? AS TEMPTORS OR CLOISTERED? AS PLAYGIRLS OR NON-PERSONS TO BE PLACED UPON RELIGIOUS PEDESTALS?

I do not know which is the greater insult to my Creation: to be forever a Daughter of Eve whom men fear through their sin-obsession; or to be forever pedestaled, protected from the storms and stresses and creativities and responsibilities of human development which produces persons and adults . . . WHAT DO I DO WITH A GOD WHO DOESN'T SEEM TO UNDERSTAND OR VALUE MY BEING OR BECOMING, MY CREATION AND MY CREATIVITY?

you are not my god, jehovah

JEHOVAH YOU ARE SO ONTOLOGICALLY MASCULINE with all of the worst cultural features of what it is to be man, prideful and vengeful, image-protecting, and loving war, jealous and insecure, omnipotent, and in so many hidden ways afraid of women. YOU WILL NOT EVEN LET ME SERVE YOU AT YOUR ALTARS . . . AND THERE MUST BE MALE MEDIARIES TO A MALE GOD.

I will speak with my brothers . . . and I will call you brother even though you will not call me sister for we must do the tasks together rather than to argue about preordained sex roles. Do you not feel your bondage too? To bear it all? To have to be that which may not be your nature either? How is a creative world to be born out of fixed natures? The tasks can be neither defined nor implemented because the partnership cannot yet even be conceptualized! . . .

For it is a time for person-recognition and for touching *through* the roles that bind us to the wrong gods . . . a time of definition which we *all* must do, and of repossessing, building and creating that which may be old *and* new . . . a time for standing there on the abyss together and affirming and acting on what we must be and do. . . .

I WILL AFFIRM MY SISTERS and they will affirm me . . . and WE will become a WE learning to trust ourselves and one another . . . and we will BE our emerging natures which are human, and can soar, choosing our direction, our responsibility and our bondage. . . .

And we will affirm our uniquenesses among ourselves and will give support to one another . . .

to the woman who is not married by 22 and experiences what it means to be a cultural disaster . . .

to the woman who is widowed and her sources of enrichment all dry up for she may not be a self in her own right . . .

to the woman young or old who is a freak because she seeks out learning, lets her spirit soar, does battle with the structures which impede her, and cries alone at being called that dreadful epithet; she's masculine . . .

to the political radical who has chosen a course of pursuing change and to the mother in the home who has chosen to remain there . . .

to the woman who retreats and lives out her dry days uncertain even of why she fears life so. . . .

Let me create you with the men, Almighty God! Let my experiences be as real as theirs, my formulations as acceptable, my accountabilities to you just as deep.

I will cry unto my God: let us free one another.

My God; surely you do not try to hide your presence so that it cannot be discerned . . . or can only be discerned by an elite . . . or can only be discerned correctly by a masculine interpreter. . . .

I will cry unto my God: let us free one another.

My God; surely you do not limit an accountability for your creation to the men. I WANT TO BE JUDGED TOO!

FOR I AM SURE THAT NEITHER DEATH, NOR LIFE, NOR ANGELS, NOR PRINCIPALITIES, NOR THINGS PRESENT, NOR THINGS TO COME, NOR POWERS, NOR HEIGHT, NOR DEPTH . . . nor abyss of the present, nor masculine structures and definitions of me, nor limits of the church itself which is absurdly called she, NOR ANYTHING ELSE IN ALL CREATION, WILL BE ABLE TO SEPARATE ME FROM THE LOVE OF GOD IN CHRIST JESUS OUR LORD.

- WHOM I would *serve* as a full human being
- *in whose name* I would speak prophetic words
- *in whose ongoing Creation* I would govern with the kings
- *in whose Presence* I would be a priest

in whom,
there is neither Jew nor Greek,
slave nor free,
male nor female

THE AFFIRMATION OF THE MORNING:

YOU ARE NOT MY GOD, JEHOVAH.

I WILL SPEAK WITH MY BROTHERS.

I WILL AFFIRM MY SISTERS.

I WILL CRY UNTO MY GOD: LET US FREE ONE ANOTHER.

AMEN.

Women's spirituality, a large and lively legacy of women's liberation, combines the metaphysical interests of feminist theology with the biological essentialism sometimes found in cultural feminism. Today there is a great variety of woman-centered spiritual practices, and this selection illustrates just one, in a description that shows the process by which a rural women's group developed a set of healing rituals. Their rituals focused on body and spirit as well as mind, and they constitute a form of self-help rather than outreach or a movement for social change. Today, practitioners such as these who focus so heavily on therapy do not usually consider themselves part of a women's movement nor do they retain a connection to a feminist political perspective; but in 1975 when this selection was published, this spirituality group identified with women's liberation. The spirituality movement particularly thrived among those hippies, New Leftists, and feminists who sought a healthier, calmer lifestyle by moving to the country, notably in Vermont, the southeastern states, California, and Oregon. Their practices form a direct bridge to today's "New Age" tastes.

Reaching Beyond Intellect
HALLIE IGLEHART AND JEANNE SCOTT-SENIOR

1975

Many of us as women have felt the need and desire to explore and express ourselves, our psyches, and our intuitive selves, to reach beyond the intellect. As in so many other areas of our lives, however, the only avenues open to us in the past have been those created, defined and ruled by man. We may recognize the value of some of the teachings of patriarchal spirituality. However, if we try to live our lives by them, we often end up at the same wall, over and over: the wall of Something Is Missing. Something is not being expressed—some deep, inner part of ourselves. We cannot force ourselves into a male-defined structure of being or thinking, nor do we want to. As long as women and women's expressions are repressed, both women and men will suffer from the imbalance.

Two of us, Jeanne and Hallie, felt the need to get together with other women, to see how we, individually and collectively, express and recognize ourselves. We thought of experiments and exercises that would allow our own creative expression to emerge, and cut through the layers of patriarchal spiritualism which we had internalized. We would like to share some of what we experienced in our group, which we called "Feminist Spirituality/Spiritual Feminism."

We ended our first meeting with a fantasy inspired by an exercise one of us had read. Here is our version, which of course can be expanded in many ways. If you can, have someone read this to you, and close your eyes. Take as much time as you like with each step.

Think of a world in which all the leaders, decision makers and creators are women.

Imagine that all the sacred books and scriptures you have ever read talk about the Goddess, and that She is always capitalized.

Remember that women have always been the spiritual teachers, models and guides.

Think about the fact that women have been the source of all wisdom and strength throughout the ages.

Recall that all the churches, temples, shrines and sacred places you have ever been to are for the worship of the Goddess.

Remember that all the sacred pictures and images you have ever seen are female, and that all the stories are of women's teachings.

Recall every Christmas as the celebration of the Winter Solstice and the birth of the Daughter. Think of the trinity of the Mother, Daughter, and Holy Spirit.

Recall the age-old story of man as the cause of the downfall of woman, and how he led her away from her essential nature.

Remember the time you have thrown the *I Ching* and found the line, "It furthers one to see the Great Woman."

Recall that almost all books, paintings, sculptures and music were and are created by women.

Think of a world where all people, women and men, walk freely and are encouraged to express their complete androgynous selves.

This fantasy left us floating on the potential of our own power, awed perhaps at how much we could yet uncover.

By reclaiming our bodies, through exploring them and strengthening them, we are able to recognize them as our own. We rediscover the energy that flows in our bodies, and the rich world of images and symbols that arise from within.

We found that Feminist Spirituality is infinite—it is not only religion; it is not only intellectualizations. It is in our bodies; it is also in our senses. It is in our voices, and in our fingers. It is the values we have re-discovered beneath the brambles and ivy that have obscured them for centuries. We've hacked at the overgrowth with pain and fear, and often discouragement, to find our Mother earth and all the soil and seeds of our Selves.

Another offshoot of radical feminism was lesbian feminism, especially in a political form that identifies lesbianism more with the status of women than with the status of gay men. This influential statement was the initial position paper of a group first known as the Lavender Menace, a name derived from an anti-gay remark attributed to Betty Friedan, chair of the National Organization for Women. Her anxiety that a lesbian presence would enable opponents to demonize the women's movement exemplified differences between the women's rights and women's liberation movements. The NOW leadership tried to disassociate their movement from lesbians, but just a year later, in 1971, NOW reversed itself and affirmed the right to sexual choice.

The Lavender Menace came out publicly in 1970 at the Second Conference to Unite Women: the lights were suddenly dimmed and twenty women wearing violet T-shirts seized the microphone to discuss discrimination against lesbians; they called for supportive audience members to step forward and about thirty did so. Similar events occurred on the West Coast, and these events marked the emergence of the previously closeted lesbianism within feminism.

The Radicalesbians' statement theorizes lesbianism as a political choice and equates it with feminist anger. (In some ways, it represents a logical response to antifeminists who baited feminists by calling them "unnatural women" or lesbians.) Note the assumption in this article that one's sexuality is completely changeable at will, with no biological component, a position that anticipated the contemporary academic postmodern emphasis on fluidity of identity. (What makes people heterosexual or homosexual is still far from resolved.) This perspective was consistent with the mood of high optimism about people's ability to make immediate sharp breaks with the past, a tendency to overestimate the possibilities of personal and political transformation through sheer will. Omitting the sexual aspect of lesbianism served not only to underscore a political definition of lesbianism but also to avoid the connotations of perversion that were associated with homosexuality at this time. Political lesbianism was a controversial proposition, because there were many lesbians who were not feminists and many feminists who were not lesbians; moreover, many feminists disliked the implication in this article that heterosexuals were somehow less committed to feminism than lesbians were.

The Woman-Identified Woman
RADICALESBIANS

1970

What is a lesbian? A lesbian is the rage of all women condensed to the point of explosion. She is the woman who, often beginning at an extremely early age, acts in accordance with her inner compulsion to be a more complete and freer human being than her society—perhaps then, but certainly later—cares to allow her. She may not be fully conscious of the political implications of what for her began as personal necessity, but on some level she has not been able to accept the limitations and oppression laid on her by the most basic role of her society—the female role. The turmoil she experiences tends to induce guilt proportional to the degree to which she feels she is not meeting social expectations, and eventually drives her to question and analyse what the rest of her society more or less accepts. She is forced to evolve her own life pattern, often living much of her life alone, learning usually much earlier than her "straight" (heterosexual) sisters about the essential aloneness of life (which the myth of marriage obscures). For she is caught somewhere between accepting society's view of her—in which case she cannot accept herself, and coming to understand what this sexist society has done to her and why it is functional and necessary for it to do so. Those of us who work that through find ourselves on the other side of a tortuous journey through a night that may have been decades long. The perspective gained from that journey, the liberation of self, the inner peace, the real love of self and of all women, is something to be shared with all women—because we are all women.

It should first be understood that lesbianism, like male homosexuality, is a category of behaviour possible only in a sexist society characterized by rigid sex roles and dominated by male supremacy. Those sex roles dehumanize women by defining us as a supportive/serving caste *in relation to* the master caste of men, and emotionally cripple men by demanding that they be alienated from their own bodies and emotions in order to perform their economic/political/military functions effectively. Homosexuality is a by-product of a particular way of setting up roles (or approved patterns of behaviour) on the basis of sex; as such it is an inauthentic (not consonant with "reality") category. In a society in which men do not oppress women, and sexual expression is allowed to follow feelings, the categories of homosexuality and heterosexuality would disappear.

But lesbianism is also different from male homosexuality, and serves a different function in the society. "Dyke" is a different kind of put-down from "faggot," although both imply you are not playing your socially assigned sex role—are not therefore a "real woman" or a "real man." The grudging admiration felt for the tomboy, and the queasiness felt around a sissy boy point to the same thing: the contempt in which women—or those who play a female role—are held. And the investment in keeping women in that contemptuous role is very great. Lesbian is the word, the label, the condition that holds women in line. When a woman hears this word tossed her way, she knows she is stepping out of line.

Lesbian is a label invented by the Man to throw at any woman who dares to be his equal, who dares to challenge his prerogatives, who dares to assert the primacy of her own needs. To have the label applied to people active in women's liberation is just the most recent instance of a long history; older women will recall that not so long ago, any woman who was successful, independent, not orienting her whole life about a man, would hear this word. For in this sexist society, for a woman to be independent means she *can't be* a woman—she must be a dyke. It says as clearly as can be said: woman and person are contradictory terms. And yet, in popular thinking, there is really only one essential difference between a lesbian and other women: that of

sexual orientation—which is to say, when you strip off all the packaging, you must finally realize that the essence of being a "woman" is to get fucked by men.

"Lesbian" is one of the sexual categories by which men have divided up humanity. For women, especially those in the movement, to perceive their lesbian sisters through this male grid of role definitions is to accept this male cultural conditioning and to oppress their sisters much as they themselves have been oppressed by men. Are we going to continue the male classification system of defining all females in sexual relation to some other category of people? Affixing the label lesbian not only to a woman who aspires to be a person, but also to any situation of real love, real solidarity, real primacy among women is a primary form of divisiveness among women: it is the condition which keeps women within the confines of the feminine role, and it is the debunking/scare term that keeps women from forming any primary attachments, groups, or associations among ourselves.

Women in the movement have in most cases gone to great lengths to avoid discussion and confrontation with the issue of lesbianism. It puts people up-tight. They are hostile, evasive, or try to incorporate it into some "broader issue." They would rather not talk about it. If they have to, they try to dismiss it as a "lavender herring." But it is no side issue. It is absolutely essential to the success and fulfillment of the women's liberation movement that this issue be dealt with. As long as the label "dyke" can be used to frighten women into a less militant stand, keep her separate from her sisters, keep her from giving primacy to anything other than men and family—then to that extent she is controlled by the male culture. Until women see in each other the possibility of a primal commitment which includes sexual love, they will be denying themselves the love and value they readily accord to men, thus affirming their second-class status. As long as male acceptability is primary—both to individual women and to the movement as a whole—the term lesbian will be used effectively against women. Insofar as women want only more privileges within the system, they do not want to antagonize male power. They instead seek acceptability for women's liberation, and the most crucial aspect of the acceptability is to deny lesbianism—i.e., deny any fundamental challenge to the basis of the female.

It should also be said that some younger, more radical women have honestly begun to discuss lesbianism, but so far it has been primarily as a sexual "alternative" to men. This, however, is still giving primacy to men, both because the idea of relating more completely to women occurs as a negative reaction to men, and because the lesbian relationship is being characterized simply by sex which is divisive and sexist. It must be understood that what is crucial is that women begin disengaging from male-defined response patterns in the privacy of our own psyches; we must cut those cords to the core. For irrespective of where our love and sexual energies flow, if we are male-identified in our heads, we cannot realize our autonomy as human beings.

As the source of self-hate and the lack of real self are rooted in our male-given identity, we must create a new sense of self. As long as we cling to the idea of "being a woman," we will sense some conflict with that incipient self, that sense of I, that sense of a whole person. It is very difficult to realize and accept that being "feminine" and being a whole person are irreconcilable. Only women can give to each other a new sense of self. That identity we have to develop with reference to ourselves, and not in relation to men. As long as women's liberation tries to free women

without facing the basic heterosexual structure that binds us in one-to-one relationship with our oppressors, tremendous energies will continue to flow into trying to straighten up each particular relationship with a man, how to get better sex, how to turn his head around—into trying to make the "new man" out of him, in the delusion that this will allow us to be the "new woman." This obviously splits out energies and commitments, leaving us unable to be committed to the construction of the new patterns which will liberate us.

It is the primacy of women relating to women, of women creating a new consciousness of and with each other which is at the heart of women's liberation, and the basis for the cultural revolution. Together we must find, reinforce and validate our authentic selves. As we do this, we confirm in each other that struggling incipient sense of pride and strength, the divisive barriers begin to melt, we feel this growing solidarity with our sisters. We see ourselves as prime, find our centers inside of ourselves. We find receding the sense of alienation, of being cut off, of being behind a locked window, of being unable to get out what we know is inside. We feel a real-ness, feel at last we are coinciding with ourselves. With that real self, with that consciousness, we begin a revolution to end the imposition of all coercive identifications, and to achieve maximum autonomy in human expression.

Very soon after "The Woman-Identified Woman" was published, other lesbian feminists began to argue with it. The anonymous authors of this selection resented the way that political lesbians could try out lesbian sex without sacrificing heterosexual privileges, such as being coupled with straight men. They also affirmed female sexuality, asserting that to be a lesbian is fundamentally sexual, not merely political, and that to deny this is to repress a basic component of liberation. They implied that sexual orientation may not be a matter of choice at all, a perspective that has become much more widespread recently.

Politicalesbians and the Women's Liberation Movement
ANONYMOUS REALESBIANS

Among politicalesbians are found women who consider homosexual relations "right on" and politically correct but who themselves abstain. Somewhat guilt-ridden, they offer

such explanations as these: 1) "I can't because that would mean I was 'self-identified,' that, in fact, I understand what my own nature could be so with that I could truly relate to another of my kind." 2) "Masturbation is just as good and besides I don't want to get emotionally involved and lose my autonomy." The first statement implies that self-identification and affirmation are solely a head trip, when, in fact, a woman can never comprehend herself in sensual isolation. It is only through sensual communication and association within her sexual peer group that she can hope to do this. The process of physical and psychic self-affirmation requires full relation with those like oneself, namely women. As to the second statement, masturbation is *not* just as good, and fear of emotional involvement, while valid enough in itself, cannot serve as reason for inactivity. It is simply non-struggle. Personal autonomy is not attained through denial of erotic involvement, aloneness, or the sublimated coziness of straight-defined "sisterhood." Women can become autonomous beings only through constant struggle with their equals, and it is a cop-out to refrain from sensual relations and thus not to deal with sexual passivity that is one of the role functions assigned them by the oppressor. The basis of feminine passivity is the suppression of female sexuality, which was so necessary to the creation of the man/woman caste system. As long as women continue to accept (and promote through their personal-political lives) this suppression of their erotic energy, they will not become liberated.

Another variety of politicalesbian is the straight-identified woman who is interested in having a Lesbian Experience. Necessary to this is an Experienced Lesbian, to whom the woman comes on as potential sexual object, laying the male trip on the Lesbian. This is the most oppressive of all women's movement routines to the gay feminist, who is personally diminished (to the state of "manhood") and sexually objectified. In this process, the Lesbian is required to function in a service role, that of the "butch." Sexual initiative on the part of a woman does not result in direct physical gratification, as it does in a man. The equation, therefore, of "butch" and male is false. In this relation the Lesbian is oppressed by the straight-defined woman in the same way that women are oppressed by straight men. Very often after this false Lesbian Experience women return to straight men and to privilege without having developed self-definition or gay pride. In the end, to them, women are an *alternative* to men.

The claim to bisexuality is commonly heard within the movement, and while bisexuality is not physiologically impossible, the term cannot be used to characterize a stable socio-sexual orientation. Because no heterosexual relationship is free of power politics and other masculine mystifications, women who assert that they are bisexual retain their definition by men and the social advantages accruing from this. Bisexuality is a transitional stage, a middle ground, through which women pass from oppressive relationships to those of equality and mutuality. It is a struggle with privilege and fear, and not all women come through it to their sisters on the other side.

But what about Lesbian behavior that is characterized by straight-identified women as sexist? There exists within the women's movement a tendency toward puritanism, which classifies almost all sexual activity as sexism. Obviously, puritanism is itself rooted in sexism, where female sexual and emotional needs are suppressed for the higher goal of child-bearing, family, and service to the man. Lesbians, on the other hand, are non-productively sensual and sexual beings, having largely reclaimed the erotic potential of the female, which she was deprived of in the process of development of the man/woman caste system.

Women's "right of control over their own bodies" cannot mean simply contraception and abortion but, most importantly, erotic liberation.

From lesbian feminism came a small women's liberation tendency that endorsed separatism from men. However, there was little agreement and a great deal of debate about what separatism actually meant: Was it working exclusively with women in political action? in earning a living? Did it mean cutting oneself off from straight women? from sons and fathers and brothers? Charlotte Bunch, a prominent lesbian feminist from southern Christian civil rights activism, promoted separatism in an article that provoked particularly intense discussion. This editorial, written in response to Bunch, attempted to spell out a more ecumenical approach to separatism, one that considered it a strategy for building feminist political strength.

On Separatism
LEE SCHWING

1973

Separatism has been one of the basic strategies of the Lesbian/feminist movement. Women's separation from men is necessary for us to become stronger women, with a self-identity as women; to create an analysis of our oppression and how to get out of this oppression; and not be giving energy to the oppressor. We see separatism as a basic tool with which to fight male supremacy.

Separatism is a necessary strategy if women wish to become a political force with a power base strong enough to challenge male power. Women must stop nurturing individual men and feeding the institution of heterosexuality.

To implement these women-identified politics we have, as Lesbian/feminists, found it necessary to build our own movement and to develop a Lesbian/Feminist ideology. We have separated from the Women's Liberation movement which lacked a comprehensive analysis of sexism. It failed to create that analysis because it could not identify heterosexuality as one of the keys to male supremacy.

This staff continues to recognize and advocate separatism from men at this point. We are forced to advocate separatism from other women in the women's movement until they are able to accept a Lesbian Feminist ideology.

Not only are there divisions between the Women's Liberation Movement and Lesbian Feminists but there are divisions within the latter, with quite different reasons for their existence and with different objectives. These divisions have occurred over class, age, and race. They are societal divisions which exist within many of us. Many of us have tried to deal with those divisions, to change ourselves, but changes take

time and energy. Some working and lower class women saw that the energy and time they were giving to middle class women would be of more value if given to other working class women. At the same time many younger women in the movement have felt a similar type of oppression. Because those women gain strengths from their subgroups it is not only valid but necessary for them to separate.

A cry for unity at all costs dismisses the potential strengths of certain types of separatism and groups with different focuses. At first glance the withdrawal of numbers of women from the often small structures and organizations that we have built up may seem to be overwhelmingly debilitating and disillusioning. It trashes the idea that with just a little work our movement would transcend all differences. What is important is that these women have not "given up" or "left the ranks." They have simply made a decision to make a primary commitment to women like them.

We cannot form coalitions with men until we have a strong revolutionary feminist movement. We should not be warning women against man-hating, nor should we be encouraging it. Instead the question must be, how do we create that movement amongst ourselves? How do we identify the oppressor and his institutions? What is the best way to build a strong women's movement and ideology; and then be a powerful enough movement to deal with men?

Now is not the time to search for coalitions. Now is the time to work out our ideology, our strategy, our goals. When we do this, coalitions will be realistic at points, although always conditional, and not static. Our strategy will change as objective conditions change.

I Am What I Am

LORNA CHEROT

1970

MY STATEMENT: The following is a dramatic sketch on my impression of a 30-minute rap that went down Oct. 24, while some film reels were being changed at the Revolutionary Women's Conference on a farm near Philadelphia.

. . .

On the stage sit 7 women—6 white and 1 black. The women sit in a vast, wide circle (possibly they are alienated from each other, possibly to suggest the presence of a great number of women). We may assume that the women who are visible represent either factions within the movement, or "types" of women.

The 6 white women sit in chairs at 6 equidistant points on the circle. The black woman sits on the floor somewhere outside the circle. When the white women speak they hold a mirror to their faces. When the black woman speaks no one listens—2 white women put their fingers in their ears and smile (these are the radical lesbians); 2 other white women sit wide-eyed and mouths agape (these are "straight" radical women); and the remaining 2 white women alternately shake their heads "no" and nod them "yes" with exaggerated speed (these are the liberal women). No one looks at the black woman when she speaks.

. . .

RADICAL LESBIANS (*Arms on each other's shoulders, chanting and moving in a circle*): Love each other, love ourselves; love each other, love ourselves; love each other, love ourselves.

(*The white women look approvingly; the black woman just looks.*)

RADICAL STRAIGHT WOMAN: I feel oppressed. The chanting has blocked out my thoughts. They make it difficult for me to relate to them as women.

RADICAL LESBIANS (*Continue chanting and do voodoo dance around 2 radical straight women*): That's sexism! That's sexism! That's sexism! That's sexism!

(*Radical straight women shrink and withdraw in their chairs.*)

BLACK WOMAN (*Raises hand*): Let's talk about racism!

(*Radical lesbians freeze their action and do stock response as do the other 4 women.*)

2 LIBERAL WOMEN (*In obvious self-mockery*): My tummy is too round; my ass spreads too much; my tits sag; I don't like my braces; I'm too fat.

(*Liberal women say these lines again. The black woman steps forward, hands to her head—no one looks at her when she speaks.*)

LIBERAL WOMEN: My tummy is too round . . .

BLACK WOMAN: Goddamn baby inside. . . . Can't afford to keep it . . . Can't afford an abortion.

LIBERAL WOMEN: My ass spreads too much . . .

BLACK WOMAN: Mama's clothing allowance didn't allow her to buy me a girdle.

LIBERAL WOMEN: My tits sag . . .

BLACK WOMAN: I hope the milk in my thin breasts can feed my baby—lord knows that the powdered milk the government gives us won't.

LIBERAL WOMEN: I don't like my braces . . .

BLACK WOMAN: My teeth are crooked. Mama said, "I can't afford no ortho— ortho— ortho— dentist. The rent's gone up again."

LIBERAL WOMEN: I'm too fat!

BLACK WOMAN: I'm skinny! I went to bed hungry at nights.

RADICAL STRAIGHT WOMEN: Let's sing a song! Let's sing a song! Let's sing a song! Let's sing a song! Let's sing a song!

RADICAL LESBIANS AND 2 LIBERAL WOMEN: Oh yes! Oh yes! Oh yes! Oh yes! Oh yes!

(*Black woman returns to her spot frustrated.*)

RADICAL STRAIGHT WOMEN: (*Singing to tune of 3 Blind Mice*):

Bourgeoisie, Bourgeoisie

See how they run

See how they run

When the revolution comes

Kill them all with knives and guns

Bourgeoisie.

(*The women now sing in round. The black woman begins the song and she is joined by the radical straight women—they sing with animation and fervour; the radical lesbians sing half-heartedly; the liberal women are silent. Suddenly the liberal women leap to their feet.*)

LIBERAL WOMEN: Stop! This is machoism! (*the singing stops*)

I think the song is silly. We put down ourselves.

WE ARE THE BOURGEOISIE!

RADICAL STRAIGHT WOMAN: I think we have to relate to working class women.

BOTH RADICAL STRAIGHT WOMEN TOGETHER: I think we have to relate to Third World women.

BLACK WOMAN: (*Runs from one group to the other*):

(*To Radical Straight Women*): I'm both but I'm alienated from this rap.

(*To liberal women*): I mean like the bourgeoisie is the *ruling class*. How can you be a revolutionary and want to rule. I won't let you rule me!

(*To radical lesbians*): I'm black and I'm alienated from my macho brothers. I'm a woman and I'm alienated from you, my professed sisters!

RADICAL LESBIANS (*To each other*): Love me! Love me! (*they begin to hug each other*) Love me! Love me!

RADICAL STRAIGHT WOMEN: I think we must declare our solidarity with all women: Vietnamese women, working class women, Puerto Rican women, black women.

LIBERAL WOMEN: I think we should love each other. Why do we put each other down so much?

(*The white women all flock to each other and exchange kisses and hugs and declarations of "I love you." The women are standing center stage huddled in a tight bunch.*

After a while they turn out towards the black woman and say):

ALL WHITE WOMEN: We love you too.

BLACK WOMAN: (*Talks with increasing agitation*): I want to speak to that. It's fine that you love me, but will you fight with me?

LIBERAL WOMEN: Violence is a male ego trip. We needn't brag about how many and who we'll kill.

BLACK WOMAN: I'm not bragging. Violent rhetoric always precedes violent action. The rhetoric is to prepare you for that fact.

RADICAL STRAIGHT WOMEN: Yes, I think we should declare our solidarity with Third World struggles.

BLACK WOMAN: But I can't deal with those chauvinistic, elitist-structured black liberation groups!

RADICAL LESBIANS (*Chanting*): Let's dance! Let's dance! Let's dance!

LIBERAL WOMEN: Well I am what I am and that's all that I am. . . . white. . . . middle-class. . . . and for god's sake let's us women get our heads together. . . . and it's time for us to stop emulating other liberation struggles.

BLACK WOMAN: NO ONE'S GONNA HAND YOU YOUR LIBERATION—YOU GOTTA TAKE IT!

RADICAL LESBIANS: Love each other, love ourselves; love each other, love ourselves.

BLACK WOMAN: WE'VE GOT TO GET READY!

RADICAL STRAIGHT WOMEN: I pledge my solidarity with Third World struggles.

BLACK WOMAN: AT LEAST ARM OURSELVES IN DEFENSE!

LIBERAL WOMEN (*To each other and together*): I want to relate to you. You're white, I'm white; I'm middle-class, you're middle-class; let's not put each other down.

BLACK WOMAN: THEN HOW CAN YOU LOVE ME?

RADICAL LESBIANS: Let's dance! Love each other, love ourselves.

BLACK WOMAN: Let's rap.

RADICAL STRAIGHT WOMEN AND LIBERAL WOMEN: Let's get together. Let's relate.

(*Chanting among all white women grows louder and stronger, then more rhythmic as black woman speaks*)

BLACK WOMAN: (*In extreme agitation and franticness*) (*To radical lesbians*): Some sisters and me got ideas to rip off the uptown Harlem Welfare Center. Will you join us?

RADICAL LESBIANS (*Chanting*): Come out! Come out! Come out! Come out!

BLACK WOMAN (*To radical straight women*): Some black sisters are gonna liberate the furniture at the uptown Harlem Welfare Center and liberate the Goodwill Industries and distribute the clothing to the people of East Harlem. Will you help us?

RADICAL STRAIGHT WOMEN: Solidarity forever, sister. But we're not ready for that step yet.

BLACK WOMAN (*To liberal women*): Some sisters and me are thinking of ripping off. . . .

LIBERAL WOMEN: Violence only begets violence. . . . It doesn't help anything. So let's just love each other.

BLACK WOMAN (*To liberal women*): Don't tell me you love me if you won't fight with me.

(*To radical straight women*): And when are you going to get ready?

(*To radical lesbians*): I'll love you when my belly is full, there's clothes on my back and shelter over me.

BLACKOUT

II
Bodies

Women's liberation had and is still having a substantial impact on women's health and health care in the U.S., because health was one of the most important arenas of feminist activism. By 1973 there were 1,200 women's health groups in the U.S. that provided direct services, promoted health education, and agitated to change the mainstream health system. And it certainly needed to change. Although women are the major "consumers" of health care, making decisions not just for themselves but for their families, and although women constitute 75–85 percent of health care workers, in the 1970s only 10 percent of doctors were women. There was widespread discrimination against and condescension toward women in medical schools, in hospitals, and in doctors' offices. In the 1970 hearings on the safety of contraceptive pills, a physician who opposed package inserts listing warnings about such drugs testified: "A misguided effort to inform such women leads only to anxiety on their part and loss of confidence in the physician. . . . They want him [the doctor] to tell them what to do, not to confuse them by asking them to make decisions beyond their comprehension." In medical research, white men were the universal subjects, and frequently men of color and all women were excluded from drug testing and other treatments. Dr. Bernadine Healy, former surgeon general, cites one example: a major study of health and fitness (with the apt name "MR-FIT") excluded women on the premise that men were "the human norm." Disproportionately less money was spent on studying diseases that affected men of color and women, such as breast cancer and sickle-cell anemia.

These problems are by no means solved, but the women's health movement has produced significant gains. Women once hid diseases like breast cancer and alcoholism; the women's movement challenged the shame attached, and its message was communicated even through such women nonfeminists as former First Lady Betty Ford. The proportion of women among physicians has doubled, though it still remains a puny 25 percent. There have been two female surgeons general and now a permanent director of women's health research at the National Institutes of Health. In 1986 the NIH adopted a policy that women could only be excluded from clinical trials if there was a clear rationale for doing so (although a recent General Accounting Office study found that the NIH only began applying the rule consistently in 1990, showing that a policy adopted is not a policy implemented). Feminist concerns and warnings about the safety risks of birth control pills (see chapter 6) produced the FDA program of patient package inserts, which for the first time required that information about dangers and side-effects associated with medications be given out with prescription medication. Feminist pressure not only won increased funding for breast cancer research, but also changed its treatment, exposing the overuse and misuse of chemotherapy and excessive surgery, and dramatically increasing research funding. From the 1880s to the 1970s, the extremely disfiguring Halsted radical mastectomy was the standard surgical treatment for breast cancer, even though the survival rates did not justify its employment. Starting in 1972 women's movement activism discredited it so thoroughly and quickly that it fell into disuse within five years. Probably most important, women's consciousness-raising changed doctors' attitude and behavior, both directly and through changing their training. Feminists challenged sexist psychiatry and psychology, and feminist psychotherapy has become a large field.

One of the major sources of the women's health movement was anger at physicians. In the course of the twentieth century, doctors had replaced the clergy as the dominant moral authorities, instructing women not only about health matters but also about sexual and reproductive behavior. In exercising this authority, many doctors patronized and infantilized women (and the few female doctors produced by the same training system did not always do better). Feminists began to see that when physicians failed to listen to their patients, dismissed complaints as illegitimate or psychosomatic, neglected to explain diagnoses or treatments, withheld information, and discouraged patients from making their own health and treatment decisions, these were not just individual shortcomings of doctors but a systematic and direct result of their training and the assumptions of the medical system. Doctors were not educated to care for people, but rather to treat separate parts of the body and discrete ailments. They considered it their responsibility to make health care decisions for patients, especially for women. The result was not simply benign neglect but actual mistreatment—for example, when dangerous high-dose oral contraceptives were promoted to women.

The feminist challenge came not only from patients but also from health care workers at every level, including nurses' aides, physicians, and public health experts. Activists focussed particularly on gynecologists and obstetricians who were trained to advise women on sexual activity as well as childbirth, birth control, and abortion. When feminists began writing critiques like the following, they were often labeled as uninformed and hysterical, and indeed they did exaggerate sometimes. But allowance for exaggeration does not mitigate the sexist and racist attitudes communicated by the Ob/Gyn textbook reviewed in this 1975 article. At first these critiques could only be published and distributed through women's movement networks, but today whole magazines, catalogs, and shelves in bookstores are devoted to encouraging people of both sexes to take responsibility for their own health and medical treatment.

What Medical Students Learn
KAY WEISS

1975

One of the cruelest forms of sexism we live with today is the unwillingness of many doctors to diagnose people's diseases with equality. The education of doctors can explain this. [Consider the messages in] the recently revised text *Obstetrics and Gynecology* (1971, 4th edition), which is used this year [1975] in 60 of the nation's medical schools.

SHE'S A CHILD

In *Obstetrics and Gynecology,* women are childlike, helpless creatures with animal-like or "instinctive" natures, who can't get through intercourse, pregnancy, labor or child-raising without "enlightened" physician intervention. The woman in childbirth is just a child herself. Her doctor, even if he is a novice and she is an old pro, is a fount of knowledge while she is "anxious," "fearful," afraid of "getting messy" and may feel "ashamed" and "guilty." The medical student is taught to believe that many symptoms of illness in pregnancy (excessive nausea, headache) are really a result of her "fear of pregnancy" rather than any physical condition he (all medical students and physicians are "he" in *Obstetrics and Gynecology*) need test for. She "may have

fears of death during childbirth" but these fears are always neurotic, never justified. They are most often caused by guilt: she may "fear that the rewards (of pregnancy) will be damaged or denied because of past sins." It is easy to see why maternal mortality is still a problem when women in childbirth are still referred to as sinners in medical texts.

SHE LOVES RAPE

Many gynecology texts reveal a greater concern with the patient's husband than with the patient herself and tend to maintain sex-role stereotypes in the interest of men and from a male perspective. But *Obstetrics and Gynecology* clearly spells out the attitudes that other texts only imply:

The normal sexual act . . . entails a masochistic surrender to the man . . . there is always an element of rape.

The traits that compose the core of the female personality are feminine narcissism, masochism, and passivity.

Every phase of a woman's life is influenced by narcissism. Women then love in a different way from men.

The woman falls in love with the idea of being loved; whereas the man loves an object for the pleasure it will give. She says, "I am valuable, important, etc. because he loves me . . ." This type of narcissism finds expression in . . . her interest in clothes, personal appearance, and beauty. Too much feminine narcissism without masochism produces a self-centered woman.

The idea of suffering is an essential part of her life.

SHE FEELS LIKE AN ANIMAL

Women are described in the text alternately as psychopathic and idiotic: "She is likely to feel that she is animal-like . . . to think of the vagina as a 'dirty cavity.' Black patients will think that the source of sexual desires is in the uterus; white patients think that it is in the ovaries. "Orgasm represents the woman's ability to accent her own feminine role in life." "Many women equate orgasm with loss of bowel control . . ." "Menstruation symbolizes her role in life . . ." "To the immature girl menstrual blood comes from the same area as feces and urine; this causes her to transfer to menstruation the feelings she has toward these excretions." The medical student is persuaded by the authors that women with dysmenorrhea (menstrual dysfunctions including painful uterine contractions) have no organic disease they need test for; these women simply have "personality disorders," "emotional difficulty in the home," or "neurotic predispositions." They need "sex education" and "mental hygiene" (does this mean their minds need cleaning?) if not "intensive psychotherapy." When treating such women "the husband can be helpful by not being too sympathetic and increasing the woman's guilt." A brief concession is made to the possible physical causes for menstrual pain, but the authors then quickly return to the problem of diagnosis:

It is important to ascertain how crippling the symptom and how much emotional gain the patient is deriving from it. For example, does the whole household revolve around whether or not the mother is having menstrual cramps? Is the dysmenorrhea the locus for the expression of depression, anger, or a need to be dependent?

The adult woman who presents this symptom very often is resentful of the feminine role. Each succeeding period reminds her of the unpleasant fact that she is a woman. . . .

SHE NEEDS A PSYCHIATRIST

The clear implication is that if the patient asks too many questions, she is abnormally demanding! "The patient should be questioned about sexual aspects of her life . . . when the patient fails to respond and seems to be unduly emotional about the discussion her transfer to a psychiatrist is indicated." If she is not "relaxed" during a pelvic examination with an "*unlubricated* speculum," she might also be referred to a psychiatrist.

Only two paragraphs in the text are devoted to the hormonal role of female sexual response: one of these enlightens us about female dogs in heat and the other informs us that the sex drive of females can be increased by giving them testosterone (male sex hormone). According to the authors, trichomonas (vaginal parasitic infection) is probably a result of sexual tension. This is no more than an unsophisticated version of the medieval belief that women with the unbearable itch really just need a good screw. "The physician can help the woman discover how she wishes to relate to men in a more meaningful manner," an incredibly pompous statement in juxtaposition with 55 pages of medical ignorance about "female sexuality." Frigidity is defined as "occasional failure to obtain orgasm," placing 99 percent of women in the category of abnormal. If pleasure is only felt from clitoral stimulation, she may be referred to a psychiatrist. The doctor may have trouble curing frigidity because of "too deep a degree of pathology in the woman," never because of her husband's poor technique. Her frigidity may develop because she "resents her husband's preoccupation with his work or his recreational activities." The physician, a "parental figure," should "discover the problem in the patient's personality" and "encourage her to mature sexually."

Twenty-seven gynecology texts written over the past three decades were reviewed by Diana Scully and Pauline Bart in the *American Journal of Sociology* in January 1973.

They confirm the idea that medical science has made little advancement for women. No text Scully and Bart examined incorporated Kinsey's 1953 findings that orgasm without stimulation "is a physical and physiological impossibility for nearly all females" or Master and Johnson's 1966 findings that portions of the vagina have no nerve endings and lack sensation and that although orgasm is felt in the vagina, the feeling derives from stimulation of clitoral nerves.

With doctors like these for friends, who needs enemies?

In changing consciousness about women's health, the single largest influence was *Our Bodies, Ourselves*, a book whose popularity puts it in the same category as the Bible or Dr. Spock's *Baby and Child Care*. In 1969, at a conference of Bread and Roses, a Boston socialist–feminist organization, a group of women came together in a workshop to vent their frustrations with physicians and then decided to continue meeting. A year and a half later they produced the first version of *Our Bodies, Ourselves*: 194 pages, printed on newsprint by a small New Left press, priced at 75 cents. The modesty of their original intentions is apparent in the excerpt below from the first edition's introduction. Through word of mouth and advertisements in women's and New Left publications, it had sold 250,000 copies by 1973. The group then signed with Simon & Schuster, a major publishing house. The authors, a collective of eleven, insisted on provisions rare in commercial publishing: all profits go to the women's health movement, and the publishers are required to make copies available at 40 percent of cover price for nonprofit health groups. By 1995 the book had sold 4.5 million copies, not including sales of three related books, *Changing Bodies, Changing Lives* (for teenagers), *Ourselves and Our Children*, and *Ourselves, Growing Older*. All of the substantial profits from the books go into a foundation that supports feminist grassroots health activism around the world.

What made *Our Bodies, Ourselves* so influential? At first the book was remarkable for its positive and explicit discussion and pictures of sexual and reproductive issues, which were quite shocking at the time. It did not defer to professionals. It assumed that readers want all the information available, that women can become their own experts and make informed judgments, an approach that seems commonplace today. Less commonplace but just as needed today were the book's critiques of the giant for-profit health care industry, the fear of fatness, the influence food and drug manufacturers exercise over the FDA and USDA, the treatment of women workers in the food and health care industries, and the substantial advertising budgets of the big pharmaceutical corporations. *Our Bodies, Ourselves* became the model for a virtual industry of self-help health advice for women, most from for-profit enterprises, rarely maintaining the critical edge of the original.

The Origins of *Our Bodies, Ourselves*
BOSTON WOMEN'S HEALTH BOOK COLLECTIVE

1970

One year ago, a group of us who were then in women's liberation (now most of us consider ourselves members of Bread and Roses) got together to work on a laywoman's course on health, women and our bodies. The impetus for this course grew out of a workshop on "women and their bodies" at a women's conference at Emmanuel College in Boston, May 1969. After that, several of us developed a questionnaire about women's feelings about their bodies and their relationship to doctors. We discovered there were no "good" doctors and we had to learn for ourselves. We talked about our own experiences and we shared our own knowledge. We went to books and to medically trained people for more information. We decided on the topics collectively. (Originally, they included: Patient as Victim; Sexuality; Anatomy; Birth Control; Abortion; Pregnancy; Prepared Childbirth; Postpartum and Childcare; Medical Institutions; Medical Laws; and Organizing for Change.) We picked the one or ones we wanted to do and worked individually and in groups to write the papers. The process that developed in the group became as important as the material we were learning. For the first time, we were doing research and writing papers that were about us and for us. We were excited and our excitement was powerful. We wanted to share both the excitement and the material we were learning with our sisters. We saw ourselves differently and our lives began to change.

As we worked, we met weekly to discuss what we were learning about ourselves, our bodies, health and women. We presented each topic to the group, gave support and helpful criticisms to each other and rewrote the papers. By the fall, we were ready to share our collective knowledge with other sisters. Excited and nervous (we were *just* women; what authority did we have in matters of medicine and health?), we offered a course to sisters in women's liberation. Singularly and in groups, we presented the topics and discussed the material; sometimes in one large group, often in smaller groups. Sisters added their experiences, questions, fears, feelings, excitement. It was dynamic! We all learned together.

So after a year and much enthusiasm and hard individual and collective thinking and working, we're publishing these papers. They are not final. They are not static. They are meant to be used by our sisters to increase consciousness about ourselves as women, to build our movement, to begin to struggle collectively for adequate health care, and in many other ways they can be useful to you. One suggestion to those of you who will use the papers to teach others: the papers in and of themselves are not very important. They should be viewed as a tool which stimulates discussion and action, which allows for new ideas and for change.

It was exciting to learn new facts about our bodies, but it was even more exciting to talk about how we felt about our bodies, how we felt about ourselves, how we could become more autonomous human beings, how we could act together on our collective knowledge to change the health care system for women and for all people.

Feminists steadily pressured health care institutions to serve women better. Women activists conducted studies of community needs, monitored patient care, picketed and demonstrated against unresponsive medical facilities. The following account details such an action, persuading a Baltimore free clinic to offer a special night just for women.

Women's Night at the Free Clinic
KATHY CAMPBELL, TERRY DALSEMER, AND JUDY WALDMAN   1972

The People's Free Medical Clinic in Baltimore had been in operation for about nine months when the push for a Women's Night began in response to these concerns. Prior to this time, our commitment to women was most clearly seen in the Women's Counseling section of the Clinic, which was then open three nights a week. The women's counselors run early pregnancy detection tests, arrange abortion referrals, and rap with women about birth control methods, VD, female sexuality, etc. The women's counselors emphasize preventive medicine (i.e., birth control). For many reasons, including the fact that we were overcrowded, the medical staff of the Clinic was more concerned with infectious diseases. Healthy women coming in for birth control were given low priority and could be seen only after people who had more immediate problems.

Women's problems, medical and otherwise, are complex, and up to then no conventional institutions had dealt with them comprehensively or adequately. In spite of our commitment to meeting women's needs, problems of space, time, and medical priorities made it increasingly apparent that another clinic night devoted only to women was necessary. Women's Night was to become a night of women sharing with women: rapping about themselves—their medical problems, family situations, personal problems. We wanted to change some of the ideas about the staff and its relationship to women coming in. We wanted to place more emphasis on relating to individuals and groups about all our mutual concerns. We hoped to further break down artificial relationships between "staff" and "patients." Certain role divisions were eliminated, allowing a freer interaction between all women who were involved in Women's Night, be they staff or patients. We wanted to continue to provide comprehensive primary medical care, along with a gynecological consult, with increased emphasis on birth control information and all kinds of counseling. We had hoped that most of our professional staff, like the general staff, would be women.

The planning meetings for Women's Night convened once a week for about six weeks. We asked ourselves what we wanted to do and how we wanted to do it. Did we want to follow the Clinic procedures we were used to or did we want to start from scratch? What were the things we wanted changed? Did we want only women doctors? Impossible.

There is an indefinable difference between Women's Night and any other Clinic night. Women sit and talk with each other. There is a calm, unhurried air, even on the most frantic nights when there are two doctors and forty patients. Women bring food or fruit to share. Someone leaves loaves of homemade bread and a sign apologizing for the price, fifty cents a loaf. There is formal counseling, but there is also informal advice, help, and support from staff members and other patients who may be sitting in a group rapping and sharing problems and solutions. The waiting room crowd on Women's Night tends to be, not little islands of one or two people, sitting reading or staring at the wall, but clusters of three to five women, talking, eating, laughing. Women leave to see the doctor, or to assist in a pelvic exam. The groups change and grow. Women talk about children, marriage, divorce, housing hassles, their successes or failures with various birth control methods. What will cure vaginitis and what won't. The state of the women's movement. The date of the next women's dance. There's a feeling of warmth, shelter, of "yes, you've come to the right place; what can we share with you?"

We wanted to stress that women are not simply "pelvics," but people, and should be treated as such. In case one of the clinic doctors should forget this, we as a group are there to confront him and talk it out.

One night we experienced a good example of how little control we have over our bodies and how Women's Night hopes to change this. A woman, complaining of cramps related to her I. U. D. was examined by a male gynecologist, new to our staff. The woman was extremely nervous and uncomfortable during the exam, and needed constant reassurance from the advocate who was there assisting both the patient and the doctor with the exam. Although he found nothing wrong, there was something he wanted another doctor to see, so that he insisted she have another examination. The advocate strongly questioned the necessity for this, and although the woman reluctantly agreed to be reexamined, the issue was brought up again at our evaluation session at the end of the evening. (This session includes everyone—patients and staff.) We then talked with this doctor and others about their using our bodies for teaching (especially without being open about this and asking our permission) and how we wanted to be sure that we control what is being done to us and our bodies. We felt good—we were speaking together as women; we were being heard and making some changes.

We are still struggling with many questions, such as why abortions cost so much, why there is no completely safe method of contraception, why women often have bad experiences with doctors, and how this society's attitude towards sex affects all of us.

One of the most important implications of Women's Night at a medical clinic is that it can be a vehicle for movement into many areas other than medical care. Many women who would not feel comfortable seeking out a women's discussion group or rap session will come to a clinic for their medical needs. Once there, they can talk with staff members and other women around them and are casually invited to a rap session (which involves no commitment) while waiting for the doctor. Through these experiences, we all have the opportunity to hear and discuss many important aspects of our lives and situations as women. It is this sharing process which is so important to the growth of the women's liberation movement.

In addition to pressuring mainstream institutions, feminists also created their own. In two areas in particular—obstetrics/gynecology and psychotherapy—feminists developed alternative treatment methods and clinics.

One gynecological health project was so iconoclastic, and therefore so much talked about, that in the 1970s the very term "self-help" came to refer to its approach. Carol Downer and Lorraine Rothman in Los Angeles realized that "in order to better understand what we are talking about we had to look." They did just that with the help of speculum and mirror, tools that allowed women to see their own vaginas and cervixes. Women thus became subjects as well as objects of health care and research. Downer and Rothman toured the country in 1971, making "self-help" so popular for a time that many women's groups, from informal get-togethers to women's studies classes, featured demonstrations of the technique. The fascination of self-discovery enabled some women to overcome their modesty, although the number who tried it in public may have been small. Feminists lost interest in gynecological self-examination after a few years, but the impetus to become well informed about one's body endures.

Self-help in the generic sense, however, led to a lasting development: the creation of alternative women's clinics all over the country, such as the one whose brochure is included below. Most of them attempted, like the feminist enterprises discussed in chapter 3, to create relatively democratic working structures: minimizing salary differences, sharing skills and learning opportunities, involving community women in governing boards, and offering sliding fee scales. The women's movement's clinics were so successful that the marketing managers for increasingly profit-oriented mainstream medical practices and hospitals had to emulate them in order to compete successfully. By the mid-1980s many HMOs and hospitals opened Women's Health Centers, semi-autonomous clinics within larger medical operations.

Wonder Woman

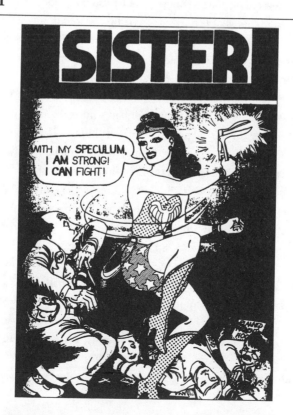

A group of women not long ago banded together to seriously consider some mutual questions concerning the care of their reproductive and sexual organs. It all came about because each of us seemed to be getting the same kind of no help from our physicians. So we decided to just rap, share experiences, and maybe as a group seek out some answers on our own. Our results were so mind blowing that we want to share them with our sisters in hopes of encouraging others to do the same. Some of the problems we first attacked were: how can I recognize vaginal infections early, before they become so advanced that I have to visit a physician and probably wind up on antibiotics$$$. Can I see early infections, especially yeast (Monilia) effectively and inexpensively? How do I recognize yeast? What does syphilis look like, and can I recognize gonorrhea—in spite of what the physicians say? Are there marked changes on the cervix of my uterus during my 28–30 day menstrual cycle? If so, does the cervix also show change due to pregnancy, and if so how soon can I see the change? We realized early in our rap sessions that being able to recognize very early pregnancy would be a great asset if we were to decide to terminate the pregnancy. Each of us at one time or another had been told by a physician that the chemical test for pregnancy wasn't foolproof. We would really have to wait for at least the 4th to 5th week after the missed period to know for sure. Too long, we all decided!

Another point in which we were all up-tight about was the present methods of health care for women. For instance: I've got an itch. So I've gotta call the doctor. When I call, the receptionist asks, "What's wrong?" and proceeds to make an appointment from one to two weeks hence. So I wait. Take sitz baths, douches, and no sex. Sometimes the waiting alone helps, usually not. Often the bladder becomes infected while waiting for the appointment interval to pass. Finally I get to see the physician and his comment on examining me, draped in a sheet so that I couldn't watch even if I wanted to—"Usual female infection, take the antibiotic prescription and come back in two weeks$$$." When I ask him if I can see what the infection looks like, the physician is appalled at the idea. "You shouldn't worry your little head about this kind of thing. After all, isn't that what I'm here for?" So I return in 2 weeks$$$, and maybe it's cleared and maybe it isn't. Another kind of antibiotic is prescribed and another appointment is made$$$. I again ask for specific information about the infection and by now the answer usually comes in Greek (which I am obviously not very fluent in).

With pregnancy it's pretty much the same thing. See him, wait, and come back $$$. I know that the longer I wait the more difficult it will be on my body to terminate the pregnancy. In addition, different states' laws offer time limiting restrictions.

So the women got together. We rapped about our common medical encounters. Then we made a discovery on that very first meeting. In order to better understand what we were talking about we had to look. So we encountered our first, last and only hangup in the entire rap/self-help clinic. And we did it with the help of 5% courage and 95% curiosity. Up on the table each of us went. Some of us were a little shy going up, all of us thoroughly with it by the time we got down. All of us were learning about our sexual organs and realizing that we were not only sharing our answers but were learning things about the cervix that was a gold mine of information. No wonder physicians have been reluctant to share the information$$$. We realized that there was a great deal that we could do for ourselves in personal health care, long before it becomes necessary to see a physician, and all because we learned a very simple self-examination procedure. We were able to purchase plastic speculums (one for each woman). The speculum opens the vaginal cavity to allow examination of the vaginal walls and the cervix. With the use of a lamp and mirror, it became quite simple to examine ourselves for irritations, infections, discharges, changes on the cervix. Since the cervix has essentially no pain nerve endings, we realized that it was quite easy to have an infection developing without giving any signs. Not until a heavy discharge has reached the vulva (outer lips) or burning and itching is taking place, do we realize what's going on. But by then it is too late to do anything but go through the ritual of visiting a physician at his convenience$$$. We also recognized that there are differences in the cervix, depending on the size of the woman, numbers of children, etc. We were able to easily recognize problems early so as to seek medical help quickly, before the problem becomes a major disease. Results of our self-help clinic were so obvious that some of us are now taking our methods and going into neighboring communities to form new self-help clinics. Every where we go we are finding the same responses: "Wow! No wonder the physicians haven't wanted us to know our own bodies."$$$ "Now I understand how the diaphragm works!" "It really isn't mysterious at all!" "It's like looking into your own mouth!"

We feel another important aspect of this clinic is to talk about the political implications of women being able to control their own bodies: giving abortion referrals, becoming fully aware of the great need for abolishing all laws that restrict and control women. We believe that getting to know yourself can save your life. Women are killing themselves with panic abortive methods, because our laws refuse them proper care. In spite of our restrictive laws, getting to know our own bodies and what we can do for them has opened up far better choices of personal care. We are continuing to live under outrageous laws and barbaric medical practices. We believe that in learning to accept the care and knowledge of our own physical selves, we will be well on the road to self determination.

Some of the findings that came of our original self-help clinic and on which we were then able to take positive action were: 1) A woman who is exposed to the risk of pregnancy, by examining herself once a week, and becoming thoroughly familiar with her own cervix, can within one week after missing her period, recognize that she is pregnant. She need not depend on chemical tests. 2) Gonorrhea is still difficult but when uterine discharges occur, we catch them early and can take positive early action. 3) Yeast infections can be recognized easily, and treated inexpensively and in many cases with positive results within 24 hours without a prescription. You need not be a highly skilled clinician to learn to recognize by name the most common vaginal infections.

Our rap sessions have no rules governing participation. We believe that the modesty hangups for each of us fall in their own time. And they do fall as our consciousness is being raised. Age makes little difference once we get our goals in mind. Our group has an R.N.—which was totally unplanned. She has been able to steer us into competent references. We also have a sympathetic physician with whom we confer. But no one lectures.

About 10 people seem to be the ideal number to participate. When our group has grown to as many as 15 we spin off into the neighboring communities.

We feel that by far the most important aspect of our self-help clinic is in its political implications that women already have the right to control their own bodies. There is nothing to fear but ignorance. Get rid of that ignorance and you are doing it!

The West Coast Sisters

The Feminist Women's Health Center Has Developed a NEW Milieu for Gynecological Examinations!

Instead of:

Sitting anxiously in a crowded waiting room for an hour

Being examined alone or with a nurse or paramedic

Being barraged by yes-or-no questions about your medical past

Seeing a hurried, usually male, gynecologist for at the most, 10 minutes

Being met with grunts, insults, or at the most, incomplete information

Being totally dependent upon the doctor's observations

Being told that tests would be run, not really knowing why they are being done

Being left with more questions than before you came

Together:

The six to eight women participating meet with three health workers and a female physician in a relaxed, woman-controlled atmosphere

We discuss and fill-out the medical "her-story" forms and talk about each woman's reason for coming to the clinic

We spend two hours in the participatory clinic as we ALL take part

We begin to share the medical information we all acquire throughout our lives as women

We share self-examination of the breasts and cervix so that we have seen, and know, our conditions for ourselves

We complete the tests, lab work and physical examinations necessary to each woman's health care with the assistance of our doctor

We can each go home with more knowledge about her body and with her own speculum in hand

In criticizing overmedicalization and overmedication, the women's health movement explored unconventional health practices, and a wing of the movement promoted alternative remedies such as homeopathy, herbal and Chinese medicines, vitamins and minerals, meditation, biofeedback, and acupuncture (many of which have now become mainstream). This popularization of alternative health measures created new problems, as the manufacture and marketing of hugely profitable but entirely unregulated products generated new health risks and inflated hopes. And the emphasis on self-help had a tendency to produce self-blaming, delivering the message that your own unhealthy lifestyle was responsible for your ailments.

Some feminist alternatives, such as the menstrual sponge, did not catch on, which is hardly surprising when you consider the inconvenience and messiness they entailed.

Using a Natural Sponge

1976

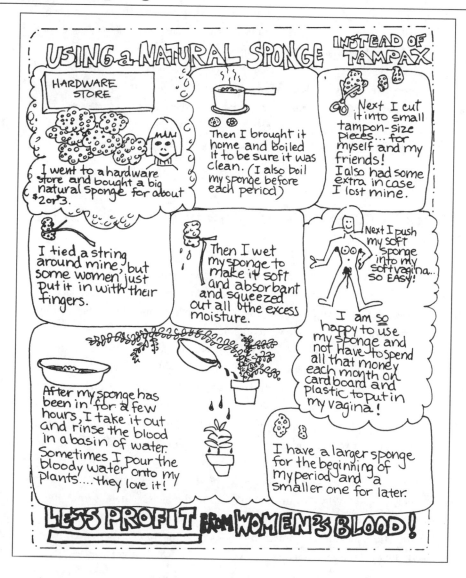

The women's health movement had its greatest impact on the conditions of childbirth and infant feeding. As a result of feminist pressure, today most women are conscious during childbirth, a big change from the mid–20th-century practice. Some women have the option of using alternative birth centers, home births, or independent midwives, although these attract less than 1 percent of birthing women.

In the late 1950s, breast-feeding had become unfashionable and only 20 percent of mothers nursed their infants. Although the organization involved in promoting breast-feeding, the La Leche League, was established in 1958, the women's movement later contributed to the large-scale return to breast-feeding. By 1995 approximately 60 percent of mothers breast-fed, with the most rapid increase occurring in the 1970s. The return to breast-feeding was part of women's challenge to mainstream medicine, which had previously discouraged the practice. Women also defied the norm that breast-feeding should only be done in private, which restricted new mothers' ability to move about in public.

The feminist attraction to breast-feeding had several roots and meanings. It derived partly from the women's health movement's emphasis on self-help as opposed to medical intervention or consumer goods. Feminists liked breast-feeding because it was more "natural," healthier, convenient, and cheaper, and they sensed that breast-feeding challenged exclusively sexual associations with the breast. Breast-feeding also resonated with an aspect of feminism that made motherhood the source of women's identity and special power. Nursing increased women's sense of bonding with infants (excluding men, some complained). Although women's liberation has been labeled anti-motherhood, influential aspects of the movement stressed the special creative power and even superiority of motherhood, in contrast to anything that men could experience. The movement was capacious enough to contain groups emphasizing mother-child bonding and groups struggling for child-care centers, groups emphasizing mothers' need to stay home with their children and groups stressing employment opportunities for women.

Breastfeeding Successfully in Spite of Doctors and Hospitals
SALLY WENDKOS OLDS   1973

A couple of weeks ago a woman pregnant for the first time said to me, "When I told my obstetrician I wanted to breast-feed, he said, 'Wait a minute—don't make up your mind so fast. Let me tell you all the *dis*advantages.'" He then went on to describe in vivid detail everything that could possibly go wrong, instead of emphasizing that with the right kind of support and encouragement, 95% of all women can nurse their babies.

Unfortunately, this woman's experience is far too typical. Doctors tell women they have the wrong kind of breasts for nursing—too big or too small or nipples that are no good. They tell them they're too nervous and that they wouldn't make good cows. They ask, "Why do you want to be a peasant?" or "What are you trying to prove?" Some go overboard in the other direction, pressuring women who do *not* want to breastfeed. But even the good doctors—and

ones who give women credit for being able to make up their own minds and support their decisions—can rarely be of much help to nursing mothers, simply because they don't know enough.

Ninety-three percent of all American doctors are men. And the psychologist Niles Anne Newton has said, "Asking a male doctor for advice on breastfeeding techniques is like asking a virgin for information on sex techniques." Also, most doctors learn practically nothing about nursing in school. One recently shouted at a patient, "Why do you keep asking me about nursing? We only had one hour about it in medical school!"

So the message here is loud and clear. We can't expect our doctors to replace the mothers and aunts, the midwives, or the more experienced friends women used to go to with their ordinary questions about child care. For advice on breastfeeding a healthy baby, we can't depend on doctors. Not only do few of them have the knowledge to help; too often they give wrong advice that sabotages the course of successful breastfeeding.

Try to choose a hospital that has family-centered maternity care and a rooming-in plan, so you can keep your baby in your room for most or all of the day. This way you can feed your baby on demand. The baby will eat when it is hungry instead of having to wait for the next scheduled feeding. The four hour feedings may be okay for bottle-fed babies, but breast milk is digested more easily and more quickly, so nursing babies want to eat more often. Furthermore, the more frequently you nurse, the sooner your milk will come in and the more you will have.

When you plan your delivery, remember that the less medication you take, the less will get through to the baby. Heavily medicated mothers have sleepy babies who are poor nursers.

Remind your doctor just before delivery that you plan to nurse and do not want any shots or pills to dry up the milk. I just heard of a horrendous case that happened last month at a Long Island hospital. The mother had had a very difficult delivery and was given general anesthesia. Twenty-four hours later, when the nurse finally brought her baby in, she handed the mother a bottle. "I don't need that—I'm going to nurse," said the mother. "It's too late for that," answered the nurse. "We gave you a shot to dry up your milk while you were still on the delivery table."

It's outrageous that this woman's doctor who knew she wanted to breastfeed should have tried to take this option away from her. But remember—even if you have received hormones to dry up your milk, you can still nurse if you put your baby to the breast as soon and as often as possible. The baby's sucking will stimulate the breasts to produce milk, despite the hormones.

Remind your doctor to leave instructions in the nursery that your baby is not to receive any formula at all—and that you are to get the baby at each feeding, even during the night. Feeding the baby formula between nursings diminishes its desire to nurse, makes the mother subject to painful engorgement, and sets up a vicious cycle whereby nursing becomes more and more difficult, the mother feels more and more rejected, and the baby becomes more and more frustrated.

Even if your doctors and hospitals do all the wrong things, you can overcome the obstacles they set in your path. But there is no reason why women should put up any longer with practices that are bad for mothers and babies. We have to make our voices heard to demand the right kind of care for our babies and ourselves.

HR 1504

A BILL TO ALLOW THE FATHER TO ATTEND BIRTH OF HIS CHILD 1973

93D CONGRESS
1ST SESSION

H. R. 1504

IN THE HOUSE OF REPRESENTATIVES

JANUARY 9, 1973

MRS. GRIFFITHS introduced the following bill; which was referred to the Committee on Interstate and Foreign Commerce

A BILL

To provide for hospitals to allow the biological father to attend the birth of his child if the woman consents.

1 *Be it enacted by the Senate and House of Representa-*
2 *tives of the United States of America in Congress assembled,*
3 That any hospital, clinic, or similar establishment set up for
4 the purpose of fostering, restoring or observing a person's
5 health and which receives Federal funds under a grant, con-
6 tract, or loan or which has loans guaranteed under any Fed-
7 eral program shall allow the biological father to be in
8 attendance during all phases of childbirth if consent is first
9 obtained from the woman involved.

RESOLUTION

Whereas it is the natural human right of a woman to determine the manner of her child's birth, Whereas the participation of the father in the childbirth process undermines rigid, traditional sex roles from the beginning, Whereas it is a sexist notion that childbirth is "woman's work"; it is rather a "family affair," Whereas there does exist the right of "familial privacy," the invasion of which is an insidious thing, Whereas there does exist a double-standard in American medicine prejudicial against women: Be it resolved that the passage of H.R. 1504, a bill of the 93d Congress to provide for hospitals to allow the biological father to attend the birth of his child if the woman consents, be made a priority of this convention.

The health care system put poor women of color into triple jeopardy: discriminated against because of their class, race, and sex. They had greater difficulty merely getting access to health care, a bitter irony because their need for medical attention was typically greater. Poor women and poor women of color in particular work in deleterious conditions, can't afford a high–quality diet, live in homes and neighborhoods that pose health risks and in communities with few doctors, clinics, and hospitals—a bitter irony because women of color so often work in health care. These disadvantages are not produced by poverty alone. Black women experience more health problems than whites at every economic level, and their disadvantage persists even among the most highly educated black women. Black women suffer a higher incidence than white women of eight of the ten leading causes of death among women (the exceptions being pulmonary disease and suicide). Even when the incidence of disease is lower among black women, as for example is the case with breast cancer, black women's mortality rates are higher. Black infant mortality rates are twice as high as whites', and black maternal mortality rates five times as high.

Black feminist activism focused on health issues from very early on in the movement. Byllye Avery founded the National Black Women's Health Project in Atlanta in 1981, having worked in the women's health movement since 1974. The NBWHP went on to engender fifteen chapters and 150 local groups throughout the U.S., as well as inspiring the Latina Women's Health Project, the Native American Community Women's Health Education Resource Center, and similar projects in several other countries.

The NBWHP, now headquartered in Washington, D.C., provides wellness education, services, and advocacy for African American women and their families. It publishes an annual newsmagazine, *Vital Signs;* a quarterly newsletter, *Sister Ink;* and many other health education materials. Because it is a black project, it has a class consciousness that is missing from some parts of the women's health movement, emphasizing affordable and equitable access to health care. At the same time it has challenged conservative black leaders through its advocacy of abortion rights and its campaigns against domestic violence and AIDS.

Breathing Life into Ourselves:
The Evolution of the National Black Women's Health Project
BYLLYE Y. AVERY

I got involved in women's health in the 1970s around the issue of abortion. There were three of us at the University of Florida, in Gainesville, who just seemed to get picked out by women who needed abortions. They came to us. I didn't know anything about abortions. In my life that word couldn't even be mentioned without having somebody look at you crazy. Then someone's talking to me about abortion. It seemed unreal. But as more women came (and at first they were mostly white women), we found out this New York number we could give them, and they could catch a plane and go there for their abortions. But then a black woman came and we gave her the number, and she looked at us in awe: "I can't get to New York. . . ." We realized we needed a different plan of action, so in May 1974 we opened up the Gainesville Women's Health Center.

As we learned more about abortions and gynecological care, we immediately started to look at birth, and to realize that we are women with a total reproductive cycle. We might have to make different decisions about our lives, but whatever the decision, we deserved the best services available. So, in 1978, we opened up Birthplace, an alternative birthing center. It was exhilarating work; I assisted in probably around two hundred births. I understood life, and working in birth, I understood death, too. I certainly learned what's missing in prenatal care and why so many of our babies die.

Through my work at Birthplace, I learned the importance of being involved in our own health. We have to create environments that say "yes." Birthplace was a wonderful space. It was a big, old turn-of-the-century house that we decorated with antiques. We went to people's houses and, if we liked something, we begged for it—things off their walls, furniture, rugs. We fixed the place so that when women walked in, they would say, "Byllye, I was excited when I got up today because this was my day to come to Birthplace." That's how prenatal care needs to be given—so that people are excited when they come.

One of the things that black women have started talking about regarding infant mortality is that many of us are like empty wells; we give a lot, but we don't get much back. We're asked to be strong. I have said, "If one more person says to me that black women are strong I'm going to scream in their face." I am so tired of that stuff. What are you going to do—just lay down and die? We have to do what's necessary to survive. It's just a part of living. But most of us are empty wells that never really get replenished. Most of us are dead inside. We are walking around dead. That's why we end up in relationships that reinforce that particular thought. So you're talking about a baby being alive inside of a dead person; it just won't work.

I left the birthing center around 1980 or '81, mostly because we needed more midwives and I wasn't willing to go to nursing school. But an important thing had happened for me in 1979. I began looking at myself as a black woman. Before that I had been looking at myself as a woman. When I left the birthing center, I went to work in a Comprehensive Employment Training Program (CETA) job at a community college and it brought me face-to-face with my sisters and face-to-face with myself. Just by the nature of the program and the population that I worked with, I had, for the first time in my life, a chance to ask a nineteen-year-old why—please give me the reason why—you have four babies and you're only nineteen years old. And I was able to listen, and bring these sisters together to talk about their lives. It was there that I started to understand the lives of black women and to realize that we live in a conspiracy of silence. It was hearing these women's stories that led me to start conceptualizing the National Black Women's Health Project.

First I wanted to do an hour-long presentation on black women's health issues, so I started doing research. I got all the books, and I was shocked at what I saw. I was angry—angry that the people who wrote these books didn't put it into a format that made sense to us, angry that nobody was saying anything to black women or to black men. I was so angry I threw one book across the room and it stayed there for three or four days, because I knew I had just seen the tip of the iceberg, but I also knew enough to know that I couldn't go back. I had opened my eyes, and I had to go on and look.

Instead of an hour-long presentation we had a conference. It didn't happen until 1983, but when it did, 2,000 women came. But I knew we couldn't just have a conference. From the health statistics I saw, I knew that there was a deeper problem. People needed to be able to work individually, and on a daily basis. So we got the idea of self-help groups. The first group we formed was in a rural area outside of Gainesville, with twenty-one women who were severely obese. I thought, "Oh this is a piece of cake. Obviously these sisters don't have any information. I'll go in there and talk to them about losing weight, talk to them about high blood pressure, talk to them about diabetes—it'll be easy."

Little did I know that when I got there, they would be able to tell me everything that went into a 1200-calorie-a-day diet. They all had been to Weight Watchers at least five or six times; they all had blood-pressure-reading machines in their homes as well as medications they were on. And when we sat down to talk, they said, "We know all that information, but what we also know is that living in the world that we are in, we feel like we are absolutely nothing." One woman said to me, "I work for General Electric making batteries, and, from the stuff they suit me up in, I know it's killing me." She said, "My home life is not working. My old man is an alcoholic. My kids got babies. Things are not well with me. And the one thing I know I can do when I come home is cook me a pot of food and sit down in front of the TV and eat it. And you can't take that away from me until you're ready to give me something in its place."

The number one issue for most of our sisters is violence—battering, sexual abuse. Same thing for their daughters, whether they are twelve or four. We have to look at how violence is used, how violence and sexism go hand in hand, and how it affects the sexual response of females. We have to stop it, because violence is the training ground for us.

When you talk to young people about being pregnant, you find out a lot of things. Number one is that most of these girls did not get pregnant by teenage boys; most of them got pregnant by their mother's boyfriends or their brothers or their daddies. We've been sitting on that. We can't just tell our daughters, "just say no." What do they do about all those feelings running around their bodies? And we need to talk to our brothers. We need to tell them, the incest makes us crazy. It's something that stays on our minds all the time. We need the men to know that. And they need to know that when they hurt us, they hurt themselves. Because we are their mothers, their sisters, their wives; we are their allies on this planet. They can't just damage one part of it without damaging themselves. We need men to stop giving consent, by their silence, to rape, to sexual abuse, to violence. You need to talk to your boyfriends, your husbands, your sons, whatever males you have around you—talk to them about talking to other men. When they are sitting around womanizing, talking bad about women, make sure you have somebody stand up and be your ally and help stop this. For future generations, this has got to stop somewhere.

6

Reproductive Rights

Reproductive rights was the issue that most distinguished second-wave feminism. It was also one of the most controversial. Controlling reproduction empowers women to play much larger public roles than had been possible when they were subject to continual pregnancies and childbirths, and it allows women to engage in heterosexual activity without the fear of involuntary motherhood. These transformations underlie the conservative hysteria about reproductive rights: the fear that women will desert their "traditional" obligations to home and motherhood, that they will enjoy the sexual freedoms that men have traditionally practiced.

In the nineteenth century, first-wave feminists campaigned to give women reproductive choice, but they were constrained by a prudish culture, lack of free speech rights, and the absence of effective birth-control technology. In contrast, the women's liberation generation grew up in a more secular, permissive culture that included higher education for many women. With the mass marketing of birth-control pills starting in 1960, the founders of women's liberation became the first generation to enter adulthood with the possibility of reliably separating sex from reproduction. This group of women would not tolerate lack of control over their destinies.

Artist Irene Peslikis's dystopian vision of women's lack of control calls upon the fundamental Marxist principle that workers must control the means of production.

Women Must Control the Means of Reproduction
IRENE PESLIKIS (DRAWING)   1967

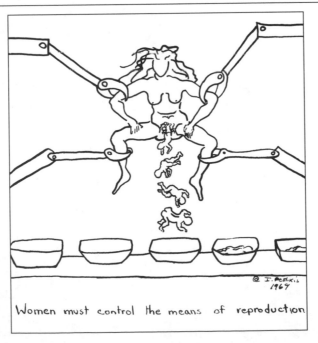

@ I. Peslikis
1969

Women must control the means of reproduction

In 1960 Patricia Robinson, a leftist African American social worker who volunteered at Planned Parenthood in Mt. Vernon, New York, started a women's group concerned with teenage pregnancy. The group's members ranged from grandmothers to teenagers, and they discussed their experiences in ways that would later be called consciousness-raising (see chapter 3). The group operated a Freedom School for children and in the early 1970s went on to agitate for welfare rights and decent housing. As this group advocated birth control and specifically the use of contraceptive pills, a birth-control method that had the advantage of being controlled by women, it ran counter to the growing black nationalist condemnation of birth control as a white conspiracy to commit genocide against African Americans—a condemnation that also expressed men's anxiety about their loss of control over women. In responding to this attack, the Mt. Vernon group's statement, which follows, did not deny white genocidal motives but argued for black women's self-determination. Although parts of black feminism came out of the civil rights movement, that was not its only path; black feminism continued a long tradition of black women's self-help, civil rights, and neighborhood organizations.

Poor Black Women

PATRICIA ROBINSON AND BLACK SISTERS

1968

September 11, 1968

Dear Brothers:

Poor black sisters decide for themselves whether to have a baby or not to have a baby. If we take the pills or practice birth control in other ways, it's because of poor black men.

Now here's how it is. Poor black men won't support their families, won't stick by their women—all they think about is the street, dope and liquor, women, a piece of ass, and their cars. That's all that counts. Poor black women would be fools to sit up in the house with a whole lot of children and eventually go crazy, sick, heartbroken, no place to go, no sign of affection—nothing. Middle class white men have always done this to their women—only more sophisticated like.

So when whitey put out the pill and poor black sisters spread the word, we saw how simple it was not to be a fool for men any more (politically we would say men could no longer exploit us sexually or for money and leave the babies with us to bring up). That was the first step in our waking up!

Black women have always been told by black men that we were black, ugly, evil, bitches and whores—in other words, we were the real niggers in this society—oppressed by whites, male and female, and the black man, too.

Now a lot of the black brothers are into a new bag. Black women are being asked by militant black brothers not to practice birth control because it is a form of whitey committing genocide on black people. Well, true enough, but it takes two to practice genocide and black women are able to decide for themselves, just like poor people all over the world, whether they will submit to genocide. For us, birth control is freedom to fight genocide of black women and children.

Like the Vietnamese have decided to fight genocide, the South American poor are beginning to fight back, and the African poor will fight back, too. Poor black women in the U.S. have to fight back out of our own experience of oppression. Having too many babies stops us from supporting our children, teaching them the truth or stopping the brainwashing as you say, and fighting black men who still want to use and exploit us.

But we don't think you are going to understand us because you are a bunch of little middle class people and we are poor black women. The middle class never understands the poor because they always need to use them as you want to use poor black women's children to gain power for yourself. You'll run the black community with your kind of black power—you on top!

Mt. Vernon, N.Y.

Patricia Haden—welfare recipient
Sue Rudolph—housewife
Joyce Hoyt—domestic
Rita Van Lew—welfare recipient
Catherine Hoyt—grandmother
Patricia Robinson—housewife and psychotherapist

The contraceptive hormonal pill, introduced in high-dosage form in 1960, was immediately used by millions of women who were denied information about its bothersome and sometimes dangerous side-effects. The women's liberation movement was responsible for exposing these dangers and challenging the drug companies' single-minded focus on profit. Women's testimony at the hearings described in this selection sparked a national movement demanding a warning label; after achieving this first goal, feminists continued the struggle and won lower-dosage pills and fuller warning labels in 1977. Oral contraceptive sales dropped steeply after these victories.

The women's movement conducted a similar campaign against unsafe IUDs in the mid-1970s. It exposed the fact that the Dalkon Shield was responsible for a high incidence of pelvic inflammatory disease, causing at least twenty deaths and hundreds of thousands of severe infections and injuries in the U.S. A class-action suit forced this IUD off the U.S. market in the 1980s (although then the manufacturer, A. H. Robins, "dumped" 35,000 of these devices onto the Third World market).

Feminist campaigns like these not only won specific victories but transformed women into more educated, vigilant, and assertive clients of health care (see chapter 5). The author of the following article, Judith Coburn, is a journalist who covered the Vietnam War as well as the women's liberation movement. Like many female journalists of the time, she combined reporting on movements with participation in them.

Off the Pill
JUDITH COBURN

"MEN, TAKE THIS PILL. WHILE YOU LISTEN TO THE HEARINGS, FEEL IT CIRCULATING THROUGH YOUR SYSTEM. CAUTION: IT MAY CAUSE CANCER, STROKE, DIABETES, BLOOD CLOTS, ETC. ETC."
—WASHINGTON, D.C.
WOMEN'S LIBERATION LEAFLET

Early this year, 30 members of Washington Women's Liberation, carrying this leaflet, disrupted Senator Gaylord Nelson's hearings on the Pill. We went to the hearings to protest the alliance of drug companies, population control experts, and the government, an alliance we believe has given the Pill a clean bill of health at women's expense. The disruption was a particular shock to Senator Nelson—a longtime foe of the drug industry—who held the hearings in what he believed to be women's interests.

To sit in the Nelson hearings was a nightmare. Male witness after male witness droned on in technical language about the more than 50 serious, sometimes fatal, side-effects which might be caused by the Pill. The catch is that most researchers say their evidence doesn't show a definite cause-and-effect relationship between the side-effects and

the Pill—yet. Women are left with enough evidence to scare them, but not enough to convince them to give up the miracle Pill and go back to the old methods.

While we pondered this choice, we listened to the most horrifying testimony of all. Dr. Roy Hertz, formerly of the National Institute of Health, told Senator Nelson he feared a Pill-caused cancer epidemic in the U.S. in the 1970's. Suddenly there was a new dimension. A woman might not escape such a catastrophe even if she had gone off the Pill immediately after the first terrifying reports of Pill side-effects came out.

Then we had to listen to the jokes. Senator Thomas McIntyre (a Pill critic) asked a witness, Dr. Robert Kistner of the Harvard Medical School, "Could you distinguish for me the differences between a side-effect and a complication?" Dr. Kistner, "Yes, one takes in estrogen, one frequently becomes nauseated. Estrogen pulls in sodium and women don't excrete the fluid, and they may become edematous and blow up. These are side-effects, but if a woman takes estrogen and gets a blood clot and dies, that is a complication." (General laughter in the hearing room.)

Women are trapped. For years, we have depended on the

Pill to feel safe from pregnancy—the spectre that haunts every relationship with a man.

After all, if a woman gets pregnant, it is she who bears the consequences. Many women, even liberated women, believe the Pill started the sexual revolution; most see their sexual liberation at least partly tied to it. It guarantees spontaneity and fulfillment of the women's magazines' ideal of romantic love. We may laugh about the hearts and flowers, but it's in the culture. Ten years of Pill success stories have convinced many of us that neither the diaphragm, foam nor any other method works. More statistics about the effectiveness of these methods can't do much about these fears, cultivated as they were by the drug companies, the medical profession and the population control movement. (The war of statistics goes on—drug companies claim the diaphragm is only 90% effective; doctors who are critics of the Pill say diaphragms are effective 98.6% of the time "in highly motivated women." That means that if a woman is serious about it, a diaphragm works.)

Lately, there has been much talk about the intra-uterine device (IUD) as an alternative to the Pill. Planned Parenthood clinics urge its use because of the side-effects resulting from the Pill. It is widely used in birth control clinics for poor women because population control experts claim these women can't remember to take the Pill. But now stories of side-effects from the IUD are seeping out: many women can't tolerate them and their use may result in bleeding or expulsion. Serious infections and perforations of the uterus are common, especially where health care is not good. Moreover, these same male doctors and population control experts who pushed the Pill are now switching their enthusiasm to the IUD. Who are women to believe?

Last year, G.D. Searle, which controls 40% of the Pill market, had net earnings of $27 million on sales of $147 million—a profit of 18%. Seven other companies—Eli Lilly, Mead-Johnson, Ortho Pharmaceutical, Parke-Davis, Syntex, Upjohn and Wyeth, shared the rest of the $120 million Pill market.

A leading customer for the Pill is the government: Last year AID bought $1,131,500 worth of pills at 16.75 cents per package from Wyeth and Syntex to pass out in birth control clinics abroad. The big money, however, is in the military: The Pentagon bought 1,755,642 packages of the Pill last year at prices ranging from 99 cents to $1.45 for a package of two-months' worth of pills. By the Defense Supply Agency's own admission, only two of these purchases were made by competitive bids—a procedure required by law. The fact that the Pentagon is not buying the Pill at cost, and not buying from the lowest bidder, suggests a big business deal in the works.

The way news travels also shows who counts (the consumer is the last to know). In the early 60's, there was an effective blackout on research detailing adverse side-effects of the Pill. When the first embarrassing reports of deaths from blood clots among Pill users began to circulate, they were not directed at women, but at the financial complex whose profits were at stake. As one UCLA professor told Morton Mintz of the *Washington Post,* "I first learned about a fatality after a patient had taken Enovid—and there had been two in the area of Los Angeles—from my broker, who telephoned me one morning and told me the news had come in over the wires from New York."

The Food and Drug Administration (FDA), the federal agency mandated to protect consumers from unsafe drugs, ruled the first Pill, Enovid, safe for contraceptive use in 1960 on the basis of tests on only 132 Puerto Rican women (Third World women are always the guinea pigs) who stayed on the Pill for only one to two years. The resignation in 1966 of FDA's top doctor, Joseph Sadusk, one of the early Pill pushers, to become vice president of Parke-Davis, symbolizes the cozy relationship between industry and the government agencies assigned to regulate them.

It is also clear that FDA, even under the most independent and "progressive" of bureaucrats Senator Nelson could find, will never move significantly against the power or profits of the private drug companies. A healthy drug and medical care industry is as crucial to a healthy American economy as Big Oil. And so the entire safety-testing process for drugs prior to marketing is left to the drug manufacturers themselves. FDA's only role is collecting post-marking reports of adverse effects of drugs sent in voluntarily by doctors and the drug companies. (Searle began hoarding its embarrassing records as far back as 1961: in less than a year after Enovid was marketed, Searle had a file of 132 cases of blood clots, including 11 deaths, which the company did not release until late 1962.

But the FDA seems to lose records just as successfully: Jack Anderson, the syndicated columnist, reports that by October 1968 the agency had records from 1965–66 of over 900 adverse reactions to the Pill, gathering dust in a back room. The FDA does protect consumers—sometimes. When cyclamates were shown to cause cancer in one species of animal, the FDA took it off the market. However, when the Pill, which causes cancer in five species of animals is involved, it's you've got a long way to go, baby.

No one has logged how many man- (and woman-) hours lobbyists for the Pill manufacturers, the Population Crisis Committee and Planned Parenthood have spent pushing the Pill with the media. When they can't squelch unfavorable stories or research reports, they counter with their own arguments. When two books, by *The Washington Post*'s Morton Mintz and *The Ladies Home Journal*'s Barbara Seaman, were published chronicling the devastating effects of the Pill and the conspiracy that foisted them off on women, the drug companies pulled out the stops. A Searle "fact sheet" sent to book review editors said of Mintz's book, "There is a danger that if certain statements from the book are given wide circulation . . . millions of American women may be thrown into a panic regarding the safety of all oral contraceptives." The long arm of the drug companies also reaches far into the academic research scene. One tale should suffice: *Medical World News* reported in 1969 that a paper detailing a study which showed a sixfold increase in cancer among 40,000 Pill users was canceled for publication by a University of Chicago magazine. The piece was withdrawn after the researcher received $1,119,000 from the Ford Foundation (the largest supporter of population control besides Rockefeller). A university spokesman told Morton Mintz, "the grants make possible a more comprehensive study and that consequently the findings set for publication were being reevaluated." Weighed down by all that gold, the results won't appear for years.

In March, women from WITCH (Woman's International Terrorist Conspiracy From Hell) hexed a population control panel at a meeting of the International Development Corporation in Washington D.C. One Witch, portraying Uncle Sam, dispensed pills, yelling, "Free Pills, Free Pills!" The demonstration was designed to show how the population control movement has often served as an arm of American imperialism overseas. It was poor women in Puerto Rico and Thailand who weren't told anything about possible dangers on which contraceptives for privileged Americans were tested. At a small dinner at a posh Washington club last fall, a Ford Foundation population expert was asked why Thai women were used to test the dangerous Pill. "Well, they could hardly be worse off than they are now," he said. Planned Parenthood and the population control movement talk about the threat to the world's resources by overpopulation. Since Americans consume 50% of the world's resources, the solution is redistribution of the wealth, not blaming the poor.

Back in America, the weapons of social control are sometimes not much less crass. The purpose of Senator Nelson's hearings was to find out whether drug companies and doctors are giving women a snow job about the Pill and whether, as a result, women can't make an informed judgement about using it. A *Newsweek* poll later summed up the matter: two-thirds of the women questioned said their doctors hadn't told them anything about serious long-term effects of the Pill. Why not? The Prescription Drug Task Force of HEW estimated in 1968 that American drug companies spend approximately $4500 per physician per year for promotions and advertising. The drug industry also supports the research and travel of a family of pro-Pill doctors like Dr. Rock and Dr. Connell, who do free flakking for the Pill. Sitting in the hearings, women had to listen to outrageous exchanges like this one between the committee counsel and again, Harvard's Dr. Robert Kistner:

COUNSEL: Why don't you tell patients there is a risk with oral contraceptives?

KISTNER: Well, they might get, if you tell them they might get headaches, they will get headaches.

COUNSEL: Well, if you told them they might get blood clots would that warning induce them to get blood clots?

In late March, Washington Women's Liberation staged a sit-in in HEW Secretary Finch's office to establish the right of women to control their own medical and personal lives. A week before, word had gone out quietly from HEW that the Pill warning was to be watered down. Women had not been involved in the preparation of the original statement or in its gutting.

"There were no politics to this," said Finch in a heated meeting with us.

"We shortened the insert after consulting with population control experts, doctors, and drug company representatives."

Women's health needs are political rights. It is up to U.S. to decide what form of contraceptive to use and whether to have abortions. But the issue of the Pill goes far beyond the content of the FDA warning. Women's liberation must fight to change society to allow women to make their own reproductive choices and whether or not to choose other careers than housewife and mother. For married women, this means round-the-clock day care centers at their place of work. For men, it means sharing equally with women the responsibilities of children, household and conception. For all women, it means redefining their lives and medical needs through political struggle and their own personal liberation.

It means learning that the sexual revolution doesn't have much to do with the Pill.

Abortion was nationally legalized by the U.S. Supreme Court in *Roe v. Wade* in 1973, but this decision only legitimated what was already happening: a wave of activism in the 1960s had produced widespread repeal of state antiabortion laws. Seventeen states had legalized or decriminalized abortion before *Roe v. Wade,* and antiabortion laws had been challenged in twenty-nine other states and the District of Columbia. This legislative action was the result of a concerted effort on the part of civil libertarians, physicians and feminists. The women's liberation movement held speak-outs; filed class-action suits; initiated referendums; and educated, lobbied, and demonstrated for reproductive rights. Additionally, feminists created networks that helped women get access to abortions while they were still illegal. Feminists saw this process not only as an opportunity to change laws, but also as a forum for educating the public about women's need for reproductive freedom.

Before the rise of women's liberation, the abortion reform movement had chipped away at the most egregious denials of legal abortion—for example, in cases of rape, insanity, and fetal deformity. In contrast the women's movement argued for repeal of all statutes criminalizing abortion; Lucinda Cisler was a pioneer of this position. In 1969, Cisler warned of the dangers of a compromise reform that would give decision-making power to doctors and the legal system instead of women. Part of Cisler's argument was recognized in the Supreme Court's creation of the constitutional rationale that women had a privacy right to control their pregnancies in the first trimester. Another part of Cisler's argument, however—that women should have a right to choice throughout pregnancy—was not recognized, and as a result physicians as well as lawmakers retain some power as women's moral guardians.

This partial legalization, precisely what Cisler warned against in the following article, opened the door to today's continuing attempts to hinder women's right to abortion, through denial of public funding, requirements for parental permission and waiting periods, bans on late abortion, and mandatory moralistic antiabortion lectures. Starting in the 1980s the "New Right" discovered that abortion was a useful issue for recruiting a grassroots following and began pouring money and other resources into nationwide antiabortion campaigns. Their intolerance created a climate that encouraged attacks on clinics and murders of health care providers. Although antiabortion-rights activists have not succeeded in recriminalizing abortion, they have put the women's movement on the defensive and forced it to continue to focus a large share of its energies on maintaining the right to abortion.

On Abortion and Abortion Law
LUCINDA CISLER

1969

ABORTION LAW REPEAL (SORT OF):
A WARNING TO WOMEN

One of the few things everyone in the women's movement seems to agree on is that we have to get rid of the abortion laws and make sure that any woman who wants an abortion can get one. We all recognize how basic this demand is; it sounds like a pretty clear and simple demand, too—hard to achieve, of course, but obviously a fundamental right just like any other method of birth control.

But just because it *sounds* so simple and so obvious and is such a great point of unity, a lot of us haven't really looked below the surface of the abortion fight and seen how complicated it may be to get what we want. The most important thing feminists have done and have to keep doing is to insist that the basic reason for repealing the laws and making abortions available is JUSTICE: women's right to abortion.

Everyone recognizes the cruder forms of opposition to abortion traditionally used by the forces of sexism and religious reaction. But a feminist philosophy must be able to deal with *all* the stumbling blocks that keep us from reaching our goal, and must develop a consciousness about the far more subtle dangers we face from many who honestly believe they are our friends.

In our disgust with the extreme oppression women experience under the present abortion laws, many of us are understandably tempted to accept insulting token changes that we would angrily shout down if they were offered to us in any other field of the struggle for women's liberation. We've waited so long for anything to happen that when we see our demands having any effect at all we're sorely tempted to convince ourselves that everything that sounds good in the short run will turn out to be good for women in the long run. And a lot of us are so fed up with "the system" that we don't even bother to find out what it's doing so we can fight it and demand what *we* want. This is the measure of our present oppression: a chain of aluminum *does* feel lighter around our necks than one made of iron, but it's still a chain, and our task is still to burst entirely free.

The abortion issue is one of the very few issues vital to the women's movement that well-meaning people outside the movement were dealing with on an organized basis even before the new feminism began to explode a couple of years ago. Whatever we may like to think, there *is* quite definitely an abortion movement that is distinct from the feminist movement, and the good intentions of most of the people in it can turn out to be either a tremendous source of support for our goals or the most tragic barrier to our ever achieving them. The choice is up to us: we must subject every proposal for change and every tactic to the clearest feminist scrutiny, demand only what is good for *all* women, and not let some of us be bought off at the expense of the rest.

Until just a couple of years ago the abortion movement was a tiny handful of good people who were still having to concentrate just on getting the taboo lifted from public discussions of the topic. They dared not even think about any proposals for legal change *beyond* "reform" (in which abortion is grudgingly parceled out by hospital committee fiat to the few women who can "prove" they've been raped, or who are crazy, or are in danger of bearing a defective baby). They spent a lot of time debating with priests about When Life Begins, and Which Abortions Are Justified. They were mostly doctors, lawyers, social workers, clergymen, professors, writers, and a few were just plain women—usually not particularly feminist.

Part of the reason the reform movement was very small was that it appealed mostly to altruism and very little to people's self-interest: the circumstances covered by "reform" *are* tragic but they affect very few women's lives, whereas repeal is compelling because most women know the fear of unwanted pregnancy and in fact get abortions for that reason.

Some people were involved with "reform"—and are in the abortion movement today—for very good reasons: they are concerned with important issues like the public health problem presented by illegal abortions, the doctor's right to provide patients with good medical care, the suffering of unwanted children and unhappy families, and the burgeoning of our population at a rate too high for *any* economic system to handle.

These people do deserve a lot of credit for their lonely and dogged insistence on raising the issue when everybody else wanted to pretend it didn't exist. But because they invested so much energy earlier in working for "reform" (and got it in ten states), they have an important stake in believing that their approach is the "realistic" one—that one must accept the small, so-called "steps in the right direction" that can be wrested from reluctant politicians, that it isn't quite dignified to demonstrate or shout what you want, that raising the women's rights issue will "alienate" politicians, and so on.

Because of course, it *is* the women's movement whose demand for *repeal*—rather than "reform"—of the abortion laws has spurred the general acceleration in the abortion movement and its influence. Unfortunately, and ironically, the very rapidity of the change for which we are responsible is threatening to bring us to the point where we are offered something so close to what we want that our demands for true radical change may never be achieved.

Most of us recognize that "reforms" of the old rape–incest–fetal deformity variety are not in women's interest and in fact, in their very specificity, are almost more of an insult to our dignity as active, self-determining humans than are the old laws that simply forbid us to have abortions unless we are about to die. But the *new* reform legislation now being proposed all over the country is not in our interest either: it looks pretty good, and the improvements it seems to promise (at least for middle-class women) are almost irresistible to those who haven't informed themselves about the complexities of the abortion situation or developed a feminist critique of abortion that goes beyond "it's our right." And the courts are now handing down decisions that look good at a glance but that contain the same restrictions as the legislation.

All of the restrictions are of the kind that would be extremely difficult to get judges and legislators to throw out later (unlike the obvious grotesqueries in the old "reform" laws, which are already being challenged successfully in some courts and legislatures). A lot of people are being seriously misled because the legislation and the court decisions that incorporate these insidious limitations are being called abortion law "repeal" by the media.

The following are the four major restrictions that have been cropping up lately in "repeal" bills, and some highly condensed reasons why feminists (and indeed anyone) must oppose them. No one can say for sure whether sexist ill-will, political horse-trading, or simple ignorance played the largest part in the lawmakers' decisions to include them, but all of them codify outmoded notions about medical technology, religion, or women's "role":

1: *Abortions may only be performed in licensed hospitals.* Abortion is almost always a simple procedure that can be carried out in a clinic or a doctor's office. Most women do need a place to lie down and rest for a while after a D&C or even a vacuum aspiration abortion, but they hardly need to occupy scarce hospital beds and go through all the hospital rigamarole that ties up the woman's money and the time of overworked staff people.

Hospital boards are extremely conservative and have always wanted to minimize the number of abortions performed within their walls: the "abortion committees" we now have were not invented by lawmakers but by hospital administrators. New laws that insure a hospital monopoly will hardly change this attitude. (The same committees reg-

ulate which women will be able to get the sterilizations they seek—even though voluntary sterilization is perfectly legal in all but one or two states.) The hospitals and accreditation agencies set up their own controls on who will get medical care, and doctors who want to retain their attending status are quite careful not to do "too many" abortions or sterilizations.

2: *Abortions may only be performed by licensed physicians.* This restriction sounds almost reasonable to most women who have always been fairly healthy and fairly prosperous, who are caught up in the medical mystique so many doctors have cultivated, and who accept the myth that abortion is incredibly risky and thus should cost a lot. But it is one of the most insidious restrictions of all, and is most oppressive to poor women.

Most doctors are not at all interested in performing abortions: even the ones who don't think it's dirty and who favor increasing the availability of abortion generally consider it a pretty boring procedure that they don't especially want to do. One reason they do find it tedious is that it is basically quite a simple operation, especially when the new vacuum aspiration technique is used, rather than the old dilation and curettage. The physicians who would like to see paramedical specialists trained to perform abortions with the aspirator (or who would like to perfect other promising new methods, such as hormone injections) would be completely thwarted by this restriction in their desire to provide efficient, inexpensive care on a mass basis. The general crisis in the medical delivery system in fact demands that paramedical people be trained to do a great many things that physicians do now.

If physicians themselves were to try to perform all the abortions that are needed, they would be swamped with requests and would have to charge a great deal for their specialized training. Childbirth is statistically eight or ten times more dangerous than abortion, and yet nurses are now being trained as midwives in many medical centers. Why can't they and other medical personnel also be specially trained to use the aspirator so that five or six of them can perform clinic abortions under the general supervision of one physician? Only if paramedicals are allowed to do abortions can we expect to have truly inexpensive (and eventually free) abortions available to all women.

3: *Abortions may not be performed beyond a certain time in pregnancy, unless the woman's life is at stake.* Significantly enough, the magic time limit varies from bill to bill, from court decision to court decision, but this kind of restriction essentially says two things to women: (a) at a certain stage, your body suddenly belongs to the state and it can force you to have a child, whatever your own reasons for wanting an abortion late in pregnancy; (b) because late abortion entails more risk to you than early abortion, the state must "protect" you even if your considered decision is that you want to run that risk and your doctor is willing to help you. This restriction insults women in the same way the present "preservation-of-life" laws do: it assumes that we must be in a state of tutelage and cannot assume responsibility for our own acts. Even many women's liberation writers are guilty of repeating the paternalistic explanation given to excuse the original passage of U.S. laws against abortion: in the nineteenth century abortion was more dangerous than childbirth, and women had to be protected against it. Was it somehow less dangerous in the eighteenth century? Were other kinds of surgery safe then? And, most important, weren't women wanting and getting abortions, even though they knew how much they were risking? "Protection" has often turned out to be but another means of control over the protected; labor law offers many examples. When childbirth becomes as safe as it should be, perhaps it will be safer than abortion: will we put back our abortion laws, to "protect women"?

And basically, of course, no one can ever know exactly when *any* stage of pregnancy is reached until birth itself. Conception can take place at any time within about three days of intercourse, so that any legal time limit reckoned from "conception" is meaningless because it cannot be determined precisely. All the talk about "quickening," "viability," and so on, is based on old religious myths (if the woman believes in them, of course, she won't look for an abortion) or tied to ever-shifting technology (who knows how soon a three-day-old fertilized egg may be considered "viable" because heroic mechanical devices allow it to survive and grow outside the woman's uterus?). To listen to judges and legislators play with the ghostly arithmetic of months and weeks is to hear the music by which angels used to dance on the head of a pin.

There are many reasons why a woman might seek a late abortion, and she should be able to find one legally if she wants it. She may suddenly discover that she had German measles in early pregnancy and that her fetus is deformed; she may have had a sudden mental breakdown; or some calamity may have changed the circumstances of her life: whatever her reasons, *she belongs to herself and not to the state.*

4: *Abortions may only be performed when the married woman's husband or the young single woman's parents give their consent.* The feminist objection to vesting a veto power in anyone other than the pregnant woman is too obvious to need any elaboration.

All women are oppressed by the present abortion laws, by old-style "reforms," and by seductive new fake-repeal bills and court decisions. But the possibility of fake repeal—if it becomes reality—is the most dangerous: it will divide women from each other. It can buy off most middle-class women and make them believe things have really changed, while it leaves poor women to suffer and keeps us all saddled with abortion laws for many more years to come.

Hernia: A Satire on Abortion Law Repeal

SARAH WERNICK LOCKERETZ

NEW MILITANT DEMAND PRESENTED TO STATE LEGISLATURE

A band of militant men recently disrupted a session of the state legislature calling for hernia operations on demand. The strident males—mostly jacket-less and tie-less, many not wearing athletic supports—puzzled and alarmed the legislators, medical experts, and others present.

The attractive blond spokesman for the radicals, who was wearing a wedding band, seized the microphone and in a gruff voice read the demands of the group. As the legislator, whose speech on public health had been interrupted, moved from the podium, she murmured, "What do these men want anyway?"

Opposition to hernia operations finds its origins in the past. The Puritans, who opposed hernia operations, believed that it violated the will of God to relieve pain through medical intervention. The laws they enacted still stand in some states. In other states, antiherniorraphy legislation was passed a century ago in an effort to prevent desperate men from seeking an operation which was then quite dangerous. In recent years, hernia legislation has been reformed considerably.

State legislation generally permits men to obtain legal hernia surgery if the reasons for which they seek the operation are valid. For example, all states permit hernia operations in order to save a man's life. Some states interpret this to allow surgery to a man if two psychiatrists testify that he will commit suicide because of his hernia. Many states allow herniorraphy on men whose mental health is judged to be seriously threatened by the hernia. Such states require hospitals to set up committees to evaluate each applicant. Many states tolerate the operation if the hernia is the result of a violent attack on the man. A few states now permit hernia operations on men whose hernias deform them.

Some have proposed additional grounds to grant herniorraphy in hardship cases. For example, reformers have advocated permitting surgery to men whose careers depend upon their lifting heavy weights. Opponents of such reform argue that men with hernias should seek training which will permit them to change their occupations if necessary. Other reformers would take into account the number of hernias a man has already, allowing operations for men who have four or five previous hernias. Conservatives oppose any liberalization of existing laws, fearing that such changes will open the way to herniorraphy on demand.

In their statement, the radicals argued that existing legislation acts to discriminate against the poor, who are most likely to have hernias. They decried the system of hospital quotas which limit the number of legal operations performed. The lads called for an end to the prevailing medical practice of requiring a married man to obtain his wife's consent to the operation. "My hernia is none of my wife's business!" shouted a brown-haired man in his thirties. Another protester, wearing a neat blue suit and a green and white striped tie, commented: "Women cannot understand how a man feels when he has a hernia. That is why we object to having nurses decide who should have the operation." Several of the dissidents carried a banner saying, "The truss is not for us." This new breed of radical men is demanding a total repeal of all legislation affecting hernias. Few present agreed with them.

Those legislators who agreed with some of the criticisms of existing laws favored reform rather than repeal. All saw the need for residence requirements to accompany reform, expressing concern that liberalized laws might attract men from other states seeking surgery. "We don't want our state to become a herniorraphy mill," said one legislator.

Most lawmakers were satisfied with existing regulations. One representative echoed popular sentiment when she said, "Everyone knows what causes hernias. Men who over-exert themselves deserve what they get."

Several doctors at the session emphasized the need for preventative measures against hernias. One doctor said, "Given the many means open to a man to avoid hernias, it is difficult to see why men can't prevent them in the first place. If we make the operation available to any man who wants it, we would be encouraging carelessness and irresponsibility."

Another doctor argued that existing hospital facilities would be over-burdened if hernia legislation were repealed. "If we gave hernia operations to any man who demanded them, we wouldn't have time for the important services a hospital should perform. I went into medicine to save lives, not to patch muscles."

A well-known psychiatrist who has written several books on the masculine mentality, spoke to reporters after the disturbance. She is currently engaged in research about the after-effects of hernia operations. "We find that most of these men are suffering from doubts about their sexual identity. The male has always been characterized by his ability to stand pain. Most of them are using the operation to avoid traditional male responsibilities. They claim the operation will help them, but how can it? Herniorraphy never solves the real problem which is their hostility towards their own masculinity. We must seek other solutions."

Many men in the audience disagreed with the protesters. One handsome man of twenty-seven shook his head and laughed. "Those boys don't represent me. They don't know what they want." His wife, listening approvingly, remarked, "My husband would never have an operation. Real men don't mind hernias."

Listeners applauded a man who stood up and said, "I have a hernia. My father had a hernia, and my grandfather had a hernia. None of us ever considered an operation. Those men should get belts. Men should be taught how to cope with hernias."

Perhaps the response of the majority was best summarized by a leading anthropologist when she remarked, "In all known human societies men have had hernias. We can't change the facts of nature."

"Jane" was an underground women's collective that grew out of Chicago's women's liberation movement. It began as a counseling and referral service, such as existed in numerous cities, connecting women with illegal abortionists and helping to preserve the safety of both. But Jane women became unique in learning to perform their own abortions, ultimately providing abortions for 11,000 women from 1969 to 1973. Although seven Jane women were arrested in 1972, they were back in practice six weeks later. Jane not only had an exemplary safety record but lowered abortion prices 400 percent, from approximately $400 to $100. When abortion was legalized, these lower prices became the norm.

Women Learn to Perform Abortions
"JANE"

1973

For the first year and a half of the service, we steadily learned more about abortions and specific medical techniques, the use of drugs and instruments, and we performed minor para-medic procedures.

We became more competent as counselors and organizers, and we recruited many new counselors as the number of patients and scope of activity grew. Fees for a D&C dropped from $500 to $350, with the number of free abortions growing as volume increased.

But we still relied on our male abortionist ("Dr." C) to do the more than 30 D&Cs a week. We, in the meantime, concentrated on expanding our service, while we were continually developing the skill and the confidence to do D&Cs ourselves.

Our biggest headaches came from the two or three cases a week when a woman turned out to be more pregnant than expected and we suddenly had to deal with an induced miscarriage instead of a simple D & C. Even with written notes from a doctor and pelvic exams beforehand, it was impossible always to predict the length of pregnancy. Some women menstruated for the first several months of their pregnancy.

Suddenly, the woman had to make major changes in plans under extreme stress. She had to deal with a process that would take days instead of minutes and involve more pain, more risk and often more money.

Suddenly, there was no way to keep the abortion a secret from intolerant parent or boyfriend, husband or employer. Women on welfare stood to lose their payments if the caseworker found out they had an abortion.

The counselor would have to be on call around the clock till the woman safely miscarried. She would have to arrange a place for the woman to stay while she was in labor; or if the woman had no one else to turn to, the counselor would have to fill in as babysitter, housekeeper and midwife till the ordeal was over. Sometimes she would receive a frantic call from a woman in labor and rush to the woman's house regardless of the hour of day or night, only to be confronted by angry husband or parents whose only response to the crisis was to yell recriminations or threaten to call the police, while the daughter or wife was in heavy labor in the bedroom.

Fear of arrest or lawsuit was only a minor consideration at times like these—the counselor's first concern was to take care of the woman. Counselors encouraged minors to tell their parents once the miscarriage had been induced. Usually the parents found out anyway, and often they turned out to be more supportive than the girl suspected.

The women who worked as assistants had become familiar with the tools and techniques for a D & C. They had been observing abortions for about ten months and were proficient at giving shots, inserting a speculum, administering injections of novacaine around the cervix and taking pap smears to determine infection and cancer. But when it came time to dilate and use a forceps or currette, the counselor/assistant stepped aside and "Dr." C took over. But he was feeling the pressure and responsibility of the workload, especially since he had a family and a life to maintain in another place. He warned us repeatedly that he would not be available forever. Sometimes "Dr." C seemed driven in his desire to teach. He constantly pushed to teach just as we constantly pushed to learn.

The women of Jane performed their first complete D & C quite unexpectedly, on a delightful young patient who was scheduled for an induced miscarriage, but turned out to be only 13 weeks pregnant. Even though we had been inducing and midwifing miscarriages for more than six months, we had avoided thinking of ourselves as actual abortionists. Now, armed with this new competence, we had no excuse for not using it if the need was there.

The need was growing daily. Jane was getting upwards of 100 calls a week now, and more than a third of these women were poor. Many would choose catheters, quinine or coathangers rather than another baby. Jane began steadily to add short-term D & Cs to our Thursday workload. Within a month, we were doing a total of twelve abortions each Thursday, with no problems. By the end of two months, the counselor who had performed the first D & C felt quite competent. The process of training other counselors to be abortionists began almost immediately and continued for the life of the service. Every counselor, after serving an apprenticeship counseling with experienced counselors, was given the opportunity to work at the apartment where the abortions were being done. She was encouraged to perform simple paramedic functions—giving shots, inserting a speculum and taking pap smears. We also switched jobs during the abortion to break down impressions of individual status. At the beginning, one counselor would hold the patient's hand and talk to her, while another inserted a speculum, took a pap smear and injected novacaine. Then the counselors changed places, and the one who was talking to the patient and getting to know her completed the abortion.

Not only did this system diffuse status, but later, when several of us had to face a judge after a major arrest, it diffused responsibility. Former patients who had been subpoenaed could not point to a single woman and say, "That's the abortionist."

The other changes that resulted from our being independent abortionists, at least part-time, were more sweeping:

—Internally, for better or worse, we had a sudden abundance of money for running the service.

—Operationally, we had to find sources for drugs and supplies—how does a lay person obtain a dilator and a set of currettes—or 1,000 ergotrate tablets . . . or 500 syringes?

—Legally, we had to face the fact that we would be considered full-fledged abortionists in the eyes of the law. We could no longer hide behind the label of "counselor," and we no longer could expect "Dr." C to act as a buffer, with his know-how and his ready cash for dealing with a bust.

—Personally, we had to cope with a range of problems, including anxiety and guilt, strains on family and friendships, and social disapproval.

—And morally, we had to be ready to accept the full consequences of our activities, even if they resulted in illness, personal tragedy or death.

Although the Catholic hierarchy condemned abortion, not all Catholics agreed. Catholic women had and have abortions more frequently than Protestants and Jews, and a 1972 study of New York State priests showed that only 68 percent fully agreed with the Church's condemnation. Some nuns even spoke out publicly in favor of reproductive choice. Catholics for a Free Choice remains a particularly active and influential group, in 1999 beginning a campaign to rescind the Vatican's status as a member country at the U.N. (a privilege enjoyed by no other religion). Catholics for a Free Choice's principles are set out in this 1974 press release.

Who Needs a Shepherd?
CATHOLICS FOR A FREE CHOICE

1974

We say that, despite all the vociferous rhetoric and lobbying of some other Catholic groups such as the "right-to-lifers," Catholics For a Free Choice believe we have a majority of the Catholic people, who are really the church, on our side as evidenced by the polls and by our mail.

Now is the time to rally Catholics of rational thinking who don't want to return to the dark ages of the crime syndicate's abortion mills and the maiming and killing of women. Many letters have been pouring in to us from all over the United States in the past month from Catholics asking us if they may join our organization. These are men and women in various occupations, housewives, students, the married and unmarried. We also have nuns supporting our stand privately.

We abhor the irreligious concept that the state should own and control a woman's means of production, her body, at any time during her lifetime. We believe that no female citizen anywhere should be forced, under threat of criminality, by any governmental body, at any time, under any circumstances, to carry to full term, a fetus, deformed or otherwise, against her own free will.

We also believe that no governmental body should enact into criminal codes, under threats and duress, any one controversial religious minority viewpoint that the majority of the citizens may find abhorrent and barbaric and which potentially affects over half the population, who are women, putting women into a subjugated sexual caste.

The Catholic church's all-male celibate hierarchy still maintains an oppressive, discriminatory and sexist code of laws regarding women, and which have not yet been successfully challenged, while at the same time it forbids women any representation on their own behalf on the policy-making and canonical, interpretative bodies.

Sinful and barbaric laws, forbidding women their human, personal right to terminate an unwanted and impossible conception, were forced upon them, in and out of marriage, and deprived them of their human and spiritual inalienable right to their own souls, conscience, free will and full personhood, reducing them to the unholy status of bondage, and slavery to a patriarchal mystique which insisted on the state and male ownership of every woman's body and mind.

To venerate the fetus above the life, health, and the religious and civil rights of the woman involved; to say that contraception and abortion are not allowed, when speaking of women, and at the same time extol celibacy for the patriarchal all-male hierarchy, thus preventing potential births; to approve of war, capital punishment and the killing of human beings in alleged "self defense" (when referring to males) is the height of hypocrisy.

Christ himself uttered not one word equating abortion with murder. Nor is there anything in the Bible forbidding contraception. Because women were unjustly and oppressively denied their voice in the making and the interpretation of the religious, civil and criminal laws regarding their domain of pregnancy, they were taken advantage of.

Many truths of history are not taught in Catholic schools, such as, that up to the year 1588 Catholic theologians and Popes condoned abortion up to 80 days for the female fetus and up to 40 days for the male, although no one could tell the difference. In 1588 Pope Sixtus V forbade all abortions, but things remained that way for only 3 years till 1591, when Pope Gregory the XIV rescinded that order and reverted back to allowing abortions up to 40 days for both the male and female fetus. The female fetus gained equality that year!

That is how the matter stood till 1869 when Pius IX forbade all abortions at any time, and the doctrine of infallibility went into effect at about the same time.

We can't forget that Joan of Arc was burned at the stake and later canonized a saint by cooler heads. Hundreds of thousands of unfortunate women were sent to the gallows or were burned at the stake as witches by so-called experts on morality, all in the name of "religion."

Women are no longer accepting in silence their shackles of religious and political socialization, the very roots of the patriarchal system which has oppressed them for millennia.

Friends of the Fetus
IRENE PESLIKIS

1969

Abortion rights faced attack not only from religious conservatives but also from African American antifeminists. Black opposition, however, also rests on some real fears and real evidence that the white establishment was trying to use birth control to reduce the black birthrate and thus strengthen white supremacy. In the 1920s and 1930s, birth-control advocates had supported racist programs of forced sterilization of the "unfit" that particularly targeted poor people of color. Although there is no evidence that abortion was ever used in this racist way, contraception was originally promoted in the U.S. as a way of reducing "inferior" populations. The abortion rights campaign has been primarily white, but by no means exclusively so, as this speech by Mary Treadwell, executive director of Pride, Inc., demonstrates.

An African American Woman Speaks Out for Abortion Rights
MARY TREADWELL

I am happy to join in supporting the campaign of the Women's National Abortion Action Coalition. As a black woman, I support the abortion campaign for reasons inherent in being a member of the black minority in racist America.

The legislators of this country are overwhelmingly white and overwhelmingly male. While rejecting legalized abortion, these very men sit in hypocritical splendor and refuse to provide an adequate guaranteed annual income for these children born to women without financial and social access to safe abortion. While rejecting legalized abortion, these very men refuse to fund quality, inexpensive pre-natal and post-natal care to women without access to abortion. While rejecting legalized abortion, these very men refuse to fund quality education and training for the children of the women—without access to abortion.

These men have never been faced with a knitting needle or coat hanger in the greasy back room of an urban garage, nor have they swallowed masses of quinine tablets or turpentine only to permanently endanger physical well being. Yet their wives, mistresses and girlfriends have ready access to (and have always had ready access to) psychiatrists and therapeutic abortions. While the wealthy, the elite and the powerful have always had this access, the masses—both black and white—have always been penalized for being the masses.

Black women have been economically and socially denied access to legal abortion or therapeutic abortion. Black women do not have more babies than white women—they have simply had fewer abortions. Very few black women have had $500 or more for illegal abortion. Very few black women have had access to the white psychiatric community granting therapeutic abortions.

At this point a few members of my community will tell me that legalized abortion is simply another white man's trick to foster racial genocide. They will say that we need to reproduce as many black children as possible—which only adds numbers. There is no magic in a home where someone has reproduced five or more black babies and cannot manage economically, educationally, spiritually nor socially to see that these five black babies become five highly trained black minds.

Black women particularly need this personal freedom to be able to fulfill themselves sexually without fear of conception. The outside pressures of this society wreak enough havoc within the black home and the black family unit. It is unspeakable that legislated racist pressures should accompany the black woman to her bedroom and creep insidiously into the center of her bed. I'll stay out of the legislature, if the legislature stays out of my bed.

Nor can black people afford to have their personal freedoms imposed upon by religious tenets or rhetoric. Let no church dare to define womb life to me when every day I see black life defiled, maimed and killed both physically and psychologically. Let no preacher ask me to religiously consider unborn life when I question the wisdom of introducing yet another black baby into life in white America. I'll stay out of church, if the church stays out of my bed.

Finally, a word to men: this society has encouraged men to view fatherhood as proof of their masculinity. Some men, in turn, have put this trip on women to conceive, to the benefit of no one concerned. Tremendous value is placed on the male heir and the continuance of the family name. We as black people have no time for these misconceptions and pervasions of values. We cannot get caught up in the misconception that fatherhood proves masculinity and motherhood reinforces femininity.

What is at stake for black women in reforming abortion legislation? In both economic and social terms, the black women have much to gain from the laws regarding this most personal of personal freedoms. Black women must consider the larger consequences in a society which is not only unwilling to provide a quality life for black children, but tries to destroy life for all black people.

The women's liberation movement popularized the concept of reproductive rights. This slogan contained a critique of the narrow focus on abortion legalization, which seemed to communicate that feminists were exclusively in favor of reducing births. An expanded reproductive rights campaign asserted women's right to bear children in safe and healthy circumstances as well as to choose not to give birth. The movement thus saw day care and child welfare as equal in importance to birth control. The movement was particularly infuriated by the Hyde Amendments to annual federal government appropriations bills, passed yearly since 1977, which banned the use of Medicaid funds for abortion except in cases of extreme danger to life; as a result Medicaid could be used to pay for sterilization but not for contraception or abortion.

The new reproductive rights organizations, such as the Committee for Abortion Rights and Against Sterilization Abuse (CARASA), also criticized the population-control establishment for its attempts to use birth control not to strengthen women's autonomy but against overpopulation, which it conceived as the root of poverty. Feminists countered that the causality went the other way—people adopted birth control as they became more prosperous and as women gained autonomy—and criticized the population controllers for not prioritizing women's choice. Two decades later, the most influential population-control foundations have been convinced that the best route to lowering population is strengthening women's economic well-being, education, and political rights.

In defending women's rights to have children and to be able to provide for them, the reproductive rights movement also attacked the widespread practice of coercive sterilization that continued in the 1970s. CARASA investigated and documented thousands of cases of forced sterilization, especially directed at people of color; welfare recipients were threatened with cutoffs of stipends unless they submitted to sterilization, and women were asked to sign sterilization consent forms while in labor, either in pain or partly anaesthetized. In 1974, responding to women's movement pressure, the U.S. Department of Health, Education and Welfare issued guidelines that required informed consent and prohibited sterilization of women under 21. Although it took over a decade to bring most hospitals into compliance with these guidelines, the campaign eventually reduced sterilization abuse considerably, another victory of the women's liberation movement.

The following CARASA position paper was written by medieval historian Joan Kelly, who was also the author of an influential early article that pioneered the rethinking of history from a female perspective.

Sterilization: Rights and Abuse of Rights
JOAN KELLY

1977

Sterilization is the fastest growing form of birth control. And sterilization-abuse is emerging as the single greatest threat to reproductive freedom. "Forced sterilization" is an ugly phrase. It recalls the race eugenics of the 1930s, and the horrifying practices of medical men and scientists that a racist Nazi state legitimated. Once again the charge is becoming increasingly familiar. But today it refers to numbers of women—poor, mostly Black, Latin, and Native

American—whose control over their own bodies is being legally and surgically terminated by white, middle-class men in the name of the society and government of the United States.

Norma Jean Serena's case, one of several pending sterilization suits, will be the first to raise sterilization-abuse as a civil rights issue. A 40-year-old mother of three children, she charges that in 1970 health and welfare officials in Armstrong County, Pa., conspired to violate her civil rights by having her sterilized without her knowledge at the time of delivery of her youngest child. Her suit, repeatedly delayed for four years, should come to trial in Pittsburgh this fall, 1977.

What is ominous about this and many such cases is the contention that race is a major factor in them. Norma Jean Serena is a Native American, and a report issued recently by the General Accounting Office (GAO), after years of such complaint by Native American groups, lends weight to her claim. In four Indian Health Service Hospitals alone, 3,406 sterilizations were performed between 1973 and 1976. Since Native Americans constitute only half of one percent of the national population, we can understand how facts such as these, and a sterilization rate said to range anywhere from 14 to 25%, revive the spectre of genocide. One study of New York City hospitals in 1973 showed that the proportion of Spanish-speaking women sterilized was almost three times that of the proportion of Black women and almost six times as great as the proportion of white women.

Puerto Rico yields startling figures. More than one third (35.3%) of the women of Puerto Rico have been sterilized, most of them in their twenties. Of course, these women chose sterilization. Or did they? Abortion was strictly illegal in Puerto Rico (except for the North American women who could afford to fly there for abortions they had difficulty obtaining at home), while sterilization was made cheap and available. Indeed, the U.S. Department of Health, Education and Welfare (HEW) subsidized these sterilizations, paying 80% of the budget of Puerto Rico's major sterilizing agency, the Family Planning Association.

A similar pattern has begun to emerge in the U.S., as independent women's groups have been quick to recognize. Public funds have been virtually cut off for abortion by the Supreme Court decisions of June 1977. And the other side of this coin is that HEW is continuing to subsidize 90% of the cost of sterilization!

There is no mistaking the race and class bias in the government's recent denial of equal access to abortion, since 38.5% of Black and other minority women have relied on Medicaid for abortion, as compared with 7% of white women. These "public funds" are now denied only for abortion but continue to be provided for sterilization.

Many women have their tubes "tied" believing they can be "untied" in the future. They are not clearly informed that tubal sterilization is an irreversible procedure.

Women are sterilized without their knowledge or consent during abortions and deliveries, as in the pending case of Rosalind Johnston, a 20-year-old Black prisoner sterilized without consent in New York City. They are pressured to sign consent forms during abortions and in labor, a practice which the HEW guidelines for sterilizing public patients do not address. The 72-hour waiting period required by HEW does commit the doctor to a second separate surgical procedure if the woman has not consented before labor or abortion (which is one of the reasons for violating consent procedures altogether). It does not give the woman time to recover from the trauma of birth or abortion, does not permit her to reflect or seek the counsel of family and friends outside the hospital, and certainly does not allow for post-partum depression.

When they do not want to consent, women are frequently threatened with loss of welfare funds. In the infamous case of Minnie Lee and Mary Alice Relf, two Black girls aged 12 and 14 were forcibly sterilized in Alabama without either them or their parents knowing the nature of the operation. It is gross abuse of this kind that the New York City legislation passed in April 1977 was meant to correct. Its guidelines apply to male and female patients in all types of institutions: public, voluntary, and proprietary. The new law requires a 30-day wait between signing the consent form and the surgery (with well-defined exceptions); counseling in the patient's preferred language, and by someone other than the doctor, on the irreversibility of sterilization and alternative methods of birth control; oral and written assurance that no other rights are jeopardized for refusing to be sterilized. And it prohibits soliciting consent from a woman hospitalized for childbirth or abortion.

Several surveys of doctors' attitudes show that an alarmingly high percentage favor compulsory sterilization of welfare mothers. Behind the doctors and the agencies, and certainly behind public agencies such as the Indian Health Service, stand the laws, programs, and policies of the U.S. government. They ultimately will determine this country's course with respect to sterilization and sterilization-abuse. But they are, or should be, subject to our guidance, and they are beginning to attract it.

Posters Against Sterilization Abuse

STOP FORCED STERILIZATION
ALTO A ESTERILIZACIÓN FORZADA

Starting Over
SONIA JAFFE ROBBINS

1977

At Washington Irving High School last Saturday, over 100 women met at a speakout sponsored by the Coalition for Abortion Rights and Against Sterilization Abuse (CARASA). They came because women's right to abortion, so recently won, is now under attack.

In 1973, the Supreme Court had held that the state has no interest in a woman's pregnancy—through the third month. (In the second trimester, the court said states could make regulations in the interest of the mother's health. Only in the last three months of pregnancy could states be concerned with the fetus and restrict abortions.) Last June, the court took this right away from poor women, practically speaking, by declaring that states are not required to provide Medicaid funds for elective abortions, nor are public hospitals required to provide elective abortions at all. At the same time, the Hyde amendment to the HEW appropriations bill, which would forbid Medicaid funds for nearly all abortions, has been passed for the second time in different forms in the House and the Senate.

Eight and a half years ago, the first abortion speakout was organized by the radical feminist group Redstockings, after a number of women had tried to testify at a state public hearing on abortion reform; the only people scheduled to talk were 14 men and a nun. At the first speakout, 12 women—white and mainly middle-class, many with a background in the radical politics of the 60's—spoke about their abortion experience in a way that women never had

before. Instead of whispered horror stories and guilt-ridden secrets, women spoke directly and openly, breaking the taboo against talking about abortion, connecting the personal and the political for the first time.

The speakout no longer has the electrifying impact it had in those early days. Abortion was still illegal or greatly restricted in 1969. Women were mobilizing state by state to liberalize or, if possible, repeal all abortion laws. In 1970 New York became one of a handful of states to make abortion legal up to 24 weeks.

Now, however, women are not fighting to gain a right. They are fighting to keep a right. We know the facts, we know what happens to women when they're faced with the decision of whether or not to have an abortion, and we know what having an abortion means.

The speakout last weekend may well be what its organizers hoped: the beginning of a broadbased counteroffensive against the reactionary tendencies of this decade. Despite limited publicity, a large number of women—and a few men as well—showed up for the kind of event that hasn't been held in many years. In a pass-the-bucket collection, $300 was taken in, an impressive sum for an organization not three months old. But as one speaker pointed out, as she described the need for, among other things, repeated lobbying both in Washington and in Albany, it's the start of a very long fight.

7

Sexuality

As women's liberation politicized the personal, sex was prominent among the newly politicized issues, and feminists exercised substantial influence in reforming American sexual culture. Feminists' attitudes were of course as variable as everyone else's, but in general there were two lines of thought: (1) that women's own sexual drives and preferences had been suppressed by a prudish and male-dominant culture and legal system, and (2) that women were often victimized and exploited by a double standard that trivialized and tolerated men's sexual aggression. These two positions were not necessarily contradictory, and most feminists hewed to a middle-of-the-road position between them, convinced that women needed more sexual freedom and men needed more sexual discipline. At either edge, however, were feminists who leaned more strongly toward one or the other of these two perspectives and thus disagreements arose within the movement. This conflict peaked in the early 1980s when the issue of pornography pitted those characterized as "pro-sex" and "anti-sex" against each other. This chapter will weight the pro-sexual freedom side more heavily because the dangerous and exploitative aspects of sex are discussed in chapter 8.

Feminist influence in making our sexual standards more open and more egalitarian showed in many areas—the media, education, politics, the economy. In the late 1960s when women's liberation first arose, a double standard regarding sex was normal. In colleges, women typically had curfews while men did not; male contraceptives were readily available while female contraceptives were not; boys were expected to tell dirty jokes while girls were not; and men's pre- and extramarital affairs were far more accepted than women's. As with so many cultural revolutions, the feminist impact on sexual norms was soon deformed by commercialization, and many feminists today find themselves objecting to gross and misogynist lyrics, films, and advertising. Nevertheless, it is important to document a feminist vision of sexual freedom without exploitation. Utopian, yes, but without utopian dreams there would be no progress at all.

A new frankness about sex was nurtured by consciousness-raising groups, in which women felt free to say what they really experienced. Women were also able to speak the previously unsayable, even unacknowledgeable, because the movement made them believe that change was possible; it is often too threatening to talk about problems when no solutions seem available. Ruth Davis's witty and painful essay shows what's wrong with labeling feminism as anti-sex, frigid, or even anti-male. She's not against sex, but her husband is oblivious to the fact that his sexual technique offers her no pleasure. It is important to note that the earliest feminist discussion of sex was overwhelmingly heterosexual, and many lesbians felt alienated or even invisible as a result.

Venus Observed
RUTH DAVIS

1972

Christ, here we go again. Why, why, why. Why wait until I'm lying still and comfortable quiet at last in the hollows and crevasses of sheet, mattress, blanket, pillow, limbs adjusted to weight and weightlessness thrust purposely into their appointed places. Feeling heavy, feeling drowsy, mind slipping into the comfortable irrationality of borderline unconsciousness.

And then the magazine. The light. A leap back, and anger as you crack the pages of *Newsweek* into order between their covers and lay it down, knocking over the clock. You turn off the light leaving red and black balls of darkness receding through my lids. No, no, not this time. See how asleep I am. Hear me groan, turn over onto my front with an exaggerated motion, settle resoundingly into the familiar lumpy contours of the mattress, hollowing a place for my cheek turned away to the darkness of my side of the room.

Why no. Why now. Why playful? You lie on your side, knees against my alien length, looking at me, inching across playfully, bouncing the mattress, smiling in the dark. How can you *hear* a smile? You can. Little noises as the corners of the mouth pull inner cheeks away from the teeth.

I am defenseless, defenses down, caught down, for lying on my stomach has left my nightgown twisted about my waist, pulled up. Your hand reaches out and finds flesh, exposed, undefended bottom, too late now to cover, clothe, hide, defend, negate. Hand on bottom. Good, good, try to pretend that it is lying casually as I sleep, that it is just a friendly hand lying on a bottom, warm and aimless.

But the mattress bounces again. Christ, to turn over, to turn over and be polite, to not hurt, to pretend, to smile, to encourage but not encourage. Oh how lovely just to sleep.

Hand hot and moist on my side, knee in my groin. Why a *knee*? No, no. Move, that's better. And your feet, cool and moist. I'm so sleepy, yet I must move my hand where it rests on your side, heavy with sleep, lifeless, a dead thing. I move it up, down, up, down, bend the fingers a little, scratch a little the way you like, effort, effort. You shudder, startle me. Effort, effort, keep moving yet do not wake up. Keep the brain heavy, drowsy, relaxed. Like having to go to the bathroom in the middle of the night, getting up and keeping eyes closed the whole time to keep from waking up. I keep my eyes closed. Roll over, come on top, finish, finish, so I may sleep.

A contradiction here, I know. In awake moments I argue about lack of foreplay, complain that you don't give me time. You laugh at that and I am angered and withdrawn. Yet here I am rushing you, hurry, end this. Is a knee in the groin foreplay? Sometimes you venture to put a hand there but don't know what to do and I pull away, hurting and angering you. Frigid wife. Incompetent husband, should read a good sex book and look at the diagrams. I should show him on myself. How humiliating, like masturbating then.

Ah, the change of position feels good. On my back, legs bent, I guide you in, looking for moisture, finding little, adjusting, moving, hurting, withdrawing, adjusting, back and forth, that's it now you are in. Ah, you say. Ah, I say (for what can it mean?), and push my legs slowly, luxuriously, into the cool of the sheets. To sleep, perchance to dream, aye, there's the rub.

Where was it that I read about the lady who said she thought about designing new hats while she made love? Relegating the whole experience to the proper perspective. Must have been in one of the early marriage manuals we have. Must look it up in the morning. Designing hats. What do I do? Carry on a monologue. Criticize. Say nasty things about your style.

But then to concentrate, to focus attention on that one part, that inward core, the introversion. To feel within and to surround the sensation within, a mind attached by some invisible cord and closed eyes looking inward down and within. But then the anxiety builds. A possibility. But no. Will I? Won't I? It is impossible, ridiculous, I don't care. Get the whole thing over with. But no. Wait.

God, it's stuffy. For God's sake, let up a bit and let me breathe. God, the wetness of my chest and belly, the stickiness between my thighs. I would roll over and sleep now, but how could I? Imagine the pain, the startled look, the incomprehension if I withdrew and simply rolled over, sighed, and slept in the cool part. On my stomach. There must be an Emily Post rule governing this; one doesn't excuse oneself from the party until the guest of honor has left.

Down comes the weight upon me again, on the ribs, pressing into the ground down down down. But after the stillness things seem better. Move a little. There. No. Christ, you are incompetent. I should have known that someone who can't dance can't make love either. It's all a matter of rhythm, of subtlety, of consistency. Just when you begin something good—three strokes—you change the style, the beat, and all is lost. Aimless confusion, chaos! How dramatic I am getting.

But Christ, what kind of rhythm is this! There is ho hope

for me. I'm sticky and numb, thoroughly uncomfortable. In fact, arc you still in there? Yes. Let's hurry it up.

Here comes my passion act. I feel like Snoopy lying on his kennel roof saying, here I am flying over Spain, searching for the Red Baron! Here I am lying in bed doing my passionate act. The girl in 100 dollar misunderstanding "doing all the work." Frantic hip twistings and it's got you, up, down, faster, faster, you're losing control and I am sweating and determined teeth clenched. Gritted. Fingers on your buttocks usually do it, right on the lower spine where your tail ought to be, just up and down on either side. This is wild! Christ, is that for me? Wait, wait, go slower, you have lost me, you have left me, wait! Maybe.

But I've done it. The master craftsman. The work of the ages, the woman, receiving the spilled seed, the last convulsions, the sweat and exhaustion, the still, dead weight of the male body. I actually feel satisfied and proud, even maternal. How can this be? I feel proud of you at *accomplishing*. What a good boy. But damn it, why do you lie there! It is

that awful, frightening moment, the relaxed one when it is all over for you and I know that the movement, the slight stir of withdrawal, will excite me. Now I am ready. Now, when there is no hardness or force, no *insistence*, but only a gentle softness. For Christ's sake get off!

Your semen drains out of me, hot and wet. I try not to think but it builds, it builds, and suddenly the tears are on my face and my mouth is contorted into a hideous shape. The silent pressure, the pressure, the force within that wants to burst, that needs to explode and shatter like a sky rocket. The silent pressure that forces the hot tears to stream down my face into my mouth, to drip onto the floor. Oh God. The desolation. The frustration.

I am a frustrated woman. I am frustrated sexually. Does one say this to one's husband? Does one thrash out, accuse, fight, tear, rip? Shall I go back and announce, I am frustrated, I am desperate? Surely people can tell. As I walk around during the day, the set of my lips and the look of my eyes must reveal my sexual non-existence. The vapid one.

What's an Orgasm?

"The Myth of the Vaginal Orgasm," which could have been an answer to Ruth Davis, became one of the most influential pieces ever produced by the women's liberation movement. At the time, it seemed extraordinarily radical. The denial of the clitoris is a striking example of the power of ideology to obscure basic physiology. Ever since Freud postulated in 1910 that women could have two types of orgasms, clitoral and vaginal, sex experts asserted, without a shred of evidence, that vaginal orgasms were somehow superior and a sign of maturity. Although Kinsey in 1953 and Masters and Johnson in 1966 had recognized the clitoris as the only site of orgasm, it took feminism to force this knowledge into the public. The recognition of clitoral orgasm seemed threatening because it showed that women did not need men for sexual satisfaction. Koedt's article released a veritable explosion of discourse and activity exploring women's sexuality without the blinders imposed by conventional assumptions or prudery. This challenge gave rise to further laboratory research, social surveys, conferences, popular and scholarly writing, instruction manuals for masturbation, and a commercial market for new sexual toys, such as vibrators.

The Myth of the Vaginal Orgasm
ANNE KOEDT
1973

Whenever female orgasm is discussed, a false distinction is made between the vaginal and the clitoral orgasm. Frigidity has generally been defined by men as the failure of women to have vaginal orgasms. Actually, the vagina is not a highly sensitive area and is not physiologically constructed to achieve orgasm. It is the clitoris which is the center of sexual sensitivity and which is the female equivalent of the penis.

I think this explains a great many things. First of all, the fact that the so-called frigidity rate among women is phenomenally high. Rather than tracing female frigidity to the false assumptions about female anatomy, our "experts" have declared frigidity a psychological problem of women. Those women who complained about it were recommended psychiatrists, so that they might discover their "problem"—diagnosed generally as a failure to adjust to their role as women.

The facts of female anatomy and sexual response tell a different story. Although there are many areas for sexual arousal, there is only one area for sexual climax; that area is the clitoris. All orgasms are extensions of sensations from this area. Since the clitoris is not necessarily stimulated sufficiently in the conventional sexual positions, we are left "frigid."

Aside from physical stimulation, which is the common cause of orgasm for most people, there is also stimulation through primarily mental processes. Some women, for example, may achieve orgasm through sexual fantasies, or through fetishes. However, while the stimulation may be psychological the orgasm manifests itself physically. Thus while the cause is psychological, the *effect* is still physical, and the orgasm necessarily takes place in the sexual organ equipped for sexual climax—the clitoris. The orgasm experience may also differ in degree of intensity—some more localized, and some more diffuse and sensitive. But they are all clitoral orgasms.

All this leads to some interesting questions about conventional sex and our role in it. Men have orgasms essentially by friction with the vagina, not the clitoral area, which is external and not able to cause friction the way penetration does. Women have thus been defined sexually in terms of what pleases men; our own biology has not been properly analyzed. Instead, we are fed the myth of the liberated woman and her vaginal orgasm—an orgasm which in fact does not exist.

What we must do is redefine our sexuality. We must discard the "normal" concepts of sex and create new guidelines which take into account mutual sexual enjoyment. While the idea of mutual enjoyment is acknowledged in marriage manuals, it is not followed to its logical conclusion. We must begin to demand that if certain sexual positions now defined as "standard" are not mutually conducive to orgasm, they no longer be defined as standard. New techniques must be used or devised which transform this particular aspect of our current sexual exploitation.

Freud contended that the clitoral orgasm was adolescent, and that upon puberty, when women began having intercourse with men, women should transfer the center of orgasm to the vagina. The vagina, it was assumed, was able to produce a parallel, but more mature orgasm than the clitoris. Much work was done to elaborate on this theory, but not much was done to challenge the basic assumptions.

To fully appreciate this incredible invention, perhaps Freud's general attitude about women must first be realized. Mary Ellman (*Thinking About Women*) said it this way:

> Everything in Freud's patronizing and fearful attitude toward women follows from their lack of a penis, but it is only in his essay *The Psychology of Women* that Freud makes explicit . . . the deprecations of women which are implicit in his work. He then describes women as intellectually less able and prescribes for them the abandonment of the life of the mind, which will interfere with their sexual function. When the psychoanalyzed patient is a male, the analyst sets himself the task of developing the man's capacities; but with women patients, the job is to resign them to the limits of their sexuality. As Mr. Rieff puts it: for Freud, "analysis cannot encourage in women new energies for success and achievement, but only teach them the lesson of rational resignation."

It was Freud's feelings about women's secondary and inferior relationship to men that formed the basis for his theories on female sexuality.

Once having laid down the law about our sexuality, Freud not so strangely discovered a tremendous problem of frigidity in women. His recommended cure for a woman who was frigid was psychiatric care. She was suffering from failure to mentally adjust to her "natural" role as a woman. Frank S. Caprio, a contemporary follower of these ideas, states:

> . . . whenever a woman is incapable of achieving an orgasm via coitus, provided the husband is an adequate partner, and prefers clitoral stimulation to any other form of sexual activity, she can be regarded as suffering from frigidity and requires psychiatric assistance. (*The Sexually Adequate Female.*)

The explanation given was that women were envious of men—"renunciation of womanhood." Thus it was diagnosed as an anti-male phenomenon.

It is important to emphasize that Freud didn't base his theory upon a study of the woman's anatomy, but rather upon his assumptions of women as an inferior appendage to the man, and her consequent social and psychological role. In their attempts to deal with the ensuing problem of mass frigidity, Freudians created elaborate mental gymnastics. Marie Bonaparte, in *Female Sexuality*, goes so far as to suggest surgery to help women back on their rightful path. Having discovered a strange connection between the non-frigid woman and the location of the clitoris near the vagina,

> It then occurred to men that where, in certain women, this gap was excessive, and the clitoridal fixation obdurate, a clitoridal-vaginal reconciliation might be effected by surgical means, which would then benefit the normal erotic function. Professor Halban, of Vienna, as much biologist as surgeon, became interested in the problem and worked out a simple operative technique. In this, the suspensory ligament of the clitoris was severed and the clitoris secured to the underlying structures, thus fixing it in a lower position, with eventual reduction of the labia minora.

But the severest damage was not in the area of surgery, where Freudians absurdly ran around trying to change the anatomy to fit their basic assumptions. The worst damage was done to the mental health of women who either suffered silently with self-blame or flocked to the psychiatrists, looking desperately for the hidden and terrible repression that kept from them their vaginal destiny.

One may perhaps at first claim that these are unknown and unexplored areas, but upon closer examination this is certainly not true today, nor was it true even in the past. For example, men have known that women suffered from frigidity often during intercourse. So the problem was there. Also, there is much specific evidence. Men knew that the clitoris was and is the essential organ for masturbation, whether in children or adult women. So obviously women made it clear where *they* thought their sexuality was located. Men also seem suspiciously aware of the clitoral powers during "foreplay" when they want to arouse women and produce the necessary lubrication for penetration. Foreplay is a concept created for male purposes, but works to the disadvantage of women since as soon as she is aroused the male changes to vaginal stimulation and leaves her both aroused and unsatisfied.

It has also been known that women need no anesthesia inside the vagina during surgery, thus pointing to the fact that the vagina is in fact not a highly sensitive area.

Today, with extensive knowledge of anatomy, with Kelly, Kinsey, and Masters and Johnson, to mention just a few sources, there is no ignorance on the subject. There are, however, social reasons why this knowledge has not been popularized. We are living in a male society which has sought change in women's role.

Rather than starting with what women *ought* to feel, it would seem logical to start out with what the anatomical facts are regarding the clitoris and vagina.

The Clitoris is a small equivalent of the penis, except for the fact that the urethra does not go through it as in the man's penis. Its erection is similar to the male erection, and the head of the clitoris has the same type of structure and function as the head of the penis. G. Lombard Kelly, in *Sexual Feeling in Married Men and Women,* says:

> The head of the clitoris is also composed of erectile tissue, and it possesses a very sensitive epithelium or surface covering, supplied with special nerve endings called genital corpuscles, which are peculiarly adapted for sensory stimulation that under proper mental conditions terminates in the sexual orgasm. No other part of the female generative tract has such corpuscles.

The clitoris has no other function than that of sexual pleasure.

The Vagina—Its functions are related to the reproductive function. Principally,

1. menstruation,
2. receive penis,
3. hold semen, and
4. birth passage.

The interior of the vagina, which according to the defenders of the vaginally caused orgasm is the center and producer of the orgasm, is:

> like nearly all other internal body structures, poorly supplied with end organs of touch. The internal entodermal origin of the lining of the vagina makes it similar in this respect to the rectum and other parts of the digestive tract. (Kinsey, *Sexual Behavior in the Human Female.*)

The degree of insensitivity inside the vagina is so high that "Among the women who were tested in our gynecologic sample, less than 14% were at all conscious that they had been touched." (Kinsey.)

Even the importance of the vagina as an *erotic* center (as opposed to an orgasmic center) has been found to be minor.

Other Areas—Labia minora and the vestibule of the vagina. These two sensitive areas may trigger off a clitoral orgasm. Because they can be effectively stimulated during "normal" coitus, though infrequently, this kind of stimulation is incorrectly thought to be vaginal orgasm. However, it is important to distinguish between areas which can stimulate the clitoris, incapable of producing the orgasm themselves, and the clitoris:

> Regardless of what means of excitation is used to bring the individual to the state of sexual climax, the sensation is perceived by the genital corpuscles and is localized where they are situated: in the head of the clitoris or penis. (Kelly)

Psychologically Stimulated Orgasm—Aside from the

above mentioned direct and indirect stimulation of the clitoris, there is a third way an orgasm may be triggered. This is through mental (cortical) stimulation, where the imagination stimulates the brain, which in turn stimulates the genital corpuscles of the glans to set off an orgasm.

Confusion—Because of the lack of knowledge of their own anatomy, some women accept the idea that an orgasm felt during "normal" intercourse was vaginally caused. This confusion is caused by a combination of 2 factors. One, failing to locate the center of the orgasm, and two, by a desire to fit her experience to the male defined idea of sexual normalcy. Considering that women know little about their anatomy, it is easy to be confused.

Deception—The vast majority of women who claim vaginal orgasm to their men are faking it to, as Ti-Grace Atkinson says, "get the job." In a new bestselling Danish book, *I Accuse*, Mette Ejlersen specifically deals with this common problem, which she calls the "sex comedy." This comedy has many causes. First of all, the man brings a great deal of pressure to bear on the woman, because he considers his ability as a lover at stake. So as not to offend his ego, the woman will comply with the prescribed role and go through simulated ecstasy. In some of the other Danish women mentioned, women who were left frigid were turned off to sex, and pretended vaginal orgasm to hurry up the sex act. Others admitted that they had faked vaginal orgasm to catch a man. In one case, the woman pretended vaginal orgasm to get him to leave his first wife, who admitted being vaginally frigid. Later she was forced to continue the deception, since obviously she couldn't tell him to stimulate her clitorally.

Many more were simply afraid to establish their right to equal enjoyment, seeing the sexual act as being primarily for the man's benefit, and any pleasure that the woman got as an added extra.

Other women, with just enough ego to reject the man's idea that they needed psychiatric care, refused to admit their frigidity. They wouldn't accept self-blame, but they didn't know how to solve the problem, not knowing the psychological facts about themselves. So they were left in a peculiar limbo.

Again, perhaps one of the most infuriating and damaging results of this whole charade has been that women who were perfectly healthy sexually were taught that they were not. So aside from being sexually deprived, these women were told to blame themselves when they deserved no blame. Looking for a cure to a problem that has none, can lead women on an endless path of self-hatred and insecurity.

WHY MEN MAINTAIN THE MYTH

1: *Sexual Penetration is Preferred*—The best stimulant for the penis is the woman's vagina. It supplies the necessary friction and lubrication. From a strictly technical point of view this position offers the best physiological condition, even though the man may try other positions for variation.

2: *The Invisible Woman*—One of the elements of male chauvinism is the refusal or inability to see women as total, separate human beings. Rather than this approach, men have chosen to define women only in terms of how they benefited men's lives. Sexually, a woman was not seen as an individual wanting to share equally in the sexual act, any more than she was seen as a person with independent desires when she did anything else in society. Thus, it was easy to make up what was convenient about women; for on top of that, society has been a function of male interests, and women were not organized to form even a vocal opposition to the male experts.

3: *The Penis As the Epitome of Masculinity*—Men define their lives greatly in terms of masculinity. It is a universal ego builder. Masculinity is defined culturally by what is the most non-female.

The essence of chauvinism is not the practical, economic, comfortable services women supply. It is the psychological superiority. This negative kind of definition of self, rather than a positive definition based upon one's own achievements and development of one's potentials, has of course chained the victim and the oppressor both. But *by far* the most brutalized of the two is the victim.

An analogy is racism, where the white racist compensates for his feelings of unworthiness by creating an image of the black man (it is primarily a male struggle) as biologically inferior to him. Because of his position in a white male power structure, the white man can socially enforce this mythical division.

To the extent that men try to rationalize and justify male superiority through physical differentiation, masculinity may be symbolized by being the *most* muscular, the most hairy, having the deepest voice, and the biggest penis. Women, on the other hand, are approved of (i.e., called feminine) if they are weak, petite; shave their legs; have high soft voices.

Since the clitoris is almost identical to the penis, one finds a great deal of evidence of men in various societies trying to either ignore the clitoris and emphasize the vagina (as did Freud), or, as in many places in the Mideast, actually performing clitoridectomy. Freud saw this ancient and still practiced custom as a way of further "feminizing" the female by removing this cardinal vestige of her masculinity. It should be noted also that a big clitoris is considered ugly and "masculine." Some cultures pour chemicals on the clitoris to make it shrivel up into proper size.

It seems clear to me that men in fact fear the clitoris as a threat to masculinity.

4: *Sexually Expendable Male*—Men fear that they will become sexually expendable if the clitoral organ is substituted for the vaginal as the basic pleasure for women. Actually this has a great deal of validity if one considers *only* the anatomy. The position of the penis inside the vagina, while perfect for reproduction, does not usually stimulate an orgasm in women because the clitoris is located externally and higher up. Women must rely upon indirect stimulation in the "normal" position.

Lesbian sexuality could make an excellent case, based on anatomical data, for the irrelevancy of the male organ.

Albert Ellis says something to the effect that a man without a penis can make a woman an excellent lover.

Considering that the vagina is very desirable from a man's point of view, purely on physical grounds, one begins to see the dilemma for men. And it forces us to discard many "physical" arguments explaining why women go to bed with men. What is left, it seems to me, are primarily psychological reasons why women select men at the exclusion of women as sexual partners.

5: *Control of Women*—One reason given to explain the Mideastern practice of clitoridectomy is that it will keep the women from straying. By removing the sexual organ capable of orgasm, it must be assumed that her sexual drive will diminish. Considering how much men look upon their women as property, particularly in very backward nations, we should begin to consider a great deal more why it is not in the men's interest to have women totally free sexually. The double standard, as practiced for example in Latin America, is set up to keep the woman as total property of the husband, while he is free to have affairs as he wishes.

6: *Lesbianism and Bisexuality*—Aside from the strictly anatomical reasons why women might seek women lovers, there is a fear on men's part that women will seek the company of other women on a full, human basis. The recognition of clitoral orgasm as fact would threaten the heterosexual *institution*. For it would indicate that sexual pleasure was obtainable from either men *or* women, thus making heterosexuality not an absolute, but an option. It would thus open up the whole question of *human* sexual relationships beyond the confines of the present male-female role system.

The Happiest Day of My Life

Liberating Masturbation
BETTY DODSON

1975

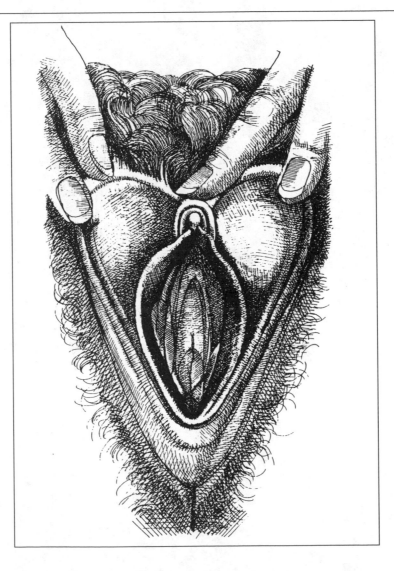

My First Orgasm

KAREN SANDLER

1974

So how would you feel if you didn't know me and I just came up to you and said, "Hi there. My name is Karen and I had my first orgasm on April 19, 1974 and my second one on April 24, and I would like to rent a billboard on Wilshire Blvd. with I CAME, I CAME, I CAME in big red letters and would you like to donate to this worthy cause?" Well, that's what I feel like doing—especially after having worked so hard in a special group to achieve this most worthy of ends.

I first heard about groups for preorgasmic women at a conference for women in psychology in February. There Lonnie Barbach spoke of her group work in the Bay Area with preorgasmic women. What turned me on the most was her success rate—over 90%. "Ain't that a kick in the ass," I thought to myself. I was ready to commute to San Francisco every week, when I heard that she was going to train therapists here in L.A.

My group started the beginning of April. At first there were four of us—ages mid 20's to mid 30's, single, married, gay and straight—plus two leaders. Later in the group one woman dropped out for health reasons.

We met two nights a week, $1^1/_2$ hours each time for five weeks with an hour's worth of homework each night. But such homework like you've never had—homework designed to acquaint yourself with how you look and what you feel like. Basically, we were told at first to just look at ourselves naked in a full length mirror and touch ourselves without thoughts of getting turned on. After that we were told to masturbate, and masturbate, and masturbate, and masturbate. Meanwhile in group we talked of our fears and the ugly messages we had received from parents and society in general concerning our sexuality. We talked of how we were taught to be sexy looking but non-sexual in actions until we married Prince Charming who would know exactly what to do in bed. Or the age-old message of "Don't masturbate. It's not nice." We had booklets showing in detail the female genitalia, women masturbating, and women climaxing. We were given excerpts from pornographic literature (so when are women going to start writing good porno instead of the male shit that's available). We talked of feeling good, fantasizing about any turn on without feeling guilty—like making it with your local naked nun, your dog, a gym teacher, your doctor, your priest, a lampost, and yes, even your lover. The only thing we didn't have was a lecture demonstration. We laughed a lot and cried and got angry and finally two of the three of us had orgasms.

Have I changed? You better believe it, Sweetie. I'm less tense, more giving to other people, stronger about myself, and hardly had any cramps during my last period (for the first time in about 3 years). Having had an orgasm has not changed my whole life like I used to fantasize it would, but it certainly has made a difference.

> Women's increasing sexual assertiveness was not, contrary to stereotype, just a white middle-class phenomenon. The following resolutions came out of the first national Chicana conference (*La Conferencia de Mujeres por la Raza*) held in Houston, Texas, in 1971, attended by over 600 women. The radicalism of these resolutions is especially great because of the power of the Catholic Church among Chicanas and its insistence on the repression of female sexuality and reproductive freedom.

Workshop Resolutions
FIRST NATIONAL CHICANA CONFERENCE

We feel that in order to provide an effective measure to correct the many sexual hangups facing the Chicano community the following resolutions should be implemented:

1. Sex is good and healthy for both Chicanos and Chicanas and we must develop this attitude.
2. We should destroy the myth that religion and culture control our sexual lives.
3. We recognize that we have been oppressed by religion and that the religious writing was done by *men* and interpreted by *men*. Therefore, for those who desire religion, they should interpret their Bible, or Catholic rulings according to their own feelings, what they think is right, without any guilt complexes.
4. Mothers should teach their sons to respect women as human beings who are equal in every respect. *No double standard.*
5. Women should go back to the communities and form discussion and action groups concerning sex education.
6. Free, legal abortions and birth control for the Chicano community, controlled by *Chicanas*. As Chicanas we have the right to control our own bodies.

"Liberate your mind and the body will follow. . . ."

"*A quitarnos todos nuestros complejos sexuales para tener una vida mejor y feliz*" (Let's cast off all our sexual complexes to have a better and happier life).

RESOLUTIONS:

1. We, as *mujeres de La Raza,* recognize the Catholic Church as an oppressive institution and do hereby resolve to break away and not go to it to bless our unions.

2. Whereas: Unwanted pregnancies are the basis of many social problems, and

Whereas: The role of Mexican-American women has traditionally been limited to the home, and

Whereas: The need for self-determination and the right to govern their own bodies is a necessity for the freedom of all people, therefore,

BE IT RESOLVED: That the National Chicana Conference go on record as supporting free family planning and free and legal abortions for all women who want or need them.

3. Whereas: Due to socio-economic and cultural conditions, Chicanas are often heads of households, i.e., widows, divorcees, unwed mothers, or deserted mothers, or must work to supplement family income, and

Whereas: Chicana motherhood should not preclude educational, political, social, and economic advancement, and

Whereas: There is a critical need for a 24-hour child-care center in Chicano communities, therefore,

BE IT RESOLVED: That the National Chicana Conference go on record as recommending that every Chicano community promote and set up 24-hour day-care facilities, and that it be further resolved that these facilities will reflect the concept of *La Raza* as the united family, and on the basis of brotherhood (*La Raza*), so that men, women, young and old assume the responsibility for the love, care, education, and orientation of all the children of *Aztlán.*

4. Whereas: Dr. Goldzieher of SWRF has conducted an experiment on Chicana women of westside San Antonio, Texas, using a new birth control drug, and

Whereas: No human being should be used for experimental purposes, therefore,

BE IT RESOLVED: That this Conference send telegrams to the American Medical Association condemning this act. Let it also be resolved that each Chicana women's group and each Chicana present at the conference begin a letter writing campaign to:

> Dr. Joseph Goldzieher
> Director, SW Foundation for Research and
>   Education
> San Antonio, Texas

Feminists, of course, did not invent lesbianism. Nevertheless women's liberation did open up protected space and opportunity for exploring a new dimension of relationships with women. Coming out is not always a process of leaping from one identity to another; in fact, the supportive feminist context made it possible for women to try out new sexual and emotional options and to resist being straight-jacketed into a fixed category. Although feminist groups provided a few small safe spaces, B.K.O. nevertheless confronted homophobia, discrimination, and the loss of heterosexual privilege. Note that she chose not to use her real name, even though she was writing for a feminist magazine.

It Just Happened
B.K.O.

1971

I am a woman, and I am in love with another woman. Through our relationship I have lost my security—my stable little "niche"—in our society. I wonder if a straight person can fully comprehend the significance of that statement. I love another woman; therefore I am queer, perverted, abnormal, and a lesbian. Oh, the connotations of that word—every time someone talks to me about those "horrible dykes" and the "disgusting" things that they do, I break up. The same thing happens when a man tells me that I am a true "man's woman" or some such nonsense. Thank heaven that I have a sense of humor. (The only defense that a gay women has in our society is her sense of humor. Without it she will die a small piece each day, until she becomes a walking shell of bitterness and disillusionment.)

I didn't plan on loving a woman—it just happened. We were very young—barely into our teens—when we fell in love. We were so happy, radiantly happy. Excited and filled with wonder; and blindly innocent and naive, we decided to share the beauty of our experience with a mutual friend. Our friend told us that we were violating the laws of nature; that we would end up destroying each other. She said that society wouldn't recognize our love, wouldn't allow us to exist, would condemn and crush us at every turn. From that moment—our love went underground.

At that time we were not even lovers. Our relationship was built on mutual love and understanding, not physical desire. It took us more than a year to shed the social barriers and become lovers. I think that some people will understand when I say that we became lovers when there were no more words.

During our years in high school and college we lived in a schizophrenic world. Alone we talked, dreamed, and loved; outwardly we were close friends. We dated frequently and eventually we both entered into emotional and sexual relationships with men, but our love did not change.

We never thought of ourselves as homosexuals. Even though we were lovers, we were still repulsed by the concept that we held of Lesbians. We thought of the sterile, bitter old spinster in severely tailored tweed suits who would literally faint if a man touched her. Or, we pictured the traditional "Butch" stereotype; the short-haired, flat-chested, heavy-set, foul-mouthed, hard-drinking, hard-fighting, masculine, male-imitator who pinches women on subways and buses, and who spends twenty-four hours a day, every day, either in bed or in rest rooms trying to lure innocent young girls into her lair.

We were both active in school and we had many friends, but we never divulged our secret. We were afraid of reprisals.

In the past year we have gradually begun to "come out." We are not completely open and I am not certain that we will ever be that open. If we were to just stop and say "Hey world: look at us, we are in love, we are happy, we are beautiful!" the repercussions would reverberate in innocent quarters. Our love would become a weapon of destruction aimed at those we hold very dear.

When we decided to emerge from our shell we told one of our closest friends. You cannot imagine our surprise and amazement when we discovered that he was also gay. Here were three people who had been friends for a number of years and who had never trusted each other enough to be honest.

We knew that to preserve our sanity we had to find people who would accept us for what we were. We had to find a place where we could be open. All too soon we discovered that the only places for homosexuals to meet were the gay bars. We didn't even know which bars were gay and we were terrified of the prospect of entering a place so foreign to our experience. Isn't it strange that the only place we could acknowledge our love was in a bar?

After weeks of coaxing, our friend finally persuaded us to accompany him to a gay bar. We were nervous and afraid, but in our desperation we knew that we had no alternative. We discovered that all of our pre-conceived opinions and ideas were false. The bar was not a cesspool of human degradation as we had supposed. It was rather nice as bars go. However, we still couldn't bring ourselves to visit the rest room. Suppose one of those tough "Butches" was hiding in there just waiting for innocent young things like ourselves?

We soon realized that the homosexual world, like its heterosexual counterpart, is male-oriented. For the most part, the bars are run by gay men for other gay men.

Through my experiences at the bars I have learned that the homosexual population is far larger than I ever imagined. I have also learned that the majority of Lesbians are just like my lover and I. My greatest shock has been seeing people at the bars that I have known in my "straight" life. Former teachers, classmates, neighbors, and dates keep appearing; and though it has happened frequently, it still amazes me.

My purpose in writing this article has been to educate. To put it bluntly, I am sick and tired of talking to women who say that they believe in the women's movement and yet, who wouldn't even be speaking to me if they knew that I was gay.

What will happen to those young girls who are just beginning to recognize their Lesbianism? Will they be relegated to the bars? Will they find acceptance in the Women's Liberation movement? We need the support of our sisters, and even though you might not think so at this point, you also need our support. Shalom, my sisters, shalom.

Smash Phallic Imperialism
SUE KATZ

Sex is an institution. In an oppressive society like amerika, it reflects the same ideology as other major institutions. It is goal-oriented, profit & productivity oriented. It is a prescribed system, with a series of correct & building activities aimed toward the production of a single goal: climax.

It's also a drag. For women, in a culture based on our oppression, heterosexual sex is a product we have had to turn out. To encourage us, we are given two minutes of this, a few moments of that, a couple minutes at something else all aimed towards the Great Penetration and the Big Come. There is great pressure to have an orgasm. Sex without orgasm is a failure, it's a drag, it's incomplete, and very very sad. (Just like marriage is not real until it is "consummated.") Because of phallic imperialism built upon Freud's ignorance of the female body, orgasm is supposed to come from intercourse. That's just terrific for boys, but since our orgasm-producing organ is the clitoris, external to the vagina—contradicting capitalist sexist physiology—many women don't produce the appropriate orgasm thru heterosexuality. By that criteria, they are frigid.

I'm a lesbian. A lot of people can't figure out "what we do," how we make love without a penis around for the final consummation. A lot of boys have these ideas of dildos and bananas. Sex as an institution is so totally tied up with the penis and its goal that boys assume there must be some poor substitute for their noble item.

I always hated sex with men. The pressure of the goal, the rigidity of the process and ends was always totally unsatisfactory. Whenever I hear the word "sex," all those shitty experiences I had with men come to mind. I cannot separate the word "sex" from the phallic tyranny I suffered from for so many years.

For me, coming out meant an end to sex. It's dead and gone in my life. I reject that institution totally. Sex means oppression, it means exploitation. It serves the needs of boys. It has little to do with pleasure for the greatest mass of oppressed people: women. Physical contact and feelings have taken a new liberatory form. And we call that sensuality. The women's movement in general, especially at the beginning, and gay feminism now is a fantastically sensual experience for me. I love my body and the bodies of my sisters. Physicality is now a creative non-institutionalized experience. It is touching and rubbing and cuddling and fondness. It is holding and rocking and kissing and licking. It's only goal is closeness and pleasure. It does not exist for the Big Orgasm. It exists for feeling nice. Our sensuality may or may not include genital experience, that may or may not be the beginning or the ending of the experience. It may be anywhere, or nowhere.

To make good love with women, I don't want to have to "produce" anything. Except pleasure. And that can be at any level or in any form. The sensuality I feel has transformed my politics, has solved the contradiction between my mind and my body because the energies for our feminist revolution are the same as the energies of our love for women. When we feel good about someone we may sleep together. That could mean a lot of things from hugs to climax to cuddling to being very close but not touching. If we feel good in a group we may have a pajama party, which would be called an "orgy" inside the institution of straight sex. That could be a genital thing or not. We are free to act without pressure. I refuse to feel like I must make a decision about whether to "put out" or not. There is no such thing as putting out among us. There is no set physical goal to our sexuality. There is no sex.

The whole language is oppressive. It is white male–oriented and heterosexual. One word that must go is "sex" because that describes a way of being physical that can only draw up very bad memories for a lot of us. We must use it only in referring to that oppressive institution, not to any new forms we are developing. Having sex means accepting a set of criteria for "success" that we did not set up and develop among ourselves.

Sensuality is formless and amorphous. It can grow and expand as we feel it. It is shared by everyone involved. It isn't something one puts out for another. Sex with boys was like doing alienated labor so that one with power could make good profit off of my surplus labor. Sexuality with women is a collective experience growing out of our struggle.

Smashing the notion of sex, getting away from these concepts so intimately tied up with the penis, helps us destroy roles. One thing we realized in our group of gay feminists is that the word "lover" doesn't describe anything for us anymore very much. It is very hard to tell who is whose lover, because that is a condition determined by genital contact in our society. But among us, we have a very brazen set-up. I don't sleep with the same women every nite. I might cuddle with one sister tonite because we were together and felt close and I might crash on some mattress with a bunch of women tomorrow because we all danced together half the nite. If your lover is someone you feel emotional and physical attractions to and where there is

some kind of mutual commitment, then we are surely the biggest group of floozies in town. It's so wonderful. Without that kind of exclusive coupling sex and lovers breed, people cannot fall into traditional roles so easily. Because each time you sleep with someone you have to make the decision that time. Dependent exclusionary relationships take away free will. It becomes an institutionalized habit to sleep together regularly and there is not usually a fresh decision each time. Amongst us, our getting together is dependent on the reality of the present, not on the promises of more. Sensuality is something that can be very collective. Sex is private and tense. Sensuality is something you want your best friends to feel and act on with your other best friends. Sex is something you want power and territorial rights over. Sex is localized in the pants and limited by that. Sensuality is all over and grows always. Sex is pinpointed in the pants because the penis is there and the penis is, if not the material source, the material basis for power in amerika. If you don't have one you are fucked over by those who do. If you don't have capital you get fucked over by those who do. Unless you attach yourself to someone who has it so that you can serve them in exchange for protection (known as marriage). Sperm is coin. And that whole system of exchange necessarily excludes us as lesbians. We can't pretend that those few flaps of skin that make up the masculine apparatus are just a few objective ectodermal gatherings. That stuff is the proof of a right to have access to privilege. Some boys reject that privilege, but they always have the possibility of whipping it out in an emergency and asserting their privilege.

We are building a revolution which isn't based on such drivel. And we must have a new language and aesthetic to describe it. Lesbianism is not a sexual perversion: it has nothing to do with sex. It is not another way to "do it": it is a whole other way to have contact. Sex is a phallic term and we are involved in building a humane world. It's like when people talk about being bisexual it blows my mind. It's like saying that if you have an apple and an orange you have two apples because they're both fruit.

Heterosexuality and lesbianism are two forms of physical contact. But that's as far as the similarity goes. I sleep with women, make love with women, am a woman, a lesbian. But I don't have sex with anyone. If I had sex, I could have it with a boy, but that would be a whole other trip from what I am feeling about my gay sensuality. It would be another experience altogether, not a different form of gay sexuality. I would be reentering an institution the structure of which is inherently oppressive to me, although particular experiences might be of reasonable fun. But radical lesbian sensuality is a form which I myself am helping create. It is not an institution existing outside of me, like sex is. It is me, us, as it comes out of our new consciousness.

In 1976 an antipornography movement was growing among feminists, although it reached its peak of visibility a decade later. By the early 1980s, when it was at its most powerful, the antiporn forces were calling for legislation and civil suits that amounted to censorship, and as a result many feminists did not agree. But in the early women's liberation period, the movement was united in focussing on violent imagery (as opposed to merely sexual imagery) and in relying on a strategy of protest and boycotts. The boycott initiated with this document followed a successful campaign to remove the Rolling Stones's "Black and Blue" billboard (which depicted a sexualized bruised woman with hands tied above her head and the slogan "I'm Black and Blue from the Rolling Stones and I love it") from the Sunset Strip in Los Angeles. This boycott was also victorious, and Warner/Elektra/Atlantic—the industry leader—prohibited images of violence against women on its album covers, but only after three years of a national campaign.

The early feminist antipornography campaign, as illustrated by the press release below, targeted pornographic representations of violence and argued that violent imagery trivialized and condoned violence against women, not that it caused such violence. By contrast, 1980s anti-porn feminists began to argue that representation of even peaceable sexual acts not only encouraged but actively caused violence against women. In fact, the leading feminist anti-porn advocates of the 1980s, such as Andrea Dworkin and Catharine MacKinnon, argue that pornography not only causes violence but is itself violence against women.

Like so many other feminist activists, Julia London came to the women's liberation movement from New Left activism. She had been an organizer for the United Farm Workers, a predominantly Mexican American union that sparked widespread support for its unionization struggle against western agribusiness. Throughout the U.S. tens of thousands joined in demonstrations, picketing and boycotting lettuce and grapes. London used her organizing skills and understanding of peaceful direct action in becoming the first staff person for the feminist antipornography campaign.

Boycotting Pornographic Record Covers
JULIA LONDON

1976

A Statement Presented by Julia London at Press Conference Held December 10, 1976 at Tower Records, Hollywood, California

California NOW, Inc. of the National Organization for Women, in conjunction with Women Against Violence Against Women (WAVAW) is calling for a boycott of Warner/Elektra/Atlantic Products. Executives of WEA Inc., Atlantic Records, Elektra Records, and Warner Brothers Records failed to indicate by December 6, 1976 compliance with NOW's demands to cease and desist from further use of sex violence and violence against women in advertising and on album covers, to cancel further abusive and offensive advertising, and to furnish by December 15th, 1976 proof of an immediate initiation of the withdrawal from retail outlets of all such advertising and promotion, including album covers. WEA labels include Atco, Atlantic, Asylum, Elektra, Reprise, Nonesuch, and Warner Brothers.

WEA has refused to assume social responsibility for its advertising policies.

WEA's album covers and/or promotion copy have included portrayals of women as willing victims of battering, as implied targets of gang rape, as victims of abduction and targets of abuse, and as being sexually attractive as victims, asking for it. Such advertising perpetuates the myth that women are willing, natural victims and contributes to an environment that trivializes and condones violent behavior towards women. This advertising is being used at a time when rape is increasing and when a conservative estimate puts the number of battered women in the United States at *one million.*

Communications research indicates that violence viewed in media results in at least indifference to violence. Advertising people acknowledge that advertising reinforces stereotypes. Members of the psychiatric profession have noted that as rape becomes a more common element in entertainment, rapists are more resistant to therapy.

Rape crisis hotline personnel and others have noted that many men, including law enforcement officers, court and rehabilitation persons and law makers do *not* perceive violent, aggressive denigrative forced sex and battering as an act of assault—a criminal act—especially in "domestic disputes." Such lack of consciousness is illustrated by two daily life examples: by Long Beach Superior Court Judge Charles Litwin's recent sentencing of a *confessed* rapist to 30 *weekends* in jail and by the rehiring of New York weather announcer Tex Antoin after an initial suspension because of the large negative audience response made to his flip comment on the report of a near rape of an 8-year old child.

We do not call for censorship. We demand social responsibility. It is demeaning and contemptuous for members of the recording industry to hide behind the gloss of artistic freedom and a pious resistance to "censorship," especially in light of the fact that the industry self-regulation with regards to glorifying and romanticizing of drug abuse acknowledges our premises. This issue is not one of obscenity but of the perpetuation and condoning of assaults, long term physical and emotional injuries, and of deaths to women. We demanded and expected WEA to be a leader in assuming social responsibility as it already is a leader in sales and prestige.

We refuse to be victims and we refuse to allow the perpetuation and promotion of myths about women being willing victims and of men being animals. We suspend our economic support of an industry that attacks our health, safety, dignity and personhood. We call on others to do the same.

To the women and men who are not with us today we ask that you go to your local stores. Point out to the managers that these types of graphics are a crime against women. Ask that they be returned to the distributor.

We urge other groups to join us in this boycott. Women's cries have not been enough. We will have to be visible through the economic vote.

The women's movement was, and still is, divided about how to approach prostitution and prostitutes' organizations, such as COYOTE, or "Call Off Your Old Tired Ethics." Some feminists condemned the commodification of the female body and sex. They compared prostitutes to wives, arguing that both were forced to exchange sex for economic support; and they emphasized the coercive aspects of prostitution. Others considered prostitution merely as a job. In comparison to other jobs available to women, prostitution could bring high pay and freedom to control one's working conditions and hours, but it was also dangerous and often controlled by male pimps. In the 1980s, as women's movements arose throughout the world, U.S. feminists became active in opposing the international sex trade. The exploitive, brutal, and coercive characteristics of sex work again became the major theme. Feminists were unanimous in calling for prosecution of clients rather than prostitutes, although only some feminists supported the decriminalization of prostitution altogether. Feminists saw in prostitution a symbolic representation of all women's situation.

HIRE (Hooking Is Real Employment)

HIRE (Hooking Is Real Employment) is the Georgia sister organization to COYOTE (Call Off Your Old Tired Ethics), which was the first prostitution advocacy effort in this country, founded in San Francisco. HIRE's goals are as follows:

- To lobby for the decriminalization of prostitution;

- To claim prostitutes' rightful place in the women's movement;

- To provide an outreach program for prostitutes.

If we agree that prostitutes should be free to pursue their work, there are two ways by which this may be done—legalization and decriminalization. By legalizing prostitution, government agencies maintain strict control and, typically, over-regulate. Our taxes would pay for yet another and unnecessary bureaucracy. If the brothels of Nevada are any indication of how the state is "helping" prostitutes by imposing twelve-hour work shifts (14–18 hour shifts are common), by forbidding a woman's right to refusal and restricting those areas that prostitutes may frequent, then we do not need or want this kind of "help." In effect, the government and the brothel-owners become the pimp in exploiting the prostitute.

If we decriminalize prostitution, then all criminal statutes regarding prostitution would be repealed from state law. All laws preventing child prostitution and those laws prohibiting the forcing of people to become prostitutes would remain. Enforcement of health inspections could be administered by the health departments as is done for the restaurant business. All aspects of the prostitution business would be removed from the Police Department.

Decriminalization maximizes the possibility for women to operate as independent contractors and to form businesses or cooperatives among themselves. *Hooking Is Real Employment.*

Many feminists consider prostitutes to be traitors to the women's movement. Prostitutes are singled out as the worst perpetrators of the subjugation of women. The scorn and self-righteous hypocrisy of feminists around the issue of prostitution betrays a "buying into" of the traditional male supremacist cultural values of good women–bad women–madonna–whore. Males in power may continue to maintain control over women as long as the fear of certain groups of women is perpetuated by women themselves. Lesbians and women of color should well understand these "divide and conquer" tactics. To be strong, we must fight together, but not against each other.

Prostitutes do *not* perpetuate the male power system any more than do secretaries or factory workers. When prostitutes are scorned and viewed as a group apart from the rest of women, this additional division of the movement limits the potential strength of women united. It is time for prostitutes to claim their rightful place in the women's movement. We are calling for your support. To be a feminist *and* a prostitute is not a contradiction in terms: prostitutes are strong, independent women who are struggling to govern their own bodies. *Hooking Is Real Employment.*

- There are approximately 1,300,000 prostitutes in the United States, or about 1% of American women, including housewives and career women moonlighting as call girls. Perhaps 13% of the female population has worked as prostitutes at some point in their lives.

- The average client is a white, middle-class, middle-aged and married businessman.

- Police officers arrest prostitutes by disguising themselves as customers. They will approach women until one is deceived into agreeing to perform sex for money. The woman is then arrested for "offering and agreeing to an act of prostitution." It is practically impossible to arrest a prostitute *without* the use of entrapment, invasion of privacy or the use of discriminatory laws or tactics. Few officers are assigned to the task of arresting pimps, although that is a more serious offense in the Penal Code.

- It cost the San Francisco taxpayers in 1978, $2,400 to arrest and keep one prostitute in jail for two weeks.

- About 45% of the women now in jail are there for prostitution; 70% were originally arrested for prostitution. That is, even if they are now serving time for another crime, i.e., bank robbery or drug smuggling, their first arrest, the one that initiated them into the penal system, was for prostitution. (This is obviously a system that breeds rather than deters criminal activity.)

- Eighty-five percent of women jailed for prostitution are women of color. Customers are rarely arrested more than once in the same city and are infrequently jailed.

Objectification, Harassment, Violence

The connection between violence against women and the culture of sexism was brought to public attention by second-wave feminism. Targets of feminist protest ranged from the ubiquitous display of women's bodies and body parts to sell goods, to Hollywood romances in which women were represented as passive, preferring sexual surrender to sexual choice. Feminists distinguished sexual freedom and appreciation for female bodies—which they affirmed—from exploitive uses, whether by advertisers or individuals. This distinction is not always easy to make, because the line between the aesthetic and sensual pleasures of sex and exploitation is often blurred. One result was disagreement among feminists about how to respond to pornography. (This conflict became public and extremely divisive in the early 1980s, when some feminists joined conservatives to demand legal measures against pornography while others insisted on freedom of expression and even regarded some forms of porn as potentially artistic, liberating, enjoyable, and/or educational. Pornography is discussed in chapter 7.)

Feminists agreed, however, about the damaging effects of the objectification of female bodies. Linda Phelps dissects the process that makes women's bodies into spectacles, alienating women from their own sexual potential. Her argument is not anti-sex. Rather, she is concerned about the damages to women resulting from being forced into sexual passivity, both by men's individual behaviors and by corporate profit-seeking.

Death in the Spectacle
LINDA PHELPS

1971

In the last few years, the so-called sexual revolution has turned sour. The end of inhibition and the release of sexual energies which have so often been documented as the innovation of the revolutionary culture are now beginning to be seen as just another fraud. After the gang-rapes at Altamont and Seattle, after the demands raised at People's Park for "Free Land, Free Dope, Free Women," after the analyses of (male) rock culture, women are beginning to realize that nothing new has happened at all. What we have is simply a new, more sophisticated (and thus more insidious) version of male sexual culture. Sexual freedom has meant more opportunity for men, not a new kind of experience for women. And it has been precisely our own experience as women which has been decisive in developing the Women's Liberation critique of the sexual revolution. The generation of women who only a few years ago saw themselves as the vanguard of the new sex, now suddenly find themselves plagued with all the problems of their grandmothers—loss of interest in sex, hatred of sex, disgust with self. This turnabout happened very fast and I think it happened because we opened ourselves up in consciousness-raising and a lot of bad feeling we thought we'd gotten rid of floated to the top. It has been good to get these feelings out and look at them. But can we *explain* them, can we understand what has happened to us in the last five years?

I would like to suggest that we can understand the destruction of female sexuality if we conceptualize it as a special case of alienation, understood as a political phenomenon. If alienation is the destruction of self which ultimately leads to schizophrenia, the widespread alienation of females from their own sexuality is a kind of rampant mental illness at the base of our experience which we must recognize for what it is.

Alienation is a much used and little explained term. Put

simply, it refers to the disintegration of our very selves and personalities which occurs when we are powerless. The opposite of powerlessness is self-actualization, and the healthy self-actualizing human being is one who moves through the world as an autonomous source of action. As Ernest Becker put in an important essay on alienation:

> People break down when they aren't "doing," when the world does not reflect the active involvement of their own creative powers. Alienated man is man separated from involvement with and responsibility for the effective use of his self-powers.

What is more difficult to understand is precisely *how* alienation comes about in certain individuals. Becker suggests three ways: (1) Alienation occurs along the dimension of time. As children we learn certain patterns of behavior which bring us approval. As we grow older, however, we must constantly adapt to new situations. If our early childhood training has been too rigid, we are unable to make the necessary adjustments and become increasingly unable to handle our experiences. (2) Alienation also occurs in terms of the roles we play. This problem affects both men and women, but we are particularly familiar with the female version. Not only are females confined to a few narrow roles, but they are also subject to contradictory messages about the roles they do play. Motherhood, for example, is viewed as a sacred task, but mothers are not taken seriously when they act outside their kitchens and homes. (3) The third dimension of alienation is more complex: the breakdown of self occurs when the gap between thought and action, theory and practice, mind and body becomes too great. The classic and extreme example of this form of alienation is the schizophrenic, living totally in a thought world of his own creation with no relation to reality.

This three-dimension model of alienation is complex but I think it can help us understand our own experience with sex. What I am about to say about female sexuality as schizophrenic will make more sense, however, if I digress for a moment to describe some attributes of schizophrenia.

This extreme form of alienation, you will recall, is produced by a split between mind and body. Such an odd condition is possible in human beings as opposed to animals because we are self-conscious beings. We have an "inner self" of reflection and thought but our body is part of the world "out there" of experience and material objects. This mind-body dualism is at the base of human power—our ability to reflect upon, then act upon the material world. Such power becomes destructive—as in schizophrenia—when the mind turns in on itself and never tests its perceptions in concrete reality.

It is in grappling with the outside world, in testing the powers of thought and emotion that the individual becomes a full, self-actualized person. In this self-directed behavior, we test ourselves, make contact with reality and gain control over ourselves and our environment. And the more positive and successful experiences we build up, the more secure we are as whole persons. This is the mechanism by which we become liberated; the reverse process is alienation.

In this reverse process, the schizophrenic fails to develop the necessary unity between mind and body, takes refuge in a world of *symbols,* and thereby forfeits *experience.* In other words, a schizophrenic is someone who becomes accustomed to relating to symbol-objects rather than person-objects and in doing so loses all self-powers.

I would argue that as females we are sexually schizophrenic, relating not to ourselves as self-directed persons, not to our partners as sexual objects of our desire, but to a false world of symbols and fantasy. This fantasy world of sex which veils our experience is the world of sex as seen through male eyes. It is a world whose eroticism is defined in terms of female powerlessness, dependency, and submission. It is the world of sado-masochistic sex. If you don't know what I mean by sado-masochism, think of the erotic themes of all the novels, comic books, movies, jokes, cartoons, songs you've experienced. The major sexual theme which appears over and over again is the drama of conquest and submission: the male takes the initiative and the female waits, waits in a thousand variations on a single theme—eagerly, coyly, shyly, angrily, and at the outer edge of pornography and fantasy, is taken against her will. Usually it is more subtle. The female stands in awe of the hero's abilities, his powers; she is willing when he takes the initiative, guides her by the elbow, puts his arm around her waist, maneuvers her into the bedroom. What is it that makes such descriptions arousing? Not a mere run-down of anatomy but the tension in the social situation as male advances on female, whether she is willing or not, submission is acceptable in our culture if the man is superior, and this leads to the search for the man who is smarter, taller, more self-confident—someone to look up to and thus worthy of giving in to.

> In each of our lives, there was a first man for whom we were prepared like lambs for the slaughter. My fantasy of him was a composite of Prince Valiant, Gary Cooper, and my father. Trained in submission, in silence, I awaited him through a series of *adolescent boyfriends who were not masterful enough to fit the dream* because I would not really graduate to the estate of womanhood until I had been taken by a strong man.

Trained in submission women instinctively look for the strong man who will continue the loving benevolence of the father. That this pattern of sexual relations is our society's model is confirmed by psychologist Abraham Maslow. In a study of sexual behavior, Maslow reported that women who find a partner more dominant than they usually make the best sexual adjustment. On the other hand, a very sexually active woman in his study failed to reach orgasm with several male partners because she considered them weaker than herself and thus could not "give in to them." Thus, "normal" sexual adjustment occurs in our society when the male plays the dominant role.

If we come to view male-dominated sexual relations as by definition healthy sex, the mechanism of this learning process is the bombardment of sexual fantasy that we experience long before we experience sex itself. Sexual images of conquest and submission pervade our imagination from an early age and lay the basis for how we will later look upon and experience sex. Through the television set and the story-book, we live out in imagination society's definition of sex and love. Rapunzel waits in her tower for years in hopes of the young prince who will free her body from its imprisonment. Sleeping Beauty's desires slumber until they are awakened and fulfilled by the kiss of the young prince. These fairy tale princesses are not unusual. There are few women, no matter how intelligent, no matter how dedicated to the pursuit of a goal, who will not finally be conquered—and like it. And if they are not conquered, it is understood that no man desired them anyway.

By experiencing such sexual fantasies at an early age, we become alienated along Becker's first dimension of time. Locked early into a set of fantasy images which define female sexual roles as passive, women are constantly denying feelings which don't fit the cultural definitions. And so all pervasive is the male bias of our culture that we seldom notice that the fantasies we take in, the images that describe to us how to act, are *male* fantasies about females. In a male world, female sex is from the beginning unable to get a clear picture of itself.

And from the beginning, women experience Becker's second dimension of alienation. The role of women as sexual beings is subject to contradictory evaluations by society. Young girls quickly become attuned to society's ambivalent view of their sexuality. Women come to see themselves as synonymous with sex, yet female sexuality is seen as valid only under certain conditions, such as marriage. Even as such narrow restrictions break down in more permissive ages like our own and the limits of female sexuality expand, we still run up against those limits at the point where a female can be labelled promiscuous. And women who initiate and direct sexual activity on a regular basis find that they have gone beyond the limits of the possible and are termed castrating. Male sexual desires, on the other hand, are affirmed throughout and are associated with prowess, power, and man(self)hood.

As females, then, we relate to symbol-objects rather than person-objects. Like the schizophrenic, we are alienated from our own experience and from our own self-powers of initiation. This form of alienation has to do with sex in a very direct way because women do not often take the initiative in relation to men.

Schizophrenic passivity is a dire abrogation of one's power in the face of the object. If you relate to an object under your own initiatory powers, then it becomes an object which enriches your own nature. If you lack initiatory powers over the object, it takes on a different value, for it then becomes an individual which crowds your own nature. A girl really comes to exist as a feminine sex object for the adolescent only as he learns to exercise active courtship powers in relation to her.

If women become objects of sexual desire for men in the social process of male-initiated relationships, how does the male become an object of sexual desire for the female? It is not clear, in fact, that the male body *per se* is deemed erotic by women, certainly not in the same way that the female body is for men. In fact, since women are bombarded with the same sex stimuli of the female body as is a man, females often respond in a narcissistic way to their own body and what is being *done* to it rather than projecting sexual desire out onto the male. The female is taught to be the object of sexual desires rather than to be a self-directed sexual being oriented toward another; she is taught to be adored rather than adoring. Is it surprising then that so many women find the male body ugly, that so many women see the drama of sex in what is done *to* them?

Two things happen to women's sexual lives. Many women have no sexual fantasies at all (since there is little male sexual imagery available in this culture). Masters and Johnson found that many women who could not focus on sexual imagery had difficulty having orgasm. The good doctors have tried to encourage sexual fantasy (by reading arousing material!) to enable these women to experience orgasm.

Females that do have fantasies often have the same sado-masochistic fantasies that men do. As Shulamith Firestone points out in *The Dialectic of Sex,*

Cultural distortion of sexuality also explains how female sexuality gets twisted in narcissism: women make love to themselves vicariously through the man rather than directly making love to him.

In these fantasy episodes, the female does not always play the masochistic role. The female who is focusing on sexual imagery can take the part either of the male, the female, or an onlooker, but in any case eroticism is still dealing in female powerlessness.

How do women tolerate a situation in which men control and define the experience of sex? I believe we solve our problem in the same way the schizophrenic does. A woman's sexuality is experienced in symbolic terms at the expense of active physical involvement. Sex is re-presented to her by society in symbolic messages of passivity and conquest. Like the symbolic world of the schizophrenic, a woman's fantasy life—her desire to be taken, overpowered, mastered—allows her to play the passive role and perhaps even to enjoy it *if she fully accepts the world as defined by men.* Caught between the demands of a male-dominated society and the demands of our own self-definition, we survive by fully accepting the masochistic symbol-world given to us by male society at the expense of our own experience. In fact, our physical experience has been denied and distorted for so long that most of us aren't even aware of the sacrifice we have made. We are only uneasy that all is not well.

Yet ultimately in the lives of those women for whom fantasy and reality become too far apart, a crisis occurs. The mechanism of crisis in some cases may be merely the demystification of the male through years of marriage. It is hard to keep intact fantasies of male power when confronted with the reality of a pot-bellied, lethargic husband. Such a crisis may result either in a transfer of fantasy to a new male or in a loss of interest in sex altogether. For women in Women's Liberation the whole fragile structure of fantasy and power often falls along with the myth of male supremacy. Males are subject to the same fantasies of conquest, yet their fantasy life is an expression of their own active powers (albeit also in a false way) and does not separate them from their own experience.

Women, then, are alienated from their sexuality along

several dimensions. From an early age, we are alienated from ourselves as sexual beings by a male society's ambivalent definition of our sexuality: we are sexy but we are pure; we are insatiable but we are frigid; we have beautiful bodies but we must shave and anoint them. We are also alienated because we are separated from our own experience by the prevailing male cultural definition of sex—the male fantasy of active man and passive woman. From an early age, our sexual impulses are trained to turn back onto ourselves in the narcissistic counterpart of the male fantasy world. In social relations with men, we are alienated from ourselves as initiating, self-directed persons. Some women hold all these contradictory parts together; most women, I suspect, have given up on sex, whether or not they have informed their husbands and lovers.

Calling into question our traditional female role has meant calling into question more and more layers of our experience. With this questioning has come the discovery that there is not much left that is valid in male-female relations as we have known them. Kate Millet showed us in *Sexual Politics* that fascism—the relations of dominance and submission that begin with sex and extend throughout our society—is at the very core of our cultural experience. So it is with little joy and much sadness that we peel back the layers of our consciousness and see our sexual experience for what it really is. And it is also with much sadness that we admit that there is no easy answer. It is too easy to say that we have been merely the victims of male power plays. The sadomasochistic content of sex is in the heads of women too. As long as female powerlessness is the unspoken underlying reality of sexual relations, women will want to be conquered. As long as our cultural vision is the projection of solely male experience, women will not be able to understand even their own alienation.

To say this is to suggest some ways out of our cultural and sexual alienation. Yet it is also too easy to blithely assume, as we often do, that all this sexual distortion is going to be easily changed in some new culture in the future. We have pushed beyond the economic revolution and the cultural revolution to come face to face with the real sexual revolution and we are not sure what we have left in the way of hope and affirmation.

Perhaps the most courageous and in the long run the most positive statement we can make is to acknowledge the pain we feel now and the perhaps irreparable damage that we have sustained. But saying this is not totally to despair. Sometimes it is necessary to touch rock bottom before we can find the strength to push up for air.

A Pretty Girl Is Like a Commodity and Ain't She Sweet

BEV GRANT

1968

(TO BE SUNG TO THE TUNE OF "A PRETTY GIRL IS LIKE A MELODY")

A pretty girl is a commodity
with stock to buy and sell.
When the market is high,
and you see her pass by,
count up your shares
in what she wears
that pay you dividends.

A pretty girl in this society
is judged by looks alone.
What you see on her face
is often the waste
of chemicals developed for the War.

(TO BE SUNG TO THE TUNE OF "AIN'T SHE SWEET")

Ain't she sweet
makin' profit off her meat.
Beauty sells she's told so she's out pluggin' it,
ain't she sweet.

Ain't she cute
walking in her bathing suit,
selling products for the corporation, now
ain't she cute.

Chorus:
Just cast an eye
in her direction.
She has to buy—
It's her oppression.

Ain't she quaint
with her face all full of paint.
After all how can she face reality,
ain't she quaint.

Ain't she nice.
Maybe they'll give her a slice
of the profits that she's bringin' in for them,
ain't she nice.

Chorus:
(repeat above)

Ain't she fine.
On her face there's not a line.
Just a packaged doll, a prize commodity,
ain't she fine.

Body Odor and Social Order
FLORIKA

The aerosol spray container reveals that the roles of the policeman and the middle-class housewife are interchangeable.

The aerosol spray, both as a weapon and as a product, has created a new distinction in social behavior: between the rioters and the consumers. Between those who have to be controlled and those who've learned to control themselves.

The police have defined as well as sanctified the function of the aerosol weapon, but it is the housewife (the consumer), with her toy aerosol, who routinizes and normalizes its use. Through the medium of weapon-toy identification, the ad men encourage the housewife to believe that germs are a substitute for human targets.

As the aerosol spray equates the drudgery of housework to that of police-work, it also reduces rebellious people to the level of germs. And what has become for the middle-class housewife an acting out of mindless routine, is to the potential victim a rehearsal for his humiliation.

The spray forms an invisible, protective shield. This is a recurring image and theme used in aerosol advertisement which is in essence the heart of the Cold War policy of containment.

Sweating, stinking, germ build-up, flying insects, are all specific contingencies which are countered with the aerosol technique of flexible response and mobility.

The mass production of aerosol sprays not only enlarged the microscopic and made it "visible"; it also magnified the puritan eye into a reactionary outlook.

The obsession with dirt, like the fear of communism, is the product of eyeing the world through the peephole of the aerosol can. And the American consumer, in trying to spray back and contain an impinging and elusive environment (enemy), has unknowingly been inside a psychological container himself.

Aerosol advertisement is extremely revealing. It has taken over the function of relating the individual to society, and interpreting society to the individual. In the case of deodorant sprays, it even pits the individual against himself.

Right Guard, for example, is a deodorant: "the perfect family deodorant." The product is promoted as a Super Ego, "the Protector," who alternately threatens—"Don't leave your family unguarded"—and reassures—"twenty-four-hour protection for the whole family."

The real social antagonisms that exist within the family, or between society and the family, which are portrayed in spot commercial deodorant dramas, are cleverly diagnosed as "perspiration problems."

Right Guard's formula, then, is to neutralize the conflict between body odor and social order by providing total sanitation through individual sterilization. It also assures each member maximum security from contact with all the rest—"Nothing touches you but the spray."

Right Guard—in its totality of concept, name, and function—is an environmental mechanism for controlling the middle class, the way the National Guard is an armed force for quelling rebellious minorities.

Right Guard even stops "wetness" too, because it regulates your emotions—which are a cause of wetness. Internal surveillance without tell-tale leakage—"Get it today."

The duty of every *Right Guard* is to whisper inside the middle-class ear, "contain yourself!"

Another group of antipersonal products are the hair sprays. Hair sprays are the "special forces" for dealing with the problem of hair-do sabotage. The threat of overthrowing the hair-do structure comes from the alliance between nature as an external liberating force and the natural movement of the hair itself. For this reason advertising lauds the merits of a hair spray by juxtaposing its capacity to hold a hair-do in place against the disintegrating powers of rain and wind.

Hair spray also acts as an invisible screen to prevent humidity from infiltrating and subverting an orderly coif into an unruly jungle.

Hair sprays are experts at "holding power." The labels even advise women on the degree of control she thinks she needs: "light" for the swinging natural look, "regular" for those who want to be sure, and "extra" for frizzy, unmanageable fly-away hair.

One commercial for *VO-5* hair spray shows two young "starlets" in the process of getting drenched by a "Hollywood rainstorm." The viewer is told that the blonde uses *VO-5* with "myrol," the brunette another favorite brand. "Watch!" Naturally, *VO-5* is the victor. The brunette's favorite hair spray could not prevent a total hair-do washout. Test proves: "*VO-5* hair spray with myrol holds [you] even in a Hollywood rainstorm."

The duel between nature and hair spray over the pretty, fragile hair-do is the ad man's recipe for selling hair-spray romance to the twentieth-century woman. Being desirable to a man, or dependent on him, becomes a stimulant for desiring a product. Hair sprays must respond to every woman's dream of a knight who will take her out of suburbia and into chivalry. The ad man caters to feudal myths as a panacea for a futile life.

You needn't always be the target.

You can go on the offensive. Extend the perimeter of defense.

Vietnam has been called "The War of the Mosquito." It is fought with aerosol technology—defoliants and herbicides.

The War of the Mosquito is also being waged right in the backyards of suburbia. With *Raid Yard Guard.*

The voice of God speaks to you over the tube: "Deep in a bug-infested jungle, two scientists are testing *Raid Yard Guard* against another leading spray."

After *Raid Yard Guard* has been proven king of the beasts, the jungle scene ends. Back to a friendly lawn somewhere in suburbia where Tarzan's family of four is about to settle down to a picnic dinner. The kiddies are playing, Tarzan is flipping over the medium-rare, charcoal-broiled burgers (with go-together-burger-buns toasting nearby) and Jane—what is Jane doing?

Jane is spraying the entire area with *Raid Yard Guard.*

The voice of God again: "Keeps out bugs, seals in protection. Get outdoor living with indoor comfort. Get *Raid Yard Guard,* the jungle-tested bug-killer."

If *Raid Yard Guard* doesn't do the job, you can try *Black Flag* insecticide—"Kills bugs on contact!"

Don't let pests, flying insects, and outside agitators drive you buggy. But if they do break through your perimeter of defense, retreat into the science-fiction environment called home: the man's castle.

Step over the threshold. You've just entered the "Invisible World" of *Lysol.*

The ad man is waiting for you, arms open: "The Invisible World surrounds every man, every woman, every child, every day of his life. It's a world of germs you can't see. It's a world of odors you can't see. It's the world *Lysol Spray* was made for. Also in new Purse and Travel size for use away from home. It kills the ugly things you can't see."

The Invisible World, like mysticism and religion, has always been used to obscure and protect those powerful few in the real world. Advertising is the invisible hand which blesses the faithful consumer.

Out of the lowest form of life, bacteria, it has created the image of conspiracy. In true Cinderella fashion, a metamorphosis takes place: the microbe is transformed into a subversive agent. Confronted with the presence of The Invisible World the consumer takes up the holy *Lysol* spray on behalf of the Free World.

Biologically, the "invisible" power of germs came to an end in the nineteenth century with Pasteur's germ theory of disease. Their threat today is no longer really physical, but political.

Unconsciousness creates invisibility. Desires and fears which we are not aware of are turned into germs which we cannot see. Germs have become a symbolic enemy. The basis for germ phobia is the fear of contact. What makes it political is that the consumer culture converts this germ phobia into a middle-class hallucination of the "masses."

The Cold War reveals the phobic character of the aerosol products and their culture. The policy of containment is the reaction induced by the powerful few in their phobic subjects. Political paranoia is a symptom not so much of the Cold War mentality but of the routine of everyday life where neurosis is skillfully substituted for class consciousness. The more we try to control the movement of microbes, the less likely we are to realize that we ourselves have become the objects of control.

With *Lysol,* they make it easier to "adjust" to your dehumanization. Being turned into an animal (i.e., a mindless creature) is OK so long as you remain docile. Otherwise they use *Lysol* on you.

In the arsenal of aerosol products there is a new disinfectant spray cleaner on your supermarket shelf. *Clean & Kill.* The brand name is the solution.

Why do you need this new weapon which "zips through dirt and zaps household germs?" Because: "Dirt & Germs are buddies." "*Clean & Kill* cleans and cleans right down to the germs. It leaves every surface so germ-free you could eat off it!"

With *Clean & Kill* you can formulate foreign policy at the push of a button—do a man's job with a woman's touch.

With *Clean & Kill* you can participate in the defense of your country without leaving the house.

With *Clean & Kill* you're honoring those commitments you made when you took the vow.

With *Clean & Kill* you're mobile. You've got options. You can contain bacterial unrest before it spreads. You can snuff out mildew and subversion, the leading causes of Staph and Stress. You can wipe out dirt and ignorance (which breed crime and germs), right off your kitchen floor.

Clean & Kill. Keeps your house germ-free, while it helps Standard International keep the world free. They make it, sister.

Pssss!

Isn't it about time we let them do their own cleaning and killing?

Poster
FLORIKA

The protest against the 1968 Miss America beauty pageant was the first women's liberation's protest covered widely by the national media, the action that first put "women's lib" on journalists' radar screen. Along with media coverage came the manufacture of myths, most famously that the feminist protestors at this event held the first bra-burning. In fact, it is not clear that any bra-burnings ever took place and certainly none took place here: the Atlantic City authorities had forbidden building a fire on the boardwalk, so the protesters threw items symbolizing the tortures of female beautification—eyelash curlers, girdles, garter belts, curling irons, and home permanent kits from Toni, one of the sponsors of the Miss America Pageant—into a freedom garbage can (associating the project with the civil rights freedom schools and freedom rides). Nevertheless, bra-burning became one of the most widespread images of feminism, no doubt because of its theatrical and sexual qualities.

The ten points of the following leaflet announcing the protest represent a coherent summary of the feminist critique of objectification of female beauty and of the practice of ranking women's attractiveness. As usual, feminists were connecting this exploitive use of women's bodies to the whole social order, including racism, militarism, and consumerism. Miss America contests still occur, of course, but they have been changed by the reach of this critique: the TV audiences are smaller (75 million in 1984 shrank to 18 million in 1998), there are women of color among the contestants, and, although beauty is still the main measure, the "girls" are expected to show "talent" as well.

Carol Hanisch, a veteran civil rights organizer and journalist, immediately scrutinized every aspect of the protest, and criticized herself and her sisters for using Left jargon, for letting a few women speak for the whole group. Most importantly, she criticized slogans that inadvertently blamed women for their own oppression. Hanisch, in the excerpt below, was asserting the "pro-woman line" (also articulated by Ellen Willis in chapter 12), which says that women's acquiescence to these beauty standards was forced upon them not only by the culture but also by economic necessity.

No More Miss America
NEW YORK RADICAL WOMEN

1968

No More Miss America!
We Protest:

1. *The degrading Mindless-Boob-Girlie Symbol.* The Pageant contestants epitomize the roles we are all forced to play as women. The parade down the runway blares the metaphor of the 4-H Club county fair, where the nervous animals are judged for teeth, fleece, etc., and where the best "specimen" gets the blue ribbon. So are women in our society forced daily, to compete for male approval, enslaved by ludicrous "beauty" standards we ourselves are conditioned to take seriously.

2. *Racism with Roses.* Since its inception in 1921, the Pageant has not had one Black finalist, and this has not been for a lack of test-case contestants. There has never been a Puerto Rican, Alaskan, Hawaiian, or Mexican-American winner. Nor has there ever been a *true* Miss America—an American Indian.

3. *Miss America as Military Death Mascot.* The highlight of her reign each year is a cheerleader-tour of American troops abroad—last year she went to Vietnam to pep-talk our husbands, fathers, sons and boyfriends into dying and killing with a better spirit. She personifies the "unstained patriotic American womanhood our boys are fighting for." The Living Bra and the Dead Soldier. We refuse to be used as Mascots for Murder.

4. *The Consumer Con-Game.* The Pageant is sponsored by Pepsi-Cola, Toni, and Oldsmobile—Miss America is a walking commercial. Wind her up and she plugs your product on promotion tours and TV—all in an "honest, objective" endorsement. What a shill.

5. *Competition Rigged and Unrigged.* We deplore the encouragement of an American myth that oppresses men as well as women: the win-or-you're-worthless competitive disease. The "beauty contest" creates only one winner to be "used" and forty-nine losers who are "useless."

6. *The Woman as Pop Culture Obsolescent Theme.* Spindle, mutilate, and then discard tomorrow. What is so ignored as last year's Miss America? This only reflects the gospel of our society, according to Saint Male: women must be young, juicy, malleable—hence age discrimination and the cult of youth. And we women are brain-washed into believing this ourselves!

7. *The Unbeatable Madonna-Whore Combination.* Miss America and *Playboy*'s centerfold are sisters over the skin. To win approval, we must be both sexy and wholesome, delicate but able to cope, demure yet titillatingly bitchy. Deviation of any sort brings, we are told, disaster: "You won't get a man!!"

8. *The Irrelevant Crown on the Throne of Mediocrity.* Miss America represents what women are supposed to be: unof-fensive, bland, apolitical. If you are tall, short, over or under what weight The Man prescribes you should be, forget it. Personality, articulateness, intelligence, commitment—unwise. Conformity is the key to the crown—and, by extension, to success in our society.

9. *Miss America as Dream Equivalent To —?* In this reput-edly democratic society, where every little boy supposedly can grow up to be President, what can every little girl hope to grow to be? Miss America. That's where it's at. Real power to control our own lives is restricted to men, while women get patronizing pseudo-power, an ermine cloak and a bunch of flowers; men are judged by their actions, women by their appearance.

10. *Miss America as Big Sister Watching You.* The Pageant exercises Thought Control, attempts to sear the Image onto our minds, to further make women oppressed and men oppressors; to enslave us all the more in high-heeled, low-status roles; to inculcate false values in young girls; to use women as basis of buying; to seduce us to prostitute our-selves before our own oppression.

Excerpt from A Critique of the Miss America Protest
CAROL HANISCH

1968

The protest of the Miss America Pageant in Atlantic City in September told the nation that a new feminist movement is afoot in the land. Due to the tremendous coverage in the mass media, millions of Americans now know there is a Women's Liberation Movement. Media coverage ranged from the front pages of several newspapers in the United States to many articles in the foreign press.

When I proposed the idea to our group, we decided to go around the room with each woman telling how she felt about the pageant. We discovered that many of us who had always put down the contest still watched it. Others, like myself, had consciously identified with it, and had cried with the winner.

From our communal thinking came the concrete plans for the action. We all agreed that our main point in the demonstration would be that all women were hurt by beauty competition—Miss America as well as ourselves. We opposed the pageant in our own self-interest, e.g. the self-interest of all women.

Yet one of the biggest mistakes of the whole pageant was our anti-womanism. A spirit of every woman "do her own thing" began to emerge. Sometimes it was because there was an open conflict about an issue. Other times, women didn't say anything at all about disagreeing with a group decision; they just went ahead and did what they wanted to do, even though it was something the group had definitely decided against. Because of this egotistic individualism, a definite strain of anti-womanism was presented to the public to the detriment of the action.

Posters which read "Up Against the Wall, Miss America," "Miss America Sells It," and "Miss America Is a Big Falsie" hardly raised any woman's consciousness and really harmed the cause of sisterhood. Miss America and all beautiful women came off as our enemy instead of as our sisters who suffer with us. A group decision had been made rejecting these anti-woman signs. A few women made them anyway. Some women who had opposed the slogans were in the room when the signs were being made and didn't confront those who were making the anti-woman signs.

A more complex situation developed around the decision of a few women to use an "underground" disruptive tactic. The action was approved by the group only after its adherents said they would do it anyway as an individual action. As it turned out, we came to the realization that there is no such thing as "individual action" in a movement. We were linked to and were committed to support our sisters whether they called their action "individual" or not. It also came to many of us that there is at this time no real need to do "underground" actions. We need to reach as many women as possible as quickly as possible with a clear message that has the power of our person behind it. At this point women have to see other women standing up and saying these things. That's why draping a women's liberation banner over the balcony that night and yelling our message was much clearer. We should have known, however, that the television network, because it was not competing with other networks for coverage, would not put the action on camera. It did get on the radio and in newspapers, however.

The problem of how to enforce group decisions is one we haven't solved. It came up in a lot of ways throughout the whole action. The group rule of not talking to male reporters was another example.

We tried to carry the democratic means we used in planning the action into the actual *doing* of it. We didn't want leaders or spokesmen. It makes the movement not only *seem* stronger and larger if everyone is a leader, but it actually *is* stronger if not dependent on a few. It also guards against the time when such leaders could be isolated and picked off one way or another. And of course many voices are more powerful than one.

Our first attempt at this was not entirely successful. We must learn how to fight against the media's desire to make leaders and some women's desire to be spokesmen. Everybody talks to the press or nobody talks to the press. The same problem came up in regard to appearances on radio and television shows after the action. We theoretically decided no one should appear more than once, but it didn't work out that way.

The Miss America protest was a zap action, as opposed to person to person group action. Zap actions are using our presence as a group and/or the media to make women's oppression into social issues. In such actions we speak to men as a group as well as to women. It is a rare opportunity to talk to men in a situation where they can't talk back. (Men must begin to learn to listen.) Our power of solidarity, not our individual intellectual exchanges will change men.

We tried to speak to individual women in the crowd and now some of us feel that it may not have been a good tactic. It put women on the spot in front of their men. We were putting them in a position which we choose to avoid ourselves when we don't allow men in our discussion groups.

It is interesting that many of the non-movement women we talked to about the protest had the same reaction as many radical women. "But I'm not oppressed," was a shared response. "I don't care about Miss America," was another. If more than half the television viewers in the country watch the pageant, somebody cares! And many of us admitted watching it too, even while putting it down.

We need to take ourselves seriously. The powers that be do. Carol Giardina of Gainesville, Florida, was fired from her job because of her activities in women's liberation and her participation in the protest. Police cars were parked outside the planning meeting one night. The next day we got a call from the mayor of Atlantic City questioning us about just what we planned to do. Pepsi Cola is withdrawing as a sponsor of the pageant. They produce a diet cola and maybe see themselves as next year's special target.

Unfortunately the best slogan for the action came up

about a month after when Ros Baxandall came out on the David Susskind show with "Every day in a woman's life is a walking Miss America Contest." We shouldn't wait for the best slogan; we should go ahead to the best of our understanding. We hope all our sisters can learn something as we did from our first foray.

> If proof were needed of the cost of violating beauty standards, here is a vivid example. (And if shaved legs were required in a San Francisco tropical fish store, you can be sure they would be required everyplace else.) Hair has notoriously gendered meanings: bringing strength to Samson and beauty to women (if it's in the right place), hair in the wrong place on women has been intensely threatening, even repulsive. But Mary Alice Carlson was connected to women's liberation, and a local group fought back and got her rehired. This action was typical of women's liberation groups, which often took up what might be considered small, individual, and usually unreported cases of injustice.

Hairy Legs Freak Fishy Liberal
SHEILAH DRUMMOND

On Nov. 5, Mary Alice Carlson, a student at San Francisco State, was called to go to work at Aquatic Specialties, 24th and Vicente, as a saleswoman. She had applied for the job along with several other women a week previously. One of the owners, Mr. X, hired her, telling her to begin work two days later. The job consisted of cleaning dead fish from the tanks, learning the names of different species, and waiting on customers.

She came to work at 2:00 p.m. About five-thirty, Mr. X asked her to come into the back room for a talk. She did. He told her that he didn't think she was going to "work out here," and, in fact, that she was fired. She asked him why.

At first he refused an explanation, but she demanded that he give her some reason, so finally he told her it was because of her "grooming." What, she asked, was wrong with her grooming? (Mary Alice was wearing a clean, simple, straight dress, flat shoes. She was neat and clean.)

X told her, "You don't shave your legs."

Mary Alice was stunned. She asked if she was incompetent on the job. She couldn't believe that she was actually being fired because she didn't shave her legs. However, it was true.

She asked how it was that he had hired her (as he claimed at the time) over 16 other applicants when, after all, he had interviewed her and apparently had not been offended at that time by her unshaven legs. He said he had not noticed this at the time or he wouldn't have hired her.

X said that he felt rather badly about the whole thing and so he would be willing to pay Mary Alice for a whole day instead of just three hours. Mary Alice declined the payoff and left for home, feeling a sense of unreality about the whole thing, as if she'd somehow gotten mixed up in someone else's scene. It was so hard to believe—but by the time she got home she was both hurt and angry. She talked with her roommates about what had happened, and women involved in San Francisco Women's Liberation began to call each other and talk about it.

Women from at least four different groups decided that some action should be taken to help this sister. A leaflet and some signs were made up, and on Saturday morning some women, some men and some kids gathered to picket Aquatic Specialties.

The picketers handed out the leaflets and rapped with people going by. People were surprised to hear the story and were mostly sympathetic. Many customers did not go into the store. Finally, Mr. X screeched up onto the curb in his huge car, in a cacophony of tires, horn and brakes. He was most upset, and agreed to talk with the women.

At first he maintained that Mary Alice was incompetent, and laid down a rap about what a lousy (and possibly dishonest) employee she was. Then he told the group that a *Chronicle* reporter had called him and asked about Mary Alice and he had told the reporter that she had been fired for incompetence and dishonesty. (A suspect amount of money in the cash register—)

Mary Alice told him that he had slandered her and was continuing to do so and she might well sue him for it.

Then X became even more upset, and opened his jacket to flash a small peace button which he had pinned discreetly inside. He told the girls they shouldn't do this to him as it was ruining his business and after all he was a liberal and he thought their movement was all about peace and love and flowers and they were costing him money, this was terrible, and wouldn't they PLEASE GO HOME!

The girls said they wouldn't go home until he did right by Mary Alice! So X finally agreed that he would call the *Chronicle* reporter and take back the slanderous things he had said about Mary Alice being incompetent and dishonest, and that he would hire her back. In the presence of the sisters he did indeed make this call and admit that he and not Mary Alice had misrepresented the situation and that he had been wrong in firing her for not having shaved her legs, and that he was hiring her back.

In a movement of people who are only just beginning to realize that they are oppressed and who have not yet got a really strong sense of unity or purpose, a victory, however small, is sweet. Mary Alice felt good about the whole action, as did all the women concerned. Women, after all, must spend far more time and money on their appearance than men, while they're making lower wages for the same work.

They must be appealing sex objects as well as competent workers to get even the low-pay jobs. (Not to mention our black sisters, who must try to look like WHITE sex objects.) This writer once quit an employment-agency job because of a hassle over a black sister I wasn't even allowed to try to place—with three years of college, she couldn't even get a lousy typing job because she was too "ugly"—that is, too black, lips too thick, and didn't straighten her hair or wear a wig.

What is Women's Liberation all about, anyway? Maybe it's idealistic, but I think it's about women using their united strength to help first themselves, then each other, then all oppressed, fucked-over people everywhere.

Only six years after the first Miss America protest, a particularly fearless high school student said it all as she challenged her mayor.

Untitled news story about a high school girl sassing a mayor

1974

Last January, Zoe Joyner, a 16-year-old senior at Terra Nova High School in Pacifica, California, decided to confront the mayor, Aubrey Lumly, and Miss Pacifica at a school assembly called to urge the women of Terra Nova to enter the Miss Pacifica Beauty Contest.

Zoe Joyner described the incident in her own words:

I walked into the cafeteria and sat down with 25 other girls. I wasn't really aware of who would be there but it didn't matter to me because I was there to say what I felt. When the mayor started talking I said, "Excuse me. Since the important thing about a woman is her measurements, as this gathering demonstrates, would you tell us the measurements of your penis before you speak, so we can tell if you're important enough to listen to?" He didn't say anything so I continued, "If you don't know them, I've got a tape measure."

After lying on the floor to prevent herself from being bodily removed, Ms. Joyner was expelled for five days. Zoe didn't seem to mind though, and neither do we.

Possibly the most destructive aspect of women's beauty standards is the tyranny of thinness. Fat women are more mercilessly ridiculed, humiliated, and discriminated against than any other category of women who do not conform to conventional appearance codes. Only 10 percent of American women like their bodies as they are. This problem and the eating disorders that result—not only anorexia and bulimia, but also chronic yo-yo dieting, binge eating, and self-hatred—are pervasive: 8 million people in the U.S. suffer from eating disorders, and 3 percent of young women and girls suffer from anorexia and 3 percent from bulimia.

Women's liberation fought these disorders through a constructive emphasis on "naturalness," health and fitness, and produced an explosion of women's participation in sports. This orientation showed the youth bias of the movement. More recently, with the decline of the movement and commercialization of women's new athletic interests, fitness became just another coercive beauty standard.

Women's liberation also challenged the thinness obsession. One California group, Fat Underground, tried to reach Spanish-speaking as well as English-speaking people. Like all the radical movements of the time, it connected the grievances of fat people with those of all other oppressed groups. Its rhetoric comes from the Left: its slogan, "Fat People of the World Unite! You Have Nothing to Lose . . . ," echoes the conclusion of the Communist Manifesto. Through women's liberation fat women also challenged stereotypes that they were weak, clumsy, lazy, and unathletic, as in the dance group portrayed by California feminist photographer Cathy Cade.

Antes de hacer dieta . . .

¿Es Usted "Gorda"? ¿Falla siempre en sus dietas y vuelve a engordar, aumentando más de peso cada vez? ¿Se critica a si misma por no tener "fuerza de voluntad"? ¿Le han dicho que usted tiene un problema emocional con la comida? ¿Que usted es autodestructiva?

.   .   .

¡Pues no está sola! ¡79 millones de americanas no son autodestructivas!

Hecho No. 1: 99% de todas las personas que se ponen a dieta para adelgazar, en cualquier tipo de dieta, vuelven a aumentar dentro de cinco años o menos, las libras que pierden.

Hecho No. 2: 90% de todas las personas que pierden peso aumentan *más* de lo que perdieron, en un período de cinco años después de dejar la dieta.

Hecho No. 3: La mayoría de las personas gordas NO COMEN más que las personas delgadas. Este hecho es el resultado de más de veinte años de estudios hechos por nutricionistas, y está bien documentado.

En otras palabras, usted *no* es quien se hace gorda. La gente delgada *no* come menos que usted. (¿Porque ha usted de pasar hambre?)

Hecho No. 4: Hasta las dietas "seguras" le hacen daño a su salud. El perder y aumentar peso una y otra vez causa daños a su corazón, músculos, nervios y riñones. La razón por la cual las personas gordas son un "riesgo" en asuntos de salud es porque debilitan sus cuerpos tratando de perder peso.

Hecho No. 5: La tensión es el mayor factor en los problemas de salud tales como la presión alta, diabetis, etc. Entre más nos presionen para que nos odiemos, mas tensión sufrimos.

Hecho No. 6: La gente gorda que vive en lugares donde está bien visto ser gorda, son tan saludables como las personas delgadas que viven alrededor de ellas.

Hecho No. 7: La industria de "dietas para rebajar de peso" gana $10 billones al año. Alguien está haciendo muchísimo dinero por el temor que el público tiene de ser gordo. Su pérdida (temporal) de peso le da a esa industria muchas ganancias, y por supuesto, ellos quieren mantener las cosas así.

Fat Chance Performance Group
CATHY CADE

Fat Liberation Manifesto

JUDY FREESPIRIT AND ALDEBARAN

1. WE believe that fat people are fully entitled to human respect and recognition.

2. WE are angry at mistreatment by commercial and sexist interests. These have exploited our bodies as objects of ridicule, thereby creating an immensely profitable market selling the false promise of avoidance of, or relief from, that ridicule.

3. WE see our struggle as allied with the struggles of other oppressed groups against classism, racism, sexism, ageism, financial exploitation, imperialism, and the like.

4. WE demand equal rights for fat people in all aspects of life, as promised in the Constitution of the United States. We demand equal access to goods and services in the public domain, and an end to discrimination against us in the areas of employment, education, public facilities and health services.

5. WE single out as our special enemies the so-called "reducing" industries. These include diet clubs, reducing salons, fat farms, diet doctors, diet books, diet foods and food supplements, surgical procedures, appetite suppressants, drugs and gadgetry such as wraps and "reducing machines."

WE demand that they take responsibility for their false claims, acknowledge that their products are harmful to the public health, and publish long-term studies proving any statistical efficacy of their products. *We make this demand knowing that over 99% of all weight loss programs, when evaluated over a five-year period, fail utterly, and also knowing the extreme, proven harmfulness of frequent large changes in weight.*

6. WE repudiate the mystified "science" which falsely claims that we are unfit. It has both caused and upheld discrimination against us, in collusion with the financial interests of insurance companies, the fashion and garment industries, reducing industries, the food and drug industries, and the medical and psychiatric establishment.

7. WE refuse to be subjugated to the interests of our enemies. We fully intend to reclaim power over our bodies and our lives. We commit ourselves to pursue these goals together.

FAT PEOPLE OF THE WORLD, UNITE! YOU HAVE NOTHING TO LOSE....

Another major victory of the women's movement was defining a new crime: sexual harassment. The range of behaviors included in this category—from whistles to "compliments" on women's figures, to indecent exposure and grabbing women, to offering favors in return for sex—would previously have been considered harmless "boys-will-be-boys" play, flirtation, or even flattery. Women had been pressed into accepting these definitions and pretending they didn't mind or didn't notice. In fact, these supposedly harmless acts of male aggression make women alienated from or even hostile to their own bodies, fearful of exploring the world on their own and, ironically, dependent on male protection against men. In entitling this selection "Little Rapes," the authors invoke a continuum between objectification of women's bodies and violent assaults.

There is probably no woman in American who has not experienced street harassment—wolf whistles, obscene remarks, quick grabs of breast or butt. But this behavior is difficult to control by law without making our streets unfree. So in 1970 women's liberation in several locales conducted "Ogle-Ins," turning the tables on the guys by directing whistles, animal noises, and evaluations of sexual organs against obnoxious men, even grabbing crotches. As Susan Brownmiller recounts in her recent memoir, *In Our Time,* Los Angeles feminists were stimulated by an official Chamber of Commerce "Girl-Watching Week." Activists carried tape measures, shouted "too small" and "Hey, fella, can you type, file, and make coffee?" The campaign turned to legal remedies against workplace harassment, but only after extensive educational work. In Ithaca, New York, women's liberation conducted what was probably the first speak-out on sexual harassment in 1975. At this extraordinary public event women who had never dared complain before— waitresses, administrators, clerks, factory workers, an assistant professor, a filmmaker—told of threats, exposure, and propositions to barter sex for jobs. Eleanor Holmes Norton, then New York City's commissioner on human rights, included testimony on sexual harassment in public hearings she was conducting on sex discrimination in employment, and it was because of her doing so that the national press first reported on the issue (see chapter 9).

Criminalizing sexual harassment has not been an uncomplicated or a perfect process. By the beginning of the 1990s consciousness had been raised to the extent that 21 percent of women said they had been harassed at work. But some encounters rest on the boundary between pleasurable flirtation and harassment, and sometimes women make false charges, so that there are legitimate differences of opinion about what constitutes harassment. Antifeminist libertarians of the 1980s and 1990s found and publicized a few cases in which efforts to protect women resulted in prudish overreactions. By contrast antifeminist conservatives of a more repressive bent reinterpreted sexual harassment, changing its meaning in both the courts and public opinion to focus on sex rather than discrimination or exploitation. Today it remains the case, however, that only about 6 percent of harassment victims ever file formal legal complaints, in part because of fear of retaliation, and even the most serious harassment commonly goes unpunished.

Little Rapes

1977

Has a man ever whistled at you while you were walking down the street?

Has a man ever made comments about your body while you stood at the busstop, minding your own business?

Has a man ever exposed himself to you while you were reading a book on the beach?

When a man sits next to you on the bus and presses his leg against you, are you afraid to say anything for fear that he will deny what he is doing, accuse you of flattering yourself, and call you paranoid?

Have you ever told a lover that you weren't in the mood, only to have him ignore your feelings and insist on making love?

Then you have been raped. Surprised? Don't be. If we define rape as "any sexual intimacy, whether by direct physical contact or not, that is forced on one person by another," it becomes clear that a woman can be raped in a situation that does not involve the stereotypical gang of Hell's Angels carrying knives, chains and guns. Sexual violence can take many forms:

- I work in a library. My first day on the job, I wore a dress. I was putting some books away in the stacks, when I became aware of a man crouched beside me. I thought he was looking for a particular book. Suddenly, he put his hand up my dress, then fled.
- While fixing breakfast one Sunday morning, I happened to glance out the kitchen window, which faces a patio. A man was standing in my yard, looking into the kitchen, and masturbating. I knelt down behind the counter so he couldn't see me and just prayed that he would go away.
- I had just returned from a Joann Little rally, and I had a roll of leaflets with me. When I got on the bus to go home, I put the leaflets in my lap. I noticed a man in front of me looking at the leaflets and I assumed he was trying to read them. He looked several times, but after a while I realized it wasn't the leaflets he was looking at, but rather, my crotch. Then I noticed he was masturbating.
- I was waiting for the light to change so I could cross the street. A man came up behind me and grabbed my breasts. By the time I realized what had happened, he had shot across the street—against the light. Too bad no cars were coming.
- I was jogging when a man came up to me and asked me for directions. We happened to be standing on the street he was asking directions to, so I knew something was amiss. He continued to follow me, despite the fact that I was only curtly answering his questions. After about a block and a half, he grabbed my arm. I swung around and screamed at him, "Get your fucking hands off me," at which point he grabbed one of my breasts and held onto my backpack with his other hand. I spit into his face to catch him off guard, then I started running as fast as I could. He was wearing bulky clothes and high shoes, and I, in my jogging clothes, could run faster. After several hundred yards, I looked back. He was lying on the sidewalk, panting and holding his stomach.

Women have the right to walk down the street without having to engage in conversation with total strangers. A woman should be able to stand on a crowded bus without wondering if the thing that keeps jabbing her in the leg is a briefcase or a less inanimate object. It shouldn't be the responsibility of women to play nursemaid to some lonely man in a bar who is intruding on a conversation she may be having with another woman. (Men wouldn't think of interrupting a woman who was talking with another man; territorial rights extend far beyond the animal world.)

And yet, we continually see women trying to pretend they didn't hear that editorial comment about their breasts. We see women walking hurriedly past groups of men, heads down, eyes fixed to the path ahead, as if they had done something wrong by just being on the street. We hear women saying "excuse me" when a man "accidentally" brushes up against them. We see women making up excuses to men in bars, fabricating male partners so they won't offend the intruder by turning him down.

It has been said that men who verbally accost women on busy streets or who attempt to touch women on crowded buses are usually not the type of men who will do further harm. It is not healthy to make this kind of generalization. Today's street hassler may be tomorrow's rapist. Men who rape often test a potential victim's vulnerability and resistance by committing a "small rape" and seeing how she responds. Don't be afraid to show your contempt for their tactics. Shout at them. Insult them. Don't let them rob you of your rightful space. Get angry. Get hostile.

On a beautiful, sunny day, I was sitting in the park reading a book. The area I was in was filled with people playing with frisbees, and young families enjoying picnics. I felt content, and safe. Then I heard someone going "Pssst, pssst," behind me. I thought it was someone I knew trying to get my attention. I turned around and saw a man standing with his pants down, exposing his penis. I was surprised more by the fact that he seemed hip, had long hair and didn't look at all grubby, or like a typical "flasher," more than I was by seeing him exposed. I think he expected me to be shocked and faint or something. But I jumped up and began chasing him, screaming at the top of my lungs, "You stupid fucker! Get out of here, God dammit, you jerk!" and so forth. I was really furious. Here I was minding my own business, and he had to ruin it for me. God, I was mad! Thinking back on it now, I feel good about my assertiveness. Not to mention the pleasure I get from remembering the sight of this guy trying to run away from me and pull his pants up at the same time.

Don't worry about offending the sensibilities of the "little rapist." Is he equally concerned about your feelings?

In short, walk down the street as if you had a right to be there because you DO.

Unlike sexual harassment, rape had long been considered a crime, although a crime often trivialized or blamed on women's provocation. It was conceived primarily as an unfortunate product of men's difficulty controlling their natural biological urges. When prosecuted, rape was primarily an offense against another man, the female victim's father or husband whose "property" had been damaged. Rape has also functioned to maintain racial and national domination. As a weapon of war, rape continues to be used to terrorize and subjugate conquered peoples, and in the U.S., false accusations of rape against African American men in particular helped maintain white dominance. Rape disproportionately victimizes poor and working-class women, who have to live and work in high-crime areas with inferior policing and lighting. Moreover, poor women face more difficulties in prosecuting rapists because they have less access to lawyers; are less likely to be believed and more likely to be blamed by police, prosecutors, and juries; and are more vulnerable to being fired or having their wages docked for taking the time to engage in legal struggles that are often protracted.

The function of rape to terrorize and subjugate women remained denied until women's movements brought it into the open and exposed its prevalence. A 1992–93 Department of Justice study estimated that 500,000 women in the U.S. were raped or otherwise sexually assaulted every year—that's 1,374 attacks a day. The result is that women are kept perpetually fearful—33 percent do not feel safe being out alone in their own neighborhood, and the proportion rises to 43 percent among black women. Women restrict their own movements as a result of fear: most women say they would never go to a movie or a laundromat alone at night, and half will not use public transportation at night. Some of these fears are ill-conceived. Since 78 percent of rapes are perpetrated by acquaintances, avoiding these activities makes no difference.

The feminist anti-rape campaign began by encouraging women to speak out, to defy the shame attached to being identified as rape victims. Then feminists conducted educational campaigns about the nature of rape, showing that: (1) it is not primarily a crime of passion but one of anger, aggression, and violence toward women; (2) there is nothing uncontrollable about the male sex drive; (3) most rapists are not strangers to their victims but acquaintances, dates, husbands, or other family members; (4) women don't "invite" rape—not only should women have the same right as men to go where and when they want, dressed as they want, but in fact rape serves to confine women. The core of the feminist critique is that rape is part of a system of male oppression in which all women, whether or not they have been raped, are made timid by the fear of rape.

Anti-rape education for men requires very basic consciousness-raising: although one in twelve male students admitted to having committed acts that met the legal definition of rape, 84 percent of them denied that it was rape. This is what the authors of "RAPE: The All American Crime" meant by their title, although of course rape is not uniquely American. Susan Brownmiller's 1975 book, *Against Our Will*, presented one influential variant of feminist thinking about rape. Brownmiller was a civil rights activist and member of New York Radical Feminists. The following fragment of her introduction illustrates a problematic and still-debated aspect of feminist rape theory. Because she called attention to anatomy as the basis of rape, her work was accused of making rape seem biologically determined and thereby letting men off the hook. In other parts of her book, Brownmiller failed to register adequately the racist use of false accusations of rape against black men. Whatever its flaws, almost inevitable in such a pioneering work, *Against Our Will* helped create a sea change in public consciousness about rape by showing that it is not an extraordinary occurrence but a mainstay of male supremacy.

Rape: The All American Crime

KAREN LINDSEY, HOLLY NEWMAN, AND FRAN TAYLOR

Rape is the perfect example of a woman's experience in a sexist society, the ultimate act of aggression which binds the victim still closer to her oppressors. Rape is both a symbolic and an actual means of keeping woman in her place: for every rape that *does* take place there are thousands of possible rapes in the back of a woman's mind every time she walks down the street. The controls exerted by this fear effectively limit the freedom of all women, and in fact encourage women to seek out men as protectors from other men. Rape functions to reinforce those institutions, like marriage, which contribute to woman's oppression. It is in the interest of the patriarchal system to condone rape while appearing to condemn it, for it is through rape that the anxieties which make women dependent on men physically, emotionally, morally, and legally, are reinforced.

Psychologically, rape is linked to the opposite kinds of conditioning males and females receive. Psychiatric studies, including those conducted by Naomi Weisstein, author of "Psychology Constructs the Female," support the hypothesis that people become what others expect them to be. In a society that defines them as the achievers, men feel compelled to live up to artificial standards of strength and forcefulness, and women learn to think of themselves as helpless and fragile. The resultant sexuality of both becomes confined to the roles of either aggressor or receptacle. This creates an emotional situation in which rape becomes an excellent possibility, even in so-called "normal" sexual relations.

The opposite of the belief that women are sexually passive is the equally misleading and disgusting myth that the use of force will bring out a woman's latent sexuality, and hence that women secretly like being raped. Violence seems to be differently perceived by men and women. Since men are used to being confident and forceful in their dealings with the world, and do not expect women to be so, a woman's "no" is perceived as "yes" or "maybe," and the ensuing violence may be seen by the man as persuasion. And the haunting fear of force in a woman's mind often acts as effectively as actual violence to pacify her. When the distinctions blur in respect to when persuasion becomes force, feminists insist that the person upon whom the attention, wanted or not, is being focused should be credited with the intelligence to determine when force actually occurred. The laws concerning rape deny this intelligence. For the conviction of rape, there must be "corroborating" evidence such as bruises and cuts—signs that the woman has actively resisted. In other words, if a woman, under threats of violence or death, submits to her assailant, she is not being raped. This puts rape in a special category of crime: If a man is mugged at knifepoint and gives the assailant his money, he is still mugged and the mugger still subject to arrest and conviction. The victim does not have to prove resistance. Obviously, the rape victim is being punished for her failure to choose death—before—dishonor.

For rape is "dishonor" in a male-dominated society. It is not the violation of a woman's person; it is the violation of a man's property. Rape is viewed not primarily in terms of the terror, pain, and indignity suffered by the victim, but in terms of the devaluation of damaged goods. This is true not only socially but legally as well. In several states, for example, an accused rapist's previous rape record cannot be used as evidence against him, but the victim's past sexual experiences can be used to discredit her "morality"; if she has lived with a man, or had provable sexual involvements outside of marriage, the defense can use this as proof that she was "asking for it." Even the *Yale Law Review* acknowledged in 1952 that rape laws exist not to protect women, but to provide a means for a man to avenge the violation of his property.

Nor is rape an uncommon crime. The statistics are high, and getting higher. According to *The New York Times*, the number of *reported* rapes in New York City alone has doubled in the past two years, while only a small fraction of arrests, and a smaller fraction of convictions, have resulted. Under existing "liberal" New York laws, for a rapist to be convicted, a witness is required. Most rapists don't wait for an audience; rape conviction is nearly impossible. In every aspect of rape, the burden is placed on the woman, first, not to get herself in any situation where rape might occur—i.e., she should not be walking out alone at night; she should not hitchhike; she should not live alone. Further, she should not dress in such a way as to "invite" rape, despite the fact that society demands that she dress enticingly in order to attract a husband, or get a job, or achieve popularity.

Even when a rapist is convicted, sentenced, and removed from the streets, a woman's freedom has not been protected. Her value as property may be restored, but the restraints on her ability to move freely in society have not been removed, and her rights to self-determination have not been recognized. A woman's observation of these conventions, however subtle or unconscious, drives her into the relationships set up by society allegedly for her protection. When rape is an everyday fact of life, marriage becomes a comforting solution (but not all that comforting, since in most states a husband *cannot* be accused of raping his wife). It is the sexual respectability conferred by the institution of marriage that is so desirable, that is so much more secure than the personal freedom and self-

determination women may enjoy outside it. So far the solutions offered vary only in degree, and not in approach. If some have begun to realize that rape is not a woman's fault, they still think it is her problem, her responsibility. Conservatives may argue that women should stay home if they don't want to be raped, and some radicals may urge women to take up karate to "disarm" rapists, but neither solution deals with the fundamental socialization that takes place in every child and fills our streets with aggressors and victims. If we continue to raise our children to conform to social expectations, if we wean our boys on John Wayne and our girls on Marilyn Monroe, rape will continue to be, as Susan Griffin terms it in her brilliant *Ramparts* article, "The All-American Crime."

Our society glamorizes rape by calling it a crime of passion. It is not. It is a crime of hate. It is the most ugly, brutal manifestation of man's power over woman. Until our bodies are truly our own, until men can no longer assert ownership over us, rape will continue. We will always be "asking for it"; we will always be "bringing it on ourselves." Because if male society really admits the crime of rape, it admits the crime it has perpetrated against us since the beginning of recorded history. And that is not a crime mankind is willing to face, or to stop.

The Mass Psychology of Rape
SUSAN BROWNMILLER   1975

Man's structural capacity to rape and woman's corresponding structural vulnerability are as basic to the physiology of both our sexes as the primal act of sex itself. Had it not been for this accident of biology, an accommodation requiring the locking together of two separate parts, penis into vagina, there would be neither copulation nor rape as we know it. Anatomically one might want to improve on the design of nature, but such speculation appears to my mind as unrealistic. The human sex act accomplishes its historic purpose of generation of the species and it also affords some intimacy and pleasure. I have no basic quarrel with the procedure. But, nevertheless, we cannot work

around the fact that in terms of human anatomy the possibility of forcible intercourse incontrovertibly exists. This single factor may have been sufficient to have caused the creation of a male ideology of rape. When men discovered that they could rape, they proceeded to do it. Later, much later, under certain circumstances they even came to consider rape a crime.

In the violent landscape inhabited by primitive woman and man, some woman somewhere had a prescient vision of her right to her own physical integrity, and in my mind's eye I can picture her fighting like hell to preserve it. After a thunderbolt of recognition that this particular incarnation of hairy, two-legged hominid was not the homo sapiens with whom she would like to freely join parts, it might have been she, and not some man, who picked up the first stone and hurled it. How surprised he must have been, and what an unexpected battle must have taken place. Fleet of foot and spirited, she would have kicked, bitten, pushed and run, *but she could not retaliate in kind.*

The dim perception that had entered prehistoric woman's consciousness must have had an equal but opposite reaction in the mind of her male assailant. For if the first rape was an unexpected battle founded on the first woman's refusal, the second rape was indubitably planned. Indeed, one of the earliest forms of male bonding must have been the gang rape of one woman by a band of marauding men. This accomplished, rape became not only a male prerogative, but man's basic weapon of force against woman, the principal agent of his will and her fear. His forcible entry into her body, despite her physical protestations and struggle, became the vehicle of his victorious conquest over her being, the ultimate test of his superior strength, the triumph of his manhood.

Man's discovery that his genitalia could serve as a weapon to generate fear must rank as one of the most important discoveries of prehistoric times, along with the use of fire and the first crude stone axe. From prehistoric times to the present, I believe rape has played a critical function. It is nothing more or less than a conscious process of intimidation by which *all men* keep *all women* in a state of fear.

Feminists in virtually every locality invented new forms of activism to combat rape and to assist rape victims. They published the names of rapists. They organized "Take Back the Night" marches in order to assert that women have a right to walk the streets in safety. By 1976 there were approximately 1,500 feminist anti-rape projects in the U.S. As a result of this activism, today there are rape crisis hot lines in most towns, escort services for women who are out late at night, hospitals and police staff members trained to respond appropriately to rape victims, and many journalists, judges, and defense attorneys who know that they can't get away with blaming rape victims.

Women of color are victims of rape disproportionately often, yet they have greater difficulty than white women in obtaining justice in a biased police and legal system. Moreover the myth of the highly sexual black woman renders black women less able to get themselves identified as victims. These cultural and legal systems have created and perpetuated tensions between white and black women about rape, because of the American legacy of false accusations by white women against black men, because of the white propensity to make rape appear as a black crime, and because racist police make reporting rape often futile or even dangerous for black women. In spite of these difficulties some women of color have worked with white women in establishing rape crisis centers and have formed their own community projects and alliances to combat rape.

Black Women Organizing Against Rape
AN INTERVIEW WITH NEKENGE TOURE AND MICHELE PLATE 1977

NEKENGE: Rape is not just another crime like bank robbery, pocketbook snatching or auto theft. It is not a crime for monetary gain or self-defense. Neither is rape a crime of survival, so why rape? Rape is sexual intimacy forced on one person by another. Women in American society are considered inferior to men and the social environment forces and enforces this concept constantly. Sex is both a beautiful and pleasurable act. When practiced by two persons of the opposite sex, it is also an act in which the male often takes the exclusive role of aggressor. Where such attitudes are fostered and promoted, the crime of rape has arrived at its inevitable destiny. Under such circumstances, men take what they feel it is their right to take. Women have no total equality and are not respected as human beings because of it. Therefore rape is an open question and forced sex on a woman is seldom considered rape. At this time America is experiencing opposition and struggle on all fronts from the people for their right of self-determination. Women must wage a struggle against rape. This struggle must be waged against all aspects of rape.

SUE: Why did you decided to become involved in the Rape Crisis Center, knowing that at the time Michele was the only Black member?

NEKENGE: I must admit that I had reservations. However, I believe the Center was really trying to diversify and reach out to the community in a more concrete manner through having Black and Third World women playing a key role in this center. Keeping in mind that the D.C. population is in excess of 80% Black, I felt a genuine responsibility to serve my sisters through the vehicle of the Rape Crisis Center. In addition, I considered the Center to be an excellent learning experience. So with that in mind I put aside my reservations and came into the Center as open-minded as I was able.

I think one thing that was good and really impressed me when I came to the D.C. Rape Crisis Center was the fact the women at the Center were trying to understand all kinds of women. When I first came to the Center it was not the most comfortable situation. Although I had worked with white people before on various things, it had been some years ago. Everything I had been doing for the last few years had, for the most part, been strictly within the confines of the Black community. I was in Third World activities here and there but not where I had to come into contact with various white women. I thought, "This is going to really be interesting, to get used to the women here, to be comfortable enough to be able to be myself, to be able to talk to people, to criticize people and to accept criticism from people." That whole thing took some time because I had certain ideas and feelings, although I consider myself somewhat political, somewhat flexible and somewhat sci-

entific. If I could feel uncomfortable coming into the Rape Crisis Center, other women who don't have the particular past experiences, ideas or outlook on life that I have could certainly feel that way.

As time went on I became used to the environment and I saw that on the whole people seemed to be very sincere. I think that any Black woman who might come here might feel that certain people around the center put you in a fishbowl and tried to analyze you in terms of why Black people do this and why Black people do that. They asked you questions but already had their own stereotyped ideas about race. However, overall I was very impressed with most of the people at the Center.

MICHELE: My friends think that I'm dealing with a problem that is important to the community. At first, there weren't other Black women here and I'd drag my friends to speaking engagements with me. But after a while, since the Center was dealing a lot more in the black community, I feel they accepted it as an organization that happened to have Black and white women involved. They could also see that the Center focused on the Black community so they didn't see me ignoring Blacks, but working on another issue that affects Blacks—rape.

NEKENGE: I haven't had that problem, because I am still a member and co-founder of Save the People, which is a Black organization that's working in the Black community. So they can say whatever they will say because my practice stands firm. I work at the Rape Crisis Center and have a lot of input and hope to have more, but I also do a hypertension screening program and different things like that. I am a Citizen of Record of the Republic of New Africa; that is, since everybody is a citizen by birth, an active citizen. I practice what I preach. I believe we need a nation of our own. At the same time, I also believe that black women need to live up to our potential—we have to be a motivating force. In a city like Washington, Black women could play a key role because we're so much of the population.

Most women who are conscious of their positions and conscious of where they are in life and society and the roles they have to play are becoming political. I think that once you become political, you organize on all levels around a number of issues; and it takes you away from being isolated. You become multifaceted because you understand interconnection. My being oppressed is related to the oppression of all people in general.

JACKIE: Acknowledging that a majority of anti-rape groups were begun by women who are white and middle-class, how can such groups become more responsive to needs and concerns of Third World women?

NEKENGE: White women cannot be responsive or sensitive by coming into an established Third World community and trying to organize to meet the needs of the women who live there. White women in organized anti-rape groups should share their resources and experience with Third World women. With those combined resources, Third World women can arrive at a point whereby they can make necessary changes and deal with expressed concerns within their own communities more rapidly. Black and Third World women will arrive at these solutions in time. However, combined resources from already organized women will hasten this process.

Coalitions could be formed between white and Third World women's groups based upon concentrated action. The objective may be, for example, an effective mass rape prevention program for the entire area. Women would be working in their own particular communities of which they have the most intimate knowledge. This would require the coordinated exchange of resources, expertise and experience between the women in different communities. It would also require a central information point. In this manner, a strong coalition could be formed.

Another equally important approach would be opening a particular Rape Crisis Center to Third World women with an acknowledged understanding that these women would concentrate more of their action within their own communities. Among the many things Third World women would contribute is knowledge concerning the special problems they face when confronting institutions.

Third World women within anti-rape groups can supply clearly defined information about the particular problems they encounter which are based upon their ethnic background, religion, historical experience, class status and even family concept.

MICHELE: With a common bond of race, the raped woman may be better able to express her feelings to a sister. For example, if she's Black, she may never tell a white woman she's been raped by a white man, and vice versa, a white woman may not tell me she's been raped by a Black man.

JACKIE: In general a center which relies on personal contacts for outreach will be very limited as to the type of people reached. If you can't afford the time and money to do widespread outreach work, your center will not develop into a multi-racial, multi-class organization.

NEKENGE: I think paying salaries is a priority in order to free the time of some dedicated people away from other jobs and into the Center. I think that paying salaries to Third World women is very important to assure that you have Third World women here. I think that to search out women who have some degree of consciousness and understanding of the community is also very important. It is these women, Black, white and Third World with community identification, who can do the things that have to be done to make sure that a Center survives, to make sure that the center builds strong coalitions and ties with other groups and to make sure that the Center's services reach the ears of the people.

MICHELE: I've talked to a lot of Black women who have been raped; they've been treated a lot differently in institutions than white women, mainly because institutions are the embodiment of the idea that Black women ask for it and it's no big deal if they get raped. When Black women go to the police they don't get the same treatment. They are asked more personal questions, usually, and if they've known the rapist they're just forgotten—they don't have a case.

Black policemen, they're chauvinistic just like white

policemen. A lot of times what they're going on is not mainly race but class assumptions. If a Black woman goes to the police and she's from a lower class they're going to say, "Well, honey, what are you coming in here crying about, because I know how you women are." They already have their myths. All men live by myths. I don't care what race they are.

It's the same thing when a Black woman who's been raped has to deal with the D.A. It shocked me no end when a white woman told me she went into the D.A.'s office and talked to him, because I had just been with a Black woman who went to see the D.A. and the D.A. wouldn't even come out the door of his office to speak to the woman. But he knew she was Black.

If she is raped by a white man and he has some money or some type of position, she can forget it because the police will warn the rapist, "Hey, this Black woman came in and told us you raped her. What are you going to do about it before she goes any further?" A black woman has to go through all of this most of the time by herself because a lot of times she doesn't have other strong people to be with her to make sure the police aren't being unfair to her.

I really think institutions are very cruel to Black women. People in institutions perpetuate not only rape myths but also Black myths. They feel that *all* Black women are "loose," so what are we complaining about. They feel that *all* Black women want sex 24 hours a day, so what's the big deal that someone took it with force. They feel that *all* Black women are cheap, so they treat Black women as tramps and with as little respect as possible. They feel that Black-on-Black crime is irrelevant, so why should they take this case seriously. I don't see how any black woman who has been raped ever gets a man convicted because she has to go through all that. She must also face a jury of middle class people, white or black, who share these same myths.

The hospitals feel it is not important when a Black woman says she's been raped. Most doctors live by myths also. They figure that any woman who has had a lot of sex can't be raped, but a lot of them also think that Black women have been having sex since they were six. Sometimes members of rape crisis centers or hot lines won't try to counsel a Black woman because they can't relate to her. They might feel, "I don't want to talk to her because I'm not really sure how she's going to respond to me." They should tell her that instead of being afraid to say anything for fear of being thought a bigot, they could just say, "I haven't counseled that much or I may not know where you're coming from, but let's give it a try," and try to work it out together.

Closely associated with the feminist anti-rape agitation was a major campaign against violence against women. Known to previous generations as "wife beating," the new label recognizes that such violence can be directed at an unmarried partner. Today, thanks in large part to the efforts of second-wave feminists, virtually all Americans agree that there is no excuse for such violence, yet in the mid-1990s an estimated million women a year experienced beating by an intimate partner, and nearly one in three women suffer at least one attack during adulthood. Shocking as these data are, they do not indicate an increase in violence against women so much as increased reporting. Before women's liberation, domestic violence stigmatized its victims more than its perpetrators and consequently was rarely discussed in public. The criminal justice system looked the other way and, when victims called, often worsened their situation by implicitly condoning assailants' complaints that women provoked and deserved the beatings.

Women's liberation forced this violence out of the closet. The movement's message—that there is never an excuse for domestic violence—was delivered not only through writing and speak-outs but also through an important innovation: shelters for battered women. While nineteenth-century feminists had spoken out against violence and even secretly harbored runaway wives, the establishment of the first shelters in 1975 created spaces in which battered women could connect with each other and with feminist staff, who emphasized that the victims were not to blame. During the next twenty-five years the domestic violence movement has made stunning achievements, such as establishing a national toll-free hot line in English and Spanish (with interpreters available for 139 additional languages) that receives 11,000 calls per month. The fullest expression of the feminist impact was the Violence Against Women Act of 1994, which established a Violence Against Women office in the Justice Department, the first federal government agency devoted to such a problem. Today this federal program helps fund approximately 1,800 shelters, telephone help lines, and education programs.

Still, the problem is difficult to police and the obstacles remain formidable. As with rape, poor women are more vulnerable to violence and have less access to protection and prosecution. Unfortunately, some victims of rape and battery become so desperate and so unable to find or even imagine legal recourse that they counterattack and sometimes kill their assailants. In recent years cases of battered women who kill have been widely publicized, and some have been acquitted or pardoned because of sympathy for their predicament. Formative in developing a battered woman's defense was the 1974 Inez Garcia case, which garnered national publicity because of a women's liberation defense campaign. The choice facing the defense in this case remains controversial today: whether to plead that a woman victim kills because she was so desperate that she became temporarily insane or because, from her perspective, her violence was a rational act of self-defense.

The Case of Inez Garcia
INTERVIEW WITH SUSAN JORDAN

When an illiterate Soledad woman shot dead a man named Miguel Jimenez in 1974, she had no idea she would become a *cause celebre* for the nascent women's movement.

Inez Garcia claimed she shot Jimenez because a half-hour earlier he had helped another man rape her, then threatened her again. But the district attorney didn't believe her and charged her with murder.

To feminists, the case symbolized the outrage of rape and the indifference of law enforcement to its victims. Gar-

cia was considered a hero—"the rape victim who fought back," as the *Ms.* magazine cover story put it. But Garcia was convicted of second-degree murder. The conviction was reversed, however, due to instructional error.

The task of defending Garcia on retrial fell to Susan B. Jordan, a young, female defense lawyer who saw the case differently—as one of self-defense. Jordan's challenge was persuading the judge and jury to see it through Garcia's eyes, and understand why she killed her assailant when there appeared to be no imminent threat of danger. "No one had ever asked a jury to look at it that way, from a rape victim's point of view," says Jordan. Shifting the focus worked: Garcia was acquitted.

Inez Garcia was an unlikely *cause celebre*. A young, devout Hispanic woman who had married at 14 and could neither read, write nor tell the time, in 1974 she was living in Soledad, to be near her husband, who was incarcerated there. One night, two men dragged her out of her house to a nearby alley, where one of them raped her while the other, who weighed some 300 pounds, held her down. A few minutes after leaving her, the accomplice, Miguel Jimenez, telephoned and told her they were going to come back and "do worse to her." Garcia didn't wait for them—less than an hour later she grabbed a .22-caliber rifle and went after the pair. When she found them a few blocks away, Jimenez had a knife in his hand. Without hesitating, Garcia shot him dead.

The district attorney charged her with murder and claimed Garcia was lying about the rape because she had never reported it. The DA insisted it was a simple case of revenge: Garcia shot Jimenez because he'd beaten up her roommate.

But to a nascent women's movement, the case represented much more: It symbolized the outrage of rape and the indifference of law enforcement to its victims. Local feminists formed a defense committee that quickly rallied around her, raising money and churning up publicity about the case.

Garcia already had drawn some attention after legendary trial lawyer Charles Garry agreed to represent her. But to the dismay of feminists, Garry chose not to argue self-defense because Garcia had shot Jimenez after the rape. Instead, he argued diminished capacity—that she was, in effect, temporarily insane when she fired the gun. The 1974 trial went badly, with Garcia enraged that no one took her rape claim seriously. "I'm not sorry I did it," she exploded at one point during cross-examination. "The only thing I'm sorry about is that I missed Luis the rapist."

With such admissions, it was no surprise when the jury convicted her of second-degree murder. That conviction, though, was reversed due to instructional error.

The 1977 retrial was what earned the case a place in history. On the second go-round Garcia was defended by Susan B. Jordan, who saw the case quite differently than Garry. "This was a classic self-defense case," says Jordan.

Many lawyers say Jordan's successful defense of Garcia laid the foundation for what is now known as the battered women's defense—the theory that a woman who kills her abuser may be acting in self-defense, even if she was not being attacked, or her abuser was unarmed, at the time of the killing. Garcia's case brought focus to a moment in time when ideas about women were changing and the once invisible crimes of rape and domestic violence were being brought to light, she says. Women were saying they had the right to fight back, and "it was the moment at which the world got the message," she says. "Without the case, the world would have gotten the message anyway, but the case was an easy way to get a handle on it."

Jordan, whose office is in Oakland, CA, talked about the Garcia case with San Francisco free-lance writer Susan Freinkel for this article.

QUESTION: [Charles] Garry was arguing a diminished capacity defense. Why didn't it work?

JORDAN: It wasn't working because Inez hated it. She couldn't stand being represented that way in court. And the judge, Monterey County Superior Court Judge Stanley Lawson, kept saying, "I don't want to hear any evidence about rape, this isn't a rape trial." To Inez, the rape was central to the whole thing.

Now the most difficult fact of the case, that Charlie couldn't get over, was she left the house with a loaded shotgun. And it was 20 to 40 minutes after she was raped. And Charlie just couldn't figure out what to do with that, and so he made her defense diminished capacity instead of something rational.

Q: If you link her decision to leave the house to the rape, then it can look like revenge. But if you link it to the fact that the assailants called her afterwards and threatened to do something worse, then it seems easier to create the context for self-defense. Was that what you did?

J: Yes, exactly. I mean this is self-defense. You're threatened, you leave, you don't have to wait to be killed.

Garry was a great lawyer. I don't want to take anything away from him. He just had no clue about women. He had a stereotypical view of women which prevented him from seeing the self-defense picture. To represent a woman or a man, or a murderer, or a terrorist, or a white collar person, you have to be able to be free of preconceptions about who they are or why they did it, in order to really look at what happened.

Q: So what did you do to get jurors to look at this free of preconceptions about rape victims?

J: I started with the men and I said something like, "Do you have any kids?" "Yes," said one man, "a boy and a girl." It was perfect. So I said, "Well, do you let your son go to the store at night?" This was a rural community. And he said, "Oh, yes, you know, no problem."

And I said, "Well, what about your daughter? Do you let your daughter go—" "Oh, no."

"Well, why not?" "Well, she might get raped."

And I said, "Well, if your daughter got raped, would she be asking for it?" "Oh, no, she'd be dressed very modestly."

I said, "Well, does she wear shorts?" "Yes." "Does she wear halter tops?" "Yeah." "Well, if she got raped, would you blame her?" "Never."

And the lights started to go off, because it was so clear that some jurors had one standard for the bad girls who get raped, and another standard for their daughters. They really began to engage in the dialogue. And

they got so engaged in the dialogue that we ended up with a jury of 10 men and two women, because those were the people who opened up the most.

It really was the moment the world was changing. Susan Brownmiller's book, *Against Our Will,* was published in '75, I think. A whole subject of rape was being opened up to scrutiny in a way which it hadn't probably for centuries.

Q: I'm curious about Garcia. She was portrayed as illiterate, as this naive, devout Catholic, devoted to her husband.

J: She was very smart, and savvy, and quick. But somehow she had missed reading and writing, and amazingly, she could not tell time. But she always knew what time it was.

Q: And was she transformed by this whole experience? Did she become politicized by it?

J: She hated every minute of it. She was a very reluctant symbol of the women's movement. She would go out there and carry on, talk about women, but this was not her milieu. She did not welcome this role. After the trial ended, she left the next morning. I haven't seen her since the verdict.

Q: You've said that once you looked at the circumstances through her eyes, it was a pretty straightforward self-defense case. Now as I understand the law of self-defense, you have to show that somebody truly believed themselves in danger, and that it's a reasonable belief. What did that mean in the context of this case?

J: That meant that at the moment Inez shot Miguel Jimenez, she had to believe that she was in danger of death or great bodily harm, and that a reasonable person in her shoes would have also believed that.

The Sexual Abuse of Children
FLORENCE RUSH   1971

The sexual abuse of children is an early manifestation of male power and oppression of the female.

There is, significantly, very little material on the subject of sexual abuse generally and particularly as it relates to children.

1. National statistics on the incidence of sexual offenses against children are wholly unavailable. The FBI's annual Information Crime Report is concerned with statistics on the offender and not the victim. It does not even carry a breakdown of the total incidence of all crimes against children. What makes an assessment even more difficult, except for rare cases of brutal attack or fatal situations, is that cases of sex offenses against children are not generally publicized by the press.

2. The problem of sexual abuse of children is of unknown national dimensions but findings strongly point to the probability of an enormous national incidence many times larger than the reported incidence of child abuse (physical abuse other than sexual). By an overwhelming ratio, 97%, offenders were male and ranged in age from 17 to 68. Victims were on a ratio of 10 girls to one boy. In 75% of the cases, the offender was known to the child or family such as a father, stepfather, mother's lover, brother, uncle or friend of the family—25% of the offenders were alleged to be strangers.

Let us consider a study which deals with 20 cases of incest and involves the fathers as offenders and daughters as victims. The preponderance of incest cases are between fathers and young daughters. The author, although sympathetic with the victim, still does not deal with the offender, but looks to the mother to control the problem.

There follow several examples of father behavior described by 13 mothers and, in every instance, corroborated by the child victim; breaking a radio over the mother's head; burning the child with hot irons, chasing the mother out of the house with a gun . . . locking mother or children in closets while he sexually abused the child victim . . . forcing sexual intercourse with the child in the mother's presence . . . etc.

After examining the character of the incest family . . . the unavoidable conclusion seems to be that the failure of the mother to protect the child against the contingency of incestuous victimization is a crucial and fruitful area of study. . . .

Considering the father offender as a possible source of control of incest behavior seems . . . like considering the fox . . . as guard in the hen-house. . . .

The mother is the only possible agent of incest control within the family group.

The father rapes and brutalizes and it turns out to be the

mother's fault and responsibility. Has anyone thought of the fantastic notion of getting rid of the father?

According to most anthropologists and sociologists, the purpose of the family is the protection of children. From what I have heard, read and seen, it would seem to me that the protectors and the offenders are one and the same. The fact is that families, generally, are given the job of socializing children to fill prescribed roles and thus supply the needs of a power society. My mother's inability to protect me from sexual abuse did not occur because she was worse than any other mother, but because, like all women, she was guilty and repulsed by her own sexuality and taught me to feel the same way. Seventy-five percent of the sexually abused children are victims of family members or friends. Children have nowhere to go outside the family. They have no options, no choices and no power. Ingrained in our present family system is the nucleus of male power and domination and no matter how often we witness the devastatingly harmful effects of this arrangement on women and children, the victims are asked to uphold the family and submit to its abuse.

We must begin to think of children's liberation as being the same as women's liberation. The female child and woman are the same person, merely at a different stage of development. The growth from childhood to adulthood is a process not a "gap" or separation. The female infant, child, woman and old woman are subject to the same evils.

One response to women's increasing rage about their vulnerability to violence was learning to fight back physically. Women's liberation enthusiastically took up martial arts. Feminists studied in private schools and also set up women's classes in women's centers. (In fact feminists contributed to popularizing Eastern martial arts in America.) Although it is doubtful that karate expertise or any kind of physical resistance is the best defense against attack, women nevertheless benefited mentally and physically from the confidence, strength, agility, and discipline of these skills. Women's increased interest in physical fitness has produced a major change in women's attitude toward their bodies and participation in athletics. Here, West Coast photographer Cathy Cade captured the excitement of women becoming powerful, and Chicana artist Ester Hernandez used karate to transform the archetypal Mexican saint, the Virgin of Guadalupe, into a feminist fighter.

Women's Martial Arts Demonstrations
CATHY CADE (PHOTOGRAPH)   1974

Karate As Self-Defense for Women

SUSAN PASCALÉ, RACHEL MOON, AND LESLIE TANNER

Women are attacked, beaten and raped every day. By Men! Women are afraid to walk certain streets after dark, and even afraid to walk into buildings where they live. It's about time that we as Women get strong in order to defend ourselves. Two of us (ages 29 and 43) and three children decided to learn Karate. We went to watch a class before signing up and if we hadn't been so determined, the classes (consisting of about 25 frighteningly strong men) would have scared us into quitting before we started. We had yet to learn how really weak we were!

When we went to our first class, we huddled in a corner, feeling inferior and somehow as though we were trespassing. The men stood directly in front of the mirrors, totally unselfconscious, to practice. We, after 3 months, are still self-conscious. We punch with our left hand, and it looks and feels like a piece of spaghetti. We are totally unaccustomed to looking in the mirror, contemplating our own gorgeous muscles. It makes us feel like fools. We are conditioned to feel that what we're doing is unfeminine. We have been taught to be passive all our lives — even for the two of us, who were sportswomen and dancers, the punching is just a little too much.

The trouble is, even now, after actually learning how to punch, we don't really want to punch at men. The first thing we think about is: "But I don't want to hurt him." Then we realized that this is really a traditional feminine cover-up for the truth which is that we are afraid of men. Women have always known to hit a man seriously means risking getting killed. We have acknowledged these "feminine attributes" to ourselves, and we try every day to overcome them. It is clear that the longer our attitudes persist, the less we learn.

Our experiences as Women, at the Dojo (the place where you learn and practice Karate) have shown us how very deep and oppressive the attitudes of men are towards Women. We have been tolerated to the point that we have sometimes felt like the "Invisible Woman." The men treat us with a patronizing air that seems to say they wish we weren't there.

The first and most obvious example of discrimination is that women are charged only half price. We don't know the actual reason for this, perhaps it's because we're considered only half-persons, or because the teacher feels guilty because he figures we'll never learn Karate anyway. We decided to take advantage of this form of oppression, and have not yet challenged it.

Secondly, the Sensei (Teacher) originally addressed the class as "Gentlemen." We let this pass for a couple of days, thinking it would take him a lesson or two to get used to us. But he continued and we confronted him, stating that we didn't care how he wished to address us, just as long as our existence was recognized, either as "ladies" with "gentlemen," or as "women" with "men," or just part of "everybody." The Sensei admitted his oversight and agreed to make amends.

Then, quite recently, Sensei got angry at the class and let loose a loud "Don't punch like that. It's too weak. You're punching like girls!" (Obviously the worst insult that can be given to a man.) At one time, we probably wouldn't have been insulted by this, thinking that he couldn't possibly mean us.

In Karate no distinctions are made in instruction between men and women. We are expected to do everything the men do: to learn the positions as fast and to do them as well. We have been rewarded on that assumption. We have advanced in rank beyond some men who were ahead of us when we started. (We are now advanced white belts and by December we should have our green belts.) Women entering a male Dojo should watch that they are not discriminated against by having less demanded of them. Women taking Karate with an all women's group should check their instruction against all-male or mixed classes.

Male chauvinism is masked by the fact that the code of the Dojo is that everyone be treated with great respect and humility, regardless of rank. We are treated *very politely*, formally and respectfully. In terms of human relationships, however, we are avoided as much as possible because the

Sensei and all the other men in the Dojo know how to treat us only in the traditional sense, i.e. as sex objects. Since we have not allowed ourselves to be treated as sex objects, we are not "women" in their eyes.

It is very difficult to figure out whether we are being treated in a certain manner because we are beginners (and weak) or because we are women. The men have tried to avoid all physical contact with us. When we need a partner for sit-ups (which means entangling our legs with theirs), they immediately try to find someone other than one of us, using the excuse (when questioned directly) that we're too light-weight or too weak. When Sensei makes the rounds to test our "stance," by touching the "butt" and thigh muscles, he just doesn't touch ours.

There are several reasons why I wanted to learn the art of self-defense. The two most important reasons were: 1) in the society we live in today I feel a great need for women to be strong; 2) karate and kata (dance forms) are really most beautiful and exciting. I feel I am getting stronger, and I feel all women should get strong and learn to fight.

Karate has made us feel much healthier and stronger than we were before (we've even cut our smoking in half). Stronger hands and arms enable us to do things we usually rely on men to do, such as carrying heavy loads from the store.

Karate gets us out of the house 3 nights (or days) a week, and because we like it, it becomes something we'll do *no matter what*. It's good for freeing us from household chores/waiting around for the man to come home/waiting around because the man *is* home/creating a good reason why a man must fit his schedule into ours, i.e. see us when *we're* available/or take care of his own children three nights a week!

Karate has mentally increased our confidence in ourselves as human beings. Simone de Beauvoir says, "Not to have confidence in one's body is to lose confidence in oneself" (*The Second Sex*). Our confidence has increased not only in confrontations with "dirty-old-men" in the street, but in non-physical confrontations with our own men and society in general.

La Virgen de Guadalupe Defendiendo los Derechos de los Xicanos

[The Virgin of Guadalupe Defending the Rights of Chicanos]
ESTER HERNANDEZ

1975

III
Institutions

A common accusation against women's liberation was that the movement was "anti-family." This myth derives from the powerful tendency to "naturalize" family, that is, to assume that one kind of family is proper or "natural" or God-ordained. Feminists challenged that assumption. They were critical of dominant family ideals such as male headship, women's exclusive responsibility for child care and housework, the sexual double standard. Feminists also saw that a majority of Americans did not live in "ideal" families, because they would not or could not, and that many forms of family served human needs. So feminists in the 1970s, as today, rejected the notion that the government should try to enforce one definition of family. To cite just one example: in 1976 feminist economist Barbara Bergmann organized a campaign to get the census to quit labeling husbands as "heads of household"; with support from Senator Pat Schroeder, the census agreed to this reform in 1980.

Yet feminists were strong proponents of family values in a democratic sense: they supported policies to strengthen family life through parental leave from jobs, campaigns against family violence, child welfare programs, sex education, and reproductive rights. And the women's-liberation critique of male-dominated families did not necessarily produce antagonism toward marriage or enthusiasm for single-mother families. Eleanor Holmes Norton, today the congresswoman (without a vote) from Washington, D.C., and in the 1960s a civil rights activist, called for the strengthening of marriage and two-parent families among African Americans, but without retreating to male domination.

Issues regarding black families have been controversial in America since slavery. Some scholars and advocates contended that slavery's legacy of shattering black families is responsible for the prevalence of black single-mother families today. In 1965 Secretary of Labor Daniel Patrick Moynihan issued a report on "The Negro Family" in which he argued that black poverty was a "pathology" created by "matriarchy." "A fundamental fact of Negro American family life is the often reversed roles of husband and wife," he argued, characterized by humiliated, submissive husbands and dominant wives. Many African Americans and some progressive whites responded angrily to the victim-blaming inherent in the report, which suggested that "defective" family structure and independent women were the cause of poverty. Feminists, black and white, were angered by the suggestion that only male-headed families could be considered healthy. Unfortunately the Moynihan Report made it difficult to discuss single motherhood and black male absence from families without great defensiveness. Just a few years later, Norton was one of the few people to be able to discuss black families in a nuanced and balanced manner.

For Sadie and Maud
ELEANOR HOLMES NORTON

Some subjects are so complex, so unyielding of facile insight, that it will not do to think about them in the ordinary way. Black women, their lot and their future, is for me such a subject. Thus, the new crop of literature concerning women—attuned to the peculiar relationship between white women and white men in America—has inspired me much, but less than the poetry of the great black poet, Gwendolyn Brooks, who writes for me and about me. Take, for example, Miss Brooks' poem, "Sadie and Maud," a sad ballad that, in a few stanzas, touches in some intimate respect all of us who are black women:

Maud went to college.
Sadie stayed at home.
Sadie scraped life
With a fine-tooth comb.

She didn't leave a tangle in.
Her comb found every strand.
Sadie was one of the livingest chits
In all the land.

Sadie bore two babies
Under her maiden name.
Maud and Ma and Papa
Nearly died of shame.

When Sadie said her last so-long
Her girls struck out from home.
(Sadie had left as heritage
Her fine-tooth comb.)

Maud, who went to college,
Is a thin brown mouse.
She is living all alone
In this old house.

Sadie and Maud are blood sisters, each in her own way living the unrequited life of the black woman. Sadie has two children out of wedlock, but the Sadies of this world also include black women who have been married, but have lost their husbands in America's wars against the black family. Maud "went to college"—or wherever black women have gone over the years to escape the perils of living the nearly predestined half-life of the black woman in this country. Maud, the "thin brown mouse" lives alone rather than incur Sadie's risks or risk Sadie's pleasures.

The difference in the lives of those two women cannot conceal the overriding problem they share—loneliness, life lacking in the chance to develop a relationship with a man or satisfactory family relationships. The complexities of the problems facing black women begin to unfold. Not only

must we work out an unoppressive relationship with our men; we must—we can at last—establish a relationship with them *de novo*.

In this respect, we conceive our mission in terms that are often different from the expressed goals of many white women revolutionaries. To be sure, our goals and theirs, in their general outlines, are the same, but black women confront a task that is as delicate as it is revolutionary. For black women are part of a preeminent struggle whose time has come—the fight for black liberation. If women were suddenly to achieve equality with men tomorrow, black women would continue to carry the entire array of utterly oppressive handicaps associated with race. Racial oppression of black people in America has done what neither class oppression nor sexual oppression, with all their pernicious qualities, has ever done: destroyed an entire people and its culture. The difference is between exploitation and slavery. Slavery partakes of all the worst excesses of exploitation—and more—but exploitation does not always sink to the miserable depths of slavery.

Yet black women cannot—must not—avoid the truth about their special subservience. They are women with all that that implies. If some have been forced into roles as providers or, out of the insecurity associated with being a black woman alone, have dared not develop independence, the result is not that black women are today liberated women. For they have been "liberated" only from love, from family life, from meaningful work, and, just as often, from the basic comforts and necessities of an ordinary existence. There is neither power nor satisfaction in such a "matriarchy." There is only the bitter knowledge that one is a victim.

Still, the stereotypic image of matriarchy has basic appeal to some black men who, in their frustration, may not see immediately the counter-revolutionary nature of such a battle cry. To allow the white oppressor to share the burden of his responsibility with the black woman is madness. It is comparable to black people blaming Puerto Ricans for competing with them for jobs, thus, relieving the government of the pressures it must have to fulfill its duty to provide full employment. Surely, after hundreds of years, black men realize that imprecision in detecting the enemy is an inexcusable fault in a revolutionary.

But our problems only begin with the reconstruction of the black family. As black men begin to find dignified work after so many generations, what roles will their women seek? Are black people to reject so many of white society's values only to accept its view of woman and of family? At the moment when the white family is caught in a maze of neurotic contradictions, and white women are supremely frustrated with their roles, are black women to take up such troubled models? Shall black women exchange their ancient insecurity for the white woman's familial cocoon? Can it serve us any better than it has served them? And how will it serve black men?

There is no reason to repeat bad history. There is no reason to envy the white woman who is sinking in a sea of close-quartered affluence, where one's world is one's house, one's peers one's children, and one's employer one's husband. Black women shall not have gained if Sadie and Maud exchange the "fine-tooth comb" and the "old house" for the empty treasures white women are trying to discard.

With black family life so clearly undermined in the American environment, blacks must remake the family unit, not imitate it. Indeed, this task is central to black liberation. The black male will not be returned to his historic strength—the foremost task of the black struggle today—if we do not re-create the strong family unit that was a part of our African heritage before it was dismembered by the slave-owning class in America. But it will be impossible to reconstruct the black family if its central characters are to be paper copies, acting out the old white family melodrama.

We are a people in search of what, for us, has been the interminably elusive goal of economic security. Wretchedly poor for 350 years in a country where most groups have thrived, we could come to see the pain of much of white family life as bearable when measured against the tortures we have borne. Our men, deliberately emasculated as the only way to enforce their servile status, might easily be tempted by a family structure which, by making them the financial head of the household, seemed to make them its actual head. In our desperation to escape so many suffering decades, we might trip down the worn path taken by so many in America before us.

If we are to avoid this disaster, the best, perhaps the only, place to begin is in our conception of the black woman. After all, the immediate tasks of the black man are laid out for him. It is the future role of the black woman that is problematical. And what she is allowed to become—or relegated to—will shape not simply her future, but that of the black family and the fate of its members.

Yet it is certain that the institution of the family will undergo radical alteration largely through the new roles women will have to seek. With birth preventatives and with world overpopulation, many couples will rethink whether it is wise to have children at all. And even though most may choose to have children, it is doubtful that it will any longer be prestigious or wise to have very many. With children no longer the universally accepted reason for marriage, marriages are going to have to exist on their own merits. Marriages are going to have to exist because they possess inherent qualities which make them worthy of existing, a plane to which the institution has never before been elevated. For marriage to develop such inherent qualities, the woman partner, heretofore oriented toward fulfilling now outmoded functions, will have to seek new functions. Whether black or white, if American women are to find themselves, they must begin looking outside the home. This will undoubtedly lead them into doing and thinking about matters now pretty much reserved for men. Inevitably, women are going to acquire new goals and a new status.

As it is, we have a chance to pioneer in forging new relationships between men and women. We have a chance to make family life a liberating experience instead of the confining experience it sometimes has been.

We have a chance to free woman and, with her, the rest of us.

What's in a Name?

JULIE CORYELL

1971

What's in a name? Plenty. Why is it that women take their husband's name on marriage? Why do we call our original names *maiden* names? Why don't we keep our names if we want to?

In studying about patriarchy, I learned that women and children came to bear the husband's and father's name because he owned them. I am no one's possession but my own self.

Social usage clarifies the potential sexual availability of a woman in her name. We are Miss so and so—fair game— or Mrs. (man's name)—safe, hands off, men—or Mrs. (woman's name)—divorced? available? Probably. Mr. does not reveal a man's marital status. After all, what does marital status have to do with one's work and attitudes? Why must women continue to be forced to declare it unless it is truly relevant?

In September I filed a petition (cost $25) in King County Superior Court, Washington, to change my name to my original name. (The lawyer's fee is negotiable—legal guidance cost me $25.) To be sure my surname comes from my father, but my mother used her poet's ear in naming me Julie Esther Coryell. My married name had always felt rhythmically incomplete. I like my name and am glad to have it back.

If you like your name and want to keep it—that is all you have to do. If you marry, simply maintain your original signature on all documents. If you divorce, arrange to have your name change as part of the settlement. Parents can bestow any name upon their children at birth on the certificate of birth—it need not be the father's surname. We do not have to continue the patriarchal tradition. Use the mother's name, hyphenate the parents' names, or use something different. But think about how you feel about your name.

While both first- and second-wave feminism tried to reform family law and relationships toward greater equality, only women's liberation challenged the deeply embedded notion that housework and child care were women's special responsibility, determined by biology. Women tried many formal and informal, serious and humorous, means of trying to get men to share the work. (Pat Mainardi's "The Politics of Housework" in chapter 11 describes male resistance in a widely circulated satire.)

Feminist criticism of men's domineering behavior and failure to share in housework crossed race and class lines. But the task of "reforming" men was more difficult among people of color and poor people. Such men felt symbolically emasculated by poverty and racism, by the obstacles they faced in achieving respect in public. Denise Oliver, a leader in the Puerto Rican Young Lords Party, encapsulates both sides of this problem.

We can see both similarities and dissimilarities in an account by someone from a more privileged position. Writer and feminist activist Alix Shulman's "Marriage Agreement" was a well-known formal approach to the problem, and after its original 1970 appearance in a women's liberation magazine, *Up from Under,* it was widely reprinted and attacked in mainstream magazines such as *Redbook* and *Life.* In retrospect, most feminists today find this draft agreement rigid, even ridiculous. Its function was more rhetorical than practical. In its time it was a powerfully educational document, pointing out how much work housework entailed and how disproportionately much of it women did. Through provocative documents like this one, women's liberation was encouraging women to make demands and nudging men to question their privileges. As a result, many heterosexual relationships shifted toward a somewhat fairer division of labor, usually without a formal agreement. As Shulman suggests at the end of her article, many men found that they also benefited and particularly enjoyed closer relations with their children.

Machismo
DENISE OLIVER

1971

Machismo is a word that is used to depict a certain tendency among Latin males. It doesn't mean that machismo doesn't exist among white males—it's just not that obvious. Among white men, their whole machismo thing is like, who can make better business deals or take over a large corporation. A man is respected by virtue of the money he has.

But since the Third World man doesn't have any money, he's respected by his fellows for how much balls he's got, and how much he can oppress women, and how many women he can take to bed and use and fuck over. So that although machismo is not just a Latin thing—and we'd like to make sure that idea gets corrected—it is more apparent in oppressed communities.

In Puerto Rican society, the woman is taught to cater to the needs of her family, in particular to the demands of her father or husband. She's taught that she is inferior in her own ways. Like, sometimes she is taught not to enjoy sex. The man, of course, can go out and enjoy it—this is being very macho.

You see a lot of women with a black eye or scars on their face, and you know what's been going on at home—their husband or their old man has been beating the shit out of 'em—and there's nothing that they can do. You can't complain to anybody—nobody else is gonna stand up for you, because that's supposedly the code of the streets. It's something that we're gonna have to educate our sisters and our brothers out of.

One of the things that I've noticed in most Puerto Rican homes is that the mealtime's really a drag. The woman cooks all day long for the family. Naturally the first person she serves is her husband—she may even serve him better food than everyone else, cause there may not be enough meat to go around. Okay, he sits down and eats a whole meal, then she serves the kids and whatever relatives are hangin' around and friends.

A lot of times there's not even enough food left for her to eat after she's been cooking since maybe two o'clock in the afternoon, or if there is, she eats by herself, and then she has all the dishes to do. Meanwhile, everybody else has gone out to watch the ball game or out on the streets.

I rebel against that when I go to people's homes and the woman is there serving me. I tell her I'm not gonna eat unless she sits down too at the table. It seems like a petty point, but after day after day of doing that, the woman starts hating the people that she's feeding. Frankly, I wouldn't blame her if she started poisoning the family.

We have to have the kind of society where a woman can determine for herself whether or not she wants to have a child—not on the basis of whether that child will eat, because all children will be eating and will be well-clothed and well-educated, but just on the basis of how many children she feels like having at that time.

A Marriage Agreement
ALIX KATES SHULMAN

1970

When my husband and I were first married a decade ago, "keeping house" was less of a burden than a game. We both worked full-time in New York City so our small apartment stayed empty most of the day and taking care of it was very little trouble. Twice a month we'd spend Saturday cleaning and doing our laundry at the laundromat. We shopped for food together after work and though I usually did the cooking, my husband was happy to help. Since our meals were simple and casual, there were few dishes to wash. We occasionally had dinner out and usually ate breakfast at a diner near our offices. We spent most of our free time doing things we enjoyed together, such as taking long walks in the evenings and spending weekends in Central Park. Our domestic life was beautifully uncomplicated.

When our son was born, our domestic life suddenly became *quite* complicated; and two years later, when our daughter was born, it became impossible. We automatically accepted the traditional sex roles that society assigns. My husband worked all day in an office; I left my job and stayed at home, taking on almost all the burdens of housekeeping and child raising.

When I was working I had grown used to seeing people during the day, to having a life outside the home. But now I was restricted to the company of two demanding preschoolers and to the four walls of an apartment. It seemed unfair that while my husband's life had changed little when the children were born, domestic life had become the only life I had.

I tried to cope with the demands of my new situation, assuming that other women were able to handle even larger families with ease and still find time for themselves. I couldn't seem to do that.

We had to move to a larger apartment to accommodate our larger family, and because of the children, keeping it reasonably neat took several hours a day. I prepared half a dozen meals every day for from one to four people at a time—and everyone ate different food. Shopping for this brood—or even just running out for a quart of milk—meant putting on snowsuits, boots, and mittens; getting strollers or carriages up and down the stairs; and scheduling the trip so it would not interfere with one of the children's feeding or nap or illness or some other domestic job. Laundry was now a daily chore. I seemed to be working every minute of the day—and still there were dishes in the sink; still there wasn't time enough to do everything.

Even more burdensome than the physical work of housekeeping was the relentless responsibility I had for the children. I loved them, but they seemed to be taking over my life. There was nothing I could do, or even contemplate, without first considering how they would be affected. As they grew older just answering their questions ruled out even a private mental life. I had once enjoyed reading, but now if there was a moment free, instead of reading for myself, I read to them. I wanted to work on my own writing, but there simply weren't enough hours in the day. I had no time for myself; the children were always *there*.

As my husband's job began keeping him at work later and later—and sometimes taking him out of town—I missed his help and companionship. I wished he would come home at six o'clock and spend time with the children so they could know him better. I continued to buy food with him in mind and dutifully set his place at the table. Yet sometimes whole weeks would go by without his having dinner with us. When he did get home the children often were asleep, and we both were too tired ourselves to do anything but sleep.

As the children grew older I began free-lance editing at home. I felt I had to squeeze it into my "free" time and not allow it to interfere with my domestic duties or the time I owed my husband—just as he felt he had to squeeze in time for the children during weekends. We were both chronically dissatisfied, but we knew no solutions.

After I had been home with the children for six years, I began to attend meetings of the newly formed Women's Liberation Movement in New York City. At these meetings I began to see that my situation was not uncommon; other women too felt drained and frustrated as housewives and mothers. When we started to talk about how we would have chosen to arrange our lives, most of us agreed that even though we might have preferred something different, we had never felt we had a choice in the matter. We realized that we had slipped into full domestic responsibility simply as a matter of course, and it seemed unfair.

Eventually, after an arduous examination of our situation, my husband and I decided that we no longer had to accept the sex roles that had turned us into a lame family. Out of equal parts love for each other and desperation at our situation, we decided to re-examine the patterns we had been living by, and starting again from scratch, to define our roles for ourselves.

We began by agreeing to share completely all responsibility for raising our children (by then aged five and seven) and caring for our household. If this new arrangement meant that my husband would have to change his job or that I would have to do more free-lance work or that we would have to live on a different scale, then we would. It would be worth it if it could make us once again equal,

independent and loving as we had been when we were first married.

Simply agreeing verbally to share domestic duties didn't work, despite our best intentions. And when we tried to divide them "spontaneously" we ended up following the traditional patterns. Our old habits were too deep-rooted. So we sat down and drew up a formal agreement, acceptable to both of us that clearly defined the responsibilities we each had.

It may sound a bit formal, but it has worked for us. Here it is:

MARRIAGE AGREEMENT

PRINCIPLES

We reject the notion that the work which brings in more money is the more valuable. The ability to earn more money is already a privilege which must not be compounded by enabling the larger earner to buy out of his/her duties and put the burden on the one who earns less, or on someone hired from outside.

We believe that each member of the family has an equal right to his/her own time, work, value, choices. As long as all duties are performed, each person may use his/her extra time any way he/she chooses. If he/she wants to use it making money, fine. If he/she wants to spend it with spouse, fine. If not, fine.

As parents we believe we must share all responsibility for taking care of our children and home—not only the work, but the responsibility. At least during the first year of this agreement, *sharing responsibility* shall mean dividing the *jobs* and dividing the *time*.

In principle, jobs should be shared equally, 50–50, but deals may be made by mutual agreement. If jobs and schedule are divided on any other than a 50–50 basis, then either party may call for a re-examination and redistribution of jobs or a revision of the schedule at any time. Any deviation from 50–50 must be for the convenience of both parties. If one party works overtime in any domestic job, she/he must be compensated by equal extra work by the other. For convenience, the schedule may be flexible, but changes must be formally agreed upon. The terms of this agreement are rights and duties, not privileges and favors.

JOB BREAKDOWN

A. Children

1. Mornings: Waking children; getting their clothes out, making their lunches; seeing that they have notes, homework, money, passes, books, etc.; brushing their hair; giving them breakfast; making coffee for us.

2. Transportation: Getting children to and from lessons, doctors, dentists, friends' houses, park, parties, movies, library, etc. Making appointments.

3. Help: Helping with homework, personal problems, projects like cooking, making gifts, experiments, planting, etc.; answering questions, explaining things.

4. Nighttime: Getting children to take baths, brush their teeth, go to bed, put away their toys and clothes; reading with them; tucking them in and having night-talks; handling if they wake and call in the night.

5. Babysitters: Getting babysitters, which sometimes takes an hour of phoning.

6. Sickcare: Calling doctors, checking out symptoms, getting prescriptions filled, remembering to give medicine, taking days off to stay home with sick child; providing special activities.

7. Weekends: All above, plus special activities (beach, park, zoo, etc.).

B. Housework

1. Cooking: Breakfasts; dinners (children, parents, guests).

2. Shopping: Food for all meals; housewares; clothing and supplies for children.

3. Cleaning: Dishes daily; apartment weekly, bi-weekly, or monthly.

4. Laundry: Home laundry; making beds; drycleaning (take and pick up).

Our agreement changed our lives. Surprisingly, once we had written it down, we had to refer to it only two or three times. But we still had to work to keep the old habits from intruding. If it was my husband's night to take care of the children, I had to be careful not to check up on how he was managing. And if the baby sitter didn't show up for him, I would have to remember that that was *his* problem.

Eventually the agreement entered our heads, and now, after two successful years of following it, we find that our new roles come to us as readily as the old ones had. I willingly help my husband clean the apartment (knowing it is his responsibility) and he often helps me with the laundry or the meals. We each have less work, more hours together and less resentment.

Before we made our agreement I had never been able to find the time to finish even one book. Over the past two years I've written three children's books, a biography and a novel and edited a collection of writings. Without our agreement I would never have been able to do this.

Perhaps the best testimonial of all to our marriage agreement is the change that has taken place in our family life. One day after it had been in effect only four months our daughter said one day to my husband, "You know, Daddy, I used to love Mommy more than you, but now I love you both the same."

Women's liberation continued a traditional division of labor in which women take responsibility for social relationships. Early second-wave feminists not only emphasized bonds among women but also tried to create and practice free and equal intimate relationships with men. Following in the tradition of utopian communitarianism from the previous century, a movement in which many women's rights advocates participated, second-wave feminists tried many different ways to envisage and construct alternative love and family relationships. Many feminists were concerned that living exclusively in couples and nuclear families kept women isolated and too dependent on men and strengthened individualism at the expense of commitment to community. In response, feminists and other members of the counterculture experimented with alternative household forms, both urban and rural. Their political ideals sometimes pushed them into uncomfortable situations, although they also often had practical motivations—needing to live more cheaply. They were also seeking less wasteful and more ecological ways to relate to the earth and the economy. These alternatives did not turn out to be panaceas, and communal living in particular was mainly a bust: with the exception of some rural communes that survive, most women found it difficult to live closely with a large number of other adults. But feminists learned from their mistakes and in the process developed their analysis—as the following three articles each demonstrates.

Communal Living

1971

We think of extended families and communal living, either all women or women and men together, as life styles which will help us learn about ourselves and about better ways of living. Living communally allows us to share the routine work of living and allows us to share ourselves with other people. As a group of people work together to "live," each individual is changed in the process. We all come out better people, having dealt with the hang ups that interfere with our relating to other people. By living communally, the possibility of sharing material possessions becomes real, as does the absurdity of so many TV sets, radios, books, records, and household items. The contradictions in society become more unbearable as we build really human relationships with one another.

Communal living can be a liberating experience for children, too. Some parents are reluctant to "experiment" with their lives because of children, but more and more parents are finding it necessary to move out of the nuclear family precisely because of their children. An only child will certainly be happier living with other children, and adults without children are often anxious to live in a family with children. Communal living arrangements can be less oppressive to children than the nuclear family, as adults struggle to relate to them in a less authoritarian, more respectful way. People are realizing that it is contradictory to talk about abuses of power in the government and economic system and then to be psychologically abusive to children. Certainly if we want our children to be critical of the status quo, we must raise them to question *our* authority over them.

Communal living offers opportunities for old people to live either together or with groups of people of different ages. We have done little thinking about the possibilities for old people and this should certainly be explored more thoroughly.

It is important to realize, however, that poor people have often been forced into extended families of blood relations out of economic need rather than choice. Solving financial problems may be an important function of extended families, but people cannot live together successfully without a shared commitment to each other based on trust and a willingness to deal honestly with their problems.

The Five of Us (With a Little Help from Our Friends)

VICKI COHN POLLARD

1971

I and my husband, Robert, and our daughter, Tanya, 2 & a half, live in a mortgaged $6,000 row house in Baltimore with another couple, Frank and Jean, who don't have any children and at this time don't plan to. Robert and I were living in the house when my women's liberation consciousness made me realize how terrible it was to raise a child in a nuclear family. Also I knew I would go nuts if I didn't figure out some way to share the burdens of raising a child. In addition we were having a hard time financially. For us, communal living offers a partial solution to these problems.

When Robert and I first started talking about living communally, I had many fears—the way women often do when faced with a new and threatening situation. I felt sure that I absolutely had to have privacy, that I was so selfish that I couldn't share my possessions, that I was such a bitch that no one could ever get along with me. Possibly the most irrational fear was that somehow I had hoodwinked Robert into not believing all these terrible things about me, and that if we lived with other people who would confront me on these things, he would come to realize how awful I actually was. I had heard stories about couples ending in divorce after living communally. So I was somewhat shocked and quite pleased to find how unrealistic my fears were. Not that these problems are easily brushed aside, but everything is part of a process and when working together and being honest and open about feelings, solutions can be found.

One of the problems we're still working on is the lack of privacy that is bound to develop before structures are worked out to insure that privacy. For us, this is a problem both with the four of us in the house and with the community of friends around us. People who live together must work out ways to be together in different groupings. We are still a long way from solving this problem, but we talk about it often, so that informal solutions take place from time to time. We have a shared babysitting arrangement, so that Robert and I are free to leave the house, to be together or with friends. Our biggest problem is having enough time

for the two of us to relate to each other alone because we are both so incredibly busy, and because when we are not busy, there are so many different friends whom we love and want to spend time with. There is an added friction because my being busy is a direct result of my involvement in women's liberation. Many times a conflict arises for me between being with Robert and being with my sisters. He has no counterpart among men at this point to make that problem easier. He fears that my very close relationships with women might draw me into an all-women's living situation.

Everything that we are doing is so challenging of everything that we were raised to expect from our lives that there is little stability in anything any more. Living out our politics means that everything is a struggle; nothing has been laid out for us ahead of time. We never know what we are leading ourselves into. But we have found that struggling through all our changes is much easier with other people sharing them. Robert and I tried to break down job patterns before Frank and Jeanie moved in and found it almost impossible. No matter what, I still felt the responsibility of checking the refrigerator in the afternoon to see whether there was any food for dinner. At first we used to make personal attacks on each other when either of us wasn't doing our job properly; now we can relate as comrades offering helpful suggestions. It used to be that if one of us didn't do a job, it could be interpreted as something being done to the other; now it can only be seen as directed to the whole house.

Another important sharing for us has been learning not only how to argue in front of Jeanie and Frank, but to actively involve them in our arguments. So often it happens that we can't see that there is some block in communication keeping us from understanding what the other is saying, and someone else can see that easily. It's painful to argue in front of others, knowing that the things they say can greatly affect the outcome of the argument. But it is also liberating. We have all been taught for so long that problems must be personal and kept to ourselves. So it becomes a political act to let others help in times of crisis and avoid the individualistic way of thinking we must solve everything alone. There has been a politicization of problems because Jeanie and I often are allies in arguments and see things from a women's liberation point of view. If either of us were living alone with our husbands, this would not be possible.

Ever since my first women's liberation discussion group, when Tanya was three months old, I began conceiving of changes I thought we should make in raising her. I knew that I wanted her to be trusting rather than competitive. I wanted her to be able to love many adults, not just her parents, and I wanted her to grow up mostly with her peers, rather than with family. I became convinced that the nuclear family was destructive for everyone in it. I feel that the more responsibility any one person bears for raising a child, the more anger that person will have for the child. To avoid what I knew would be a problem if I kept taking care of her we began early, when Tanya was 3 months old, involving her in a more child-centered environment, first sending her to a babysitter with another child for four hours a day, and then, when she was one and a half, sending her to an all-day care center. When she first started attending her Mini-school, some people responded with horror at the thought that we were sending her away for so long so early. But she really loved Mini-school.

Before this we tried to break down her image of us as the only people who could take care of her. As our friendship with Dick and Kay, our friends across the street, developed, a sharing of Tanya developed also. It's remarkable how difficult this process is—being able to give up the privileges and burdens that are involved in being the only people to whom a child can turn. At some level, it is scary to think that she can so easily learn to trust and love lots of other people, to be so independent that she might need us a lot less than we need her. On the other hand, while struggling to get over these feelings of possessiveness, there are so many happy and beautiful experiences with sharing her that we know we are doing the right thing, that many parents are better than two, for everyone.

When Frank and Jeanie moved in, there was no discussion at all of how or if child care would be divided up. Our house in many ways was founded on practical needs, and we had done little political thinking about what we were going to do. We were fairly aware that Frank was not particularly fond of kids. It was only through much discussion that we realized that he was inexperienced and afraid more than anything, and we had to figure out ways to break down these feelings. Mothers have awful fears about asking other people to take responsibility for their children, because traditionally that has meant mothers were unable to do their job. This fear has to be broken down on mothers' parts. Often people unsure of taking care of children won't volunteer, but they actually might very much like to begin trying and need to be asked.

Because of my fears, I was not able to propose that child-rearing be shared in our house. We have moved slowly, but wonderful things are beginning to happen now. Frank has gone through the steps of first reading books to Tanya, to really talking to her about what she is doing, to putting her to bed at night, and even having a wonderful time lying down with her and having her shut her eyes and tell him what pictures she sees. Robert and I share Tanya absolutely equally. For example, I don't even see her before four in the afternoon when she comes home from Mini-school because every morning Robert gets up with her, dresses and feeds her, and takes her with other children to Mini-school. Since she is so close to Robert, she has always been fantastically receptive to Frank, and this has helped the two of them learn to love each other. It is still a new and unusual enough thing that it is slightly touching when Tanya goes all by herself to Frank's room to play with him.

In addition to Dick and Kay and Jeanie and Frank, there is our whole radical community who share Tanya. Almost all of our close friends live within two blocks of our house, so it is fairly easy to call on others to help out. Everyone makes it clear that when either of us really need someone to take care of Tanya, they will always be glad to do it. In our larger group, so far we have done almost nothing in the way of structured child-sharing, but people are anxious to, and we are beginning to schedule such things as taking the kids on weekends or to each other's houses for dinner. We realized, recently, when Tanya was eating dinner away from us, the huge difference there is in not having a child present at a meal. We carried on a conversation that just couldn't have happened with her there, because of her needs to be included in things. Most important to me about our community is that Tanya is growing up feeling a sense of love and support from the many adults close to her, and that the children of that community have special feelings about each other that we probably can't begin to comprehend.

We have been fairly astonished at the response our house has had from our neighbors. Our street is divided into apartments on one side, where mostly hippies and students live, and houses on the other side which are owned by working class families who have lived there for many years. I grew up being the only Jewish family in a neighborhood of non-Jews and had never really experienced being accepted by my neighbors. So, in our situation, four quite obvious freaks, living what has to appear to be some kind of orgiastic existence, I had no hopes for anything but hostility. While everyone else on the block has a house painted the same dull brown, our house is bright red. But our neighbors have been warm and friendly to us. At this time, we count six households who have actively reached out to us, and many others who smile and talk to us. We have been given several presents for Tanya, including a doll bigger than she is from a woman across the street, and a pumpkin and other fall decorations from a man who said he got them at a fair.

Discussions about politics have come about very slowly with our neighbors. We have big posters on our front windows, some permanent revolutionary ones, and the changing type that announce things like the August 26th Women's Strike, a street festival for our People's Free Medical Clinic, and an anti-repression rally. They know where we stand and if they don't agree, at least some of them respect what we are doing. One man who works at a newspaper office sent over with his son a photo of cops in Washington beating a guy badly. It seemed he sent it over to show his sympathy with us. He also sent over some AP news clips about Nixon's plans for concentration camps for radicals.

The elderly man who lives next door is very friendly with us and talks to us regularly, helping us with our garden and other things around the house. We once had a very heated discussion with him because during the summer Tanya would play naked in her wading pool. This freaked our neighbor out badly. We had previously discussed it with him in a more calm fashion and had agreed that whenever his grandchildren were around, we would put a bathing suit on Tanya. He didn't want his grandchildren to grow up thinking it was all right to "go around naked." But one afternoon Tanya was naked with another friend, Bruce, and this was more than our neighbor could bear. During the screaming and yelling that took place, he said some nasty things about our politics. We tried to explain to him what we thought freedom was and why it didn't exist in the United States, and to prevent Tanya from going naked would be a part of that. After a great deal of discussion, it all ended amicably. We aren't trying to organize him, but it's nice to honestly communicate what we believe.

Hippie Communes
VIVIAN ESTELLACHILD

In this article I will discuss two rural hippie communes in which I lived for a total of 10 months. Those experiences served as a catalyst to my becoming a feminist.

What I have seen is a lot of very boorish men on some very heavy ego trips, and a million little self-appointed, self-infatuated male (you'll never see a female) gurus running around. I see women treated as groovy objects to possess and adorn the male ego. Wanted: groovy, well-built chick to share apartment and do the cooking and cleaning, must be "clean." Does that ad sound familiar? Rent a "chick" prices range from $0 to free bath and rent.

Men have told me that they couldn't remember the name of the girl (they always say "chick" but I just cannot) they slept with the night before, in some cases they had not even asked. Who cares? Hippie men act like suburban studs, who look good but are selfish and rarely know how to do anything more than gain a little pleasure for themselves. Hippie women over thirty have that lean and desperate look. If they remain hippies they become the big mamas. It seems that no one wants a woman, just a "chick." If a woman objects, she is "uptight," a "dyke," a "bitch," frigid and subject to physical and mental abuse. Many women are made to feel sick and neurotic for stepping out of any of the traditional female roles. Most damaging of all is the feeling that it is "all in your own head." If you could only get that straight then everything would be groovy and you would be liberated.

The talk of love is profuse but the quality of relationships is otherwise. The hip man like his straight counterpart is nothing more, nothing less, than a predator. His sexual experience is largely an act of conquest or rape and certainly nothing more than an expression of hostility. The idea of sexual liberation for the woman means she is not so much free to fuck but free to get fucked over. All of this and it's free of charge. A woman can hope for a place to "crash." The sons have really outdone the fathers. Our mothers could get a home and security, a prostitute—money, but the hippie woman is bereft of all that.

With that introduction I would like to talk about Grow Farm, a commune of 30–50 people in Oregon. It consists of

310 acres financed by loans and parents to the tune of $75,000. (Sound like the house in the suburbs?) The men do odd jobs like tree pruning while the women take care of the babies and wash the unending pile of dirty dishes. They contribute their welfare checks to the communal bank account. It takes $2500/mo. for expenses. Despite the communal handling of money there is continual squabbling and distrust as to who gets more and who is "stashing" money and other articles. This is particularly true among the men.

The men come in a few simple varieties. The first is the Bill C., Ph.D., mathematician with 2 wives and 7 kids, too good to work with his hands, but not too good to fuck everything that moves. At the same time always making it clear by putting you down that he had the market for brains. To him I was always the idealist whose head he never quite understood.

The major problems of the commune were male chauvinism, insensitivity, and stagnation. New ideas met with incredible resistance. In order that people notice that you were upset about something it was necessary to do a total hysterical freakout scene. New suggestions met with laughter and ridicule. It is impossible to live in such conditions. When I saw Lottie freak out precisely over the unwillingness of people to change I saw her old man hit her in the face so badly that she was blinded for two weeks. She and I were called the "dykes" because we were uppity. Only she was braver and paid a higher price.

The second type of "man" was the big Jim C. variety. He was a big macho alcoholic (as were at least 6 other men). He has sired 6 children but will never be a father. I have seen his wife thrown around and come close to a concussion.

While the men played all-American on an $8,000 caterpillar, and wrecked all the cars, the women were criticized for their driving and told things like "there are three kids with dirty diapers in here and three chicks—get to it!" Of course the men had just been sitting there all that time while the women had been baking bread, making supper, and doing the endless pile of dishes left from the interminable snacks. On one occasion I was crazy enough to leave a friendly note on the wall suggesting that each person wash his own dish. The response was angry derision from the men. The note also asked to cook three meals a day and make meals and dishes simpler. What! Infringe on people doing their own thing? Schedule their lives? Well, hell, my life was becoming one long round of dishes and meals. I finally stopped helping but then the burden fell on the other women since we really did not have our shit together.

There was a schoolhouse in which one woman worked tirelessly. Education was more of an all-day living experi-ence. So we were successfully raising kids who were free of time zones but into heavy "masculine" and "feminine" role playing. The ten year old boy was getting to be an unnerv-ing copy of his father.

Another problem was the rapid turnover of people and transients. The atmosphere left me with no bearings at all. I left and so did a few other women. (This seems to be a trend—so there is hope.) The next time I saw the men they were in town looking for "some ass," and only four women were left on the farm.

Benjamin Spock's *Baby and Child Care*, first published in 1946, was a virtual bible for many American parents for several gen-erations, in part because it empathized with and reassured mothers. However, progressive peace activist Dr. Spock was a crea-ture of his time in his gender assumptions, and he assumed that the conventional family ideal—headed by a father who was the only wage-earner with a wife responsible for the children—was in fact how all families lived. These assumptions, not surpris-ingly, raised feminist hackles and numerous feminist mothers criticized his sexist advice. It is evidence both of Spock's openness and of the women's movement's power that he revised later editions of his book in accord with just the kinds of crit-icisms made here by Jo Ann Hoit.

Speaking of Spock
JO ANN HOIT

1970

In his most widely read book, *Baby and Child Care*, Dr. Spock assumes from the beginning that the mother will be taking care of the children, rather than expecting that both parents will share this 24-hour job, even when both are at home. In his first general statements about his philosophy of child-rearing, Spock speaks about "parents," but as he gives concrete examples and begins discussing the actual care of the child, he refers almost exclusively to mothers.

This is a typical sequence: "If *parents* are too hesitant in asking for reasonable behavior . . . they can't help resenting the bad behavior that comes instead . . . If, for example, a baby acquires a taste for staying up late in the evening and his *mother* is afraid to deny him this pleasure, he may, over a period of several months, turn into a disagreeable tyrant who keeps *her* walking for hours." This example is particu-larly interesting since it deals with one problem—bed-time—which occurs when most fathers are home. Yet it is the mother's problem and the baby will keep *her* walking all night.

Clearly then, it is the job of the mother—not of the "parents"—that Spock is describing when he says about child care: "At best, there's lots of hard work and depriva-tion . . . preparing the proper diet, washing diapers and clothes, cleaning up messes . . . stopping [the children's] fights." This list goes on for a paragraph and includes trips to zoos and such, juggling the tighter family budget, and staying home from most parties and other entertainment. Later Spock adds that the mother must also remember to give her husband some attention so he won't feel left out!

Spock is well aware of the detrimental effect this role has on women. He devotes several pages to such topics as "needless self-sacrifice sours everybody," "parents are bound to get cross," "parental impatience," "mixed feelings about pregnancy," "the blue feeling," "a feeling of depression," being "anxious," and the mother's feeling "convinced that she is inadequate" and "inferior." Spock admits these feelings are the result of the living situation, which he has already said requires self-sacrifice ("deprivation"). He emphasizes that many mothers have these feelings and that they are, therefore, "normal" feelings. Yet he does not criticize the conditions which create them; instead he recommends seeking psychiatric help to adjust to the life which he says is "*at best* . . . lots of hard work and deprivation." In other words (presuming you can afford this expensive prescription), change your feelings instead of the conditions which caused them.

At one point it does look as if Spock is about to suggest that fathers accept their responsibility for the care of their children—a change which might ease the pressure on the mother. He says: "Some fathers have been brought up to think that the care of babies and children is the mother's job entirely. But a man can be a warm father and a real man at the same time . . . Of course, I don't mean that the father has to give just as many bottles or change just as many diapers as the mother. But it's fine for him to do these things occasionally. He might make the formula on Sunday . . ." Fatherhood, then, is still primarily the 8-hour job (more, if he works overtime) of earning the family's income, while motherhood remains a 24-hour job with no nights or weekends off.

Because of these problems, which result from the way we live, many people are beginning to consider alternatives to the nuclear family, some of which I will discuss later. Spock, however, proceeds to tell you how to rear your little boy and little girl so that they will live their lives in the same way.

The process is called "identification": "A boy now wants to be like his father. By the age of three a boy is beginning to realize more clearly that he is a boy and will grow up to be a man like his father. This gives him a special admiration for his father and other men and boys. He watches them carefully and works hard to be as much like them as he can in appearance and behavior and interests. In his play he concentrates on propelling toy trucks, trains, and planes, pretending his tricycle is a car, being a policeman or fireman, making deliveries, building houses and bridges. He

copies his father's remarks in his father's tone of voice. He takes on his father's attitude toward other males and toward women."

Notice the variety of toys and the number of roles Spock expects the little boy to use in his play. Notice the amount of movement and the opportunity for creating ideas and objects. Contrast that with the limited possibilities offered little girls: "A girl wants to be like her mother. The girl at this age [three years] realizes that it is her destiny to be a woman and this makes it particularly exciting and challenging for her to be like her mother and other women. She turns with more concentration to housework and baby (doll) care if these are her mother's occupations. In caring for her dolls, she takes on the very same attitudes and tone of voice her mother uses toward children. She absorbs her mother's point of view toward men and boys."

Spock notes that a father can further the feminine development of his daughter "by complimenting her on her dress, or hairdo, or the cookies she's made." Her "feminine" skills will be the basis for their early relationship and it will matter little that "When she is older, he can show her that he's interested in her opinions."

Spock uses the nuclear family as the understood setting for *Baby and Child Care*. The only exception is eight pages in a section in the back titled "Special Problems." Here are three short pieces on other family forms: "Separated Parents," "The Working Mother," and "The Fatherless Child." Dr. Spock can call these living situations "problems" only because he considers the nuclear family the model and predominant family form in the United States. The nuclear family's desirability as a model, however, is already in question, and the U.S. Census indicates that if it is the predominant form, it holds only a slight lead.

In 1968 there were an estimated 50 million families; 44 percent were without children, leaving some 28 million families. If you also consider the unspecified number in which grandparents and other relatives live, families where the father is not present because of divorce, death, or is effectively absent because of military or work demands, and the 12 million working mothers, you are left with relatively few groups that can qualify as nuclear families without "Special Problems"—even if you allow for the fact that many of these conditions exist simultaneously in one family.

This suggests that *Baby and Child Care* was not written for the general public, but for a select group of families, largely middle class—where the mother can stay home because her income is not needed—and predominantly white.

Percent of Mothers Working

with children under 3	18% white
	30% non-white
with children 3–5 years old	25% white
	52% non-white
with children 6–17 years old	40% white
	57% non-white

The working mother receives particularly harsh treatment from Dr. Spock: "Some mothers *have* to work to make a living. Usually their children turn out alright . . . But others grow up neglected and maladjusted." A 1963 research study found that "children of working mothers are no more likely than children of non-working mothers to become delinquent, to show neurotic symptoms, to feel deprived of maternal affection . . ." Other studies have found that the mother's working had a positive effect on the development of her children, both boys and girls. While it cannot be said that Spock actually misrepresents the facts, his negative interpretation can hardly fail to frighten any mother working or considering going to work.

Although single motherhood has increased rapidly since the 1970s, and more than half of all children today will live with a single parent for some part of their lives, it is not a new phenomenon: as early as 1900 almost 10 percent of American children lived with single mothers. Recently the women's movement has been blamed for creating single motherhood through allegedly destroying marriage and licensing nonmarital sex. Except for a small proportion of women, primarily prosperous women, who choose to become single mothers deliberately, whether by childbirth or by adoption, single mothers do not choose that situation. The great recent increase in single motherhood is mainly due to increasing poverty, unemployment, male unreliability, the disproportionate number of poor men of color in prison or dead, and the lack of good jobs for poor women. In 1960, well before the women's movement, 22 percent of black households were single-mother families.

Women's liberation defended women's rights to raise children on their own, and insisted that a single-parent family is not necessarily or always inferior, although it is more difficult for one adult alone to bear the responsibility of supporting and raising children and above all because most single-mother families are poor. Because of below-subsistence welfare stipends, the low wages that most women earn, and the lack of affordable child care, mothers trying to raise children without the help of a male wage have always had a hard time. The women's movement organized numerous projects by and for single mothers. In Los Angeles a group attempted to create a newspaper devoted to single mothers. In Brooklyn, New York, the Sisterhood of Black Single Mothers, founded by Daphne Busby, operated home day care, out-of-the-home children's activities, a big-sister program for pregnant single women, a monthly newsletter, and an exchange for clothes and books.

The Single Mother Experience
KAROL HOPE

1972

My daughter says she doesn't have a family, only a mother.

She wants a daddy and a baby and a crazy, raucous, family dinner hour. My heart saddens. I want those good feelings for her.

Something is missing.

I am missing the familiarity of one man's body, the warmth of him beside me.

I am missing old friends, family. They wonder, and sometimes pull away.

I am missing the satisfaction of a life unfolding according to plan, ordained by God, my mother and the President of the PTA.

Rhythm is interrupted. Permanence is gone. So is security.

We are all going through it. SEVEN MILLION of us

divorced, separated, widowed, never-been-married mothers in the United States with children under 18. We vary in age. We are a racial mixture. Some of us are broke. Some of us are rich. Together we share a unique life style. We are solely responsible for the care and well-being of ourselves and our children.

Perhaps the world really is too turned upside down for anyone to figure out. Perhaps there is too much change, confusion, anger in the air. I've tried to rationalize it all away, let it mend itself without me. The reality of my life continues. I am sad. My daughter is resigned.

What to do?

I am not willing to wait for the shrinks and the social workers and the politicians to decide how the ideal family operates. They will be years at it, even if they do know what they're talking about.

I am not willing to wait for the next man. Maybe he will

come, maybe he won't. Maybe I will stay with him, maybe I won't. I refuse to continue my life as a "stage between marriages."

I am a single mother *now*. I want a fulfilling life *now*.

I want responsible work.

I want lots of friends, for me and for my daughter.

I want mobility.

I want enough money.

I want a nice place to live.

I want a good place for my daughter to spend her days.

I want leisure time.

RIGHT NOW.

How? How for me? How for all of us?

We can't change something we know little or nothing about.

What is the single mother experience? What is our commonality? I am not unique. What is my experience? What do I do? How do I feel?

ALONE. RESPONSIBLE. OVERWORKED. TIRED. PLEASED. AFRAID. HILARIOUS. TOUCHED. PROGRESSING. ANGRY. HOPEFUL. ON TOP OF IT ALL.

Sound familiar?

ALONE. Late at night. Full of things to talk about, wonder about, questions to be answered, tickles to be tickled, jokes to be cracked, backs to be rubbed, love to be made. But alone. Tonight I don't like it.

RESPONSIBLE. Brandace (my daughter) is crying. Lost her shoes. Someone scared her. She's spending the night with a friend. O.K. Mom? Needs her allowance. No money. Damn. Money.

OVERWORKED. Too much to do. Strung out. Meetings, papers, organizing, decisions, dinner. Too much. My energy is gone. I should have more. What's the matter with me?

TIRED. Let's not even eat dinner!

PLEASED. Brandace told me she was afraid she was pregnant (she is nine). She'd been "playing" with the neighborhood kids. I reassured her. She was glad she talked to me. I was too. Pleased that we are so close. She's been invited away for the weekend. Pleased I have some time for myself.

AFRAID. There is something terribly wrong. Nobody is getting along with anybody. Splitting up. Arguing. Moving on. I can't cope with this confusion, this uprootedness. The lies I get told. The lies I tell. The fraud on people's faces. The stiff bodies. The words. Nobody is moving. Nothing is happening. We are all stuck in a lonely, nobody-knows place. We are doomed.

HILARIOUS. Larry making faces, horrible faces, after he has promised to do my week-old dishes and takes his first look in my sink. Brandace does a Joe Namath commercial and wags her bottom. Beverly and Leo admit that their self-proclaimed model relationship is not perfect (they are psychologists).

TOUCHED. Bob and Sydelle and Sybil and Mike and Cory and Amy sit beside me, hug me, while I am crying and being sad because I haven't felt cared for in awhile. Sylvia offers to lend me $200 when I am broke and getting desperate (panicking). Germaine Greer tells a national television audience that she "blew" her last relationship—did it all wrong.

PROGRESSING. Telling a male friend who is having a

problem with Brandace to talk to her about it, not me. Getting the oil changed in my car when the red light FIRST comes on, not three days later. Being aware that I didn't ask that friendly man in the clothing store to have coffee with me because I was scared he would think I was crazy knowing that I'll do it next time I meet a friendly man.

ANGRY. Brandace went on a camping trip and took the only toothbrush. And the toothpaste. Having my mother call me up long distance to tell me that my sister is blissfully happy in her three-year marriage. My landlady won't get me a new hot water heater. Discovering a new man won't let me get upset. I *am* upset!

HOPEFUL. Someone understood what I was talking about. Brandace tells me a secret. I meet five new interesting people. Someone is honest with me, even though it hurts. Having a fight with a friend and still being friends when it's over. An old lover shows up for coffee (we're still friends).

ON TOP OF IT ALL. Money in the bank, food in the refrigerator, work done, Brandace laughing, a new friend coming over.

No, I am not unique. We all share the delights and the difficulties of independence. Seven million of us—divorced, widowed, separated, never-been-married mothers with children under 18. We pursue careers, choose lovers when we please, raise our children as we like, run away for the weekend at a moment's notice.

But jobs are hard to get, much less careers. Lovers are gone and hated. We long for a rest from a child's cry. The weekend jaunt doesn't get past the local drive-in movie. We overdraw at the bank.

There are times, late at night, when we are certain that our personalities are marred by a tragic flaw. "I am incompetent, a failure, I can't keep anything together," we whisper harshly.

I don't want us to be so hard on ourselves. You know we never really expected to "handle all of this," shape our own individuality. Since we were little girls we have been taught, expected, to revolve our lives around the center of our existence, a man. He was our father, then our husband, and for some he's now our paternal "friend," the government. We are inexperienced; we don't know how to create, control, maintain our own lives.

Some of us are ready. Really ready.

We lack the resources. The tools. The recognition.

Quality child care is simply unavailable. The little that is there costs too much, for anyone ($100 per month per well child). The job. We are competing in an overloaded, white male–oriented job market. That means we get the dumb jobs and at lower salaries, even if we do have the skills. Child support and alimony are considered unstable income by most credit bureaus. They are right. Counseling centers assure us that everything will be fine "once we marry again."

And we lack a community. Our parents take the kids for the weekend, sometimes. They don't know any more than we do about single parent-hood. Our media is vacant—no books, magazine articles, television shows that educate us or anyone else to the realities of raising children, with or without a man, with or without a housekeeper. Our neighborhood bars, our single's clubs, are not places to develop warm, caring friendships with anyone, regardless of sex.

We are not in touch with ourselves or with each other.

We are not getting what we need.

This isolation must end.

There is an opportunity here, with MOMMA. The opportunity has to do with openness. Discovery. Risk. Sharing. Another woman's solutions reveal our own alternatives.

Another woman's feelings soften the bitter sting of our own isolation.

We must talk to each other.

Learn from each other.

Discover ourselves.

Be recognized.

We have no other choice. Nobody else knows what we're all about.

Just us.

The Sisterhood of Black Single Mothers
DAPHNE BUSBY

We'd like at this time to remind everyone
About "Sisterhood" and the work to be done.

Now with the demands of being single mothers
Some may have more time to contribute than others.

We don't expect what you can't spare
But we do expect you all to care.

Make it your business to keep in touch
and to participate/Is that asking too much?

In this society we have changes to make
We can't neglect this for our own sake.

By working together through the Sisterhood
We can undo the bad and bring about some good.

We can maintain communication in person or by phone
So that no sister feels isolated from being alone.

"I don't have any problems" some of you may say.
Well, we need to know how you got that way.

Your constructive criticism will make us grow
We respect your opinions so just let them flow.

We must view each other with respect and trust
And the Sisterhood will grow, our progress is a must.

So the next time you have an idea or problem to share
Just call on the Sisterhood and we'll be there.

Lesbian Mothers and Their Children   1972

The lesbian who is also a mother faces a unique oppression in this society. Lesbians without children may, in a certain way, escape the scrutiny of society in their personal lives, simply because of the low visibility given to female homosexuality in comparison to male homosexuality. However, even this small security, and its worth is certainly minor when compared with all the other negative forces facing gay women, is withdrawn from the lesbian mother.

Children raised in lesbian households have a chance to experience the world differently from the children of the heterosexual couples. They see women not in positions of inferiority and subservience to men but as independent human beings. Many of them see a love relationship significantly different from the traditional sexual role stereotypes. Many have the possibility of being encouraged to develop in freer and less limited ways than the conventional "boy" or "girl" roles.

One of the main threats facing a lesbian mother [is] that of losing her children because of a social system that labels her behavior as "unfit" for a mother. The fear that her children may reveal something to an in-law, or to their father, thus precipitating a custody fight, is ever present.

For many lesbians, the court fight comes just after they leave their husbands, or the fathers of their children. If a woman has publicly declared her wish to live with another woman, she is particularly vulnerable.

In California, the law states that a court cannot find a mother "unfit" on the basis of homosexuality. It must consider the best interests of the child. This almost always means that the judge will find in favor of the father, or the in-laws, because they represent the heterosexual value system and thus must be in the "best interest of the child."

Even when a judge is forced to find in favor of the woman (because he takes the law at its word?) the father can appeal—this happened recently in California when a woman won custody of her children in the first suit and in the second suit retained their custody, but with these restrictions:

1. The woman and her lover could never live together, or she would lose the children,

2. Her lover may never visit her when the children are in the house, and

3. The woman may not leave her house to visit her lover when her children are at home (even if they have child care).

Day care was the subject of a great deal of analysis and activism by women's liberation. In every locality, women's liberation groups fought for day care—one of several ways in which women's liberation was a pro-child, pro-motherhood, and pro-family movement. Even childless feminists grasped the importance of day care to women's equality and often joined struggles for day care. Campaigns for day care included organizing cooperative nurseries, lobbying for government funding, and pressuring employers and universities to provide day care, often through demonstrations designed to highlight the problem. For example, in several locations women's groups organized "child-ins," that is, they brought their babies and toddlers to workplaces to dramatize their need for day care facilities. The modest gains achieved were spurred on by the women's movement and the increased employment of mothers. In 1995, of approximately 21 million preschool children, 12.9 million were in child care, of which 30 percent were in day care centers. The federal government now spends $11.7 billion annually on child care support programs. But with the increase in mothers' employment and the abolition of Aid to Families with Dependent Children (known colloquially as "welfare"), progress has fallen far behind need. Between 10 and 20 percent of women do not seek employment, and 20 to 25 percent do not seek full-time employment, because they cannot get affordable child care, and half of all working parents prefer day care centers to babysitters but cannot find places. By and large the poorest children who could benefit most from professionally run, stimulating child care have the least access to it.

The women's movement never considered day care only a women's issue, and tried to involve entire communities and workplaces. Feminists routinely made a point of asking men to support women's liberation by providing child care for women's events. Involving men came about partly because women did not only want babysitting; they wanted to change the way children were raised. They believed that being with men was important for children and that being with children was important for men. Feminists wanted to challenge sex-role stereotyping, to encourage girls in playing sports, working with tools, and becoming more assertive, and to encourage boys in verbalizing thoughts, expressing feelings, and learning interpersonal skills. Feminists often enunciated what Head Start has proven: that early social experiences for children, especially those from poor backgrounds, enhance children's later academic and social development.

Why Day Care?
LOUISE GROSS AND PHYLLIS TAUBE GREENLEAF   1970

Day Care has become one of the central issues of the Women's Liberation Movement. It is quite clear that free and public day care centers would be an important means for liberating women from the traditional tasks of child rearing.

The authors of this discussion paper think it is a mistake to view day care solely as an issue of Women's Liberation. We would like to assert that day care centers in which children are raised in groups by men and women could be as important for the liberation of children as it would be for the liberation of women. Group child care—if well conceived—has a radical potential through the impact it could have on children's early development.

The underlying reason for the failure of day care programs to develop in this country exists in the traditional ideology that young children and their mothers belong in the home. Even today a strong bias exists against the concept that day care is potentially good for children and mothers. That women should *have* to work and therefore *have* to put their children in day care centers are circumstances which are generally considered to be necessary evils in this society.

The current demand for day care by the Women's Liberation Movement springs from a rejection of the ideology which says that women belong in the home. Yet the Movement's present demand parallels the historical attitude toward day care in its non child-centered approach. The primary reason for demanding day care is the liberation of women.

The majority of existing U.S. day care centers, which are run as profit-making enterprises, are glorified baby sitting services—dumping grounds—where children are bored most of the time. In these centers children are emotionally brutalized; they learn the values of obedience and passivity. They are programmed through a daily routine in which opportunities for personal choice and meaningful social relationships with adults and other children are minimal. Eating and naptime are managed in a mass production style which values efficiency over dignity. The adults as well as the children become routinized and enslaved to the daily schedule.

In contrast, there are a few day care centers where children have meaningful social and educational experiences, and where they participate in non-alienating play/work activities. In these centers self-directed learning and discovery are valued, and curriculum is developed in terms of the children's interests. Social cooperation is based on a rational group-problem-solving approach, rather than on rules impersonally established. Eating and resting activities are designed to be responsive to children's individual and group needs, rather than to meet the efficiency goals of the day care operation.

We feel the differences among existing day care centers reflect a conflict in values and attitudes toward human development. This conflict in the care and education of young children is directly related to conflicting values and attitudes expressed in the economic and political behavior of adults. Values in competitive enterprise and individual rather than social achievement, respect for private property, adoration of the nuclear family—are attitudes that are nurtured in childhood and expressed in adult society.

As radicals we must understand that *our* goals for children are in conflict with those of the institutions—corporations and universities—from whom we will be demanding day care services. This implies that when we make demands for day care they should be solely in terms of money and space. The corporations and universities should have no control.

The kind of interaction that takes place between the child and the human and physical environment (be it a home or a day care center) affects the kind of capacities that the child will have as an adult. The capacity to feel deeply and be sensitive toward other people, the capacity to trust oneself and use one's initiative, the capacity to solve problems in a creative and collective way—these are all capacities that can be given their foundation or stifled in the first five years.

By the age of 4, children are assimilating the idea that a woman's place is in the home. Three and four-year old children are already learning that it's better to be white. They are learning to follow directions and rules without asking why. They are learning how to deny their own feelings and needs in order to win approval from adults.

To a young child curriculum in a day care center is everything that he or she experiences: painting a picture, having to take a nap, experimenting with sand and water, wetting your pants or making it there on time, listening to an interesting story, eating lunch, riding a trike, being socked in the nose and having it bleed, observing one teacher being bossed by the other teacher, being told that blue is called blue, figuring out a hard puzzle, being hugged by the teacher, watching a building be demolished, seeing the mother guinea pig give birth, having everyone sing happy birthday to you, hammering a nail hard, and waiting to be picked up.

Although as adults we can place these events into categories of social, intellectual, emotional and physical experiences, for the young child each event is experienced in a total way. That is, the experience of painting a picture simultaneously involves emotional, intellectual, physical, and even social capacities. Emotionally a child may be using paint to express feelings of anger, loneliness, contentment, or boredom. Intellectually a child may be using the paint to discover what happens when different colors are mixed or learning how to write different letters. Physically, the child uses the paint brush to explore her/his own coordination, movement, and rhythm. Socially, painting can give the child an opportunity to be alone, with a friend, or in a group—depending on how the teacher has structured the painting experience.

The teacher's values and attitudes form the base from which the structure and therefore the style of the group are formed. A single activity such as "juice time" illustrates how a teacher's goals and attitudes affect the way the situation is structured. One teacher might have three year olds pour her/his own juice from a pitcher, whereas another would have the children take already filled cups from a tray. What underlies the difference? Presumably both teachers know that three year olds are in the process of developing muscle as well as eye-hand coordination. Also, three year olds are usually concerned with becoming independent and self-sufficient. By letting children pour their own juice the teacher is structuring the situation to allow for growth—however groping—in the areas of self reliance and manual dexterity. By filling cups for the children, the other teacher is structuring the situation for maximum efficiency and neatness: to keep the routine running smoothly. One teacher uses juice time as an opportunity for children to gain some control over their activity, while the other teacher uses juice time to take control. In the first case the child gets to act upon the environment, while in the second case the child is treated as a passive recipient.

Let us take two teachers who have undergone similar training in early childhood education and have learned that the housekeeping corner provides an opportunity for children to "act out" adult roles thus contributing to their "ego growth" and "sex identification." One of the teachers sets up a housekeeping corner which encourages girls to be Mommy, the Housewife, and boys to be Daddy, the Worker. The other teacher sets up an area in the classroom in which both boys and girls are given opportunities to cook, play with dolls and trucks, sew, hammer, build with blocks, wash clothes and dishes, dress up as doctors, firemen and firewomen, construction workers, and other interesting occupations. In other words, one teacher uses the housekeeping corner to promote the learning of traditional stereotyped roles, while the other transforms the housekeeping corner into an area where children can explore and test out various adult activities.

Another way that children learn the traditional stereotyped roles is through observing that almost all day care teachers are women. The children quickly comprehend the concept that there is "women's work" and "men's work." This in itself would be sufficient argument for us to insist that men be included at all levels in the day care staff.

There is another good reason that *both* men and women should be involved in the day care center. Teaching-working-playing with children can be an extraordinarily creative and non-alienating job. What often makes the caretakers of young children—teachers and mothers—feel apologetic about their occupation and what deprives men the opportunity of working with children is the fact that our society considers child care "women's work"—a low-status/cheap labor occupation biologically relegated to the weaker, "sensitive" sex.

A day care program which had a sexually integrated staff—and salaries in keeping with the value of this work—would make child-rearing a desirable and rewarding occupation. Finally, it seems self-evident that it's best for children—emotionally, socially and politically—that they be cared for equally by both men and women.

10
Education

Feminists were not only engaged in raising their own consciousnesses but were concerned with education at all levels—from the daily reproduction of gendered existence to the formal educational system to the construction of alternative educational institutions.

Understanding that gender itself is in large part a product of education—that people *learn* what is masculine and feminine—women's liberation set about challenging the subtle, everyday conditioning that oppressed women. Consciousness-raising was a process of uncovering that which is invisible because it has been taken for granted as natural, so that it could be challenged (see chapter 3). Through those challenges, in turn, feminists learned more about how sexism operates and shared those insights in further educational activism.

Verne Moberg's leaflet was originally published by The Feminist Press, an independent feminist publishing house established by Florence Howe and Paul Lauter in 1970 that is still operating. Evidence of the leaflet's success in outreach was its distribution by the mainstream National Education Association.

Consciousness Razors
VERNE MOBERG

1970

1.

Go to a playground in a park and watch some children. Pick one boy and imagine the rest of his life. Make a list of all the things people will tell him he shouldn't do because he's a boy. Then pick a girl and think about how she'll be spending her time from now on. Make a list of all the things everybody will tell her are illegal because she's a girl. Compare the lists. Get up and go over to the boy and girl and give them each a list; tell them it's all right to do all those things.

Walk home slowly, observing the adults who pass you by.

2.

At 11 p.m. on the nineteenth day of every month think about what you've done all day. Next consider what you might have done that day if you had been a man (woman). By January 1 figure out what to do about this.

3.

Ask the neighbor girl what she wants to be when she grows up. Then ask her what she would want to be *if she were a boy.* Find her brother and ask him what he wants to be when he grows up. Then ask him what *he* would want to be *if he were a girl.*

Later, mention to their parents what they said.

4.

Force yourself to watch television for six hours. Write down every innuendo you see and hear that denigrates women. Translate all those into insults aimed at midgets. Ask yourself: Would midgets allow that? Would the FCC allow that? Would you allow that if *you* were a midget? If you weren't?

If these things offend you, telephone the TV station to let them know, since they say they are interested in public service.

5.

Go to your nearest children's library and pick out twenty picture books at random. Page through them and count the number of aprons, checking to see who is wearing each one (males or females, both humans and animals). Go home and count the number of aprons you own. Ask your neighbors how many they own.

Spend time wondering who is drawing all those aprons, and why?

6.

Ask your seven-year-old daughter (or somebody else's) to play this game with you. Just before Christmas, take her down to the toy department in a big department store and go along with her to visit Santa Claus. When she sits on Santa's knee and he inquires what she wants for Christmas, ask her (in advance) to say: "A set of building blocks and a chemistry set and an electric train and a fire engine." Watch the look on Santa's face. Next go to the toy department of a rival store and this time ask your daughter to tell Santa (as she's sitting on his knee and he asks what she wants): "A Barbie doll and a play kitchen and a toy vacuum sweeper." Check *this* Santa's face.

Afterwards, take your daughter out for an ice cream soda and ask her what she *really* wants for Christmas. Also ask her if she thinks that's right, that people should always *get* things just on Christmas, and usually only things they're *allowed* to get.

7.

Call up your local school board and ask how many girls have won athletic scholarships over the past ten years? How many boys? If more boys than girls are winning these scholarships, ask if there are other scholarships available to girls, as compensation.

8.

Some Saturday morning when everybody in your family has just had a good breakfast and is in a mellow mood, sit down together around the kitchen table and draw up a list of all the fights you have had over the past year (give each one a name and write that down in the first column on a piece of paper). Then write down, for each fight, who was the angriest (in the second column), what that person really wanted to get out of it (third column), how they expressed their anger (fourth column) and finally whether or not they got their way (fifth column).

Then figure out if one style of anger (crying, shouting, fist-pounding, name-calling, pouting, etc.) is more "efficient" in your family than any other. Do the males or the females in the family practice the "efficient" style of anger most frequently?

At this point somebody will accuse the person who drew up the lists of cheating. During the fight that follows, every member of the family should try to express her or his anger in the style that is most efficient for this particular family. The winner gets to make lunch.

9.

Ask your kids to ask all their women teachers if they ever wanted to be school administrators.

10.

Stand in front of a large mirror together with one or two or three people you are extremely fond of (either males or females, of any age; everybody should be wearing everyday clothes, and preening is prohibited). When everybody is gazing into the mirror, all repeat, in unison: "Mirror, mirror, on the wall, who's the *fairest* of them all?"

Then everybody close their eyes for one minute and listen hard for the mirror's answer.

11.

Pick up a copy of *The New York Times* (or any other daily newspaper) for every child in your class (or your family). Give each child one newspaper, one pencil and a slip of paper. Ask everybody to look through the entire newspaper keeping score of how many pictures there are of men and how many pictures there are of women (both newsphotos and ads). Also, on each picture, ask the children to write down one adjective describing how they think that person felt about having his or her picture taken in that particular way. When everybody's finished, compare results.

If the findings upset you or the children, write a letter to the editor-in-chief of the newspaper reporting on your experiment and ask him if he thinks his photographers are doing a good job. While you're at it, also ask him to print your letter along with his reply in the letters-to-the-editor column.

12.

This game is called "Meanwhile, back in the kitchen—." It is played in a group of mixed couples (children or adults).

To begin the game the female in the first couple thinks up some great achievement in history performed by a man. For instance: "In 1492 Columbus discovered America." Her male partner must then say what the great man's wife was doing at that particular moment: "Meanwhile, *Mrs.* Columbus was discovering _____." If he does not know what the great man's wife was doing at the moment, he must forfeit and reply: "Meanwhile, back in the kitchen, Mrs. Columbus was doing the dishes" (or fixing supper, or any of those fascinating chores one does in the kitchen). In which case his partner wins the point. The play continues around the room in this fashion until one side (males *or* females) has accumulated twenty-one points.

Afterwards, the group will want to discuss why they don't know more about what women were doing and how they could go about finding out. Did all those women really spend all that time in the kitchen? If so, should the females now playing the game get extra points? How did history really happen? In the future, who will be kept in the kitchen?

There is no winner in this game.

Feminists devoted a great deal of thought and effort to early-childhood education. In their efforts to transform curricula, they gave equal consideration to how men and women were both deprived in the conventional gender system, and developed new curricula for boys as well as girls. These efforts were particularly deeply felt because many feminists were parents, and because women, precisely because of the unequal division of parenting that they were trying to change, were socialized to be uniquely concerned with child raising. A typical example of the problem: in a 1970s curriculum for teaching language skills, the vowels were identified as female and therefore unable to stand alone, pictured as leaning, needing the support of the male consonants.

Teachers as well as parents became active in attempts to transform schools. In addition to criticizing existing curricula and pedagogy, feminists wrote detailed nonsexist (and usually antiracist) lesson plans and lobbied schools to adopt them. Children's book publication was radically transformed with the appearance of anti-sexist books, first from the alternative presses, but very soon promoted by large trade presses as well. Soon textbooks and official curricula began to move away from sex stereotyping and showed girls being physically active, heroic, and assertive. Women's liberation's influence also made it possible to show alternative families—single mothers, divorced parents, even gay parents—although this development gave rise to a vigorous conservative backlash.

Gender in the Fourth Grade
KEVIN KARKAU

Being an account of how I tried
to make fourth-graders aware
of sex roles, stereotypes, and POTOS;
and how I in turn became aware
of cooties, girl-touch,
and the illegibility of fourth-graders' handwriting.

[In the class in which I was a student-teacher,] there was a definite problem, in that boys and girls rarely associated with each other. The children could place their desks wherever they wished, but the result was that boys and girls did not sit together. They formed two separate lines whenever they went to art class or math lab although the teacher had never asked them to do so. Boys played soccer at recess while most girls played pom-pom or tag. In art class boys and girls sat at separate tables. In math lab, they played sep-arate math games. They teased each other when someone touched a Person of the Opposite Sex (which I will call a POTOS), formed all-girl and all-boy groups for creative writing exercises, sat in two rows for music class, and worst of all, rarely talked with each other.

The children's segregated behavior could be attributed to a "natural stage" that children go through, but I believed that the behavior was a result of socialization processes. Surely this segregation was unhealthy and limiting.

Change must first begin with the teacher. Learning by example can only lead so far, though. For this classroom, some consciousness-raising activities were needed. [He asked the class to list characteristics of ideal men and women and of typical men and women.] On looking over the groups' ideal persons, most of the characteristics that the groups decided on were unisexual—that is, they could be important to both sexes. In the first column (the typical man or woman), traditional views showed up. Men were brave, strong, healthy, humorous, kind; women were gentle, pretty, good cooks, clean, and smart.

I then asked the group if anyone could think of qualities that were peculiarly masculine or feminine. No one could think of any. "I don't understand something," I said. "Here you have listed characteristics that could apply to both men and women, you have agreed that males and females should have equal opportunities, that there are no distinctly masculine or feminine qualities, yet in the classroom and at recess, boys and girls hardly ever associate with each other. Why?" No one replied, so I moved the discussion to a more concrete area—that of sports. I asked the class why girls didn't play soccer more at recess—was there any discrimination on the boys' part? Some boys were upset at that thought and quickly defended themselves. "They can play if they want to," said the boys, "but they just don't want to." I asked the girls if they felt free to play soccer. Most replied affirmatively, but said they simply didn't want to play soccer. But one girl who played soccer occasionally brought out some real reasons for the lack of female participation. "First of all," she said, "the boys never ask us to play, then when we do play only boys are chosen to be captains. And girls don't get the ball passed to them very often, and when a girl scores a goal, the boys don't cheer." I asked the boys if that was true, and they argued a great deal, but finally agreed that the girls had legitimate complaints.

I [then] pointed out the way they were currently sitting. The children looked around as if they had never realized the segregation before, then let out a collective sigh of amazement. I then asked them why they formed two lines whenever they went out of the classroom. Some of the boys said that the teacher had told them to do so, but the teacher and the girls quickly corrected that statement. The teacher then asked if previous teachers had told them to form two lines. No teachers had, which showed that the segregation by sex was voluntary, and thus deeply socialized into the children by their experiences outside school.

The first discussion ended and the children went out for recess. There were some immediately noticeable results.

Eight girls played soccer, more so than ever before. There were at least three occasions where boys and girls talked to each other. One girl kept touching a boy she liked, teasing him about his hair, but really seeking for some sign of interest. When the students returned and lined up for art class, one girl formed the girls' line on the side where the boys usually stood. "Hey that's the boys' side," said some boys, whereupon the girls dared the boys to stand on their usual side. The boys weren't quite ready yet to stand close to girls, so that day two lines were still formed.

I asked the class "why don't you talk with or even go near POTOS more?" The answers—"People will think you're 'in love' with the person," said many girls; while for the boys, "if you touch a girl you get 'cooties' or 'girl-touch'" (a mysterious quality which can only be removed by saying "no gives"). So I asked the kids why people say such things, and why they themselves take the sayings seriously. There were no explanations, except that people have always done it, and everyone agreed that the sayings were not necessarily true, but that it was difficult to ignore the laughter and ridicule. Everyone believed privately that talking with or touching a POTOS signified next to nothing in itself, but as long as the group enforced its opinion on interactions, it was difficult to disregard the group.

In the third section of the discussion I asked the children if they could think of specific activities they could perform in the classroom to help reduce the separation between the sexes. "Invite the girls to play soccer," said one boy. "Stand in the boys' line," said a girl. After that, though, there were no other suggestions and although many people were interacting more with a POTOS, some were clearly uninterested in the whole issue. I decided to simply list some activities they could do with a POTOS, but not reward people with candy (simply praise) for doing the activities. The list included sitting near, helping standing in line, talking, playing sports, saying something nice about a POTOS, and not laughing when people associated with a POTOS.

There was a group of about four boys who seemed to take no interest in the subjects of sex stereotyping and interaction with a POTOS. The reason was fairly simple. In changing their behavior to a situation where unlimited opportunities for living one's life are available, many people lose their security of an already-defined role. The boys didn't understand the long-term benefits of such a change, and felt threatened by loss of their male status. They were afraid of being coerced into changing their behavior. Individual attention and explanation is necessary for such people, but they must also be given the option of not changing.

The next logical step, since the class as a group was not completely prepared for natural interaction, was small group discussions. I brought in some advertisements that showed women and men in stereotyped manner, and prepared some questions on the effects of advertising. The ads showed women in passive roles, concerned with beauty and pleasing men; while men were shown in tough, outdoorsy roles, such as racing, canoeing, and herding horses. Two discussions of about a half-hour each were held over the same material, with volunteer groups of six people each. I had previously asked the four boys who seemed uninterested in the subject to volunteer, and two of them did so.

But more important than the discussion that day was a change in the children's behavior. Four days had elapsed between the second discussion and the small group discussions, and in that time the girls and boys occasionally played together at recess, and another good discussion over an article in the weekly news-magazine had taken place. The article concerned sex roles, and the kids were strongly critical of some unfair views in the article. I state these facts to illustrate how long it took for some fundamental behavior changes to occur.

Anyway, after the small group discussion, two girls decided to integrate the boys' line. The lines were just forming and the two girls stepped behind two boys, while I was the only male in the girls' line. Immediately the two boys left the line and tried to stand behind me, but some girls arrived first. The boys looked around, realized they would have to stand next to a girl, and as the rest of the class arrived, the lines dissolved into one big integrated line. There was much excited teasing and talking between boys and girls as we walked to the art room, and once there, boys and girls sat together at tables, although not too closely.

Another discussion was held to examine the children's feelings towards the changes in the classroom and to suggest or entertain ideas for further change. The consensus was that people enjoyed the opportunities for increased association with POTOS, felt more free to interact, and teased others less when they interacted with a POTOS. But there were no further suggestions for change, except to try individually to be less sensitive to unjust ridicule.

The last activity was a student evaluation of the changes in the classroom. A high percentage indicated that they felt more at ease with a POTOS. Student evaluations must always be taken with a grain of salt, however, as young children tend to answer as the teacher wants them to. But taking into consideration the behavior and attitude changes in the classroom, there is no other interpretation than that these evaluations represent fairly accurately the increased association.

There have been some definite and seemingly permanent behavior and attitude changes. There is more communication between the sexes, boys and girls feel freer to sit, talk, and play together, and they remain sensitive to sexual stereotyping. For those who didn't become more free to associate with a POTOS, there was nothing completely wrong with that, either. They *must* certainly be allowed the option of not associating with a POTOS, as the goal was not to *force* people to interact, but to *expand* their opportunities for interaction.

In a way, these activities have required the children to act in a more mature way than adults do—to ignore a person's gender as a measure of ability, to allow people to define their own role, to tolerate various behaviors—but that is exactly the point of education. The value of such education can be seen in the increased associations between boys and girls in the classroom, in their more sociable personalities, and in their positive comments about the activities. The difficulties of the project, such as lack of interest inside the classroom and not understanding outside the classroom, are only symptomatic of what the children may face in the future. In that sense, the final value of the project depends on the degree to which the ideas I've attempted to communicate can help the children in their future.

Women's liberation found it difficult to reach adolescents. Teenagers are particularly in need of peer approval as they are taking first steps toward independence from parents, developing sexually and establishing a sense of themselves as attractive, and worrying about being "popular." These things make teenage girls leery of criticizing boys or rejecting the powerful unwritten rules of womanhood, and teenage boys—often still smaller and less mature than girls—wary of deviating from the equally constricting rules of assertive manhood. Understanding teenagers' hostility to being told what to do, feminists looked for entertaining, nonlinear, and nondidactic methods of communicating their nonconformist messages.

Many women's liberation organizations established outreach projects aimed at high schools and tried to form groups within high schools, with occasional success. The leaflet below is an example of an outreach tool produced by adult feminists in conjunction with high school girls. It does something quite radical for the time—suggesting that sex, masturbation, and birth control should be openly discussed in classrooms.

What Every Young Girl Should Ask!
HIGH SCHOOL WOMEN'S LIBERATION COALITION

1. Can you play basketball, soccer, football?
2. Were you ever taught to use a saw?
3. Did you ever pretend to be dumb?
4. Do you babysit? What do boys do for bread?
5. Do your brothers have more freedom than you? In what way? Why?
6. Are your brothers asked to help clean house?
7. Is education more important for you or your brothers? Why?
8. How many boys are there in your typing class?
9. Would you be interested in birth control information as a service in your school?
10. Did you discuss masturbation and lesbianism in your sex education class? Did you discuss intercourse? Orgasm? Abortion?
11. Would you know what to do if you needed an abortion?
12. What do you want sex education to be?
13. How many famous women do you know about (not counting Presidents' wives and movie stars)?
14. How many paragraphs (pages) cover the women's suffrage movement in your history texts?
15. Who are Susan B. Anthony, Lucretia Mott, Elizabeth Cady Stanton, Mother Jones, Harriet Tubman, Sojourner Truth?
16. How are women portrayed in the books you read?
17. How do your classes react to "ugly" women teachers?
18. Have you noticed that there are college scholarships that discriminate against girls (football scholarships!)?
19. In extra-curricular coed organizations, do girls make decisions? Or do they take minutes?
20. Did you ever hesitate to speak up in a coed organization?
21. Are girls with boyfriends winners? What did they win?
22. Did you ever lie about having a boyfriend? Why?
23. Do you ask boys out? If not, why not?
24. Do you believe boys get sexually aroused faster, at a younger age, and more often than girls? Who told you *that?*
25. Are you hung up about being/not being a virgin? Why?
26. Should boys be more experienced sexually? Why?
27. Do you ever hug or kiss your girl friend?
28. If you were in a dangerous situation would you rather have a man defend you or defend yourself? *Can* you defend yourself?
29. Are you the teenybopper, bitch, cheater, foxy lady, or "honey"-type portrayed in rock music?
30. Are you flattered by catcalls on the street?
31. Do you like your body?
32. How much time and money do you spend on your makeup? Why?
33. Why did you start wearing nylons and bras?
34. Will you be a failure if you don't get married?
35. Do you think of unmarried women as "bachelor girls" or "old maids"?
36. Are these the best years of a woman's life? Why?
37. Is your mother an oppressed woman?

Women's liberation produced a startling revolution in women's athletics. The greatest achievements of this transformation—breaking records at a very rapid rate, proving that women could be stronger than had been imagined, creating professional teams with loyal audiences, and increasing the number of women who participate in amateur athletics—occurred later than the period of this book. But their source was women's liberation's early campaigns in the areas of education, health, and the conception of what a beautiful female body is.

The degree to which women and girls were once excluded, and excluded themselves, from sports, on the grounds that they were physically unable to compete, has receded from public memory. Until 1972 women were not allowed in the Boston Marathon. Until 1973 girls were widely excluded from Little League teams. Schools and universities provided few resources for women's sports and girls were discouraged from participating in athletics. Girls were regularly excused from physical education classes if they were menstruating, and pregnant women were urged to remain physically inactive.

The testimony below was part of a widespread feminist campaign against unequal access to sports opportunities in the universities, a campaign that produced in 1972 the now celebrated Title IX of the Education Act, barring sex discrimination in any educational programs. At hearings on the bill, introduced by Oregon Congresswoman Edith Green, women testified passionately about the many barriers to women's athleticism: fewer and lower-paid coaches, few if any athletic scholarships, inferior facilities, and derogatory attitudes. Title IX benefits not only superstar female athletes, but also the millions of girls and women who now enjoy recreational sports and are healthier and happier as a result. Just ten years after Title IX, participation in women's college athletics increased by 100 percent, in high school athletics by 500 percent. In two decades the ratio of girls to boys in interscholastic sports went from 1:12 to 1:1.8. The source of these gains was the women's movement, of course, but not just the direct campaign against discrimination in athletics. Women's new athleticism also derived from feminist campaigns for women's health, for women's knowledge of their bodies, and against sexist advertising, the stereotype of women as weak, the use of sexualized images of women's bodies, and incapacitating fashions—indeed, the whole project of feminist challenge to established authority and the confidence that came with women's collective activism.

Testimony of a High School Pitcher
RUTH COLKER

In second grade, boys and girls in my district were separated for physical education. For girls, the emphasis was on skills such as tumbling and scooter racing, whereas for boys the emphasis was on life-long sports such as softball, football, basketball, and soccer. The result was that I lacked confidence in game situations as well as the fact that it made me recognize the uselessness of athletic skills for me as a girl. For instance, when I was in elementary school I wanted to be a baseball pitcher like many nine or ten year-olds. Therefore the summers of third and fourth grades I spent throwing a baseball against a target on the wall. But I gave up in fifth grade because I realized I would never have a chance to test my skill in a game situation.

My junior high school sponsored an intramural and interscholastic program for boys in wrestling, football, basketball and track. The intramural program was open to any boy who wanted to participate. As a girl, however, the only program open to me was one which you had to try out for and was thereby limited to twenty or twenty-five girls. Personally, I had no skills to show at a tryout—only interest—so that no athletic opportunities were open to me.

I then progressed to high school where my district claimed it gave girls and boys equal opportunities to participate in athletics. Their proof consisted of the fact that they offered boys nine varsity sports and girls seven, which met the interest that the girls had demonstrated. However, in reality the girls' program was unequal in all respects.

GYMS—The boys have exclusive use of a double gym which is centrally located, has a seating capacity of 2,400, modern electronic scoreboard, two locker rooms, whirlpool bath, and excellent lighting. The girls have exclusive use of the oldest gym, which is a single gym with a seating capacity of 800, has fold-out bleachers which go against the foul lines and often interfere with play, very poor lighting, and is located at the extreme end of the building far from the parking lot. The boys have exclusive use of a football, soccer, and double basketball field. By contrast, the girls have to share a boys' Little League field which they must vacate by six p.m.

INSTRUCTION—Officials: Unlike the boys, the girls do not pay clock operators or score-keepers, which often promotes cheating especially in track and basketball. Coaches: Boys and girls varsity teams are the same sizes but the girls have less coaching. When the boys have two coaches for a particular sport, the girls have one, and where the boys have three the girls have two. Although the girls' coach must do more work because she or he is responsible for more girls, the girls' coach gets paid far less. A boys' intramural coach is on the same pay scale as a girls' varsity coach, although the intramural coach works at least ten hours less a week than a varsity coach.

Here is a comparison of the coaches' salaries for the same years experience and the percentage, girls' of boys'.

Boys' basketball	$1680	50%
Girls' basketball	$840	
Boys' baseball	$673	63%
Girls' softball	$421	
Boys' track	$1121	55%
Girls' track	$617	
Boys' swimming	$1121	70%
Girls' swimming	$784	

On the whole, the girls' coaching is far inferior to that of the boys'. Personally, I played varsity fast-pitch softball in eleventh and twelfth grades. Although I was the starting pitcher for the team, I received no pitching assistance and was never even told that I would be pitching until it was time for the team to go on the field. I often strained muscles because I could not adequately warm up. The next year, however, the coaching was even worse. The coach often displayed even an ignorance of the rules. The coach for the boys' intramural softball would have been willing to coach girls' varsity softball except that the salary for the intramurals was the same and it required much less work.

NUMBER OF ACTIVITIES—I have already mentioned that my school offered nine varsity sports for boys and seven for girls, but when one studies the details of their opportunities, it is clear that many more boys can and do participate than girls. For instance, the boys' track team has a no-cut rule so that fifty to one hundred boys can be on the team, whereas the girls' team cuts to twenty-five girls. The boys also have a special program for freshmen in football, wrestling, and basketball, which the girls do not have. In 1973, Mt. Lebanon estimated that 470 boys participated in interscholastic athletics and only 210 girls did.

EQUIPMENT, SUPPLIES, AND SERVICES—Swimming: The boys are allowed to keep their T-shirts and suits at the end of the season whereas the girls must return theirs, and in fact, have an insufficient number of suits for the full team. Track: The girls get nothing for practice and wear old warm ups in meets. They have only twenty uniforms for twenty-five girls. By contrast, the boys allocate money each year for new meet shorts, shirts, sweats, shoes, and spikes. For practice, they allocate money for new shorts, T-shirts, hoods, and sweats. Basketball: The boys allocate $284 for equipment and supplies whereas the girls allocate nothing. In terms of quantity and quality, the boys have a cartload of leather balls whereas the girls have a few old rubber balls from the gym program. Publicity: The school graphic arts department prints the boys' schedule in a leaflet which is passed out to all students. In addition, the boys have several trophy cases in a Hall of Champions. The girls have none of these advantages.

In funding per participant in both intramural and

interscholastic athletics combined, at the high school level the girls receive 40% of what the boys receive; at the junior high level, 49%, and at the elementary level, 52%. Next, I tried to compare expenditures per sport because many people argued that football expenditures caused the boys' inflated budget. Comparing the totals for girls' and boys' swimming, track, baseball/softball, and basketball expen-ditures, the expenditures for girls are only 57% of the expenditures for boys. Here, of course, the boys and girls have the same number of participants. I also analyzed the available data a third way—per pupil. There are the same number of boys and girls in the school system; however the athletics expenditures for girls are only 37% of that for boys.

Baseball Family
CATHY CADE

1972

The widespread development of independent women's liberation courses and schools was another example of civil rights influence. Throughout the South, the civil rights movement established "Freedom Schools" and "Citizenship Schools," teaching black history, politics, and basic literacy to children and adults who had been denied educational opportunities. The women's schools, like the civil rights schools, were counterinstitutions, established, administered, and taught by women's liberation members. They were usually democratically run by collectives, often open to anyone who volunteered, and the frequent staff meetings could often last for many hours. In an attempt to minimize authority and hierarchy, teachers were often called "conveners" and students were expected to take some responsibility for the shape of the course; many courses were conducted in a consciousness-raising format, with everyone sitting in a circle and participating equally. Many of these generally short-lived schools were part of women's liberation organizations or women's centers, such as the Chicago Liberation School for Women, one of the biggest and longest lasting, which grew from the Chicago Women's Liberation Union. This school charged a typical $4 per course, but was free to those who could not afford it.

The range of courses described in the two selections below exemplified the women's liberation sensibility, extending from the most abstract theory to the most practical skills, and from the most traditionally female practice, such as childbirth or nutrition, to that which was traditionally male, such as auto mechanics and martial arts. Some of these innovations were picked up by mainstream institutions: prepared childbirth is now taught by hospitals, martial arts by commercial enterprises, feminist theory by universities.

Courses, Spring 1973
CHICAGO LIBERATION SCHOOL FOR WOMEN   1973

READINGS IN FEMINISM: We will be discussing de Beauvoir's *The Second Sex* and Herschberger's *Adam's Rib* with emphasis on their analyses of modern woman's life.

WOMEN IN JUDAISM: In Judaism, as in all patriarchal cultures, women have never been full-fledged participants. The purpose of this course is to explore just what has been the role of women as defined in Judaism, historically, religiously and culturally, to the end of determining whether there are any positive models for us as Jewish women to look to today, or whether we must develop these.

WOMEN AND THEIR BODIES: The purpose of this course is to enable us, as women, to gain greater control over our lives through understanding "our bodies and our selves."

FOOD CONSCIOUSNESS: Women are looking for alternatives to the chemically treated, often non-nutritive, food being served up in American grocery stores and restaurants. We will examine good nutrition, looking at diets in other countries with special emphasis on alternative sources of protein.

POLITICS OF SANITY: This course will analyze the mental health structures of our society and how they are oppressive to people, particularly women. We want to study who determines what is "healthy," what causes people to have difficulty functioning, and the treatment of people in mental institutions.

KARATE: A class for developing confidence and control of your body as well as an opportunity to develop a feeling of solidarity with other women.

PREPARED CHILDBIRTH: In this course we will introduce the Lamaze method and practice relaxation, body building and breathing technique. We will discuss the history of childbirth, home and hospital deliveries, progressive advances in maternal care, and general baby care.

GODDESSES AND AMAZONS, THE HISTORY WE NEVER HEAR: This course discusses ancient matriarchal societies and feminine godhead, and how later mythology and the modern state reinterpreted those.

PHOTOGRAPHY: Basic techniques of photography, including film developing and printing, types of film, uses of light, composition, cropping, what makes a good picture, elimination of the camera mystique.

AUTO MECHANICS FOR VOLKSWAGENS

SELF DEFENSE AT THE WORK PLACE: How to conduct a fight for your rights at work.

MARXISM STUDY GROUP: A study group for women interested in developing and convening an introductory Marxism course.

WOMEN AND IMPERIALISM STUDY GROUP: In this study group we will explore various aspects of imperialism such as imperialist wars, internal welfare, missionary activity, and how they affect women and family structure.

Nuts to Bolts

1974

In coming issues we plan to carry articles which we hope will be of assistance to women who wish to become more capable in doing their own repairs on automobiles. By sharing our knowledge we can overcome the embarrassment of having to ask a man for help and the encumbering problem of having him do it all, depriving us of the exhilarating feeling of having some control over the mechanical services which seem to run our lives. We feel that the most important problem any of us must overcome is the *feeling* that we can't!

Tools are available for any task and with the proper frame of mind and knowledge of the tools and methods nothing is impossible. This first article deals with tools that should ideally be carried in every car, and future articles will involve their use.

Clip and save these articles and stow them in your tool box for reference.

1. *TOOL BOX:* No need to get elaborate, Sears or the Mart have them for about $4. Get one with a single insert tray to avoid having to dig for the tool you want.
2. *RATCHET WRENCH & SOCKETS:* The most important item, and the most

costly. Best buy I've seen is the 20-piece set by Kraeuter Tools at the Value House for around $18 (#30260-MDR). This set will really shorten time spent on loosening and tightening those annoying nuts.

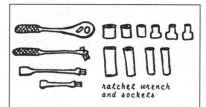

ratchet wrench and sockets

3. *BOX-END WRENCHES:* Preferred because of their ability to grab the nut and turn the wrench in tight places. Also easier to set on a nut or bolt head when they are out of sight and you're just using your fingers to see with. A set can be found in Sears for $6.49.

4. *SCREW DRIVERS:* A good start will be these—1/89'29 regular tip (1/89 wide by 29 long); 3/169'49 regular; 1/49'49 regular; 2 1/29'#0 Philips tip (#0 is a convention used to standardize sizes of the Philips head screw recognized by its crossed grooves); 49'#2 Philips: Always be sure that your screw driver fits the groove in the screw before attempting to turn. Damaged grooves make it next to impossible to turn.

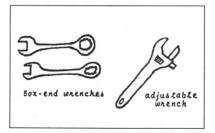

Box-end wrenches   adjustable wrench

5. *ADJUSTABLE WRENCH:* Very handy. Always be sure that the wrench is adjusted to fit the nut as tight as possible to prevent rounding the corners. $5.49 at Sears for an 8" long wrench.
6. *VICE GRIP PLIERS:* Many people swear by this tool for a variety of tough jobs. Lets you adjust to approximately the size of the piece you want to hold, then by squeezing the handle closed you get one hell of a grip. $3.59 at Sears.

7. *PLIERS:* Common pliers can be used for twisting, holding, pulling, etc. $1.59

8. *NEEDLE NOSE PLIERS:* Good for getting into the tight spots and for holding small items. $2.39

9. *THICKNESS GAUGE:* For setting spark plug gaps and ignition points in a tune-up. $1.09 at Sears.

10. *TIRE PRESSURE GAUGE:* Overinflated or underinflated tires can be dangerous in fast stops and turns. Also you can get the longest wear from your tires with proper inflation. Check the side-walls of your tires for the recommended inflation, and also your auto manual for any difference between front and rear tires. $1.25 at Sears.

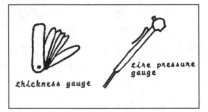

thickness gauge

tire pressure gauge

11. *PENETRATING OIL* (Liquid Wrench): Often frees fastenings that have been frozen by rust. Also helps get rust off tools. Kerosene also works well. 49¢

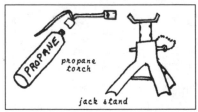

propane torch

jack stand

12. *PROPANE TORCH:* This device is safe and will not explode, so don't be nervous about using one. They are invaluable in freeing things that are heavily rusted beneath your car. Heating expands different shapes and kinds of metals at different rates and nearly always works, especially on the lug nuts (tire nuts) that have been

put on with an air pressure wrench in a garage. $5.49 for a tip and bottle set at Sears.

13. *JACK STAND:* Used to support the car in lieu of a jack when you need to crawl under the car. An absolutely necessary safety device. Get two of them for when you need to support the whole front or rear of the car. Never trust the jack except for changing tires. They tip too easily! A 1 1/2 ton capacity stand can be found at Sears for $3.99.

14. *OIL SPOUT:* For pushing into a can of oil to avoid spilling on the engine when pouring. 99¢ at Sears.

15. *GREASE GUN:* For $5.59 at Sears you can get 10 or 12 grease jobs out of one 69¢ refill of grease. Check your auto manual for the location of your car's lube points and frequency of greasing.

16. *JUMPER CABLES:* Make sure the wires are copper. The aluminum wires are just about worthless. Really useful in our cold Maine winters. $12.79 at Sears, but shop around.

17. *IGNITION FILE:* A very small, narrow file used to get corrosion off electrical contacts. It's really amazing how much this can affect starting a car and gas mileage. 69¢

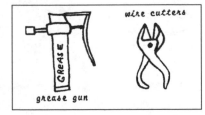

wire cutters

GREASE

grease gun

18. *WIRE CUTTERS:* A useful tool. Get the small size with the pincer like tips for about $2.39.

19. *HACK SAW:* Sometimes you just have to cut a piece of steel, especially when

working on the exhaust pipes and muffler. $3.49

20. *COLD CHISEL:* Sometimes a nut is too rusty or bruised by wrenches to come off. When this happens set this chisel against it pointed to the center of the nut, and rap hard with a hammer until it splits. It is made of very hard steel and can be kept sharp with a file or grind stone. You can find new nuts in a hardware store for pennies. $1.50 at Sears.

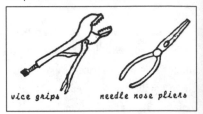

vice grips

needle nose pliers

21. *HAMMER:* Several years ago during the second moon walk, I was watching them try to use the most sophisticated color movie camera in the world which wasn't working. Suddenly a picture came into view and mission control asked, "What did you do?" The voice from the Commander, PHD physicist, on the moon said, "I hit it with my hammer." $3–$5 at Sears.

Most of these tool prices are of the Craftsman (woman!) brand from Sears, and I quoted them for two reasons. First, they are of reasonably good quality and second, they have a "You break'm we replace 'm" guarantee which they are very good about honoring.

If you add the prices you'll find the sum in the vicinity of $100. It's worth it. Once you've got the tools and begin to use them, they'll seem worth a lot more.

Until feminists challenged the conventional historical narrative, women were rarely mentioned in history books or courses. Male power was so taken for granted that it was invisible, and courses frequently used titles such as "The History of Mankind." In the late 1960s some scholars embarked on historical research about women and gender, usually independently of academic institutions that rarely recognized the legitimacy of such topics. Many of these self-taught women's historians went on to academic jobs and succeeded in establishing and legitimizing what is today a large academic field, with designated faculty lines, numerous courses in almost every college and university, conferences, research centers, archives, journals, and a dizzying number of scholarly and popular books. Historians concerned with gender also examined the way masculinity and gay identity were constructed and reconstructed. They practiced the feminist slogan, "The personal is political," and exploring the "private" and the "public" have been mutually developed. Gradually the field of women's history is changing the way all history is taught—much research and teaching that is not explicitly about women or gender now incorporates women's history materials. The success of "bottom-up" history, that is, history that includes the less powerful members of society, produced a significant backlash that protests what it falsely labels excessive emphasis on women, working-class people, gays, and people of color. In fact, the inclusion of women is still inadequate, and the traditional subjects of historical narratives—powerful white men—still predominate overwhelmingly in history books and courses.

In the photograph below, a Berkeley women's liberation group sat in at the public library in 1973 to demand a women's history collection; they were so determined that five of them were arrested for refusing to move. In this photo celebrated New York lawyer and author Flo Kennedy is reading a statement.

Women's liberation often used women's history in inventive and popular forms—skits, slide shows, poetry, demonstrations, posters, and songs. Early women's history discovered unsung heroes in the past. Feminists wanted to link the second to the first wave of the women's movement, to learn from the past as well as to transcend it. Activists used the past for inspiration in the present, while understanding earlier feminists not as invulnerable but as humans with limitations.

Library Sit-in for Women's History
CATHY CADE

1973

Dear Sisters

NEW YORK RADICAL FEMINISTS CABARET

Oh, Lucy Stone
Dear Lucy Stone.
There's a question I might ask now
    we're alone.
Henry Blackwell was your spouse.
You shared his bed, his board, his
    house.
But you never shared his name,
    O Lucy Stone.

Oh, Susan B.
Dear Susan B.
Married women could not own their
    property.
For this very fact alone
I remained Ms. Lucy Stone.
And as Lucy Stone am known in
    history.

Oh, Miss George Sand
Oh, Miss George Sand.
By a man's name you are known
    across the land.
When you wrote your sexy books
Didn't you think that with your looks
You'd do better as a female than a
    man?

Oh, Miss George Eliot
Dear Miss George Eliot.
Women writers weren't in any great
    demand.
So, to get my books to bloom
I assumed a nom-de-plume.
That's that reason, Miss George Eliot.
—Well, I knew that, Miss George
    Sand.

Oh, Susan B.
Dear Susan B.
You did so much to set all women
    free.
Your work was so sublime.
Where did you find the time?
—I'll try to answer, Mrs. Mott.
—I wish you would, Miss Anthony.

Oh, Mrs. Mott
Lucretia Mott.
There are some things I did well &
    some things not.
Speaking, writing were my fears
But ORGANIZE I did for years.
—Weren't you harried, Susan B.?
—I never married, Mrs. Mott.

Oh, Gertrude Stein
Dear Sister Stein.
I would like to get your sex life on the
    line.
You lived throughout your life
With Alice Toklas as your wife.
What did you do at night, Miss
    Gertrude Stein?

Oh, Mrs. Stanton
Dear Mrs. Stanton.
With seven kids I know just why
    you're askin'.
At night I'd write my book.
While Alice B. just cooked and
    cooked.
—Did you abuse her, sister Gertrude?
—I amused her, Mrs. Stanton.

Oh, Margaret Sanger
Dear Margaret Sanger.
I'm inclined to ask you this and risk
    your anger.
In your affair with Havelock Ellis
Was your husband ever jealous,
Did you wear your diaphragm,
    O Margaret Sanger?

Oh, Emma Goldman
Dear Emma Goldman.
Your path and mine diverged as we
    grew older.
While you became more red,
I took Havelock E. to bed.
But in fact he was impotent,
Emma Goldman.

Oh Sojourner
Oh Dear Sojourner.
In Truth, you were so wise,
    Oh Sojourner.
After forty years a slave
You remained so very brave
—Ain't I a woman, oh my sisters?
—You're a hero, oh Sojourner.

Oh Sisters Dear
Dear Sisters Dear.
I implore you not to doubt, or wait,
    or fear.
Be united in our fight.
Sally forth for all our Rights.
Feminism is the Truth.
Oh Sisters Dear.

The women's liberation movement flowed into colleges and universities, creating women's studies programs for the first time in 1969. These programs were won through struggle: activists engaged in agitation, demonstrations, and sit-ins in order to gain administrative support. By 1974, the time of the national conference at which poet Adrienne Rich's speech below was given, approximately 1,000 institutions offered women's studies courses and over eighty had established formal programs. New Left writer Lillian Robinson, in her poem below, expressed the movement's sense of continuity between academic and nonacademic learning. The programs often began by offering one or two interdisciplinary courses, with titles like "Women in Society," and have by now become large departments within which faculty and courses are highly specialized. Soon women's studies was spreading into the most conservative areas of the U.S., as Judith Jones's article describes, and into the most resistant of academic fields, such as economics and biology. Women's studies faculty tried to change not only the content of their fields but the way knowledge is communicated, challenging authoritarian lecture styles, encouraging critical thinking among students, and experimenting with more participatory teaching methods.

The successful institutionalization of women's studies had costs. Just as feminists influenced the academy, so academic success influenced women's studies. Some of its activist and outreach orientation was lost as faculty became more focussed on professional priorities. Today, few feminist scholars write for popular audiences. As the women's movement has declined, there is less feminist pressure from below and the faculty often find themselves more radical than the students they teach, who have been brought up in a conservative era. And academic institutions have proved far more resistant to change than feminist faculty had hoped, and many fields of research and teaching remain largely unchanged by feminist insights.

Nevertheless, women's gains in the colleges and universities have been substantial. There are more female graduate students and faculty, especially in the humanities and professional schools, to a lesser extent in the sciences. The campus atmosphere has improved considerably over the last three decades, with fewer female students feeling alienated, discouraged, and neglected; more women receiving scholarships, fellowships, and teaching assistantships; and many single-sex institutions becoming coeducational. Studies of women, gender, and homosexuality have won acceptance, again especially in the humanities. In the U.S. there are several high-status academic journals focussed on women and gender, such as *Signs* and *Feminist Studies*, and some of the dominant disciplinary journals, notably in history, literature, art, sociology, anthropology, and psychology, are alive with feminist research.

Women's Studies As a Pledge of Resistance
ADRIENNE RICH

1974

I think of women's studies as a pledge of resistance: *Man shall no longer make the world in his image.* Flowing from that resistance, that pledge, women have been moving with passion and energy to possess the knowledge we need to think, and act, further.

Women's studies within the university can become an especially false illusion of power. Even when we are learning more and more about our own past and present. Even while we are learning to analyze the social/political forces against which every female thought has had to risk itself,

against which every line was written, against which every act of self-determination has been leveled. Women's studies can be institutionalized, therefore perceived, as an "alternate lifestyle" of the mind. Until every classroom and syllabus in the self-described "mainstream" is persistently being criticized for its androcentrism, its binary assumptions, its contribution to the Great Silence, we have not gone far enough. As long as we ourselves go on acting and writing as if the androcentric world-view is really the mainstream, and that the history, thought, experience, work of women are merely a broadening of the "real" curriculum or culture, we have not gone far enough. We are then simply accruing information on a special subject—not changing the nature of knowledge itself, and therefore changing the nature of power.

We are the age-long, world-wide, culture and class-wide outsiders in patriarchy. We have only the faintest idea what the brains and imaginations of women will be capable of, once we fully understand that our need of each other transcends time, space, culture, and class, and that we are the *only* group which can criticize and challenge every aspect and product of patriarchy.

Women's Studies
LILLIAN ROBINSON   1973

But this class
goes on
all
the time!

Feminism in the Bible Belt
JUDITH P. JONES   1977

Drive only a few miles from the metropolitan centers of Arkansas, Mississippi, Alabama, Georgia, Northern Florida, North and South Carolina, Tennessee, and Virginia and you begin to sense what Flannery O'Connor meant when she said that the South, though hardly Christ-centered, was "most certainly Christ-haunted." The sides of barns and even the hillsides are painted with slogans declaring that "Jesus Saves" and "The Lord is Coming"; and there is the predictable proliferation of bumper-stickers that admonish drivers to "Honk if they Love Jesus." Closely linked to the Christ-hauntedness of the Bible Belt is a chauvinistic loyalty to the region. The "Bible Belt Syndrome" is characterized by a bedrock conservatism which holds to traditional ways of thinking and being because they are God-given and thus unquestionably "right." At the moment, not surprisingly, all the forces that fundamentalist patriarchy can muster are being directed against the vast changes implicit in the women's movement.

I am a feminist born and raised in the Bible Belt. I have until quite recently found it difficult to express my feminism visibly and vocally in political action. Coming from a background that combined traditionally Southern and immigrant heritages, I spent the early years of my adulthood trying—despite great personal conflict—to conform to the pressures of the society I have described. And I am still learning painful lessons about what will and will not work politically and in my teaching.

I am an assistant professor of Modern and Renaissance literature at Auburn University in Montgomery, a commuter-community university whose students come largely from middle and lower-middle class families with extremely conservative, rural, white Southern backgrounds.

In the 1976 class, most of the students resisted being bombarded with opinions that seemed more foreign and more dangerous to them than I had expected. The women who were moving in the direction of feminism were encouraged and I made two good friends, but in effect I lost the rest of the class. I saw early that these students resented my trying to force strange opinions on them. Eventually I realized that much of what I said simply baffled them; I was asking them to respond to concepts for which they had no frame of reference.

Not being one to give up easily, I planned to offer "Women in Literature" again the next year. This time I intended to concentrate on recent women poets, particularly the "Women's Poetry Movement" that has become such a significant expression of the developing consciousness of American women. Some months before I started making specific plans for the 1977 course, I stumbled upon Freire's *Pedagogy of the Oppressed*.

According to Freire, we cannot teach people what they are not ready to learn; liberation comes only from the experience of individuals who are learning to "deal critically and creatively with reality and discover how to participate in the transformation of their world." The oppressed must free themselves; it cannot be done *for* them.

Much influenced by Freire, I organized the 1977 class differently. I had chosen to work with feminist poets, rather than novelists, because I had myself become interested in how much women from varied backgrounds are turning to poetry as a medium for expressing a "new being." It seems to me that it was a lucky choice. Many students do write poems now and then, and therefore know more about its composition than about writing novels. By encouraging the writing of poetry as well as the reading of it, I was able to enhance the "project" aspect of the classroom situation. Thus the insights of the students were allowed to grow out of their experience, rather than out of my politics.

Instead of starting with feminism, we started with the meaning of poetry—how and why it is written. We used David Swanger's *The Poem as Process* as a guide. Soon most of the students were writing and discussing their own poetry, although no one was required either to write it or bring it to class.

The poetry class included fifteen students, five mature women with various degrees of identification with the Women's Movement. Two young men took the course, but often did not attend class. This fact undoubtedly accounts for some of the differences in the two courses, for the women students were always more free in discussing their resentment of their roles and the difficulties of male-female relationships when no men were present. The other students in the class were young women very much influenced by their Southern patriarchal training. Several of them believed, and still believe, that in a family the man should make the decisions and that the Bible is paramount in determining the relationship between men, women, and God. But all the students broadened their perspectives, and there was much less resistance to the perceptions of the writers we studied than there had been in the other class. The experience by older students of motherhood, the problems of early marriages and of middle age deeply affected the thinking of the younger women. A particularly provocative session evolved from our discussion of Sylvia Plath's love-hate response to motherhood. And conflicts that arose between the men and the women in the class forced us to define carefully such terms as "masculine" and "feminine."

I do not mean to suggest that my new approach to teaching feminist literature altogether eliminated the kind of fear and hostility that dominated the other course. It did not. Especially at the beginning of the session, some of the students objected to the feminist tone of both the poetry and the literary criticism. They often responded to the essays in the Donovan collection with the familiar complaint: "But *these* women just go *too* far."

One of the most dramatic events of the quarter occurred as a result of a book report given by one of the male students on *Beyond God the Father*. The student is the only child in a rigidly fundamentalist family. His method of reporting on the book was to take issue with Daly on Biblical grounds: God intended that man be the head of the family and civilization; God created men for certain purposes and women for others. The student insisted that he did not think men were superior to women, but that it was essential to the survival of Christian civilization that men and women adhere to the positions assigned by God. A quiet young woman with similar religious training (who up until now had prefaced everything she said with: "I'm not really for women's lib, but . . ."), admitting that she had been reading Daly and other feminist thinkers, in an emotional speech challenged fundamentalist constraints on the spirituality of women. She concluded, with no apologies for the feminist tone of her statements, that what Daly was really saying was that the patriarchal church separated women from God. "And that," she said, "is what I call a sin."

11

Work

The women's liberation movement arose, in part, because of the increase in women's labor force participation. By 1970, not only were over 40 percent of women employed but so were over 40 percent of married women. Women's liberation struggled for equality and opportunity in work, and made considerable gains.

However, not all women workers benefited equally from the demands made by the women's movement on the government and employers. The differences were primarily due to class, race and ethnicity, age, disability, family status, and geographic location. Growing numbers of professional women were frustrated by the lack of advancement and acknowledgement in their careers, and women supporting families needed work but could not get by on women's wages. As more women entered college, university attendance soared and educated women came to expect the same jobs when they graduated as did their male peers, but met instead discrimination.

The general economic expansion of the 1950s and 1960s and the demand for women's labor led to a new confidence but also to new frustrations. In 1970 over two-thirds of women were still concentrated in low-paid, so-called female jobs—clerical work, nursing, sales, cleaning, food service, and elementary education.

It was not easy sailing for working women. With increased employment, many women put in what came to be called a "double day," that is, working full-time for wages and returning home to work many more hours without pay. An important theoretical contribution of second-wave feminism was the recognition of housework as labor, and labor that could also be done by men. Housework had often been invisible to those who didn't do it, or seen as a virtually biological behavior of the female sex, rather like breast-feeding. The vast majority of Americans at this time assumed that housework and child care were exclusively women's responsibility, regardless of whether they were employed outside their homes or not. Many men "helped" with the housework but it was clear that they were helping women, not sharing responsibility. In the typical sexual division of labor in American households, men characteristically did the outside tasks—putting out the garbage, mowing the lawn, putting up screens, shoveling snow—jobs that were seasonal or occasional and rarely amounted to a significant part of the work that had to be done.

The feminist demand that men share the housework was one of the radical challenges set out by the movement. Underlying this demand were some new experiences of the 1960s generation: middle-class young women were living away from home, first at college and then, often, in apartments, and in these situations they were not accustomed to having to clean up after others; there were fewer children in families and children were doing much less housework than in previous generations. In consciousness-raising groups women gained the confidence to quit blaming themselves for their resentments over men's resistance to doing housework and came to understand that women's domestic labor often constituted a serious injustice that kept them from political activities, careers, higher education, and leisure.

Women's liberation convinced most Americans that housework should be shared and that men would not lose their manliness by doing it. But getting men to share housework was easier said than done. Recent surveys show that even today men rarely pull their weight in the household.

Pat Mainardi, an art historian from Redstockings, decoded typical male excuses about housework in this widely circulated article of the early movement.

The Politics of Housework

PAT MAINARDI

1968

Though women do not complain of the power of husbands, each complains of her own husband, or of the husbands of her friends. It is the same in all other cases of servitude; at least in the commencement of the emancipatory movement. The serfs did not at first complain of the power of their lords, but only of their tyranny.

—John Stuart Mill, *On the Subjugation of Women*

Liberated women—very different from Women's Liberation! The first signals all kinds of goodies, to warm the hearts (not to mention other parts) of the most radical men. The other signals—*housework*. The first brings sex without marriage, sex before marriage, cozy housekeeping arrangements ("You see, I'm living with this chick") and the self-content of knowing that you're not the kind of man who wants a doormat instead of a woman. That will come later.

On the other hand is Women's Liberation—and housework. What? You say this is all trivial? Wonderful! That's what I thought. It seems perfectly reasonable. We both had careers, both had to work a couple of days a week to earn enough to live on, so why shouldn't we share the housework? So I suggested it to my mate and he agreed—most men are too hip to turn you down flat. You're right, he said. It's only fair.

Then an interesting thing happened. I can only explain it by stating that we women have been brainwashed more than even we can imagine. Probably too many years of seeing media-women coming over their shiny waxed floors or breaking down over their dirty shirt collars. Men have no such conditioning. They recognize the essential fact of housework right from the very beginning. Which is that it stinks.

Here's my list of dirty chores: buying groceries, carting them home and putting them away; cooking meals and washing dishes and pots; doing the laundry; digging out the place when things get out of control; washing floors.

The list could go on but the sheer necessities are bad enough. All of us have to do these jobs, or get someone else to do them for us. The longer my husband contemplated these chores, the more repulsed he became, and so proceeded the change from the normally sweet considerate Dr. Jekyll into the crafty Mr. Hyde who would stop at nothing to avoid the horrors of—housework. As he felt himself backed into a corner laden with dirty dishes, brooms, mops and reeking garbage, his front teeth grew longer and pointier, his fingernails haggled and his eyes grew wild. Housework trivial? Not on your life! Just try to share the burden.

So ensued a dialogue that's been going on for several years. Here are some of the high points.

"I don't mind sharing the housework, but I don't do it very well. We should each do the things we're best at."

Meaning: Unfortunately I'm no good at things like washing dishes or cooking. What I do best is a little light carpentry, changing light bulbs, moving furniture. (How often do you move furniture?)

Also meaning: Historically the lower classes (Blacks and women) have had hundreds of years doing menial jobs. It would be a waste of manpower to train someone else to do them now.

Also meaning: I don't like the dull stupid boring jobs, so you should do them.

"I don't mind sharing the work, but you'll have to show me how to do it."

Meaning: I ask a lot of questions and you'll have to show me everything, every time I do it because I don't remember so good. Also, don't try to sit down and read while I'm doing my jobs because I'm going to annoy hell out of you until it's easier to do them yourself.

"We used to be so happy!" (said whenever it was his turn to do something)

WORK   255

Meaning: I used to be so happy.

Meaning: Life without housework is bliss. No quarrel here. Perfect agreement.

"We have different standards, and why should I have to work to your standards? That's unfair."

Meaning: If I begin to get bugged by the dirt and crap, I will say "This place sure is a sty" or "How can anyone live like this?" and wait for your reaction. I know that all women have a sore called *guilt over a messy house* or *housework is ultimately my responsibility.* If I rub this sore long and hard enough it'll bleed and you'll do the work. I can outwait you.

Also meaning: I can provoke innumerable scenes over the housework issue. Eventually, doing all the housework yourself will be less painful to you than trying to get me to do half.

"I've got nothing against sharing the housework, but you can't make me do it on your schedule."

Meaning: passive resistance. I'll do it when I damn well please, if at all. If my job is doing dishes, it's easier to do them once a week. If taking out laundry, once a month. If washing the floors, once a year. If you don't like it, do it yourself oftener, and then I won't do it at all.

"I hate it more than you. You don't mind it so much."

Meaning: Housework is shitwork. It's the worst crap I've ever done. It's degrading and humiliating for someone of my intelligence to do it. But for someone of your intelligence . . .

"Housework is too trivial to even talk about."

Meaning: It's even more trivial to do. Housework is beneath my status. My purpose in life is to deal with matters of significance. Yours is to deal with matters of insignificance. You should do the housework.

"In animal societies, wolves, for example, the top animal is usually a male even where he is not chosen for brute strength but on the basis of cunning and intelligence. Isn't that interesting?"

Meaning: I have historical, psychological, anthropological and biological justification for keeping you down. How can you ask the top wolf to be equal?

"Women's Liberation isn't really a political movement."

Meaning: The Revolution is coming too close to home.

Also meaning: I am only interested in how I am oppressed, not how I oppress others. Therefore the war, the draft and the university are political. Women's Liberation is not.

"Man's accomplishments have always depended on getting help from other people, mostly women. What great man would have accomplished what he did if he had to do his own housework?"

Meaning: Oppression is built into the system and I as the white American male receive the benefits of this system. I don't want to give them up.

POSTSCRIPT

Participatory democracy begins at home. If you are planning to implement your politics there are certain things to remember.

1. He is feeling it more than you. He's losing some leisure and you're gaining it. The measure of your oppression is his resistance.

2. Most men are not accustomed to doing monotonous, repetitive work which never issues in any lasting let alone important achievement. This is why they would rather repair a cabinet than wash dishes. If human endeavors are like a pyramid with man's highest achievements at the top, then keeping oneself alive is at the bottom. Men have always had servants (you) to take care of this bottom stratum of life while he has confined his efforts to the rarefied upper regions. It is thus ironic when they ask of women: "Where are your great painters, statesmen, etc." Mrs. Matisse ran a millinery shop so he could paint. Mrs. Martin Luther King kept his house and raised his babies.

3. It is a traumatizing experience for someone who has always thought of himself as being against any oppression or exploitation of one human being by another to realize that in his daily life he has been accepting and implementing (and benefiting from) this exploitation: that his rationalization is little different from that of the racist who says "Niggers don't feel pain" (women don't mind doing the shitwork), and that the oldest form of oppression in history has been the oppression of 50% of the population by the other 50%.

4. Arm yourself with some knowledge of the psychology of oppressed peoples everywhere and a few facts about the animal kingdom. I admit playing top wolf or who runs the gorillas is silly but as a last resort men bring it up all the time. Talk about bees. If you feel really hostile, bring up the sex life of spiders. After sex, she bites off his head.

The psychology of oppressed peoples is not silly. Blacks, women, and immigrants have all employed the same psychological mechanisms to survive. Admiring the oppressor, glorifying the oppressor, wanting to be like the oppressor, wanting the oppressor to like them.

5. In a sense all men everywhere are slightly schizoid—divorced from the reality of maintaining life. This makes it easier for them to play games with it. It is almost a cliche that women feel greater grief at sending a son off to war or losing him to that war because they bore him, suckled him, and raised him. The men who foment those wars did none of those things and have a more superficial estimate of the worth of human life. One hour a day is a low estimate of the amount of time one has to spend "keeping" oneself. By foisting this off on others, man has seven hours a week—one working day—more to play with his mind and not his human needs. Over the course of generations it is easy to see whence evolved the horrifying abstractions of modern life.

6. With the death of each form of oppression, life changes and new forms evolve. English aristocrats at the turn of the century were horrified at the idea of enfranchising working

men, were sure that it signalled the death of civilization and a return to barbarism. Some working men even fell for this line. Similarly with the minimum wage, abolition of slavery and female suffrage. Life changes but it goes on—don't fall for any crap about the death of everything if men take a turn at the dishes. They will imply that you are holding back the Revolution (their Revolution). But you are advancing it.

7. Keep checking up. Periodically consider who's actually doing the jobs. These things have a way of backsliding so that a year later once again the woman is doing everything. Use timesheets if necessary. Also bear in mind what the worst jobs are, namely the ones that have to be done every day or several times a day. Also the ones that are dirty—it's more pleasant to pick up books, newspapers, etc., than to wash dishes. Alternate the bad jobs. It's the daily grind that gets you down. Also make sure that you don't have the responsibility for the housework with occasional help from him. "I'll cook dinner for you tonight" implies that it's really your job and isn't he a nice guy to do some of it for you.

8. Most men had a bachelor life during which they did not starve or become encrusted with crud or buried under the litter. There is a taboo that says that women mustn't strain themselves in the presence of men—we haul around fifty pounds of groceries if we have to but aren't allowed to open a jar if there is someone around to do it for us. The reverse side of the coin is that men aren't supposed to be able to take care of themselves without a woman. Both are excuses for making women do the housework.

9. Beware of the double whammy. He won't do the little things he always did because you're now a "Liberated Woman," right? Of course, he won't do anything else either.

I was just finishing this when my husband came in and asked what I was doing. Writing a paper on housework. Housework? he said. *Housework?* Oh my god how trivial can you get. A paper on housework.

Wages for Housework

NOTICE TO ALL GOVERNMENTS

The women of the world are serving notice. We clean your homes and factories. We raise the next generation of workers for you. Whatever else we may do, we are the housewives of the world. In return for our work, you have only asked us to work harder.

We are serving notice to you that we intend to be paid for the work we do. We want wages for every dirty toilet, every painful childbirth, every indecent assault, every cup of coffee and every smile. And if we don't get what we want, then we will simply refuse to work any longer.

We have brought up our children to be good citizens and to respect your laws and you have put them in factories, in prisons, in ghettos and in typing pools. Our children deserve more than you can offer and now we will bring them up to EXPECT more.

We have borne babies for you when you needed more workers, and we have submitted to sterilization when you didn't. Our wombs are not government property any longer.

We have scrubbed and polished and oiled and waxed and scoured until our arms and backs ached, and you have only created more dirt. Now you will rot in your own garbage.

We have worked in the isolation of our homes when you needed us to and we have taken on a second job too when you needed that. Now we want to decide WHEN we work, HOW we work, and WHO we work for. We want to be able to decide NOT TO WORK AT ALL—like you.

We are teachers and nurses and secretaries and prostitutes and actresses and childcare workers and hostesses and waitresses and cooks and cleaning ladies and workers of every variety. We havesweated while you have grown rich. Now we want back the wealth we have produced.

WE WANT IT IN CASH, RETROACTIVE AND IMMEDIATELY. AND WE WANT ALL OF IT.

THE CAMPAIGN FOR WAGES FOR HOUSEWORK

Wages Against Housework
SYLVIA FEDERICI

They say it is love. We say it is unwaged work.

They call it frigidity. We call it absenteeism.

Every miscarriage is a work accident.

Homosexuality and heterosexuality are both working conditions . . . but homosexuality is workers' control of production, not the end of work.

More smiles? More money. Nothing will be so powerful in destroying the healing virtues of a smile.

Neuroses, suicides, desexualisation: occupational diseases of the housewife.

Many times the difficulties and ambiguities which women express in discussing wages for housework stem from the reduction of wages for housework to a thing, a lump of money, instead of viewing it as a political perspective. The difference between these two standpoints is enormous. To view wages for housework as a thing rather than a perspective is to detach the end result of our struggle from the struggle itself and to miss its significance in demystifying and subverting the role to which women have been confined in capitalist society.

The wage gives the impression of a fair deal: you work and you get paid, hence you and your boss are equal; while in reality the wage, rather than paying for the work you do, hides all the unpaid work that goes into profit. But the wage at least recognises that you are a worker, and you can bargain and struggle around and against the terms and the quantity of that wage, the terms and the quantity of that work.

But in the case of housework the situation is qualitatively different. The difference lies in the fact that not only has housework been imposed on women, but it has been transformed into a natural attribute of our female physique and personality, an internal need, an aspiration, supposedly coming from the depth of our female character.

In its turn, the unwaged condition of housework has been the most powerful weapon in reinforcing the common assumption that *housework is not work*, thus preventing women from struggling against it, except in the privatised kitchen-bedroom quarrel that all society agrees to ridicule, thereby further reducing the protagonist of a struggle. We are seen as nagging bitches, not workers in struggle.

Yet just how natural it is to be a housewife is shown by the fact that it takes at least twenty years of socialisation—day-to-day training, performed by an unwaged mother—to prepare a woman for this role, to convince her that children and husband are the best she can expect from life. Even so, it hardly succeeds. No matter how well trained we are, few are the women who do not feel cheated when the bride's day is over and they find themselves in front of a dirty sink. Many of us still have the illusion that we marry for love. A lot of us recognise that we marry for money and security; but it is time to make it clear that while the love or money involved is very little, the work which awaits us is enormous.

We must admit that capital has been very successful in hiding our work. It has created a true masterpiece at the expense of women. By denying housework a wage and transforming it into an act of love, capital has killed many birds with one stone. First of all, it has got a hell of a lot of work almost for free, and it has made sure that women, far from struggling against it, would seek that work as the best thing in life (the magic words: "Yes, darling, you are a real woman"). At the same time, it has disciplined the male worker also, by making *his* woman dependent on *his* work and *his* wage, and trapped him in this discipline by giving him a servant after he himself has done so much serving at the factory or the office. In fact, our role as women is to be the unwaged but happy, and most of all loving, servants of the "working class," i.e. those strata of the proletariat to which capital was forced to grant more social power. In the same way as god created Eve to give pleasure to Adam, so did capital create the housewife to service the male worker physically, emotionally and sexually—to raise *his* children, mend his socks, patch up his ego when it is crushed by the work and the social relations (which are relations of loneliness) that capital has reserved for him. It is precisely this peculiar combination of physical, emotional and sexual services that are involved in the role women must perform for capital that creates the specific character of that servant which is the housewife, that makes her work so burdensome and at the same time invisible. It is not an accident that most men start thinking of getting married as soon as they get their first job. This is not only because now they can afford it, but because having somebody at home who takes care of you is the only condition not to go crazy after a day spent on an assembly line or at a desk. It is no accident that we find the most unsophisticated machismo in the working class family: the more blows the man gets at work the more his wife must be trained to absorb them, the more he is allowed to recover his ego at her expense.

This fraud that goes under the name of love and marriage affects all of us, even if we are not married, because *once housework was totally naturalised and sexualised,* once it became a feminine attribute, all of us as females are characterised by it.

If we start from this analysis we can see the revolutionary implications of the demand for wages for housework. *It is the demand by which our nature ends and our struggle begins because just to want wages for housework means to refuse that work as the expression of our nature,* and therefore to refuse precisely the female role that capital has invented for us.

To ask for wages for housework will by itself undermine the expectations society has of us, since these expectations—the essence of our socialisation—are all functional to our wageless condition in the home. In this sense, it is absurd to compare the struggle of women for wages to the struggle of male workers in the factory for more wages. The waged worker in struggling for more wages challenges his social role but remains within it. When we struggle for wages *we struggle unambiguously and directly against our social role.* In the same way there is a qualitative difference between the struggles of the waged worker and the struggles of the slave *for a wage against that slavery.* It should be clear, however, that when we struggle for a wage we do not struggle to enter capitalist relations, because we have never been out of them. We struggle to break capital's plan for women, which is an essential moment of that planned division of labour and social power within the working class, through which capital has been able to maintain its power. Wages for housework, then, is a revolutionary demand not because by itself it destroys capital, but because it attacks capital and forces it to restructure social relations in terms more favourable to us and consequently *more favourable to the unity of the class.* In fact, to demand wages for housework does not mean to say that if we are paid we will continue to do it. It means precisely the opposite. To say that we want money for housework is the first step towards refusing to do it, because the demand for a wage makes our work visible, which is the most indispensable condition to begin to struggle against it, both in its immediate aspect as housework and its more insidious character as femininity.

Wages for housework is only the beginning, but its message is clear: *from now on they have to pay us because as females we do not guarantee anything any longer.* We want to call work what is work so that eventually we might rediscover what is love and create what will be our sexuality which we have never known.

Unfortunately, many women—particularly single women—are afraid of the perspective of wages for housework because they are afraid of identifying even for a second with the housewife. They know that this is the most powerless position in society and so they do not want to realise that they are housewives too. This is precisely their weakness, a weakness which is maintained and perpetuated through the lack of self-identification. We want and have to say that we are all housewives, we are all prostitutes and we are all gay, because until we recognise our slavery we cannot recognise our struggle against it.

Margaret F. Stewart, Our Lady of Guadalupe
YOLANDA M. LÓPEZ

1978

Luring Women into the Armed Forces
KATE WALL

1974

What do recruiters do to lure women into the Armed Forces? Almost anything, according to personnel reports and case studies. Apparently, the deception recruiters use on men is minute compared to what they use for a choice catch—a woman. The military is trying to *double* its recruiting of women within five years. Methods include the "wining and dining" of potential recruits in fancy restaurants with fancy limousines. Misleading promises about travel, job training, and pay, lure young women into the military just as they do men. This is all very tempting and impressive to someone who has not had such opportunities and luxuries.

Besides these reasons for "joining up," women may have other unique motives. Women from lower socio-economic backgrounds, from racial minorities, and from small, rural towns have even fewer economic options than the men in these groups and more social stigma against "striking out on their own" (as well as fear of it) than young men have. The military offers a package deal, within an authoritarian structure that leaves little risk of having to make choices and decisions about one's life.

Women are taught to be sexy for men. One WAF said she was *required* to attend GI parties once a week. Other military women, told by recruiters that they'd be respected and put on a pedestal by military men, found that, once inside, they were looked upon by men as "government-paid whores."

Not only are women given courses in grooming during basic training and told to look sexy for the officers, but at the same time they are also made to feel ashamed of their bodies. Men have to look clean and neat; women are *required,* in the regulations, to look "attractive." One example is the regulation regarding skirt length, which allows women with attractive legs to wear their skirts two inches higher than the standard length.

Besides much harassment, when women disobey orders, they are disciplined differently than men. Instead of an Article 15 or time in the brig, for example, a woman with a "disciplinary" problem or even a physical complaint, is usually sent to "Mental Hygiene."

Unfortunately, both military women and military wives, called "dependents" whether or not they hold a job outside the home, have an additional problem. Even marching songs use obscene language to refer to women, and a lot of these expressions are then used in addressing women in service. For example, part of a marching chant is: "Let your left foot drag if your wife is on the rag . . ."

AFT Resolution on Women's Rights   1970

RESOLUTION passed at American Federation of Teachers National Convention, Pittsburgh, Pa., 1970
WOMEN'S RIGHTS

WHEREAS   women remain highly concentrated in the lowest paid, least skilled jobs and experience far higher rates of unemployment than men—fifty percent higher in March, 1970, and

WHEREAS   women suffer disproportionately the heavy burdens of poverty partly due to high birth rates and inadequate medical attention and medical compensation, and

WHEREAS   the Equal Rights Amendment which reads: "Equality of rights under the law shall not be denied or abridged by the United States or any State, on account of sex," has been introduced in every session of Congress since 1923, and

WHEREAS   state laws on abortion exist which force up to one million women a year to resort to illegal abortions; and one out of every three births is conceived out of wedlock, therefore be it

RESOLVED   that the American Federation of Teachers urge the AFL-CIO to:

1. Change its stand and support the Equal Rights Amendment and struggle for the continuance of protective rights labor laws, and their extension to *all* workers, female and male, in all jobs.

2. Encourage women to enter apprentice training programs that will lead to better paying jobs.

3. Seek paid maternity leaves for all women with no loss of employment or contract rights, plus full medical expenses, and be it

FURTHER RESOLVED that the American Federation of Teachers and its locals endorse the following:

1. School and vocational counseling that does not limit career choices for girls and boys.

2. Vocational education programs that are open to boys and girls equally.

3. To work in all states for the adoption of legislation to secure the implementation of the above mentioned goals, and be it

FURTHER RESOLVED that the AFT Executive Council recognize the rights of women and direct the Executive Council to observe the equal employment opportunity provisions of the AFT constitution with respect to employment of national organizers.

Women's liberation pressured unions to admit women to apprenticeships in the skilled trades, desirable because they pay higher wages as well as provide better benefits and working conditions. The women's movement also set up training programs—like the one pictured here—and published articles, leaflets, and children's books encouraging women to take up what had been men's trades. Note the Chinese poster of the woman tractor driver and mechanic in this photograph; at this time Chinese images and slogans inspired some feminists, who often failed to distinguish Maoist propaganda from the actual subordination of Chinese women.

Unfortunately, the resistance has been such that women's progress in the skilled trades has been less than what feminists once hoped for.

Learning Auto Repair
CATHY CADE
1973

Title VII of the Civil Rights Act of 1964 prohibited discrimination in employment; although primarily directed against racism, it also banned sex discrimination. It set up the Equal Employment Opportunity Commission to hear workers' complaints, and women workers used this provision vigorously. In fiscal year 1971–72, women filed 10,500 complaints with the EEOC. Although the EEOC's powers and budget were very limited, the women's movement's pressure produced some significant results. For example, in a record-breaking settlement to a sex-discrimination complaint, in 1973 the EEOC ordered AT&T to pay $15 million in back pay and up to $23 million in wage increases, mostly to female workers.

Such victories also brought further problems, as when women fought their way into union-wage, traditionally male jobs, such as carpentry, plumbing, forestry, and firefighting. In response some male workers drove women out by making their lives miserable through harassment and sabotage. In this selection, women from a steel plant faced resentment from male coworkers who saw the women as competition. In response, women brought pressure on their union, the United Steel Workers, to defend their newly won rights.

Because so many male-dominated unions refused to defend women's equal right to jobs, working women, influenced by feminism, formed their own organizations. In 1974, 3,200 women from fifty-eight different unions met in Chicago with great optimism to found the Coalition of Labor Union Women (CLUW). For a brief time CLUW had chapters in many cities, trained women for union leadership, and pressured unions to include women in apprenticeship programs, to make child care a priority, to fight sexual harassment, and to get unions to support abortion rights and the ERA. In contrast to the dominant stereotype that feminism was exclusively middle-class, it was developing strongly within labor unions. Although CLUW was short-lived, labor union feminism remains very much alive. Wherever unionization is growing today, it is largely through recruiting women, especially women of color, not only as members but also as organizers.

Open Letter to Local #1299
UNITED STEELWORKERS OF AMERICA

1973

Dear Union Representatives:

In the past four months since Great Lakes Steel was FORCED to hire women, they have followed a policy of rampant discrimination. Many women, especially Black women, have been fired for no reason at all. Before a woman really gets into the department she is told that the foreman doesn't want women in his department at all, and from that point on she is picked on until they find some "cause" to fire her. She is also forced to lift twice as much as a man just to prove that she can do the job.

Examples:

1. This one woman's husband was a weight lifter and she could also lift weights. She worked in the masonry department. She could carry two buckets when most of the men carried only one. She got fired because she was too short and they said it was unsafe for her.

2. The foreman's always complimenting the women on how good they work, and then they get fired for "not being able to do the work." Women really don't have a chance to pick their jobs like many of the men do, even if they might have more seniority than some of the men. One foreman would give out all the jobs before starting time. When the women got there he would turn to them and say, "All I have left is . . . !!"

There were two Black women working in the BOP #2, and although they had the most seniority in their department, a white woman was given a bid job, when the black women didn't know about it. They were given the impression you couldn't bid on a job until you got your 35 days in.

3. In one particular case two Black women were given the job of rod straightening and were told to do 15. When the foreman came around to check on them they had already done eight. The foreman told them to stop. So they didn't do any more. The next day they were off. The following day when they were supposed to go back to work, they got calls telling them they were terminated.

4. In another incident one woman was told by one foreman to do a certain job in general labor. Then another foreman came along and told her to do something else. She got fired by the first foreman for leaving her job. So either way you lose, because there are too many people telling you what to do.

These are just a few examples of some of the women who have been fired. After all don't think any woman would be working in a steel plant if she didn't have to work. Most women are the head of their household just like the men working there. They have the nerve to apply there in the first place; and most of them work harder than some of the men there just to prove that they can do the job.

We call on Local #1299 to do its best to get these women their jobs back. Although many of these women weren't allowed to keep their jobs long enough to get in the union, we're asking the union Reps to please fight for these jobs, regardless of your specific contract obligations.

A failure to fight against such open discrimination will hurt all union efforts. Please don't allow the company to continue such divide and conquer tactics between women and men, Black and white.

Must women lift twice as much as men in order to keep their jobs?

Waiting For Our Jobs,
Women Fired by Great Lakes Steel

The Civil Rights Act and the EEOC did not prohibit discrimination on the basis of sexual preference, and gay workers faced harassment and firings with little legal recourse. Even today, in most states homosexuals do not have the same rights as heterosexuals: for example, they can be fired without recourse for being gay, they can be deprived of benefits for their partners, and they can be discriminated against in housing and employment. Many unions refuse to take on their grievances so they have been forced to rely on gay and feminist organizations for assistance. Despite their vulnerability, lesbians were disproportionately active leaders in workplace struggles, although they usually had to remain in the closet.

Does Your Boss Know You're Gay? 1974

Most working Lesbians are working under the constant concern that their foreman or supervisor will learn about their lifestyle and fire them, often on some other contrived grounds. In 1972 Peggy Bruton, a schoolteacher in Portland, Oregon was fired for being gay. After a long court battle and appeal, the State allowed her to keep her job and have back pay. The judge said the statute under which she was fired was too vague, because it referred to morality in a very general and over-broad way, and therefore it was unconstitutional. (One can guess what would have happened with a more specific statute.)

The constitutional requirement of "due process" has been interpreted to mean that a person cannot be fired from a job unless a violation of a requirement related to the job has occurred. That is, you can't be fired for being a Lesbian—the boss has to show that your Lesbianism was directly detrimental to your job. This interpretation has cast a shadow over gay women who work with other persons—doctors, teachers, psychologists, counselors—because the State could probably find that Lesbianism, as a "disease," is a valid reason for firing.

A Washington, D.C. court has recently outlawed firing homosexuals working with the Federal Civil Service Commission. The court said homosexuality did not directly interfere with the person's job. A case now pending before the Wisconsin Supreme Court deals with a male homosexual fired from his job because he was working with young retarded boys. During the oral argument, Justice Hefferman implied that there was a distinction between a homosexual working with income tax returns for the Department of Taxation, and one working with small children for a state home. Again, a misconception of homosexuals as child molesters or as disease-ridden perverts.

But even if you know you were fired for being a Lesbian,

you will probably have a hard time proving it in court. It all depends on your employer's failure to show a connection between Lesbianism and your job, having a lot of money for the lawyer and court costs, and having a sympathetic judge. Good luck. Keep in mind, however, the case of the male homosexual who taught eighth grade in Washington, D.C. last year: the court said his homosexuality was an insufficient reason to fire him, but because he went to the press and caused publicity, the firing was upheld.

Most Lesbians who've been in the Army, Navy, or Air Force have horror stories to tell of the tactics the military uses against women who are suspected of being gay. One will tell of a house where four women lived which was bugged and planted with hidden cameras. Another will tell of day-long interrogations under the hot light about suspected homosexuals. Another will tell of signed confessions and dishonorable discharges. And these are just the official effects of the military's anti-gay stance. The real insidiousness lies in the forced psychological trauma and paranoia,

the hidden meetings, the fear of surveillance, and the hesitancy to trust anyone in the micro-world of the military.

As mentioned earlier, schoolteachers, doctors, etc. will have the added burden of showing that their Lesbianism is not detrimental to their jobs, that it is not a disease to be caught by innocent children. The State had decided that it will determine who will teach, cure or help its children based on the person's sexuality. The State's preoccupation with homosexuality has resulted in witch-hunts and paranoia-engendering periods in professional circles.

Lesbian lawyers? A survey last year of state bar associations (you must belong to one in order to practice law) showed that many states would not allow open homosexuals to become lawyers. A resolution is now pending before the American Bar Association, however, which would support the right of gay persons to be lawyers. There are at least two relatively open Lesbian lawyers in the country, and countless others justifiably waiting for the weather to change before coming out of their closets.

The new militance against sex discrimination also affected professional women, and here, too, new problems arose from the women's movement's victories. More women became doctors, lawyers, accountants, and college professors, but they often faced discrimination, lower salaries, and heavier workloads. In 1960 women earned 5.5 percent of medical degrees and 2.5 percent of law degrees; today half the students in medical and law schools are female, which suggests that soon women will be half the lawyers or doctors. (It may be much longer before women have equal numbers among elite groups within professions, like corporate lawyers or surgeons.) Here, medieval historian Caroline Walker Bynum evaluates the more subtle forms of discrimination that continued to plague professional women.

The Era of Tokenism and the Role Model Trap
CAROLINE WALKER BYNUM

1973

The 12th-century historians whom I study saw universal history as divided into three ages: the era before the law, the era under the law, and the era under grace. In the era before the law, men did not know the right: in the era under the law, men knew right from wrong and stood condemned by this knowledge, for they did not yet do the right: in the era of grace, supernatural aid made the doing of right possible for mortals. If we apply this division of time to the history of women on the Harvard faculty, we can say that the two

years since the Report of the Committee on the Status of Women was issued in April, 1971, were a transition from the era before the law to the era under the law: but the era of grace seems as far away as ever.

We might also call the era under the law the "era of tokenism."

The era of tokenism is an era of sweet reasonableness. Members of the university community now know that discrimination against women is wrong; and this "knowledge of the law" manifests itself in at least four ways: the production of a vast array of procedures; the virtual disappearance of the most blatant statements of prejudice; some statistical improvement; and a new self-confidence among all women at the university.

Knowledge of the law has also driven underground the most blatant forms of discrimination and sexism. Male faculty members no longer say to me, with obvious malice, "I suppose you think you're going to get tenure for yourself by stirring up all this trouble" or "Why are academic women all so sexually unattractive?" A letter I received recently arguing for the genetic inferiority of women (the author was not a geneticist) felt compelled to add, "Of course I would hire a woman if she were qualified"; and a faculty member who tried to insult me by scheduling an interview for 12:25 p.m. when I said I was free all day except for a 12:30 p.m. lunch engagement, conducted himself with almost exaggerated courtesy when he finally met me face to face. Three years ago one of my undergraduate tutees was told in writing, "Your paper does not disprove the cliche that women are irrational"; one of my graduate students was brushed aside after an oral exam with the comment, "I won't shake hands with a woman." Such comments are rarer now, although it is not clear that the sentiments they express have also disappeared from the minds of men.

The era of tokenism has brought an increase in the number of women on the faculty. For an institution which had, in March of 1970, only 10 female assistant professors (out of 195) and no female full professors (out of 444), even tokenism is a considerable improvement. The era of tokenism has itself brought a new self-assurance to female graduate students, who now have some hope of attaining jobs and salaries commensurate with their abilities; to Radcliffe students, who are frequently more assured (perhaps unrealistically so) about their career plans than male students; and to women faculty, who are less isolated, more hopeful of promotion and recognition, than previously.

But it is unlikely that the era of tokenism will soon lead to an era of grace. Our visits to department chairmen and search committees have often met the reply, "there aren't any women in my field"—and this from disciplines like literature and art where women scholars have long excelled.

One of the ideas most commonly used, by women as well as men, to argue for an increase of female faculty is the idea of the role model. And this idea has an obvious truth. It is hard for a female undergraduate to visualize herself 15 years hence as a lawyer, professor, forest ranger, grocery-store owner, etc. But the role model argument is a dangerous one, and can easily become a subtle reinforcement of the worst aspects of tokenism. In a self-contradictory way, the adjustment both defines human beings by their careers and then refuses to women the possibility of being hired for their scholarly abilities, rather than their personalities and lifestyles.

Surely any teacher is more a model of how to examine ideas, make decisions (moral and non-moral), write prose, and analyze arguments, than a model of a specific career.

The role model argument leads to the assumption that, while male faculty members may be bachelors and bald, female faculty must be super-women, attractive, married, and prolific in children as well as scholarship. One of the first reports on the status of woman produced by a major university began with a sensible analysis of employment and salary statistics, but ended by waxing lyrical about the "lovely young woman professor" with her "attractive surgeon husband and two children" driving away from the campus in her station wagon, and thus supposedly providing for her students a model of what it means to be a woman academic. But most teachers and scholars find it difficult enough to be responsible and intelligent in their work without the additional strain of being models, and women deserve as much chance as men to be hired for their academic credentials alone, not for their beauty or marital patterns.

Women on the faculty are still a tiny minority in the era of tokenism. A token is conspicuous and apt to arouse hostility. A token who is also a role model has no private life, and, because she is not allowed to make any mistakes, no individuality. But Harvard should move beyond tokenism, not because of the difficulties of its present female faculty, not because women have special needs, not in order to provide role models, but because it is right. Study after study has shown that qualified women are available; Harvard has only to hire them. We on the faculty know what is just; we "know the law." But the metaphor from medieval historiography breaks down in the final analysis. We must demand and create the "era of grace" ourselves; no supernatural aid is going to do it for us.

When women first went into clerical work on a large scale, early in the twentieth century, it was a privileged job, attracting well-educated, white young women. But by the 1970s almost one-third of working women did office work, and the job category was 99 percent female. It was a characteristically female job: low paying, with little or no upward mobility, and requiring women to dress well and perform personal services.

Unions had been uninterested in organizing office workers until the women's movement did it for them. The popularity and militance of labor organizations in traditional female jobs took both employers and union leaders by surprise. Women Office Workers of New York, which distributed the consciousness-raising mock dollar on page 272, was one such feminist group. Women's earnings, which were about 59 percent of men's when women's liberation broke out, were actually losing ground in the 1950s. Today women's wages have reached 76 percent of men's, and among unionized workers, women have gained even more equity, earning 84 percent of men's wages on average.

The most well-known women's union is 9 to 5, which benefited from the Hollywood hit movie of the same name starring Jane Fonda, Dolly Parton, and Lily Tomlin. A key to 9 to 5's success was its retention of an independent identity as a women's movement organization even after it joined the AFL-CIO. The women's movement stimulated similar campaigns to organize stewardesses, bank tellers, and waitresses. Women came to constitute an increasingly large proportion of unionized workers.

The women's movement was quick to reach out to clerical workers even when organizing working women was not the central issue. Feminists in Cambridge noticed that clerical workers at MIT had been left out when anti–Vietnam War activists initiated a moratorium. Did the antiwar movement assume that secretaries lacked political opinions? The leaflet on p. 273 suggested both that the clerical workers should join the protest and that they had a right to time off from work to do so.

When women first became flight attendants, this job, like clerical work, was considered privileged and even glamorous, attracting well-educated, young white women. But it became clear before long that it was just one more service job, dolled-up waitressing with long hours, no tips, much harassment, and paternalistic regulation of dress, hairstyle, and body shape. Women's liberation stimulated union drives and strikes as stewardesses fought for respect and control over their working conditions. Their victories are evident on airplanes today, where you can see flight attendants of color, middle-aged and married, who would previously have been banned from the job; less visibly, they have also won better health benefits, wages, and schedules.

The Secretary's Chant
MARGE PIERCY

My hips are a desk.
From my ears hang
chains of paperclips.
Rubber bands form my hair.
My breasts are wells of mimeograph ink.
My feet bear casters.
Buzz. Click.
My head
is a badly organized file.

My head is a switchboard
where crossed lines crackle.
My head is a wastebasket
of worn ideas.
Press my fingers
and in my eyes appear
credit and debit
zing. Tinkle.
My navel is a reject button.

From my mouth issue cancelled reams.
Swollen, heavy, rectangular
I am about to be delivered
of a baby
xerox machine.
File me under W
because I wonce
was
a woman.

Women Unionize Office Jobs

RENEE BLAKKAN

1974

Can office workers be organized?

For years a myth held that this job—done mainly by women—couldn't be unionized. It was "women's" work. The turnover rate was high—an estimated 25 to 45 percent—and it was usually a temporary occupation, a stepping stone to better things or marriage.

But in the light of the organizing going on in offices today, these rationales are being stripped of their veneer, exposing their male supremacist content.

One of the fastest-growing areas of employment and union organizing today is office work. There now are 11 million office workers in the U.S. and 76 percent of them are women. One in every three working women spends her day in an office. Their ranks will swell to an estimated 20 million in the next decade.

Today less than 10 percent of office workers are organized, the great majority of whom are government employees. While white-collar workers have jumped 46 percent in union representation in the last 20 years, the main increases so far have been among service workers, mainly teachers and hospital workers.

Women office workers are thus a vast reservoir of unorganized labor for unions that until now have ignored them due to class collaboration and sexism.

But the millions of secretaries, file clerks, stenographers, key-punch operators, typists, book-keepers, cashiers, receptionists and others may be on the threshold of a new era.

Among the unions moving most successfully into offices are District 65 of the Distributive Workers of America, Teamsters, Office and Professional Employees, American Federation of State, County and Municipal Employees and Service Employees International Union.

SPARKED BY WOMEN'S MOVEMENT

Some of the first office workers to organize themselves were more educated women who were influenced by the women's movement. Margie Albert, an office-work organizer and steward for District 65 in New York City, wrote in the *New York Times:* "The beginning of the new spirit in offices came a few years ago (1969–70) when employers imposed dress codes that decreed we couldn't wear pants to work. Women rebelled. They petitioned, sent delegations to management or simply agreed that on a particular day they'd all wear pants. Employers who thought their 'girls' were immune to the subversive ideas of 'feminism' found these women suddenly making demands—to be treated with respect, to earn more money, to define their duties, to advance and to get fringe benefits other workers enjoy.

"Now, in various spots around the country, we see the beginning of a potentially powerful alliance between the labor movement and the women's movement. Those unions with the vision to understand what's happening among women have started to address themselves to women's issues."

An example of one successful organizing drive was District 65's efforts at Barnard, an exclusive women's college in New York. Organizer Sue Costello noted that "a year before we organized, we (office workers) were closeted in our separate departments. The first ripples in the waves we started to make were centered around salaries. We started with a few women meeting on their lunch hour and after work, comparing salaries, office conditions and getting angry. Long buried grievances about job classifications, titles, salaries, department head attitudes and benefits began to surface and in turn inspired more and more women to examine their places in the 'Barnard community.'

"We started a pledge card drive and within a month and a half had signed up a wide majority of employees. Barnard warned (us) about 'outsiders,' unfamiliar with our operation, without understanding the seemingly peculiar ways of a college. Another amusing college argument was that unionization would result in an adversary relationship which would destroy the atmosphere of cooperation which blossomed at Barnard. A close examination of many administrative offices revealed them to be as oppressive to work in as any sweatshop. Our anger helped us. It became clear there was no 'Barnard community' or, if there was, we were not a part of it and never had been.

"Unionizing has been a tremendous leap forward for the women who work at Barnard. It is giving us benefits and a security we have not had before. We have written a contract that not only contains the standard labor benefits, but we have written in clauses that specifically deal with the problems of women workers: daycare, parental leave, flexible hours to take care of family or educational needs."

In the last few years, in addition to organizing, the women have held speakouts and hearings on their working conditions and wages, filed job-discrimination suits, published agitational and informational literature and formed several citywide alliances to better their conditions. Many office-worker locals sent representatives to the March founding of the Coalition of Labor Union Women.

"BILL OF RIGHTS"

In Boston, Mass., a group of several hundred women, calling themselves "9 to 5," has ratified an "office workers' bill of rights," demanding equal pay and promotion opportunities, detailed job descriptions, maternity benefits, overtime pay and the right to refuse to do personal errands for the employer.

In Chicago's Loop area some 300 women have formed Women Employed (WE). In addition to campaigning for better working conditions they have done much to expose the sexist hiring policies of the Kraft corporation, a major employer in the area. WE formed, explains one leaflet, "because we feel we are not receiving decent wages, our work is not respected and we don't have promotion opportunities. Many of us have tried individually to change the situation but have come to realize that only when women form a pressure group will real changes be possible. We discovered that women are 45 percent of the Loop labor force but earn only 25 percent of the wages."

On the West Coast, Union WAGE (Women Act to Gain Equality) provides information, legal advice and picketing support to women office workers who are trying to organize their co-workers in the Bay Area.

And in New York last October over 300 office workers held a conference where they discussed their working conditions and moved to form a citywide Women Office Workers (WOW) group. "Our labor supports New York City as the financial, administrative and communications capital of our country," wrote a conference organizer. "We process the materials in corporate headquarters, banks and insurance companies, government offices and behind desks in publishing, advertising and media. But despite our numbers and our importance, our wages are low. For Black and Puerto Rican women, wages are even lower."

In addition to organizing, women office workers around the country have closely analyzed their situation. Some of their first articles were published in newspapers and magazines put out by the women's movement.

• The women discovered, for example, how they are channeled into their dead-end jobs. Madeline Belkin wrote in *Up From Under*, published in New York, that living in a working-class neighborhood, she had no choice but to "accept my guidance counselor's advice to take a commercial course in high school. This was standard advice for the majority of girls in my class. I know now that the programming of children—particularly girls and children of the poor—into subservient job training is no accident. It is the very core of our educational system."

Barbara Bergmann, an economist, wrote: "Everybody knows which jobs are 'fit' for women: domestic and light factory work for the least educated ones, clerical and retail sales work for the high-school graduates and even some of the college graduates and teaching, nursing, social work for those with professional inclinations."

• Suzanne Paul, writing for the New York WOW conference wrote: "Employers use a variety of techniques to divide and isolate us from the day we are interviewed when they tell us to keep our salaries secret." (The average male clerical worker earned $9716 last year. The average female clerical worker received $6054.)

"First," Paul went on, "they use age. Employers, choosing among young workers, get cheap labor and avoid paying older women for the experience gained on previous jobs. Second, they use race. Once at our desk, we find that job titles, pay differentials, unequal privileges and status divide us. But whatever the job almost every office worker finds that she's doing much of her boss' job at a fraction of his salary—writing the letters, composing orders, drafting speeches, even dropping personal notes to his special friends. We do this to set him free for more vital tasks—playing golf, business trips, early cocktails."

• The women are patronized. One office worker told the WOW gathering a typical story. One day she was reading a magazine at her desk while on her coffee break. "My boss asked me what I was reading and when I said *Partisan Review,* he said: '*Partisan Review!* That's amazing!'"

• "I was working as a receptionist where 400 people had to sign in and out twice a day," another beleaguered office worker told the conference. "One time when someone stepped off the elevator—one of the 800 times someone would pass my desk—I didn't smile. He rapped his knuckles on my desk and said, 'You didn't smile when I got off the elevator.' Obviously, smiling was part of my job."

• Albert has written of the typical job pattern of women office workers. "I moved from job to job, looking for more money and better conditions as many office workers do. I often came out ahead in my paycheck but lost the benefits that come with seniority, like longer vacations. What seems obvious now—that it's better to stay on a job and work for change than to quit—wasn't so clear before."

Noting the fact that women seem to quit their jobs more often than men, Bergmann wrote that some calculations "indicate that about half of the gap in quit rates is due to the fact that women are heavily employed in the kinds of occupation where men and women tend to quit more often, while the men are heavily employed in the kinds of jobs in which stability of employment is rewarded."

Overall, the office workers are demanding just wages and working conditions, equal opportunity for training and advancement and the benefits that other organized workers won long ago. The women also want an end to the image of sex object in the front office.

They want their employers to recognize that in the U.S. today office workers, as one file clerk put it, are "no less essential in our places of employment than cooks in restaurants or welders on the assembly line."

59 Cents, A Woman's Dollar

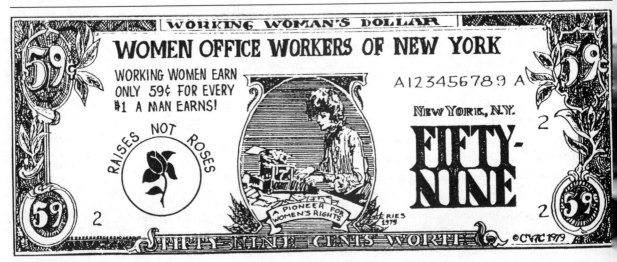

What About the Secretaries?

BREAD AND ROSES

MIT secretaries & office staff:
students and faculty are planning for the October 15 Moratorium.
What about us? Aren't we part of the Institute too?

Undergraduate association presidents, campus newspaper editors and other concerned students from more than 200 universities from across the nation have called for a recurring moratorium on "business as usual" until the war in Vietnam is ended. Wednesday, October 15th, has been set aside as a day for members of the academic community to join with citizens everywhere in voicing the demand for an immediate end of the war.

At M.I.T. there is now no provision for secretaries and office staff to join the moratorium. As long as women are required to keep the offices operating, the Institute continues to carry on its "business as usual."

Bring your lunch for a discussion about the Moratorium.
Friday, Oct. 10, 12–2 p.m. Room 400, the Student Center.

TWA Stewardesses on Strike

CATHY CADE

1973

Sexual Harassment: Working Women's Dilemma

DIERDRE SILVERMAN   1976–77

In May of 1975 Working Women United, an organization in Ithaca, New York, held a Speak-Out on Sexual Harassment. We defined sexual harassment as the treatment of women workers as sexual objects. This problem permeates all aspects of women's work.

Sexual harassment begins with hiring procedures, in which women applicants are judged not only for their work skills but also for their physical attractiveness (and, in some instances, sexual receptivity). It continues when job retention, raises or promotions depend on tolerating, or submitting to, unwanted sexual advances from co-workers, customers or supervisors. The form of these advances varies from clearly suggestive looks and/or remarks, to mild physical encounters (pinching, kissing, etc.) to outright sexual assault. In all instances, the message is clear: A woman's existence as a sexual being is more important than her work.

Respondents to a recent survey were asked to describe the most recent instance of sexual harassment they had experienced. The statistics presented refer to the description each woman gave of that one instance. In more than half of the incidents described, the man or men doing the harassing were in work positions superior to the respondent. Another 18% were customers or clients. Thus, about two thirds of the men were in a position to exert some economic pressure on the respondent. In addition, 41% of the respondents described harassment involving more than one man.

In popular literature, sexual harassment is treated as a joke of little consequence. The actress who "succeeds" by means of the casting couch, the "Fly Me" airline stewardess and other stereotypes permeate American/male humor. Are women laughing along?

Respondents were asked to describe how they felt after being harassed. Table 1 shows their responses.

TABLE 1.

PERCENT OF RESPONDENTS MENTIONING EACH REACTION

Angry	78%
Upset	48%
Frightened	23%
Guilty	22%
Flattered	10%
Indifferent	7%
Other (alienated, alone, helpless)	27%

Many respondents indicated multiple reactions, so the percentage total is more than 100%. When asked, "Did this experience have any emotional or physical effect on you?", 78% answered yes. Consider the following comments:

"As I remember all the sexual abuse and negative work experiences I am left feeling sick and helpless and upset instead of angry."

"Reinforced feelings of no control—sense of doom."

"I have difficulty dropping the emotion barrier I work behind when I come home from work. My husband turns into just another man."

"Kept me in a constant state of emotional agitation and frustration. I drank a lot."

"Soured the essential delight in the work."

"Stomach ache, migraines, cried every night, no appetite."

Many women commented on how the harassment, or their reactions to it, interfered with their job performance. The economic consequences of impaired performance are difficult to measure.

What actions do women take in response to sexual harassment? Respondents' descriptions of their most recent experience are summarized in Table 2.

Table 2.

Percent of Respondents Taking Each Action

Complain to the man harassing you	25%
Ignore it	23%
Pretend not to notice	13%
Complain through channels	12%
Quit the job	9%
Ask for transfer	2%
Other	16%

Ignoring the harassment is an ineffective response. For 76% of the respondents who tried this tactic the behavior continued, and sometimes got worse. In fact, almost one-third of these women were penalized on the job for not responding positively to the harassment. When asked why they didn't "complain through channels," women's responses indicated their weaknesses in the work situation. Forty-two percent felt that nothing would be done; 33% feared some negative consequences for themselves, varying from blame and ridicule to concrete penalties at work. For about 20% of the respondents, either there were no channels, or the harassing man was a part of them.

When respondents did officially complain, no action was taken in one third of the cases. One third of the respondents who complained were themselves penalized at work. In a small number of cases, action was taken against the man. The most severe of these was transfer to another work place or ejection of a customer.

When asked why they did not lodge formal complaints, respondents replied:

"I thought it was *my* problem."

"The importance I have been trained to place on what other people think of me—trying to please other people rather than finding my own rewards, fulfillment, etc."

"HoJo's pride themselves on their friendly, pretty girls—in a sense, they promote my sexual harassment."

"I did not want to get him (the harasser) in trouble."

"No one would believe me."

"I felt I couldn't make a scene by telling anyone in authority over him. I felt powerless and, oddly, honor-bound not to publicly embarrass him."

"I would be seen as cruel and unprofessional."

When the sexual harassment issue surfaced in Ithaca last year, women's reactions were dramatically divided. Many expressed strong support along with relief that what had been seen as a personal problem was in fact a public issue. There was also, even from feminists, a certain amount of resistance. This was expressed in comments like:

"Any woman who has it together can handle something like that."

"That sort of thing only happens to women who are asking for it." (Often accompanied by, "It's never happened to me, because I know how to present myself.")

"Just because one weird guy does something that doesn't mean it's a real problem."

(These comments are all direct quotes from women I spoke with. Any resemblance to discussions of rape five years ago is not at all a coincidence.)

Why were some women denying the relevance of sexual harassment to women's oppression? It was clear that women with class and/or educational privilege were most likely to feel this way. These women, who are the most successful and highly skilled, may be the most threatened by the idea that even they will still be judged as sexual objects. The fact that sexual harassment of these women is more often purely verbal and more subtle than that directed at working-class women may lead to their willingness to deny its relevancy.

It is also important to recognize that middle-class women have far greater job mobility than working-class women. If a problem such as sexual harassment arises, the privileged woman may just find another job, perhaps denying that there ever was such a problem. (I did that myself, at least once.) These women are also more likely to be able to leave the job market entirely. Therefore, for many reasons, sexual harassment is not as harsh an issue for them.

The more male-identified a woman is, the less likely she

is to respond to sexual harassment as a serious problem. The fact that experiences with sexual harassment are so common for women suggests that the act of harassing is quite normal for men. When women begin to think of their fathers, husbands, lovers, etc. as the people doing the harassing, resistance stiffens. Defenses that place the blame on women are developed.

At the Working Women United speak-out, women spoke about the "other side" of sexual harassment: being rejected as a worker because one is "unattractive." They felt resentment of the men in power who made those judgments, but they also felt resentment of the women who were hired because of the way they look. This jealousy and competition keeps women fighting among themselves, and not questioning the standards men are using or their right to use them.

Feminists should also regard sexual harassment as a workplace organizing issue. We should push for its recognition as a serious grievance, an intolerable working condition. We should make it clear that sexual exploitation of workers is not a joke.

Recognition and discussion of the issue in workplaces is important, so that women do not feel guilt or fear when they complain about sexual harassment. And it is important to provide organized support for individual cases, to follow up complaints and to insure the development of workplace policies that make sexual harassment unacceptable.

Just one month's news items prepared for a women's radio news show illustrate the range of women's liberation–inspired workplace activism. One of these items focuses on an issue of significance to women workers—health and safety dangers. Women have played a particularly impressive role in raising consciousness about these issues in homes, offices, factories, and farms, and in agitating for corrective action.

Radio News
WOMEN'S CLEARINGHOUSE   1974

El Paso Natural Gas and EEOC have signed an agreement committing the utility company to implement a $130,000/ year personal development program to train, counsel and educate minority and women employees so that they can reach their fullest potential within the company. The agreement also specifies that 56.8–70% of new employees in 1974 will be women and minority group members, and provides $250,000 in retroactive pay adjustments plus $70,000 in 1974 pay increases to 140 employees.

In Montgomery, Alabama, Lovemans department store has been ordered to pay more than $150,000 in back wages to 96 former and present women employees. The district court ruling followed a May 1973 appeals court decision that Lovemans violated the federal equal pay act by paying salesmen and tailors in the men's clothing department more than saleswomen and seamstresses in the women's clothing dept.

A 109-day-old strike by textile workers at the Levi-Strauss warehouse in Florence, Kentucky, ended in February when the workers won their 1st union contract. Workers at the warehouse voted in the Textile Workers Union of America (TWUA) last August, but the company had refused to negotiate a contract. The strike began Nov. 11, when 380 workers walked off the job after Levi's refused to bargain in good faith, leaving them without a contract. Along with union recognition, TWUA organizer Dan Cripe cited discrimination against women and minorities as reasons for the strike. Women, he said, were consistently put on the worst jobs for less money than the men were making. At the time of the strike, only 2 black workers were employed and strikers knew of instances when Levi's was hiring and qualified blacks were turned down. Levi blue jeans made in this country are shipped to the Kentucky warehouse for sorting. The peak business period for the warehouse began in Feb., but low production due to the strike forced the company to begin bargaining with the textile workers union. The strikers won a seniority system, more money on maternity leave, a system of raises to replace the formerly used merit system, and a modified union shop. The Florence warehouse is located in the middle of the Northern Kentucky industrial park. The park was conceived about 10 years ago, in the words of the Chamber of Commerce, to "bring jobs to northern Kentucky." To entice companies such as Levi-Strauss the sponsors of the park publicized the low inventory taxes in Kentucky, the large reserve of labor and the low profile of unions in the area. After setting up their operation the companies in the industrial park drew up and circulated blacklists of militant workers. Films were taken of union organizers and dossiers on them were compiled. In addition one union organizer suspects that yellow dogging, having workers sign statements to the effect that they will not join a union, is a frequent practice in the industrial park.

Office work is not free of occupational hazards. It has been discovered that the air in urban office buildings is sometimes contaminated by the asbestos or fibrous glass which lines the ducts of the air conditioning systems. Inhalation of these substances has been linked to asbestosis, lung cancer, cancer of the chest lining and gastrointestinal cancer. The electronic stencil machines which make stencils from a master copy give off ozone generated by the high voltage arc. According to the Public Health Service, "there is no exposure to ozone without some risk to health. . . . Even in low concentrations, inhaled ozone may cause dryness of the mouth, throat irritation, coughing, headaches, and pressure or pain in the lower chest, followed by difficulty in breathing . . . ozone also depresses the nervous system thus slowing the heart and respiration and producing drowsiness and sleep . . . exposure to sufficient quantities for 2 hours results in a marked reduction in the capacity of the lungs. Exposure for 4 hours can cause the lungs to fill with fluid and start bleeding." The stress often associated with office work can cause indecision, headache, backache, nervousness, poor memory and irritability in its early stages. These symptoms are often written off as female problems and menopause, thus contributing to the negative stereotype of the office secretary. Stress is caused by noise, fast work, monotony, job insecurity and financial difficulties, all of which are a part of the life of an office worker. Diseases associated with stress or aggravated by it include ulcers, migraine, asthma, ulcerative colitis and coronary heart disease. Office workers can work for safe working conditions through union contracts if they have a union, non-union office workers must rely on inspection by government agencies or organize work slow downs or organize a union.

A federal judge in Richmond, VA, has ruled that the General Electric Co. practices sexual discrimination by failure to provide pregnant employees with sickness and accident benefits. U.S. district judge Robert Merhige yesterday barred GE from continuing the policy. The decision affects some 100-thousand company employees across the nation.

A woman civilian secretary demoted for refusing to make coffee for her boss was restored to her old job recently at the Naval Air Station in Brunswick, Maine. The navy claimed that the job held by Alice Johnson, a navy veteran, had been abolished due to lack of funds. Her boss, however, proceeded to look for a replacement for Johnson. The civil service commission ruled that Johnson's resisting the sexist chore was justified and restored her former position.

Every Mother a Working Mother

DIANA MARA HENRY

The problems of welfare mothers are inseparable from the problems of working women and poor mothers in general. Single-mother families are disproportionately poor because of the low wages of women's jobs, the high cost of child care, and the lack of medical insurance in most low-wage jobs. This is an increasingly widespread problem: over half of all children today will spend some time in single-mother families. The early women's liberation movement offered the first analysis of welfare to connect single mothers' poverty to sex discrimination, women's economic dependence on men, and women's sole responsibility for children.

The welfare-rights movement was a women's movement as well as a civil-rights movement. It is not usually defined as part of women's liberation because poor welfare recipients do not fit the usual media image of feminists and few feminists were able to recognize welfare mothers as part of the women's movement. The following article by Johnnie Tillmon, the first national president of the National Welfare Rights Organization (NWRO), illustrates how much welfare-rights campaigns focused on poverty as a women's problem. Tillmon's analysis resembles that of the wages-for-housework stream of thought. The NWRO, active in the late 1960s, built a network of local groups which helped poor mothers navagiate the confusing welfare bureaucracy and combat pejorative stereotypes of welfare recipients. The NWRO also helped recipients defend their rights and resist harassment by landlords, merchants, and welfare caseworkers. Its successful court challenges eliminated humiliating and unconstitutional welfare practices such as unannounced midnight searches of homes, residency requirements and cut-offs of welfare without prior hearings. Some women's-liberation groups, particularly socialist-feminist organizations such as Bread and Roses in Boston and the Chicago Women's Liberation Union, helped organize local welfare-rights groups.

The 1960s and 1970s alliance of the NWRO with community organizing, the women's movement, and progressive lawyers produced significant victories in the U.S. Supreme Court, which recognized that welfare recipients were entitled to the same legal protections as other citizens. But in the 1980s and 1990s, a resurgent conservatism scapegoated welfare mothers, particularly women of color. Its ultimate achievement was the 1996 repeal of AFDC, popularly known as "welfare," which now leaves poor mothers and children with almost no guaranteed source of support. Unfortunately virtually no major progressive organizations made support for poor mothers and children a priority—not feminism, not civil rights, not labor unions.

Welfare Is a Women's Issue
JOHNNIE TILLMON

1973

The problems of welfare mothers are inseparable from the problems of working women and poor mothers in general. Single-mother families are disproportionately poor because of the low wages of women's jobs, the high cost of child care, and the lack of medical insurance in most low-wage jobs. This is an increasingly widespread problem: over half of all children today will spend some time in single-mother families. The early women's liberation movement offered the first analysis of welfare to connect single mothers' poverty to sex discrimination, women's economic dependence on men, and women's sole responsibility for children.

The welfare-rights movement was a women's movement as well as a civil-rights movement. It is not usually defined as part of women's liberation because poor welfare recipients do not fit the usual media image of feminists and few feminists were able to recognize welfare mothers as part of the women's movement. The following article by Johnnie Tillmon, the first national president of the National Welfare Rights Organization (NWRO), illustrates how much welfare-rights campaigns focused on poverty as a women's problem. Tillmon's analysis resembles that of the Wages-for-Housework stream of thought.

The NWRO, active in the late 1960s, built a network of local groups which helped poor mothers navigate the confusing welfare bureaucracy and combat pejorative stereotypes of welfare recipients. The NWRO helped recipients resist harassment by landlords, merchants, and welfare caseworkers. Its successful court challenges eliminated humiliating and unconstitutional welfare practices such as unannounced midnight searches of homes, residency requirements, and cut-offs of welfare without prior hearings. Some women's-liberation groups, particularly socialist-feminist organizations such as Bread and Roses in Boston and the Chicago Women's Liberation Union, helped organize local welfare-rights groups.

The 1960s and 1970s alliance of the NWRO with women's community organizing and progressive lawyers produced significant victories in the U.S. Supreme Court, which recognized that welfare recipients were entitled to the same legal protections as other citizens. But in the 1980s and 1990s, a resurgent conservatism scapegoated welfare mothers, particularly women of color. Its ultimate achievement was the 1996 repeal of AFDC, popularly known as "welfare," which now leaves poor mothers and children with almost no guaranteed source of support. Unfortunately, virtually no major progressive organizations made support for poor mothers and children a priority—not feminism, not civil rights, not labor unions.

And that is why welfare is a women's issue. For a lot of middle class women in this country, Women's Liberation is a matter of concern. For women on welfare it's a matter of survival.

Forty-four per cent of all poor families are headed by women. That's bad enough. But the *families* on A.F.D.C. aren't really families. Because 99 per cent of them are headed by women. That means there is no man around. In half the states there really can't be men around because A.F.D.C. says if there is an "able-bodied" man around, then you can't be on welfare. If the kids are going to eat, and the man can't get a job, then he's got to go. So his kids can eat.

The truth is that A.F.D.C. is like a supersexist marriage. You trade in *a* man for *the* man. But you can't divorce him if he treats you bad. He can divorce you, of course, cut you off anytime he wants. But in that case, *he* keeps the kids, not you.

The man runs everything. In ordinary marriage, sex is supposed to be for your husband. On A.F.D.C. you're not supposed to have any sex at all. You give up control of your own body. It's a condition of aid. You may even have to agree to get your tubes tied so you can never have more children just to avoid being cut off welfare.

The man, the welfare system, controls your money. He tells you what to buy, what not to buy, where to buy it, and how much things cost. If things—rent, for instance—really cost more than he says they do, it's just too bad for you.

There are other welfare programs, other kinds of people on welfare—the blind, the disabled, the aged. (Many of them are women, too, especially the aged.) Those others make up just over a third of all the welfare caseloads. We A.F.D.C.s are two-thirds.

But when the politicians talk about the "welfare cancer eating at our vitals," they're not talking about the aged, blind, and disabled. Nobody minds them. They're the "deserving poor." Politicians are talking about A.F.D.C. Politicians are talking about us—the women who head up 99 per cent of the A.F.D.C. families—and our kids. We're the "cancer," the "undeserving poor." Mothers and children.

In this country we believe in something called the "work ethic." That means that your work is what gives you human worth. But the work ethic itself is a double standard. It applies to men and to women on welfare. It doesn't apply to all women. If you're a society lady from Scarsdale and you spend all your time sitting on your prosperity paring your nails, well, that's okay.

The truth is a job doesn't necessarily mean an adequate income. A woman with three kids—not twelve kids, mind you, just three kids—that woman earning the full federal minimum wage of $2.00 an hour is still stuck in poverty. She is below the Government's own official poverty line. There are some ten million jobs that now pay less than the minimum wage, and if you're a woman, you've got the best chance of getting one.

The President keeps repeating the "dignity of work" idea. What dignity? Wages are the measure of dignity that society puts on a job. Wages and nothing else. There is no dignity in starvation. Nobody denies, least of all poor women, that there is dignity and satisfaction in being able to support your kids through honest labor.

We wish we could do it.

The problem is that our country's economic policies deny the dignity and satisfaction of self-sufficiency to millions of people—the millions who suffer every day in underpaid dirty jobs—and still don't have enough to survive.

People still believe that old lie that A.F.D.C. mothers keep on having kids just to get a bigger welfare check. On the average, another baby means another $35 a month— barely enough for food and clothing. Having babies for profit is a lie that only men could make up, and only men could believe. Men, who never have to bear the babies or have to raise them and maybe send them to war.

There are a lot of other lies that male society tells about welfare mothers; that A.F.D.C. mothers are immoral, that A.F.D.C. mothers are lazy, misuse their welfare checks, spend it all on booze and are stupid and incompetent.

If people are willing to believe these lies, it's partly because they're just special versions of the lies that society tells about *all* women.

For instance, the notion that all A.F.D.C. mothers are lazy: that's just a negative version of the idea that women don't work and don't want to. It's a way of rationalizing the male policy of keeping women as domestic slaves.

The notion that A.F.D.C. mothers are immoral is another way of saying that all women are likely to become whores unless they're kept under control by men and marriage. Even many of my own sisters on welfare believe these things about themselves.

On TV, a woman learns that human worth means beauty and that beauty means being thin, white, young and rich.

She learns that her body is really disgusting the way it is, and that she needs all kinds of expensive cosmetics to cover it up.

She learns that a "real woman" spends her time worrying about how her bathroom bowl smells; that being important means being middle class, having two cars, a house in the suburbs, and a minidress under your maxi-coat. In other words, an A.F.D.C. mother learns that being a "real woman" means being all the things she isn't and having all the things she can't have.

Either it breaks you, and you start hating yourself, or you break it.

There's one good thing about welfare. It kills your illusions about yourself, and about where this society is really at. It's laid out for you straight. You have to learn to fight, to be aggressive, or you just don't make it. If you can survive being on welfare, you can survive anything. It gives you a kind of freedom, a sense of your own power and togetherness with other women.

Maybe it is we poor welfare women who will really liberate women in this country. We've already started on our welfare plan.

Along with other welfare recipients, we have organized together so we can have some voice. Our group is called the National Welfare Rights Organization (N.W.R.O.). We put together our own welfare plan, called Guaranteed Adequate Income (G.A.I.), which would eliminate sexism from welfare.

There would be no "categories"—men, women, children, single, married, kids, no kids—just poor people who need aid. You'd get paid according to need and family size only—$6,500 for a family of four (which is the Department of Labor's estimate of what's adequate), and that would be upped as the cost of living goes up.

If I were president, I would solve this so-called welfare crisis in a minute and go a long way toward liberating every woman. I'd just issue a proclamation that women's work is *real* work.

In other words, I'd start paying women a living wage for doing the work we are already doing—child-raising and housekeeping. And the welfare crisis would be over, just like that. Housewives would be getting wages, too—a legally determined percentage of their husband's salary— instead of having to ask for and account for money they've already earned.

For me, Women's Liberation is simple. No woman in this country can feel dignified, no woman can be liberated, until all women get off their knees. That's what N.W.R.O. is all about—women standing together, on their feet.

12
Culture

Cultural critique was among the earliest themes of women's liberation. Drawing on civil rights and New Left analyses, the early feminists understood that women's subordination was established not only through economic and political relationships, but also through many aspects of culture, from fine art to comics to billboards to fashion.

Feminists rejected the use of "Miss" and "Mrs." as a way of marking women by their marital status, and introduced "Ms." The notion that gender was different from biological sex difference, a notion central to second-wave feminism, led to a new way of thinking about the female body: feminists saw that the pervasive sexualization and objectification of women's bodies were by no means an inevitable, "natural" aspect of femaleness or of sexuality, but a social construction. Women's liberation activists protested the use of stereotypical images of sexy women to sell everything from cars to liquor to cosmetics, and decried the privileged and WASP norms of beauty that dominated these images. Feminists tried to redefine sexy. They were outraged by assumptions about women's passivity, domesticity, shallowness, and dependence that pervaded novels, textbooks, paintings, movies, and TV programs. Feminists saw cultural artifacts not as superficial aspects of society but as the major force in defining and confining what it meant to be a woman. Cultural chains were binding women's minds as well as bodies. Feminist art exposed, condemned, and satirized these constraints.

At Home in San José
JUDY LINHARES

1972

Samplers: One of the Lesser American Arts

TONI FLORES FRATTO

Three years ago Patricia Mainardi published in the *Feminist Art Journal* an article which has since become rather well-known, "Quilts: The Great American Art." In it, she cogently argued for the recognition of quilt-making, not as simply a pleasing, useful exercise, not even as a worthwhile art form, but as *the* great American art. When I read the article, just this year, I was struck by the merits of her argument, but even more struck by the contrast between her conclusions about quilts and the conclusions I had reached about another form of needlework, the sampler. I think she is right, and that quilt-makers have produced some of the strongest, most original and imaginative, and most skillful art America has yet seen, and that the tradition of quilt-making was and possibly still is a live one with an integrity and impetus all its own. I don't think I could say the same for sampler-making. Certainly there have been handsome samplers, some sewn with consummate skill, some imaginative in their use of design and color, some animated with an Emily Dickinson–like sensibility which unites the sombre or grotesque with the fey or lovely. Samplers make up a large body of undeniably interesting art works. Yet, somehow, the form never fulfilled the promise so apparent in the pieces of the sixteenth and early seventeenth century. It never developed an impetus and integrity internal to its own purposes and possibilities. It never challenged or developed the evident skills and imagination lying semi-dormant in its practitioners. Why is this? Surely it isn't in the medium, cloth and thread; the quilts themselves, not to mention domestic decoration or ecclesiastical or courtly garb would deny this. It isn't in the juxtaposition of pictorial design and letters; manuscript illumination and, indeed, Chinese calligraphy-paintings suggest that this isn't the problem. What I suggest is that it is the social uses for which samplers were intended that inhibited the creativity of the sampler-makers and the development of a powerful sampler-style.

A sampler is a piece of cloth which bears samples or examples of embroidered pictures, design elements, alphabets, or verses. It's not a peculiarly American art and it occurred in all of the countries of Western Europe, but it reached the height of its popularity in America and here it took a most revealing course of development.

The earliest pieces are wonders of intricacy, imagination, and grace. The stitching is technically superb. The designs exist within a definite tradition, but each enlarges and develops the tradition in a subtly new direction. By the time of the sampler's greatest popularity, however, in the early decades of the nineteenth century, the form shows a real degeneration. Interest has shifted from the visual designs to the verses, which are mainly grotesquely moralizing pieces on the values of industriousness and the imminence of death. Designs have been reduced to frilling. The verses and alphabets may be and usually are done in even, fine stitches. The stiff little strawberries or roses or churches or pet dogs are charming and sometimes startling in their unexpected juxtaposition with the borders or verses. Colors are effective and sometimes subtle. The effect, in general, is pleasing, amusing, charming, but not, like the best of the quilt-work, vital and inventive. What happened? I suspect that the clue lies in the purposes for which samplers were made, in their social functioning.

The ostensible purpose of the sampler was to demonstrate a young woman's skill in embroidery and most particularly in the embroidering of letters. The ability to mark cloth with letters of the alphabet was especially important in an era when household linen was very dear and a major expense as well as a major sign of a household's prosperity; clearly marking it with the owner's initials was both necessary as a sign of its ownership and pleasurable as an act of ownership. Samplers were made, then, largely by young people at the end of their "apprenticeship"; they were visible notices that they were, in this skill and by implication also in the other household arts, able to perform the duties of a householder.

I say girls, because of all rarities, a sampler made by a boy is one of the rarest; I've seen hundreds and hundreds of samplers, and only two made by a boy. It was a "female" art and meant to display *and* inculcate the virtues deemed appropriate to a proper female. That is, the sampler was to demonstrate neatness, cleanliness, industriousness, obedience, cheerfulness, modesty, and most especially piety. It was most explicitly an instrument of socialization, and the socialization was aimed at producing an acceptable female. Flowers, sweet and pleasant to look at, were among the most common designs, but they were not wild flowers, luxuriant and undisciplined, but flowers marshalled into borders and bunches and safely held in pots, vases, urns, and baskets. Tombs and graves, mourning ladies and weeping willows were frequent reminders of the end of life and of its insignificance. Churches were common, and so were domestic scenes of houses and fences, dogs and cats, cows and stiff little humans.

There was, however, another and perhaps even more powerful function for the sampler. Like the painting on glass, theorem work on velvet, and watercolor painting of the time, the sampler was meant to serve as the sign of gentility, to establish the girl's credentials as "a lady."

The America of the late eighteenth and early nineteenth centuries was hardly a class-less paradise of equality. It was a nation with a hierarchy, a nation of marked social distinctions based on wealth, birth, learning, political power and length of residence.

Girlhood, then, was for a woman the time of her greatest chance for social mobility. Most of her socialization was aimed for that end, and virtually all of her education. After a child had acquired the basic skills of reading, writing, and ciphering, once she could read her Bible and her Isaac Watts hymn-book, her parents, if they could at all afford it, turned to the "accomplishments" which marked a lady— French, music, drawing, and embroidery.

Next to beauty, they are the best tickets of admission into society which she can produce; and everybody knows that on the company she keeps depends the chance of a young woman's settling advantageously in the world.

Quilts were "functional art"; they had an obvious, ostensible purpose, which was to cover beds. In addition, they were the product of women's work. These two facts served to keep them free of the academy. The official world of high art, of Culture, had nothing to do with this woman's craft, and so it was free to develop internally, building its own style and exploring its own possibilities. It was also an activity which brought women together, physically *and* figuratively, for the exchange of ideas and inspiration, for the exchange of snippets of fabric, and for the final and necessarily joint act of quilting the finished layers together. Quilt making brought women together and fostered a community of artists. This does not imply that the women-artists were not individuals, because almost all of the work, gathering of materials, conception of design, and execution of the process was done by one woman right up until the final piecing, which was done by the group but under the direction of the primary artist herself.

The samplers, like the quilts, began as a functional art and, like them, were regarded as woman's work quite outside the interests of the art academy, but what they gained by not being Art they lost by being a symbol of genteel Culture. An art style judged by its ability to be sentimental, dutiful, restrained, and sweet has no chance to develop. What is perhaps even more important, an art form which serves as a symbol of competition with the division of its practitioners into classes, an art which serves to divide rather than foster a community of artists, has little chance to enrich itself internally or develop its own strong tradition. The young women were too busy proving their "accomplishments" to improve their art. They were too busy competing with each other for social place to compete *or* cooperate in the development of their art.

How to Name *Baby*

IF A PERSON IS:	CALL HER:	CALL HIM:
INGRATIATING	SWEET	ASS-LICKER
SUPPORTIVE	HELPFUL	YES-MAN
INTELLIGENT	BRIGHT	SMART
HELPFUL	GOOD GIRL	HELPFUL
INNOVATIVE	PUSHY	ORIGINAL
INSISTENT	HYSTERICAL	PERSISTENT
TOUGH	IMPOSSIBLE	GO-GETTER
CUTE & TIMID	A SWEETHEART	A FAIRY
SEXY	A PIECE	HANDSOME
DUMB	NOT TOO BRIGHT	AN IDIOT
PLAIN LOOKING	HOMELY, UGLY	NO COMMENT
SUCCESSFUL	BALL-BREAKER	SUCCESSFUL
	UP-TIGHT	
	HARD DAME	
	BITCH	
	THE ONLY SUCCESSFUL WOMAN I'VE EVER MET WHO ISN'T A BALL-BREAKER, UP-TIGHT, HARD BITCH, etc.)	
POLITICALLY INVOLVED	OVER-EMOTIONAL	COMMITTED
GENTLE	A REAL WOMAN	A MINISTER'S SON
SUPPORTIVE		
HELPFUL		
INGRATIATING		
PASSIVE		

Anatomy Is Destiny or . . . Just Like Daddy

VIRGINIA W. MORGAN

PREFACE:

It is now the 21st century, and man is no longer the dominant sex with wo-man being the "second sex," the way it had been and indeed the way it was "supposed to be" in all previous centuries. Superior musculature, which made the male first for many centuries, is no longer the deciding factor in this advanced age. Indeed, the stronger genetic make-up of woman, her superior resistance and longevity, have made *her* the representative sex of the human race with man (or rather, "no-woman," as he is now termed) having become a sort of appendage—necessary mainly for the propagation of the species. Given his vital role in procreation, he is relegated the task of childcare and lesser, mundane tasks necessary for the day-to-day routines of living. His musculature well equips him for such work, for as we have all known for some time, "Anatomy is destiny" (Freud) and "Function determines role" (Margaret Mead).

. . . .

The following is an article appearing in "Ladiesman's Home Journal." Another in the series of "The No-woman Behind the Woman," it is an interview with Mr. Henrietta Jean Cosby, husband of the renowned astro-physicist, Henrietta Jean Cosby. The interviewer is the distinguished newspaper no-woman and author of *The Masculine Mistaque*, Bobby Freedom. Mister Freedom is a well-known masculinist and campaigner for masculine rights; he is chairman of the L.L.L. (Ladiesman's Liberation League) and has been active in the recent demonstrations in Miami Beach protesting the Master America Handsomeness Pageant.

B. FREEDEM: I found Mr. Henrietta Jean Cosby, husband of the world-renowned astro-physicist, Dr. Henrietta Jean Cosby, relaxing in the living room of the spacious, no-level, dome-shaped subterranean home. As the earth's surface became increasingly less habitable, there has been a mass exodus by the middle and upper classes to the subterrains, leaving the terrain to the lower classes. Mr. Cosby looked "fetching" in his bright mini-pants, which showed off to advantage his trim, virile measure-ments. As we sat down for the interview, I commented on his stylish lounge outfit.

MR. COSBY: Oh, thank you. I do try to keep myself "fixed-up" for Henrietta. I don't believe in the way some husbands let themselves go the minute the minister says "I now pronounce you woman and husband."

B. FREEDEM: Um-mm. Yes . . . Uh, Mr. Cosby . . .

MR. COSBY: Oh, *do* call me Peter.

B. FREEDEM: Uh, certainly, uh, Peter. First of all, Peter, how does it feel to be married to Dr. Henrietta Jean Cosby, the world-famous astrophysicist?

PETER: Oh, how can I tell you? Why, it's made my whole life! I was nothing until that glorious day I met Henrietta. I was so desperate—not getting any younger and so terrified that I would be a spinster, an "old lad" that nobody wanted, a failure in life, doomed to spend the rest of my days waiting, hoping, marking time in the steno pool or perhaps as a "Pal Friday." But even if I'd made it to private secretary—and I do have awfully good legs—still I would have been so unfulfilled, so *nothing!*

B. FREEDEM: But, Mr. Cosby, uh, Peter, I understand that before you were married you were the well-known Master Peter Lee Williams, who was graduated summa cum laude from college, had two years of graduate study abroad, and was commencing on a very promising career in architecture. Why did you give up those plans—just nip them in the bud, so to speak?

PETER: Well, it was sort of exciting, I have to admit. But, well, one day I just woke up and saw the light. I took a good, long look at my cousin Alfred. Alfred is 30 now and hasn't snared himself a woman yet. Well, I didn't want that to happen to me. Poor Alfred, it's such a shame! He's so attractive, too. It's just that he was always, well . . . too ambitious and too independent. He never learned that "it's not smart to be too smart" . . . and well, he just scared off all his "prospects." I mean it's O.K. to know as much math and physics as a woman, only don't let her *know* you do.

He's got a job with the same firm as my wife, only

he's not as high up . . . you know . . . he's got the right degrees and everything; it's just that it's really a woman's world. Poor Alfred! He just never could realize or maybe just never could accept that. He keeps right on bumping his head up against the brick wall. I'm so glad that I've been able to *adjust* to my masculine role as father and househusband. I've found *true fulfillment!*

(*A loud crash-bang is heard, and then the stomp of little feet.*)

Oh, the children are home from school!

KID: Daddy, Daddy, I'm hungry and I want a peanut butter sandwich with-real-chunks-of-fresh-roasted-peanuts-on-Wunderbar-bread-that-builds-strong-bodies-twelve-million-ways!

PETER (Springing up from the lounge as if he had been recalled to life): Could you excuse me for a minute, Mr. Freedem? You see, I'm always here when the children get home from school, because, you see, they need me so. I just don't approve of these "working fathers." I want my children to grow up secure, knowing that I'm *always here.*

(*A howl commences from the direction of the kitchen.*)

Daddy's coming, Regina!

(*A few minutes later, the hue and cry subdues and Mr. Cosby returns to the living room, followed by two children—a little girl of about seven and a little boy of about six. The children retire to a corner with their dripping peanut butter sandwiches to play with their Astro-Blocks.*)

PETER (sinking down on the lounge): Ah, where were we?

B. FREEDEM: We were talking about, uh, "fulfillment." Mr. Cosby, Peter, may I ask you a candid question? Do you really think you've found complete fulfillment in being just a househusband? I mean, with so many modern conveniences and everything, don't you sometimes get—well, just plain *bored?*

PETER: Well, I admit that I do have a lot of modern conveniences—Henrietta is so sweet to me! Why, just three months ago we had installed a central cleaning unit. You just push the button and it automatically cleans the whole house. I don't know what I ever did without it!

B. FREEDEM: But if all you have to do is push a button, do you really feel as needed in the home?

PETER: Ah, but you have to select the correct button, depending on whether you want vacuum, supersonic beams, or sound waves. I guess I could set the unit on "automatic" and let it select, depending on its Dirt-Gauge. But when you do it yourself, it adds that "personal touch," which shows your family you care. And with meals, I do even more myself. I push the button to select what we'll have for supper and it's immediately thawed and cooked electronically. But when it pops out on the table, I always sprinkle on a little paprika or seasoning or something to give it that special, "home-cooked" touch.

B. FREEDEM: I agree that sounds very nice. But is it challenging? I mean, after college and graduate study. . . .

PETER: Ah, but I've even found a truly masculine way to utilize the art and philosophy I studied in college—I'm chairman of the Enrichment Committee of the PTA!

(*Before I could inquire further about his work on the Enrichment Committee, Mr. Cosby had again leaped from the lounge.*)

Oh, please excuse me for just a minute or two. I don't want to seem rude, but I just *have* to find out how Uncle Barry is recovering from his ailment . . .

(*I thought that there must be someone ill in the family, and that Peter was going to make a phone call, but instead of turning on the phone-o-vision, he flicked on the wall-size TV screen, which seemed actually to become an extension of the room with its big-as-life characters actually there in our presence, so we could share in the drama of their lives. Eerie electronic organ music filled the room and then subsided, as a beautiful young doctor in a white lab coat speaks to several worried-looking people in a reassuring fashion.*)

DOCTOR: "Yes, I'm afraid that's true. Uncle Barry has indeed suffered from Emotional Trauma as a result of his fractured metatarsal. You see, I can tell that your Uncle Barry was a no-woman to whom his masculine charm meant everything . . . And, well, deep down I can tell he's afraid he won't be as desirable and alluring. As a matter of fact, I called in the staff psychiatrist, and she prescribed "Pretty Feet," as well as "Brick," the shampoo for troubled hair . . . And, well, it seems that your Uncle Barry is going to be his old gay, vivacious self in no time at all!"

(The electronic organ music swells triumphantly and then fades away as a commercial overtakes the living room.)

"Just because you're a no-woman, you solve 50% more problems, make 50% more 'executive decisions' (such as what to do about runny noses), and, for most of your life, need 50% more Vitamin V. Yes, Vitamin V, the 'Virility Vitamin,' usually found in adequate amounts only in clam juice, is now contained in our Vitamins Plus V . . ."

(Peter erased the screen by remote control, and we were alone again.)

PETER: Please excuse the interruption. I was so worried about Uncle Barry, but it seems that he is going to be O.K. . . . Where were we? Oh, yes, fulfillment. Yes, I definitely feel that adjustment to one's masculine role as a househusband and father is the key to a rich, full life . . .

(Peter turns and looks devotedly at his little son and daughter building toy rockets in the corner. The little boy is saying to his sister, "When I grow up, I'm going to be a space-woman!" Peter corrects his little boy in a gentle voice, "No, honey, when you grow up, you're going to be a househusband, just like Daddy.")

The context for the following article was a New Left critique of consumption as frivolous, conformist, manipulated, and wasteful. Many feminists shared and extended this approach, furious at the way women were forced into a standard mold of femininity, and thus encouraged women to reject the girdles, hair curlers, and hair straighteners that bound them. Feminists began what was to become a mass consumer movement toward comfortable, casual dress: including blue jeans and corduroy slacks, sneakers and running shoes, T-shirts and cotton underwear. This rejection of "fashion" soon became fashionable; as always, victories brought new problems—designer jeans that cost $60, sneakers that cost $120, and a new tyranny of muscular thinness.

Journalist Ellen Willis, a radical feminist, took a contrarian path, defending women's fashion consciousness and buying habits as a form of work assigned to women by the gender system, necessary to secure the jobs and men upon which they depended. This reinterpretation of women's alleged superficiality became known as the "pro-woman line," also represented by selections in chapter 4. Willis, significantly, did not address another aspect of consumerism—its playful, aesthetic, and pleasure-seeking impulses.

Women and the Myth of Consumerism
ELLEN WILLIS

1969

If white radicals are serious about revolution, they are going to have to discard a lot of bullshit ideology created by and for educated white middle-class males. A good example of what has to go is the popular theory of consumerism.

As expounded by many leftist thinkers, notably Marcuse, this theory maintains that consumers are psychically manipulated by the mass media to crave more and more consumer goods, and thus power an economy that depends on constantly expanding sales. The theory is said to be particularly applicable to women, for women do most of the actual buying, their consumption is often directly related to their oppression (e.g. makeup, soap flakes), and they are a special target of advertisers. According to this view, the society defines women as consumers, and the purpose of the prevailing media image of women as passive sexual objects is to sell products. It follows that the beneficiaries of this depreciation of women are not men but the corporate power structure.

First of all, there is nothing inherently wrong with consumption. Shopping and consuming are enjoyable human activities and the marketplace has been a center of social life for thousands of years.

The locus of the oppression resides in the production function: people have no control over which commodities are produced (or services performed), in what amounts, under what conditions, or how these commodities are distributed. Corporations make these decisions and base them solely on their profit potential.

As it is, the profusion of commodities is a genuine and powerful compensation for oppression. It is a bribe, but like all bribes it offers concrete benefits—in the average American's case, a degree of physical comfort unparalleled in history. Under present conditions, people are preoccupied with consumer goods not because they are brainwashed but because buying is the one pleasurable activity not only permitted but actively encouraged by our rulers. The pleasure of eating an ice cream cone may be minor compared to the pleasure of meaningful, autonomous work, but the former is easily available and the latter is not. A poor family would undoubtedly rather have a decent apartment than a new TV, but since they are unlikely to get the apartment, what is to be gained by not getting the TV?

The confusion between cause and effect is particularly apparent in the consumerist analysis of women's oppression. Women are not manipulated by the media into being domestic servants and mindless sexual decorations, the

better to sell soap and hair spray. Rather, the image reflects women as they are forced by men in a sexist society to behave. Male supremacy is the oldest and most basic form of class exploitation: it was not invented by a smart ad man. The real evil of the media image of women is that it supports the sexist status quo. In a sense, the fashion, cosmetics and "feminine hygiene" ads are aimed more at men than at women. They encourage men to expect women to sport all the latest trappings of sexual slavery—expectations women must then fulfill if they are to survive. That advertisers exploit women's subordination rather than cause it can be clearly seen now that *male* fashions and toiletries have become big business. In contrast to ads for women's products, whose appeal is "use this and he will want you" (or "if you don't use this, he won't want you"), ads for the male counterparts urge, "You too can enjoy perfume and bright-colored clothes; don't worry, it doesn't make you feminine." Although advertisers are careful to emphasize how *virile* these products are (giving them names like "Brut," showing the man who uses them hunting or flirting with admiring women—who, incidentally, remain decorative objects when the sell is aimed directly at men), it is never claimed that the product is *essential* to masculinity (as make-up is essential to femininity), only *compatible* with it. To convince a man to buy, an ad must appeal to his desire for autonomy and freedom from conventional restrictions: to convince a woman, an ad must appeal to her need to please the male oppressor.

For women, buying and wearing clothes and beauty aids is not so much consumption as work. One of a woman's jobs in this society is to be an attractive sexual object, and clothes and make up are tools of the trade. Similarly, buying food and household furnishings is a domestic task; it is the wife's chore to pick out the commodities that will be consumed by the whole family. Appliances and cleaning materials are tools that facilitate her domestic function. When a woman spends a lot of money and time decorating her home or herself, or hunting down the latest in vacuum cleaners, it is not idle self-indulgence (let alone the result of psychic manipulation) but a healthy attempt to find outlets for her creative energies within her circumscribed role.

There is a persistent myth that a wife has control over her husband's money because she gets to spend it. Actually, she does not have much more financial autonomy than the employee of a corporation who is delegated to buy office furniture or supplies. The husband, especially if he is rich, may allow his wife wide latitude in spending—he may reason that since she has to work in the home she is entitled to furnish it to her taste, or he may simply not want to bother with domestic details—but he retains the ultimate veto power. If he doesn't like the way his wife handles his money, she will hear about it. In most households, particularly in the working class, a wife cannot make significant expenditures, either personal or in her role as object-servant, without consulting her husband. And more often than not, according to statistics, it is the husband who makes the final decisions about furniture and appliances as well as about other major expenditures like houses, cars and vacations.

Consumerism as applied to women is blatantly sexist. The pervasive image of the empty-headed female consumer constantly trying her husband's patience with her extravagant purchases contributes to the myth of male superiority: we are incapable of spending money rationally: all we need to make us happy is a new hat now and then. (There is an analogous racial stereotype—the black with his Cadillac and his magenta shirts.) Furthermore, the consumerism line allows Movement men to avoid recognizing that they exploit women by attributing women's oppression solely to capitalism. It fits neatly into already existing radical theory and concerns, saving the Movement the trouble of tackling the real problems of women's liberation. And it retards the struggle against male supremacy by dividing women. Just as in the male movement, the belief in consumerism encourages radical women to patronize and put down other women for trying to survive as best they can, and maintains individualist illusions.

If we are to build a mass movement we must recognize that no individual decision, like rejecting consumption, can liberate us. We must stop arguing about whose life style is better (and secretly believing ours is) and tend to the task of collectively fighting our own oppression and the ways in which we oppress others. When we create a political alternative to sexism, racism and capitalism, the consumer problem, if it is a problem, will take care of itself.

Feminist artists both explored the nature of women's confinement and imagined pathways of escape. There is a remarkable coincidence between two works created out of two different cultures in California: Chicana artist Carrasco's image of a pregnant woman bound into a ball of yarn from which a bootie is being crocheted—an image of creativity but also of enclosure—and art student Orgel's image of a woman both closeted by her domesticity and emerging from her linen closet.

Pregnant Woman in a Ball of Yarn
BARBARA CARRASCO

1978

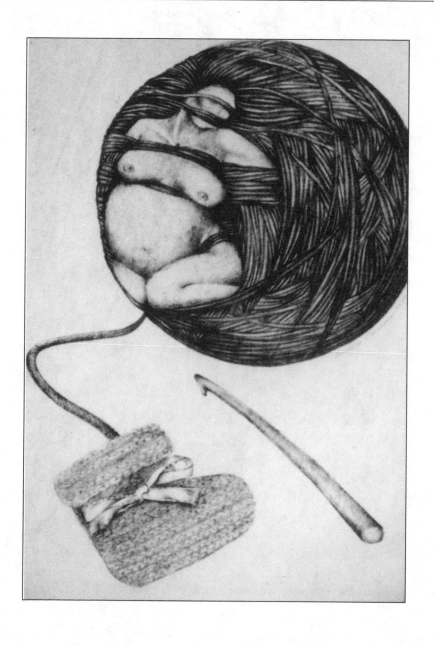

Linen Closet
SANDY ORGEL

"There Was a Young Woman Who Swallowed a Lie . . . ,"
MEREDITH TAX

1969

There was a young woman who swallowed a lie,
We all know why she swallowed
that lie,
PERHAPS SHE'LL DIE!

There was a young woman who
swallowed a rule.
"Live to serve others," she
learned it in school.
She swallowed the rule to go with
the lie.
We all know why she swallowed
that lie.
PERHAPS SHE'LL DIE!

There was a young woman who
swallowed some fluff.
Lipstick & candy & powder & puff—

She swallowed the fluff to
sweeten the rule.
She swallowed the rule to go with
the lie.
We all know why she swallowed
that lie.
PERHAPS SHE'LL DIE!

There was a young woman who
swallowed a line,
"I like 'em dumb, baby, you suit
me fine."

She swallowed the line to go with
the fluff.
She swallowed the fluff to
sweeten the rule.
She swallowed the rule to go with
the lie.
We all know why she swallowed
that lie.
PERHAPS SHE'LL DIE!

There was a young woman who
swallowed a pill,
Prescribed by the doctor though
it made her ill.
She swallowed the pill to go with
the line.
She swallowed the line to go with
the fluff.
She swallowed the fluff to
sweeten the rule.
She swallowed the rule to go with
the lie.
We all know why she swallowed
that lie.
PERHAPS SHE'LL DIE!

Reclaiming previously pejorative images of and derogatory names for women constituted another tactic in the feminist culture wars. Feminists refused to be called "ladies." Words like "bitch," "shrew," "witch," "hussy," "virago," and "amazon" became the titles of feminist publications and organizations. Feminists appropriated legends about powerful women warriors, and frequently engaged in romantic "herstory" writing of dubious accuracy in order to mythologize their "(s)heroes." Role models were important in this alternative culture, and feminists wrote children's books about Sojourner Truth, Marie Curie, and ordinary women doing extraordinary jobs, from mail carrier to astronaut.

The feminists' amazons—such as Judy Grahn's woman of strong purpose who reshapes the very earth, Gayle Two Eagles's woman warrior, or the superwoman with speculum from chapter 5—were meant to inspire an everyday, workaday kind of heroism that would provide role models for escape from various prisons. The escapes seemed more possible when the bonds holding women back were understood to be only individual and cultural rather than social and economic. Many feminists attempted to make radical personal transformations—leaving husbands and careers, learning new skills, becoming physically strong and mentally assertive, trying to create supportive new communities—and hoped that these would lead to freedom. This utopianism sometimes had negative consequences for women themselves: feminists underestimated the difficulty of making such total transformations, in part because they mistakenly thought culture more plastic than it actually was, and in part because they underestimated the satisfaction many women got from traditional cultural forms. They were too impatient and self-critical when these attempts at change produced only marginal results. Their strivings to create cultural alternatives reproduced social hierarchy and confirmed for many observers the image of the women's movement as young, white, and elite, because for many women cultural transformation was an unattainable privilege. Most American women lacked the wealth, education, and leisure to choose to live in a commune, to find a new career, to study karate, or to find a job that did not require wearing makeup or a bra. Furthermore, many women lacked the space and time to devote to political activism.

Still, we are all in debt to this utopianism. These radical dreams allowed many women to defy the dominant culture's certainty that women's position was a natural, unchangeable phenomenon, and to move further and faster than even they had imagined possible.

The Reception
JEAN JORDAN — **JUNE JORDAN**

1967

Doretha wore the short blue lace last night
and William watched her drinking so she fight
with him in flying collar slim-jim orange
tie and alligator belt below the navel pants uptight

"I flirt. You hear me? Yes I flirt.
Been on my pretty knees all week
to clean the rich white downtown dirt
the greedy garbage money reek.

I flirt. Damned right. You look at me."
But William watched her carefully
his mustache shaky she could see
him jealous, "which is how he always be

at parties." Clementine and Wilhelmina
looked at trouble in the light blue lace
and held to George while Roosevelt Senior
circled by the yella high and bitterly light blue face

he liked because she worked
the crowded room like clay like molding men
from dust to muscle jerked
and arms and shoulders moving when

she moved. The Lord Almighty Seagrams bless
Doretha in her short blue dress
and Roosevelt waiting for his chance:
a true gut-funky blues to make her really dance.

Witch
JEAN TEPPERMAN

1969

They told me
I smile prettier with my mouth closed.
They said—
better cut your hair—
long, it's all frizzy,
looks Jewish.
They hushed me in restaurants
looking around them
while the mirrors above the table
jeered infinite reflections
of a raw, square face.
They questioned me
when I sang in the street.
They stood taller at tea
smoothly explaining
my eyes on the saucers,
trying to hide the hand grenade
in my pants pocket,

or crouched behind the piano.
They mocked me with magazines
full of breasts and lace,
published their triumph
when the doctor's oldest son
married a nice sweet girl.
They told me tweed-suit stories
of various careers of ladies.
I woke up at night
afraid of dying.
They built screens and room dividers
to hide unsightly desire
sixteen years old
raw and hopeless
they buttoned me into dresses
covered with pink flowers.
They waited for me to finish
then continued the conversation.

I have been invisible,
weird and supernatural.
I want my black dress.
I want my hair
curling wild around me.
I want my broomstick
from the closet where I hid it.
Tonight I meet my sisters
in the graveyard.
Around midnight
if you stop at a red light
in the wet city traffic,
watch for us against the moon.
We are screaming,
we are flying,
laughing, and won't stop.

A Geology Lesson
JUDY GRAHN

1972

Here, the sea strains to climb up on the land
and the wind blows dust in a single direction.
The trees bend themselves all one way
and volcanoes explode often.

Why is this? Many years back
a woman of strong purpose
passed through this section
and everything else tried to follow.

The Young Warrior
GAYLE TWO EAGLES

The young warrior,
Seeing the world through brand-new eyes,
Brought up thinking she was special and good.

Lakota people can be proud again.

When an injustice is done to one of "the people,"
The warriors gather.

The woman warrior is among them,
Proud and strong,
Because she is a fighter.

The words flow off the tongues of the new orators,
Telling of the old ways,
And why being Indian is worth fighting for,
Mesmerized by the sense of strength and duty,
To become a warrior and keep the Lakota ways alive.

Tradition as told by men,
Written in history books by white men,
Religion didn't escape their influence.

Despite being told the women's squad is assigned the
    kitchen,
She guards the rooms and buildings from passing racists.

While the Lakota people make their stand,
Quiet defiance to the men who say, "respect your brother's
    vision,"
She mutters, "respect your sister's vision too."

She supported you in Wounded Knee,
She was with you at Sioux Falls,

Custer,
And Sturgis,
And has always remembered you,
Her Indian people,
In her prayers.

She has listened to women who were beaten by the men
    they love,
Or their husbands,
And gave strength to women who were raped,
As has the Sacred Mother Earth.

At some point asking where Tradition for women was
    being decided.

As a Traditional Lakota woman you are asked to approach
    a relative
or your spouse to speak your thoughts and feelings at a
    public meeting,
Not to touch a feather, or not to handle food at what the
    white culture
once referred to as the "sick time."

Woman warrior once told to break the stereotype of the
    white people,
She is also told to walk ten steps behind a man.

The new eyes that once were in awe at what the world had
    to offer,
Looks down at this new girl child,
The Lakota woman warrior knows her daughter also has a
    vision.

Mountain-Moving Day
CHICAGO WOMEN'S GRAPHIC COLLECTIVE

The mountain-moving day is coming.
I say so, yet others doubt.
Only a while the mountain sleeps.
In the past
All mountains moved in fire,
Yet you may not believe it.
Oh man, this alone believe,
All sleeping women
Now will awake and move.

-Yosano Akiko

IN CELEBRATION OF AMAZONS...

MIDWEST LESBIAN CONFERENCE
AND MUSIC FESTIVAL

Feminists made concrete demands of the mainstream media, some of which were won. In Boston the women's movement conducted a demonstration at *The Boston Globe*, the liberal elite daily newspaper, protesting not only advertising but the paper's editorial content. Feminists objected to the sexist language of disk jockeys and talk show hosts, to condescending portrayals of women and demeaning representations of gays and lesbians. The fact that there are female and even some feminist columnists and reporters today was a direct result of this kind of pressure.

In several cities feminists created stickers to challenge advertising messages and raise public consciousness. Activists carried packets of labels like those shown on page 301 and stuck them on subway and bus ads, rock-and-roll posters, even magazines in doctors' offices. The labels provided a way to condemn pornography or anti-woman statements without endorsing a strategy of censorship that less civil-libertarian feminists later proposed.

Another inventive, if unsuccessful, project attempted to get women drivers to pick up women hitchhikers, as in the leaflet on page 302. (Hitchhiking was less dangerous in the early 1970s than it is today.)

Women Invade *The Boston Globe*

LYNN EVANS

1970

On Monday, April 6 about 50 women from Bread and Roses crowded into the MTA [Boston's subway] on our way to the *Boston Globe* to present a series of demands based on the fact that the *Globe* is an actively racist, sexist institution which bombards us daily with blatant symbols of our oppression. When Pinkerton guards blocked the Up escalator, we ran up the Down escalator to leaflet and talk to the women employees. Women's jobs at the *Globe* include secretaries, switchboard operators, classified ad writers and a few "professional women" who write for the "Living" section of the paper.

While leafleting many of us were invited into the cafeteria where the *Globe* bigwigs tried to buy us off with free lunch. One woman demanded that all women employees be given free lunch also and several of us carried trays of doughnuts and sandwiches down to the women still working. Many women were receptive to our leaflets and spoke with us.

At 2 p.m. we met with Editor Winship.

Us: We demand 1) 3 paid columns a week to be placed in the "Living" section on Sun., Wed. and Fri. in all editions, with full editorial control by Bread and Roses; 2) An end to all sexist and racist advertising which uses women's bodies sexually to sell products; 3) An immediate end to segregated classified ads.

WINSHIP: "I don't think you have any idea how seriously we take these demands that have been made in the general area of women's liberation. We don't consider them a joke at all."

Us: We demand to edit our own columns to ensure that our point of view is presented, not slanted, or slurred or laughed at as is usually the case by people such as Art Buchwald or George Frazier. We can write best of our oppression and liberation.

WINSHIP: "We are going to do a better job covering the Bread and Roses and other liberation groups than you can do. In the course of a week if we get about 18 people requesting to do a column you would have no room for the news."

Us: We feel that women's bodies are used to sell products and create needs within women which eventually feed money into the *Globe*'s profit machine.

WINSHIP: "No, we will not throw out all of these ads immediately."

Us: Women should have the right to apply for and be hired for any job they feel qualified for, not just ones that have been labeled "female." The *Globe* must end its segregated classifieds.

Globe Assistant Editor Healy speaks for Winship: "This [the sex segregation of classified ads] is a simple courtesy to people who want to find jobs."

Us: A simple courtesy to exploiters.

Globe: The ads are your problem.

No, said the *Globe* to all our demands. We exited singing "Move on over or we'll move on over you." One of the editors was heard to say, "seems like we really flunked out, didn't we?"

On Wednesday we went back to the *Globe* to picket. The signs repeated our demands and that we will decide what "Living" means for us and it ain't just dieting and keeping house.

The *Globe* met us with the police and told us to move off their property. It seems that they too took our demands seriously, as a threat to their male-oriented newspaper. We moved to a public sidewalk in front of the *Globe* and continued our picket. Picketing continued Thursday and Friday mornings.

The purpose of the picket is not to prevent workers from entering the *Globe,* but to have them think about what the *Globe* does to women as readers and workers. Women from the *Globe* who showed interest in the leaflet were invited to meet at the Bread and Roses office on Monday at 5 p.m.

Stickers to Paste on Advertisements
BREAD AND ROSES

1970

NOT WITH MY BODY YOU DON'T

WE ARE FIGHTING FOR OUR OWN IMAGE – WE WON'T BUY THEIRS !

women's liberation   bread and roses 492 4130

BEAUTY IS <u>NOT</u> IN THE EYES OF THE BEHOLDER!
bread & roses 492 4130

I am being psychologically raped !

i've been in her shoes

Stuck with the shopping, the kids, and no transportation.
Hard to force myself to do all the things I have to do and go
all the places I have to go when there's no easy way of getting there.

Another woman knows what it's like.
Another woman who's driving can help.
If you're driving and you see a woman
walking or waiting at a bus stop,
offer her a ride in your direction.
You've been in her shoes.
Share your car with her.

share your car with other women

Since you can't hear music in a book, we rely here on retrospective accounts of several aspects of early feminist musical projects. These looks backward are engaging precisely because women's music has become big business. Today's successes are indebted to early feminist *chutzpah,* even if today's feminist musicians don't know their own history.

Women's liberation not only challenged the commercial media, but attempted also to create noncommercial cultural forms of its own. In doing this, democratic structure and organization were as important as feminist content. Feminists created non-hierarchical publishing companies, theater and dance groups, film collectives, radio shows, cooperative bookstores, recording companies, photography workshops, galleries, and even a few art schools. The career of the Chicago Women's Liberation Rock Band, as analyzed by its founder Naomi Weisstein—also a psychologist and feminist theorist—is instructive about the vision and the problems of this project: structurelessness, ultra-democracy, and the denial of expertise inhibited this music group from development as they did many other feminist political and artistic projects.

Women had been active performers of many types of popular and folk music, but at the time of women's liberation's birth, rock and roll ruled, as far as young people were concerned, and women were completely subordinated in this genre. There were some exceptions, such as Janis Joplin, and some female vocalists, such as Grace Slick of the Jefferson Airplane, but the instrumental groups were all male. Jennifer Baumgardner, a young feminist journalist, recounts the history of Olivia Records and the Ladyslipper distribution company, groups that rejected rock and roll in favor of the sweeter, softer sound of women's music from the 1970s and earlier (they rejected a chance to record Yoko Ono, John Lennon's widow and avant-garde rock musician). Nevertheless, by demonstrating that women constituted a profitable market for music, they prepared the way for the Ani Di Francos and Lauryn Hills of 2000.

Days of Celebration and Resistance: The Chicago Women's Liberation Rock Band, 1970–1973
NAOMI WEISSTEIN

The mountain moving day is coming.
I say so, yet others doubt it.
Only a while the mountain sleeps.
In the past, all mountains moved in fire.
Yet you might not believe this.
Oh man, this alone believe:
All sleeping women now awake and move

Yosano Akiko, 1913
Adapted and performed by
the Chicago Women's Liberation Rock Band

In Chicago, one cold and sunny day in March of 1970, I decided to organize a feminist rock band. I was lying on the sofa listening to the radio—a rare bit of free time in those early hectic days of the women's movement. First, Mick Jagger crowed that his once feisty girlfriend was now "under my thumb." Then Janis Joplin moaned with thrilled resignation that love was like "a ball and chain." Then the Band, a self-consciously left-wing group, sang:

"Jemima surrender.
I'm gonna give it to you."

I somersaulted off the sofa, leapt up into the air, and came down howling at the radio: "every fourteen-year-old girl in this city listens to rock! How criminal to make the subjugation and suffering of women so sexy! We'll . . . We'll organize our own rock band!"

My epiphany was influenced by the fact that my closest friend, Virginia Blaisdell had a feminist rock band in New Haven. Judy Miller, a fellow political activist, decided that she wanted to play drums. She bought herself the glitziest, snazziest, lights-blinking-on-and-off drum set she could find, and parked it on Virginia's doorstep. "Teach me how to play these things, and we'll start a rock band," she said.

But until that cold sunny day in March I didn't think we

could pull off a feminist rock band in Mayor Daley's brutally repressive Chicago. Chicago was not a city you wanted to venture out in after dark, even to hear your favorite rock group. White Chicago was a scared, silent, violent balkanized city. It seethed with ethnic tensions. Rape was epidemic. Vivian Rothstein, co-founder of the Chicago Women's Liberation Union (CWLU, the magnificent city-wide umbrella organization we had created), told me that most women she knew in Chicago had been raped by a stranger, an unusual and chilling observation, since most rapists know their victims. Except for a couple of streets on the north fringes of Old Town, there were no "free spaces" like San Francisco's North Beach or New York's Greenwich Village, where a seriously dissenting culture might start to develop. One couldn't hold as much as a poetry reading without the Red Squad showing up.

But that day I said to myself, "Fuck it." If I were able to find musicians in a city where no family would teach their daughter "devil" instruments like drums and electric guitar, then I would form a rock band. If the police broke it up but didn't kill us, then it would just be good publicity. Why not?

The idea of direct cultural intervention in order to bring about feminist change was held in low esteem by most of the CWLU leadership at that time. This was due to an assumption we had inherited from the New Left, namely, that if we changed the structures which maintain our oppression (such as if we won equal pay for equal work), feminist consciousness would emerge. I had started to disagree. Structural change is absolutely necessary if we are to overthrow our oppression, but it is not sufficient; we also need to change our consciousness. Structure is the tip of the patriarchal iceberg. Submission gets inside our heads, and we're only going to get it out if we create alternatives to the dominant and dominating culture. We had to go through the culture, both mainstream and Left, with a fine tooth comb, confronting every thing from why we thought that a working-class revolution—indeed any revolution—was more important than a feminist revolution, all the way to why we believed, along with the mainstream culture, that male domination and a little bit of cruelty would always turn us on.

"What about rock?" I said to myself, boiling over with my new idea. Rock, with its drive, power and energy, its insistent erotic rhythms, its big bright major triads, its take-no-prisoners chord progressions, was surely the kind of transforming medium that could help to alter the culture in which we lived, and thus help us to change our consciousness, to refuse to continue our frenzied worship of men.

The task would be to change the politics while retaining rock's impact. My goals were much too ambitious—a common problem at the time—but the band turned out to be remarkably successful in achieving many of the goals. For starters, we actually got an effective band together. After the first shake-down months (at our first performance in Grant Park in August of 1970, we had thirteen singers all bellowing happily to their individual muses), we grew into a distinctive group of hip, even talented if inexperienced musicians. High school dropout Sherry Jenkins was our resident rock genius with her wonderful alto whiskey voice and lyrical lead guitar. There was no rhythm that our hippy rhythm guitarist Pat Solo, then Miller, couldn't master. She was also wildly comical. Bass guitarist Susan Abod was steeped in rock, if just starting out on the fret board. Both her bass line and her song lines were lyrical and inventive. Fanya Montalvo and Susanne Prescott provided a double drumming rhythm. As for myself, I had seven years of classical training on the piano plus an additional two years of jazz piano. But my more important function as a performer in the band was to provide and direct theater and comedy, two areas in which I had some talent and experience.

We were explicitly, self consciously political about our performances, while avoiding leaden sloganeering. To combat the fascism of the typical rock performance where the performers disdain audiences and the sound is turned up beyond human endurance, we were extremely interactive with our audiences, rapping with them and asking them which songs they liked and keeping the sound level at a reasonable roar. We were playful, theatrical and comical, always attentive to performance. We sang "Papa don't lay that shit on me," to the tune of the old-time dirty song,

"Keep on Truckin', Mama," in carnival fashion with slide whistles and whoops of derision, the audience laughing and singing along:

> Poppa don't lay that shit on me,
> It just don't compensate.
> Poppa don't lay that shit on me,
> I can't accommodate.
> You bring me down,
> It makes you cool.
> You think I like it?
> You're a goddamn fool.
> Poppa don't lay that shit on me,
> I can't accommodate.

"Don't Fuck Around with Love" offered a parodic voice-over above a sentimental fifties doo-wop chorus: "Love is wonderful / Love is peace / Love moves the mountains / Love cuts the grease." "Secretary" described a typical pissed-off working day: ("Get up, downtown / don't you wish you could get out of this? / no trust / big bust /doesn't all those mumbles ever bother you?") At all times we wanted our politics to be artful, to be revolutionary poetry.

We were an image of feminist solidarity, resistance, and power, and audiences loved us. Just the fact that we were all women standing up on the stage playing our heavy-duty instruments into our heavy-duty amplifiers was enough to turn many women on, but we received a wildly enthusiastic response not only from women in the movement but also from a wide range of different groups including the crowd at the Second Annual Third World Transvestite Ball, and the fourteen-year-old black girls at a summer camp for inner-city children. At Cornell University, where we played with the New Haven Women's Liberation Rock Band, women stripped to the waist and danced together in undulating circles. Outside the room, angry fraternity boys were threatening to jump us. "Put your clothes back on," sang Jennifer Abod (Susie's sister) without shaving a beat, "We're in a hostile situation." The women kept dancing. "No we won't," they sang back. "We're free. We are . . . FREE." At the inner-city camp, the girls made us play Amy Kesselman's "VD Blues" six times before they would let us pack our bags and go home:

> I went to the preacher, said preacher can you help me please?
> . . . He looked at me sadly and said, girl, get on your knees.
> I went to the doctor and said doctor can you help me please?
> . . . He looked at me cross-eyed and said,
> You've got A SOCIAL DISEASE!

We were on stage and at our instruments before the audience showed up. (This was a rule with us. In accord with our subversive resolve to be audience-friendly— unheard of with male rockers—we tried always to be on time for a performance.) Assuming the sneering voice of your average low-life male sexist, I began, "A women's liberation rock band. Farrrr Out! Farrrrr fucking out. Hey, I'd like to see you chicks in your gold lame short shorts and feathers on your tits." I went on to imitate Mick Jagger singing "Under My Thumb": "There is a squirrelly dog, who once had her way . . ." Then I asked the audience: "and do you know what he says then? he says, 'it's alright.' Pause. "It's alright? *It's alright?* Well, it's not alright, Mick Jagger, and IT'S NEVER GOING TO BE ALRIGHT AGAIN. [CHEERS FROM THE AUDIENCE] *IT'S NEVER GOING TO BE ALRIGHT AGAIN!*"

Folks in the audience began to scream, and didn't stop until we stopped playing. Everywhere we went, we would end with the audience hugging the band and other members of the audience. And the band hugging the audience. And all of our faces wet with tears of joy. Surely, we felt, we had produced a new world that would never go away, that would never fail us.

Every weekend we crisscrossed the Chicago area, flew or drove to Colorado Springs, Bloomington, Madison, Pittsburgh, Lewisburg, Toronto, Ithaca, Indianapolis, Buffalo, Boston. (I flew as "Susan Young" at youth fare.) Audiences invited us back and by the second visit knew half our lyrics.

A cult began to form. We flew east to Boston to make a record with the New Haven Women's Liberation Rock Band for Rounder Records (1972), which became an underground classic for many feminists.

But ultimately we failed. The band lasted three years and broke up in an agony of hatred and hidden agendas. There were many reasons for this, but two conflicts in particular finished us. These conflicts lay at the millenarian heart of the prefigurative and utopian politics of the women's liberation movement.

The movement's utopianism included the ideas that: 1) any woman should be able to do anything as well as any other woman; and 2) there should be no leaders. We soon learned these ideas were untenable, but we persisted in hoping that if we were good enough feminists, we could abolish inequality of skills and function without leaders. The contradictions between what we knew to be true, versus what we pretended was true, destroyed us.

In our band, the first conflict expressed itself as a tension between expertise on the one hand and, on the other, enthusiasm-in-place-of-expertise (or "militant amateurism"). Our early women's movement said that any woman could do anything, if given the right social context and sufficient social support. I think this principle worked at the beginning, when our rock band was the first of its kind. Women appreciated our rough edges, our ragged style which conveyed the message that the audience itself could do things formerly considered taboo for women. But we owed it to our audience to be the best musicians we could. Some members of the band were willing to take up this challenge, but others were not. Feeling that the band needed a sharper beat, one day I suggested to one of our drummers that she take some lessons. She replied somewhat contemptuously, "I'm good enough for *this* band." The telling thing about this exchange was that nobody followed up. The myth about equality in skills was so strong that not one of us had the temerity to say, "You're not good enough for this band. Get better, or quit."

The second, and related conflict involved the question of leadership. This question was to rend the women's movement from coast to coast. Committed, as I have said, to what turned out to be a myth of equal skills, the movement applied the same kind of thinking to leadership, declaring that there should be none. For instance, as my reputation as a public speaker increased and my speaking invitations multiplied, the CWLU decided that I should refuse further invitations, lest I emerge as a "star." I willingly went along with this. (Instead, I organized intensive speaker training sessions, where I taught inexperienced women the skills that I had picked up.) But no matter how self-abnegating leaders were, it was not enough. The utopian vision became cannibalism, and the movement ate its leaders: in city after city, they went down.

Here is how the leadership conflict played out in the band. We built the group painstakingly, and through much interpersonal struggle, to be an egalitarian collective. Thus, for instance, every member wrote songs, and these were accepted by everyone in the band with few questions asked, although friendly adaptations and amendments were usually received enthusiastically. But, in spite of our laid-back social style and our values of structurelessness and leaderlessness, I was clearly the theatrical director, theoretician, and spiritual healer of wounds. If only by dint of a slight chronological advantage and a frenzied drive—and totally committed as I was to a deeply utopian egalitarianism—I was nevertheless "mother" to the band, its *de facto* leader. When the women's movement started trashing its leaders, the band turned on me for all the roles I had played. Its solidarity split open, and I came under attack. After I and Virginia Blaisdell published a piece in *Ms.* on the band's strengths and triumphs, I was attacked by the band for egotism: "Why did you sign your name to the article?" some members asked. Interestingly, nobody questioned the importance of the article, just that I should take credit for it.

The band needed my experience and skills, but they did not want to admit this. A gig we played at Bucknell University in 1972 made this clear to me. The audience was ferociously hostile, riled by an earlier speaker and angered by the fact that only half the band showed up. (In pre-performance confusion, they had taken the wrong plane.) Huge fraternity boys were screaming and baring their canines in the middle of the floor like turf-threatened gorillas. At one point, Sherry put an empty coke bottle on my piano and grabbed an empty microphone stand because she thought they were going to rush the stage. I offered to calm the audience with a stand-up comedy introduction. Concerned about my leadership role, the band refused to let me do this. Instead, another band member, inexperienced in such situations, made a stumbling presentation which further enraged the audience. At this point I—gulp—improvised a new monologue, producing (eventually) giggles, then guffaws. Afterwards the band was furious at me for my success in reversing the audience's mood.

I should point out, however, that by talking about "the band" I don't mean to imply a monolithic consensus about trashing me. As these dynamics go, one person started the attack. As it turned out, when I left the band she attacked the leader who took my place. In varying degrees, the rest of the band was reluctant to join the confrontation she had set up, but their silence gave the trashing the appearance of unanimity. Their inability to stand up for me stemmed

from the ideology and culture that had so recently infected the women's movement. Band members were just plain scared to oppose the new dogmatism. They didn't want to appear politically stupid. After all, hadn't the CWLU decreed that I should stay silent? Maybe, reasoned some of the band members, I shouldn't be performing at all.

How much the band actually relied on me was to be sadly revealed when I left Chicago. (I took a six-month leave of absence from the band, in part because the group's attacks on me as leader had become intolerable.) When I had been gone three months, I read in the CWLU newsletter that the band had dissolved.

I will mourn the break-up of the band for the rest of my life. Though from the seventies to the nineties, many wonderful kinds of women's music developed, it was rarely the kind played by the CWLRB: bust-out bad-ass visionary political poetry. It is an irony that the revolutionary vision of utopia that had made our performance so powerful was the same ingredient that had destroyed us.

Women's Music 101

JENNIFER BAUMGARDNER   1999

You've heard of Lilith Fair and the fact that women dominated the Grammys in 1998, but do you know about the radical women who seeded this flower?

In 1976, feminism had just found its way to a commune in the rural South and Laurie Fuchs, age 24, was electrified. After attending the women's music festival in Champagne-Urbana she discovered her inability to find music by women who weren't the token Joni, Joan or Judy. Fuchs discovered a rich history of women taking control of their careers. But when Fuchs made visits to the libraries of University of North Carolina and Duke to expand her research, each library had a measly two or three recordings by women—"basically Bessie Smith and that's it"—among thousands and thousands by men. Fuchs created a mail order catalog, Ladyslipper, devoted to distributing women's music. Fuchs realized that Ladyslipper had to function on two levels: uncover the history of women in music and

make recordings by female artists available. "In the catalog right now, we run between 1500 and 2000 titles—it's more than we find other places but it doesn't begin to touch the entire body of work."

Olivia, named for a feisty heroine in a pulp novel who fell in love with her headmistress at a French boarding school, was the brainchild of ten radical feminists (Furies and Radicalesbians) living in Washington, DC. In 1973 the collective put out a 45 with Meg Christian on one side and Cris Williamson on the other. Yoko Ono responded and said that she wanted to do a side project with Olivia, but the collective lovingly declined. Founder Judy Dlugacz explained, "The image that we were projecting was that we had our own music and vision and we weren't smart enough at the time to realize that [Yoko] could have been a good thing." Without hooking up with anyone high-profile, they made $12,000 with that 45, enough to put out

Meg's first record, and soon after, Williamson's. Williamson's album changed the alternative women's music scene, giving it an economic spine that supported Olivia, Ladyslipper, and countless feminist bookstores.

The Reagan-Bush years hit, and the folk music that was cutting edge when Olivia began was not going to be the music for the next generation of women. Ladyslipper, which had fought for years to have separate bins in record stores for the genre of "Women's Music" was feeling that innovation backfire. Women's music felt like a ghetto.

More than a decade later, Riot grrrl seemed to spring out of nowhere, Athena-style again, with the media's discovery of the young punk feminists in 1992. In actuality, activists such as Kathleen Hanna and Tobi Vail (from the band Bikini Kill) were not only reacting to a boy-dominated "boring" punk scene, they were drawing from feminist history. Hanna spent an entire semester studying *The Second Sex* in 1989 and worked at a battered women's shelter by day.

Now loads of other women are carrying on the spirit if not the name of the women's music movement. They own labels, produce shows, and organize mail order distribution so that girls and women can avoid the macho record store experience if they so desire. For some women, having their own sound and culture is critical. Amy Ray started her own label, Daemon records, in 1989 and uses her major label career to bankroll the independent community to which she is more committed. Daemon is a co-op, which means the artists are obligating to give 15 hours of work for each record they do, finding a co-op printing company to print your catalog, using a credit union instead of a bank, hiring women employees. The women's music revolution has had a profound impact. Artists who happen to be gay or bisexual and didn't look or sound a certain boiler-plate way—Ani, Melissa Etheridge, and Tracy Chapman—all had a place. Lilith grossed 35 million dollars in just two tours, and women bought millions of CDs last year.

The feminist movement contributed to the recognition of women's participation in contemporary Chicano art and in turn feminist content influenced that rich field. Chicano art grew particularly through a mural movement (much influenced by the epic Mexican mural movement of the 1930s–50s) which began in Tucson in the mid 1970s as part of the growing Chicano movement of the American West and Southwest. The art celebrated Chicano cultural identity and political victories. Chicano activist artists emphasized posters and murals because they wanted to reach a larger public, literate and non-literate, as an alternative to producing art for galleries, and their murals were often conceived and painted with community input.

Women soon became integral to this artistic renaissance. Sometimes the feminist content of their work aroused hostility and even defacement. In one dramatic case, a mural of a famous woman on a Chicago wall was almost immediately attacked with big splashes of white paint, but the result was, to the artist, even more powerful than her original, for it suggested women struggling to become visible against attempts to blot them out.

We have chosen to use paintings and prints rather than murals to represent Chicana art in this collection (chapters 10 and 11 contain additional selections) because the murals do not appear to their best advantage in a book. In this painting, Yolanda M. López completes the transformation of the Virgin of Guadalupe into a full-fledged feminist new woman—athletic, independent, running into a new age.

Portrait of the Artist As the Virgin of Guadalupe
YOLANDA M. LÓPEZ

Among the Things That Use to Be
WILLIE M. COLEMAN

Use to be

Ya could learn

a whole lot of stuff
sitting in them
beauty shop chairs

Use to be

Ya could meet
a whole lot of other women
sittin there
along with hair frying
         spit flying
            and babies crying

Use to be

you could learn

a whole lot about
how to catch up
        with yourself
and some other folks
        in your household.
Lots more got taken care of
          than hair
Cause in our mutual obvious dislike
           for nappiness
we came   together
        under the hot comb
to share
        and share
          and share

In the Beauty Parlor

PHYLLIS EWEN

Sources

Casey Hayden and Mary King, "Sex and Caste," mimeographed leaflet, 1965

"We Don't Need the Men" words and music by Malvina Reynolds copyright © 1958, Schroder Music Co. (ASCAP) Renewed 1986 used by permission. All rights reserved.

Mother's Day demonstration photograph, the Wisconsin State Historical Society, Visual Materials Archive (W Hi (x3) 26513)

Mother's Draft Resistance, "An Appeal to Mothers," mimeographed leaflet, 1968, Schlesinger Library

Radical Women's Group, "Burial of Weeping Womanhood," leaflet, Baxandall/Gordon papers, Tamiment Institute Library, NYU Bobst Library

Shirley Willer, "What Concrete Steps Can Be Taken to Further the Homophile Movement," *The Ladder,* 1966

Del Martin, "The Lesbian's Other Identity," 1968

Wilda Chase, "Lesbianism and Feminism," 1969

SDS Women, "To the Women of the Left," *New Left Notes,* November 13, 1967

Susie Ling, "The Mountain Movers," *Amerasia* 15:1 (1989), 51–67

New York Radical Women, "Principles," 1968, Baxandall/Gordon papers, Tamiment Institute Library, NYU Bobst Library

Bread and Roses (Boston), letter, 1970, Baxandall/Gordon papers, Tamiment Institute Library, NYU Bobst Library

"Cocktales," leaflet, 1969, Baxandall/Gordon papers, Tamiment Institute Library, NYU Bobst Library

Doris Wright, "Angry Notes from a Black Feminist," mimeographed position paper, distributed by FEM, New York, 1970

Young Lords Party, "Position Paper on Women," *Palante,* New York, n.d.

"American Foot Binding: Stamp Out High Heels," poster, Houston, n.d., Duke University Library Special Collections, ALFA Collection, Box 12

Mary Moylan, "Underground Woman," *Off Our Backs* 1:7, 1970

"Women Unite! Free the Panthers!" leaflet, New Haven, CT

Bread and Roses, "Declaration of Women's Independence,"

mimeographed leaflet, Boston, 1970, Meredith Tax personal collection

Susan Sutheim, "Women Shake Up SDS Session," *The Guardian* June 22, 1968

Cartoon, *Radical America* brochure, 1968

Ellen Willis, "Letter to the Left," unpublished letter to the *Guardian,* author's personal collection

"Sisters in Struggle," comic strip, *Hard Times,* April 13, 1970

"Goodbye to All That (1970)," by Robin Morgan, from *The Word of a Woman: Feminist Dispatches,* second edition (1968–1992) by Robin Morgan. Copyright © 1994 by Robin Morgan. By permission of Edite Kroll Literary Agency Inc.

"Unite to Win," poster, Chicago Women's Graphics Collective

"Pissed Off About the War in Cambodia," leaflet, Boston, 1970

WUNTRAC, satirical leaflet, New York City, n.d., Wisconsin State Historical Society

Cartoons and letter criticizing sexist cartoons, *Voice of the Women's Liberation Movement,* August 1968, cartoon © 1968 by Naomi Weisstein

Third World Gay Revolution, "16 Point Platform," mimeographed leaflet, 1970

Third World Women's Alliance, "Statement," *Triple Jeopardy*

Pamela Allen, "The Small Group Process," mimeographed pamphlet, San Francisco, 1969, Wisconsin State Historical Society Archives. By permission of Chude Pamela Allen, author of *Free Space: A Perspective on the Small Group in Women's Liberation* (Times Change Press, 1970) and *Jean Maddox: Labor Heroine* (Union WAGE, 1976), collaborator with Robert L. Allen on *Reluctant Reformers: Racism and Social Reform Movements in the United States* (Howard University Press, 1974) and former editor of *Union WAGE.*

Gainesville (Florida) Women's Liberation, "What We Do at Meetings," mimeographed pamphlet, 1970. This Gainesville Women's Liberation Document and other women's liberation materials from the 1960s and from current women's liberation organizing available from Redstocking's Women's Liberation Archives Distribution Project, P.O. Box 2625, Gainesville, FL 32602-2625. Please enclose a SASE. Web site: http://www.afn.org/~redstock

Jo Freeman, "The Tyranny of Structurelessness," *The Second Wave* 2:1, 1970

Gainesville Women's Liberation, "What Men Can Do for Women's Liberation," mimeographed pamphlet, 1970

Women of *La Raza* Unite! San Jose, 1972, from *La Mujer en Pie de Lucha* (Mexico City: Espina del Norte Publications, 1973), 263–68

Laura Shapiro, "You Are Where You Eat," *The Real Paper,* July 23, 1975, Cambridge, MA

Jenny Knauss and other members of the Chicago Women's Liberation School Work Group, "Analysis of Chicago Women's Liberation School," mimeographed pamphlet, Chicago, n.d., Northwestern University Archives

Norma Allen, "What Is a Woman?" handmade booklet, Washington, D.C., 1970–71, Duke University Library Special Collections, ALFA Collection

Jayne West, "Are Men Really the Enemy?" *No More Fun and Games: A Journal of Female Liberation (The Dialectics of Sexism)* #3, Cell 16, November 1969, Cambridge, MA

Redstockings, "Manifesto," mimeographed position paper, New York, 1969

Ti-Grace Atkinson, "Radical Feminism and Love," for the October 17th Movement, New York, 1969, Schlesinger Library

Patricia Haden, Donna Middleton, and Patricia Robinson, "A Historical and Critical Essay for Black Women," mimeographed position paper, Mt. Vernon, NY, 1969–70, Duke University Library Special Collections, ALFA Collection

Chicago Women's Liberation Union, "Socialist Feminism," Chicago, 1972, Vivian Rothstein personal collection

Barbara Burris, "Fourth World Manifesto," mimeographed position paper, Detroit, 1971, University of Texas, Austin, Library, Special Collections

Rev. Peggy Way, "You Are Not My God, Jehovah," Loveland, Ohio, 1970, Schlesinger Library

Hallie Iglehart and Jeanne Scott-Senior, "Reaching Beyond Intellect," Wolf Creek, Oregon, 1975, Schlesinger Library

Radicalesbians, "The Woman-Identified Woman," 1970, Susan O'Malley personal collection

Anonymous Realesbians, "Politicalesbians and the Women's Liberation Movement," *Ecstasy* #1, Carol Morton personal collection

Lee Schwing, Editorial on Separatism, *Women: A Journal of Liberation,* April 1973, Washington, D.C., Charlotte Bunch personal collection

Lorna Cherot, "I Am What I Am," *Liberation News Service,* #24, October 29, 1970, Philadelphia

Kay Weiss, "What Medical Students Learn," KNOW pamphlet #310, Pittsburgh

Boston Women's Health Book Collective, "The Origins of *Our Bodies Ourselves,*" mimeographed booklet, 1970, Linda Gordon personal collection. For the most updated version of the book, see Boston Women's Health Collective, *Our Bodies, Ourselves for the New Century* (New York: Simon & Schuster, 1998)

Kathy Campbell, Terry Dalsemer and Judy Waldman, "Women's Night at the Free Clinic," *Women, a Journal of Liberation,* 2:4, 1972

Wonder Woman cartoon, 1973, Northwestern University Archives

The West Coast Sisters, "Self-Help Clinic," 1971

Feminist Women's Health Center, brochure, Los Angeles

"Using a Natural Sponge," *Country Lesbians: The Story of the Womanshare Collective* (Grants Pass, Oregon: Womanshare Books, 1976)

Sally Wendkos Olds, "Breastfeeding Successfully in Spite of Doctors and Hospitals," International Childbirth Conference, 1973, Schlesinger Library. Sally Wendkos Olds is co-author of *The Complete Book of Breastfeeding,* 3rd ed., by Marvin S. Eiger, M.D. and Sally Wendkos Olds (Workman Publishing Co., 1999)

Byllye Y. Avery, "Breathing Life into Ourselves: The Evolution of the National Black Women's Health Project," *Black Women's Health Book* (Seattle: Seal Press, 1990)

Irene Peslikis, "Women Must Control the Means of Reproduction," drawing, New York, 1969, artist's personal collection

Patricia Robinson and Black Sisters, "Poor Black Women," pamphlet (Mt. Vernon, NY: New England Free Press, 1968)

Judith Coburn, "Off the Pill," *Ramparts* 8:12, June 1970

Lucinda Cisler, "On Abortion and Abortion Law," *Notes from the Second Year* (New York: New York Radical Women, 1969)

Sarah Wernick Lockeretz, "Hernia: A Satire," KNOW pub. #15101 Pittsburgh, n.d., Duke University Library Special Collections, ALFA Collection

"Jane," "Women Learn to Perform Abortions," *Voices,* October 1973, Chicago

Catholics for Free Choice, "Who Needs a Shepherd?" *What She Wants* 1:8, March 1974, Cleveland

Irene Peslikis, "Friends of the Fetus," 1969, artist's personal collection

Mary Treadwell, "An African American Woman Speaks Out for Abortion Rights," statement for WONAAC press conference, Detroit, n.d., Northwestern University Archives

Joan Kelly, "Sterilization: Right and Abuse of Rights," 1977, from Meredith Tax personal collection

Posters against sterilization abuse, *Liberation News Service,* 1973

Sonia Jaffe Robbins, "Starting Over," *Village Voice,* September 19, 1977

Ruth Davis, "Venus Observed," *Women: A Journal of Liberation,* 1972, Davis, CA

Anne Koedt, "The Myth of the Vaginal Orgasm," *Radical Feminism,* Anne Koedt, Ellen Levine, and Anita Rapone, eds. (New York: Quadrangle/New York Times Books, 1973). Copyright © by Anne Koedt, 1970. Originally appeared in *Notes from the Second Year* (New York: New York Radical Women, 1969)

Betty Dodson, "Liberating Masturbation," drawing, 1975

Karen Sandler, "My First Orgasm," letter, *Ain't I a Woman,* 1974, Los Angeles

"Workshop Resolutions," First National Chicana Conference, Houston, 1971

B.K.O., "It Just Happened," *Women: A Journal of Liberation,* 1971

Sue Katz, "Smash Phallic Imperialism," mimeographed leaflet, n.d., University of Michigan Library, Marge Piercy papers

Julia London, A Statement Presented by Julia London at Press Conference Held December 10, 1976 at Tower Records, Hollywood, CA, Northeastern University Library, WAVAW Papers

"Hooking Is Real Employment," Atlanta, Schlesinger Library

Linda Phelps, "Death in the Spectacle," *Liberation,* May 1971, Kansas City

Bev Grant, "A Pretty Girl Is a Commodity," 1968, author's personal collection

Florika, "Body Odor and Social Order," 1968, Harriet Fraad personal collection

Florika, poster, Linda Gordon personal collection.

New York Radical Women, "No More Miss America," leaflet, 1968, Susan Brownmiller personal collection

Carol Hanisch, "A Critique of the Miss America Pageant," copyright © 1968 Carol Hanisch. All rights reserved. New York, author's personal collection

Sheilah Drummond, "Hairy Legs Freak Fishy Liberal," *Berkeley Tribe,* from Mitchell Goodman, *The Movement.*

Untitled news story about high school girl badmouthing a mayor, *Desperate Living* 1:5, Winter 1974

Fat Underground, "*Antes de hacer dieta,*" brochure, Venice, CA, n.d., Schlesinger Library

Cathy Cade, "Fat Chance Performance Group," photograph, 1979

Judith Freespirit and Aldebaran, "Fat Liberation Manifesto," 1973, Ann Forfreedom personal collection

"Little Rapes," *A Handbook on Rape,* San Francisco, 1977

Karen Lindsey, Holly Newman, and Fran Taylor, "Rape: The All American Crime," *What She Wants* 1:5, October 1973, Cleveland

Susan Brownmiller, "The Mass Psychology of Rape." Reprinted with the permission of Simon & Schuster from *Against Our Will* by Susan Brownmiller. Copyright © 1975 by Susan Brownmiller.

"Black Women Organizing Against Rape," *How to Start a Rape Crisis Center,* Washington, D.C., 1977

"The Case of Inez Garcia," interview with Susan Jordan, *The Recorder,* American Lawyer Media, L.P., 1997

Florence Rush, "The Sexual Abuse of Children," *Radical Therapist* 2:4, December 1971

Cathy Cade, "Women's Martial Arts Demonstrations," photograph, artist's personal collection

Susan Pascalé, Rachel Moon and Leslie Tanner, "Karate As Self-Defense for Women," *Women: A Journal of Liberation,* Winter 1970

Ester Hernandez, "*La Virgen de Guadalupe Defendiendo los Derechos de los Xicanos,*" print, from artist's personal collection

Eleanor Holmes Norton, "For Sadie and Maud," n.d. Poem: Gwendolyn Brooks, "Sadie and Maud," from *Blacks* by Gwendolyn Brooks © 1991. Published by Third World Press (Chicago, 1991)

Julie Coryell, "What's in a Name?" *Women: A Journal of Liberation,* Winter 1971

Denise Oliver, "Machismo," *Palante,* 1971

Alix Kates Shulman, "A Marriage Agreement," *Up from Under,* 1:2, August-September 1970

Communal Living, unsigned editorial, *Women: A Journal of Liberation,* Winter 1971

Vicki Cohn Pollard, "The Five of Us," *Women: A Journal of Liberation,* Winter 1971

Vivian Estellachild, "Hippie Communes," *Women: A Journal of Liberation,* Winter 1971

Jo Ann Hoit, "Speaking of Spock," *Up from Under,* 1:2, August-September 1970

Karol Hope, "The Single Mother Experience," *MOMMA,* 1972, Los Angeles

Daphne Busby, Editorial, "The Sisterhood of Black Single Mothers," newsletter, n.d., Schlesinger Library

Anonymous, "Lesbian Mothers and their Children," *Womankind,* 1972

Louise Gross and Phyllis Taube Greenleaf, "Why Day Care?" 1970, Sheli Wortis personal collection

Verne Moberg, "Consciousness Razors," National Education Association brochure, Schlesinger Library. Reprinted by permission of the author. All rights reserved.

Kevin Karkau, "Gender in the Fourth Grade," KNOW pamphlet, Minneapolis, n.d.

High School Women's Liberation Coalition, "What Every Young Girl Should Ask," n.d., Barnard College Women's Studies archive

Cathy Cade, "Baseball Family," photograph, 1972, artist's personal collection

Ruth Colker, "Testimony of a High School Pitcher," KNOW pamphlet, Mt. Lebanon, Pennsylvania, n.d.

Chicago Liberation School for Women, brochure, 1973, Amy Kesselman personal collection

"Nuts to Bolts," *Freewoman's Herald,* vol. 2, 3. May, 1974

Cathy Cade, "Library Sit-in for Women's History," photograph, 1973, artist's personal collection

NY Radical Feminists Cabaret, "Dear Sisters," 1973, Susan Brownmiller personal collection

Adrienne Rich, "Women's Studies As a Pledge of Resistance," excerpt from speech at Philadelphia Women's Studies Conference, 1974, Florence Howe, Feminist Press collection

Lillian Robinson, "Women's Studies," from *Robinson on the Woman Question* (Buffalo: Earth Daughters, 1973), by Lillian Robinson; reprinted by permission.

Judith P. Jones, "Feminism in the Bible Belt," *Radical Teacher,* December 1977, Alabama

Pat Mainardi, "The Politics of Housework," New England Free Press pamphlet, 1968

"Wages for Housework," leaflet, n.d., Northwestern University Archives

Silvia Federici, "Wages Against Housework," 1975, Sheila Rowbotham personal collection

Yolanda M. López, "Margaret F. Stewart, Our Lady of Guadalupe," painting, 1978, artist's personal collection

Kate Wall, "Luring Women into the Armed Forces," Washington Peace Center *Peace Letter,* March 1974

AFT Resolution on Women's Rights, Pittsburgh, 1970, Wisconsin State Historical Society, Joan Jordan papers

Cathy Cade, "Learning Auto Repair," photograph, artist's personal collection

United Steelworkers of America, "Open Letter to Local #1299," 1973, from the Wayne State University Archives of Labor, History and Urban Affairs

"Does Your Boss Know You're Gay?" *Desperate Living* 1, Winter 1974

Caroline Walker Bynum, "The Era of Tokenism and the Role Model Trap," *Radcliffe Quarterly,* December 1973

Marge Piercy, "The Secretary's Chant," from *Circles on the Water* by Marge Piercy. Copyright © 1982 by Marge Piercy. Reprinted by permission of Alfred A. Knopf, a Division of Random House Inc.

Renee Blakkan, "Women Unionize Office Jobs," *The Guardian,* May 15, 1974

Women Office Workers, "59 cents, A Woman's Dollar," MIT secretaries' leaflet, 1970, Baxandall/Gordon papers, Tamiment Institute Library, NYU Bobst Library

Cathy Cade, "TWA Stewardesses on Strike," photograph, 1973, artist's personal collection

Dierdre Silverman, "Sexual Harassment: Working Women's Dilemma," *Quest* 3:3, Winter 1976–77, Ithaca, NY

Women's Clearinghouse, Radio News, 1974, Duke University Library Special Collections, ALFA Collection

Johnnie Tillmon, "Welfare Is a Women's Issue," *Liberation News Service,* February 26, 1972

Judy Linhares, "At Home in San José," drawing, Oakland, 1972

Toni Flores Fratto, "Samplers: One of the Lesser American Arts," *Feminist Art Journal,* Winter 1976–77, Pennsylvania

"How to Name Baby," leaflet, New York Media Project, Charlotte Bunch personal collection

Virginia W. Morgan, "Anatomy Is Destiny or . . . Just Like Daddy," New York

Ellen Willis, "Women and the Myth of Consumerism," *Ramparts,* 1969

Barbara Carrasco, "Pregnant Woman in a Ball of Yarn," lithograph, artist's personal collection

Sandy Orgel, "Linen Closet," installation, Womanhouse, Los Angeles, 1972

Meredith Tax, "There Was a Young Woman Who Swallowed a Lie . . . ," 1969. Lyrics, Meredith Tax, to the tune of "There Was an Old Woman Who Swallowed a Fly," © Alan Mills. Author's personal collection

"Breaking Out," comic strip, *It Ain't Me Babe,* San Francisco, 1970

June Jordan, "The Reception," original poem 1967, reprinted in *No More Masks: An Anthology of Poems by Women,* Florence Howe and Ellen Bass, eds. (Doubleday, 1973)

Jean Tepperman, "Witch," 1969, *Motive Magazine,* March-April 1969

Medusa, drawing, *Dykes and Gorgons* 1:1, 1973

Judy Grahn, "A Geology Lesson," *Amazon Quarterly* 1:1, Fall 1972

Gayle Two Eagles, "The Young Warrior," from *A Gathering of Spirit* edited by Beth Brant (Ithaca, New York: Firebrand Books). Copyright © 1984 by Beth Brant

Chicago Women's Graphic Collective, "Mountain-Moving Day," poster, c. 1971, Lincoln Cushing personal collection

Lynn Evans, "Women Invade *The Boston Globe,*" *The Old Mole,* April 1970

Bread and Roses, stickers to paste on advertisements, Cambridge Women's Center, 1970

"I've Been in Her Shoes," leaflet, n.d., Baxandall/Gordon papers, Tamiment Institute Library, NYU Bobst Library

Naomi Weisstein, "Days of Celebration and Resistance: The Chicago Women's Liberation Rock Band, 1970–1973," Naomi Weisstein personal collection. Copyright © Naomi Weisstein 1998

Jennifer Baumgardner, "Women's Music 101," *Z Magazine,* September 1999

Yolanda M. López, "Portrait of the Artist as the Virgin of Guadalupe," artist's personal collection

Willie M. Coleman, "Among the Things that Used to Be," *Conditions 5,* 1979

Phyllis Ewen, "In the Beauty Parlor," photograph, artist's personal collection

Further Reading

Karen Anderson, *Changing Woman: A History of Racial Ethnic Women in Modern America.* Oxford, 1996.

Susan Brownmiller, *In Our Time: Memoir of a Revolution.* Dial Press, 1999.

Flora Davis, *Moving the Mountain: The Women's Movement in America Since 1960.* Simon & Schuster, 1991.

Alice Echols, *Daring to Be Bad: Radical Feminism in America, 1967–75.* University of Minnesota Press, 1989.

Hester Eisenstein, *Contemporary Feminist Thought.* G. K. Hall, 1983.

Sara Evans, *Personal Politics: The Roots of Women's Liberation in the Civil Rights Movement and the New Left.* Knopf, 1979.

Myra Marx Ferree and Beth B. Hess, *Controversy and Coalition: The New Women's Movement.* Twayne, 1985.

Alma M. García, ed., *Chicana Feminist Thought: The Basic Historical Writings.* Routledge, 1997.

Darlene Clark Hine, ed., *Black Women in U.S. History: Theory and Practice, the Twentieth Century,* vols. 9–10. Carlson Publishing, 1990.

Ruth Rosen, *The World Split Open: How the Modern Women's Movement Changed America.* Viking, 2000.

Sheila Rowbotham, *A Century of Women: The History of Women in Britain and the United States in the Twentieth Century.* Viking, 1997.

Vicki L. Ruiz, *From Out of the Shadows: Mexican Women in Twentieth-Century America.* Oxford, 1998.

Vicki L. Ruiz and Ellen Carol DuBois, eds., *Unequal Sisters: A Multicultural Reader in U.S. Women's History,* Third Edition. Routledge, 2000.

Acknowledgments

Our acknowledgments ideally ought to include every participant in the women's liberation movement. Because this book is a collective product of that movement, we are donating our royalties to feminist activism. Here we only have room to express our gratitude to those who helped us immediately and directly, by sending us papers, by giving us clues in tracking down other papers, in reading and commenting on our drafts, and through their own scholarship. They include Mimi Abramowitz, Pam Parker Allen, Fran Ansley, Ellen Baker, Megan Balzer, Debra Bernhardt, Martha Boethel, Heather Booth, Carolyn Bronstein, Dorothea Browder, Susan Brownmiller, Charlotte Bunch, Judith Coburn, Ginny Daley, Drew Darien, Sue Davis, Alice Echols, Hester Eisenstein, Dionne Espinoza, Nancy Falk, Myra Marx Ferree, Ann Forfreedom, Alma García, Carol Hanisch, Daniel Horowitz, Diane Hurwitz, Temma Kaplan, L. A. Kaufman, Amy Kesselman, Helen Kritzler, Ward Larkin, Kate Millett, Carol Morton, Eva Moseley, Judy Norsigian, Lynn O'Connor, Susan O'Malley, Irene Peslikis, Lynn Phillips, Marge Piercy, Rivka Polatnick, Katha Pollitt, Annie Popkin, Barbara Ransby, Naomi Rosenthal, Vivian Rothstein, Sheila Rowbotham, Vicki Ruiz, Pat Ryan, Marjorie Seyler, Alix Kates Shulman, Margaret Strobel, Meredith Tax, Jules Unsel, Naomi Weisstein, Ellen Willis, Barbara Winslow, Kerry Woodward, Sheli Wortis.

Several institutions contributed valuable resources to the project and we are grateful to the Russell Sage Foundation, the University of Wisconsin, the SUNY–Old Westbury Foundation, and New York University.

While we were preparing this book, we worked on a committee with an international group of feminist scholars whose wisdom informs some of our ideas: Shireen Hassim, Luisa Passerini, Raka Ray, Sheila Rowbotham, Gina Vargas.

Thanks to our agent, Charlotte Sheedy, the editorial staff at Basic Books—Jo Ann Miller, Donya Levine, Jessica Callaway, and Richard Fumosa—and Libby Garland, who did the arduous work of collecting permissions.

A number of good friends supported us and influenced us through conversation, their own scholarship, and their comments on this book in its earlier stages: Wini Breines, Sara Evans, Elizabeth Ewen, Stuart Ewen, Harriet Fraad, Susan Stanford Friedman, Onita Estes Hicks, Allen Hunter, Ira Jacobson, Linda Kerber, Nancy Krieger, Judith Walzer Leavitt, Gail Pellet, and Sheila Rowbotham.

Index of Contributors